AN INFORMAL
HISTORY
OF THE
HUGOS

TOR BOOKS BY JO WALTON

AN INFORMAL
HISTORY
OF THE
HUGOS

A PERSONAL LOOK BACK
AT THE HUGO AWARDS,

1953–2000

JO WALTON

TOR

A TOM DOHERTY ASSOCIATES BOOK

NEW YORK

This book is for Gardner Dozois and Rich Horton, who awaited each original post with such enthusiasm, and whose well-informed comments make this their book almost as much as mine. And it is for Kevin Standlee, in recognition of his tireless and mostly thankless work for the Hugos and WSFS over many years.

AN INFORMAL HISTORY OF THE HUGOS

Copyright © 2018 by Jo Walton

All rights reserved.

Edited by Patrick and Teresa Nielsen Hayden

A Tor Book
Published by Tom Doherty Associates
175 Fifth Avenue
New York, NY 10010

www.tor-forge.com

Tor® is a registered trademark of Macmillan Publishing Group, LLC.

The Library of Congress Cataloging-in-Publication Data is available upon request.

ISBN 978-0-7653-7908-5 (hardcover)
ISBN 978-1-4668-6573-0 (ebook)

Our books may be purchased in bulk for promotional, educational, or business use. Please contact your local bookseller or the Macmillan Corporate and Premium Sales Department at 1-800-221-7945, extension 5442, or by email at MacmillanSpecialMarkets@macmillan.com.

First Edition: August 2018

Printed in the United States of America

0 9 8 7 6 5 4 3 2 1

TABLE OF CONTENTS

AN INFORMAL
HISTORY
OF THE
HUGOS

INTRODUCTION

In 2010, for the third time in history, there was a tie for the Best Novel Hugo Award. China Miéville's *The City & the City* and Paolo Bacigalupi's *The Windup Girl* had both won. Naturally, this caused discussion of the two other times there had been a tie. Mike Glyer posted on the *File 770* website, saying that everyone agreed that Frank Herbert's *Dune* was a better book than Roger Zelazny's *This Immortal,* and Connie Willis's *Doomsday Book* was better than Vernor Vinge's *A Fire upon the Deep.* He said this with casual assurance, as if nobody could disagree—but I disagreed strongly, in both cases. After I was done defending Zelazny and Vinge, I started thinking about the Hugos.

They're science fiction's most important award—and they're entirely fan voted and fan administered. I care about them passionately, not just as a writer but also as a fan. I have voted for them every time I've gone to a Worldcon and therefore been entitled to vote. There's no financial prize, but I've been told that it's the only genre award that actually affects sales of a book. The winner gets a distinctive rocket ship trophy, instantly recognizable although the inscribed bases are different every year.

I don't think the best novel always wins. I think it's very hard to say what *the* best book of the year is. Most years, there's no single obvious best. It's much easier to say what the top five are. I thought it might be interesting to take a historical look at the individual years and consider what was nominated and what won, to look at what else could have been nominated and wasn't, and how well the selected books have stood the test of time. I wanted to look at the nominees to see whether the Hugos were picking the best five books, not only at the winners. It's easy to find consideration of Hugo winners. I wanted to do something different—to revisit the winners and nominees in context.

At first I thought I couldn't do it. I wasn't qualified. I hadn't read all the nominees—I hadn't even read all the winners. (What *have* I been doing with my time?) The Hugo Awards were first given in 1953, and have been given continuously since 1955. If I stopped in 2000, the logical stopping point, that would be more than 250 books. I'd read a lot of them, of course, but I hadn't read all of them. If I hadn't read them, it was probably because I didn't want to. Reading hundreds of books I didn't want to read seemed like a lot of work and not much fun. Then I realized that the fact I'd not read a book was a data point. It was itself interesting. Some of it is my own taste, but some of it does depend on whether people were talking about a book. I read a lot, and I spend a lot of time talking about books. There are years where I've read all the nominees. So I decided I wouldn't read anything extra for this project. If you want to read about somebody reading all the Hugo winners, or all the winners and nominees, you need to find a different book. (It wouldn't be all that hard to find. Google offers a number of blogs where people are reading their way through Hugo winners.)

I also wanted to consider the five nominees in the context of all the other eligible books of the year, which meant looking at nominees for other awards, and also what else was available. I haven't read all these things either, but I used my general knowledge of the history of SF to look at each year's nominees in context.

I began a series of posts for Tor.com called *Revisiting the Hugos*. This was my own idiosyncratic reconsideration of all of the field, from 1953 until 2000, looking at all the Hugo nominees, at what they were, at how well they have lasted, and how well they represented the field in their year. I did this entirely from my personal knowledge and prior reading. I leaned heavily on the *Locus* database of awards, the Internet Speculative Fiction Database, the Fantastic Fiction UK website, and to a lesser extent on Wikipedia.

I only looked seriously at novels, though I listed all the winners in all the categories. I talked about the short fiction sometimes. I mentioned when new categories were introduced. I mentioned fanzines and fan writers from time to time. I looked at the Campbell nominees. I am a reader. I'm really not qualified to say anything about the visual categories. (In 1958, "No Award" won for Dramatic Presentation, and I cheered when I saw that. I think this excellent precedent could have been followed much more often since.) I made no attempt to be impersonal or objective—indeed, the opposite, this was very much my personal assessment of how the Hugos were doing.

As the series went on, it became very popular. Many people started commenting on it. Gardner Dozois, Rich Horton, and James Nicoll started considering the other available short fiction in the comment threads. People started to post reminiscences of their reading and the Worldcons where the awards were given. The comment threads became a fannish event, happening every Sunday morning. People argued with me about books. It became clear that I wasn't the only one who cared about the Hugos and how well they represented the field.

What you have here is a compilation of those posts and a selection of the most interesting comments, all from 2010 and 2011, together with my posts on individual Hugo winners and nominees, all arranged chronologically, and revised slightly to avoid repetition. Updates are provided in footnotes.

The Hugo Awards are awarded annually by the World Science Fiction Society, which is to say the members of each annual World Science Fiction Convention (Worldcon). As the rules stand now, the members of the previous, current, and next Worldcons can nominate, but only members of the current Worldcon can vote. This has been slightly different at various times in the past, but the award has always been voted on by Worldcon members. In very early years, no nominees were announced and votes were made by show of hands actually at the Worldcon. This was replaced with a sensible system of transferable votes, which count preferences. Fandom has tried to keep this system as clear and open as possible, and thanks are especially due to Kevin Standlee for his efforts in this direction.

Since the Hugos have had nominees, from 1959, the nominations have been made up into short lists of the five top selections in each category, which are then voted on, in advance and by transferable votes. The winners are announced at a ceremony at the con. The long lists of all nominations with more than a certain number of votes have often been released at the same time, at least in recent years, but unfortunately not in most of the years I was looking at.

One of the metrics I used for how well books lasted was whether they were in print and whether they were in the library. For these purposes, I used my local library, the Grande Bibliothèque in Montreal. I used it because it's my library—I had the online catalog bookmarked. It gave me an additional fortuitous advantage—I could see whether they had the book in both French and English or in only one language, which became another useful metric for judging lasting popularity.

In considering other possible nominees, I didn't limit myself to what was plausible in the year in question. The Hugo has always been open to fantasy and to YA novels, and in recent years we have given the Hugo to things in those categories. The nominators of earlier years wouldn't have considered them, but since we do now, I decided to take the broad view. I'm not thinking here about what the voters of any specific year considered the best. We know that, from what they selected. I'm considering whether, with the benefit of hindsight, I'm in agreement with their view.

I stopped in 2000 for three reasons. First, the ticking clock of the century seemed like a good end point. Second, it was ten years before the time when I began to write the posts, and it didn't seem possible to have perspective on anything any closer to the present than that. If you're considering whether a book from 1958 or 1978 has lasted, knowing it's in print in 2010 is useful. This doesn't work so well for a book from 1998, never mind 2008. Historical perspective takes time. The third reason was personal—I began to be published myself in 2000, and I didn't want to either consider or not consider my own work in this context. It felt tacky. I was nominated for the John W. Campbell Award in 2001, and won it in 2002. I wanted to write about the Campbells, and I wanted to stop before I came into the frame myself.

And of course, in 2012, after I had finished this series, I won the Best Novel Hugo myself for my novel *Among Others*. I described my feelings about this at the time as "stunned and awed," which I really was. I was thrilled enough to be nominated. That would have been enough. I'd written all these posts explaining how the nominees were what was important, and I truly believe that. Actually winning a Hugo myself, after writing these posts and thinking deeply about how important they were can be described only in terms of old magazine titles— *Astounding, Amazing, Fantastic, Fantasy and Science Fiction*!

1953

Best Novel

Winner: *The Demolished Man,* by Alfred Bester

Nominees:
None

Between 1953 and 1958, the Hugo Awards were fairly disorganized. The categories weren't fixed, and there was only one round of voting— no nominees were announced. The 1953 first-ever Hugo Awards were presented at Philcon II, in Philadelphia. The winning novel was Alfred Bester's *The Demolished Man.* It's not in print, but it was recently, in Gollancz's SF Masterworks series, and it's never been hard to find. I first read it when I was reading my way through all the science fiction in the library when I was twelve. It's an examination of how it might be possible to commit a murder in a world of telepaths where not even your thoughts are private. There are some aspects of it that seem dated, but I'd say it is an enduring classic, and a worthy winner.

So, what else might have been considered?

The International Fantasy Awards for 1953 had three nominees, all of which I think might well have been Hugo nominees too. The winner was Clifford Simak's *City,* one of his best books, a gentle pastoral and typically Simak story of post-civilization. It was a fix-up of short stories published in the '40s, put into novel form for the first time. It's in print in a beautiful small-press hardcover from Old Earth Books.

The other nominees were Kurt Vonnegut's first and very science-fictional novel, *Player Piano,* and C. M. Kornbluth's *Takeoff. Player*

Piano, like most of Vonnegut, has leanings toward both surrealism and science fiction, but was published as mainstream. It is still in print.

Takeoff was one of Doubleday's early attempts at doing hardcover science fiction. *Takeoff* is not in print, and isn't one of Kornbluth's best-known works. I honestly can't remember whether I've read it or not. I think I must have, but I don't remember it.

The interesting thing about both of these is the reminder that there really wasn't much science fiction being published in book form back then—the real action was still in the magazines. It's also interesting that the Hugos emerged just as science fiction book publishing was getting established.

It's worth noting here that the Hugos and the International Fantasy Awards, a juried British award started in 1951, were the only awards for the genre in 1953, according to *Locus*'s awesome database. It's easy to lose sight of that given the huge number of awards there are today.

Looking for novels published in 1952, I see a few other things that might have made the short list. Isaac Asimov had two adult books out that year: *The Currents of Space* and *Foundation and Empire.* Both of them had had earlier magazine publication, both of them are in series, which might have impeded their chances. But they're both in print, and I think they're both fairly well known almost fifty years later. There was also A. E. van Vogt's gloriously pulpy *The Weapon Makers.* I wouldn't have been surprised to see this on the short list, if there had been a short list. There's Cyril Judd's (C. M. Kornbluth and Judith Merril's) *Gunner Cade,* James Blish's *Jack of Eagles,* and Lester del Rey's *Marooned on Mars.*

In young adult and children's books, possibly E. B. White's *Charlotte's Web,* Mary Norton's *The Borrowers,* or C. S. Lewis's *The Voyage of the Dawn Treader* might have made it on. In straight SF juveniles, we have Lester del Rey's *Rocket Jockey,* Arthur C. Clarke's *Islands in the Sky,* Robert A. Heinlein's *Space Family Stone* (aka *The Rolling Stones*), or Asimov's *David Starr: Space Ranger.*

Other possibilities about which I know nothing: John Taine, *The Crystal Horde,* and Raymond F. Jones, *This Island Earth.*

So, did a good book win, worthy of the Hugo? I'd say yes. Was it the best book of the year? Well, arguably. I'd argue for *City* or *More*

Than Human, or *Foundation and Empire* as worthy of consideration, but I certainly don't have any problem with *The Demolished Man* as a winner.

Was anything left out of the short list? Well, since there was no short list, everything was.

OTHER CATEGORIES

BEST PROFESSIONAL MAGAZINE

Winner: *Astounding Science Fiction* and *Galaxy Science Fiction*

This was clearly a tie. The interesting thing to me is that there isn't a category for professional magazines today. But John W. Campbell's *Astounding* and H. L. Gold's *Galaxy* were unquestionably the best magazines of 1953. I think the real reason for stopping giving this award is that there just weren't enough professional magazines at the time to make a good short list. You don't just need five nominees, which they might have managed; you need a tail of things almost good enough, or which might be good enough next year. There should be at least ten worthy nominees for there to be a category.

BEST INTERIOR ILLUSTRATION

Winner: Virgil Finlay

BEST COVER ARTIST

Winner: Hannes Bok and Ed Emshwiller

My only comment is that this is another indication that we are still in the time of magazine prominence here. We don't divide art by "interior" and "cover" anymore.

Best New Author or Artist

Winner: Philip José Farmer

Farmer had recently burst onto the scene and taken science fiction by storm. He wasn't brand new in 1953; indeed, he wouldn't have been eligible by today's Campbell rules, as he'd been publishing for longer than two years. But he was a good winner nevertheless, as he was near the start of his career and he became a major science fiction writer.

Excellence in Fact Articles

Winner: Willy Ley

Yes, his scientific articles were in fact excellent. No argument there. I'm not sure who any other nominees might have been—had Asimov started writing his *Fantasy & Science Fiction* science essays then?

#1 Fan Personality

Winner: Forry Ackerman

Well, he certainly was a memorable fan personality, who was a prominent fan then and remained a prominent fan until his death in 2008. So the Hugos did recognize lasting ability with this one.

Comments on 1953

7. Bob

Jo, the years were rather fluid in those first years of the award. You'll find that the awards for 1958 and 1959 both cover the same year—1958! I would add one other 1952 novel—*Limbo*, by Bernard Wolfe. It was not published as SF but is pure quill dystopian fiction along the lines of *We, 1984,* and *Brave New World*. Still surprisingly good and has just been republished. I would have to include *The Paradox Men,* by Charles L. Harness, and *Ring Around the Sun,* by Clifford Simak.

9. Rich Horton

You're quite right, of course, about the fluidity of the time eligibility rules for the early Hugos. Anything published from the calendar year preceding the Worldcon up to the time of the con itself seemed to be eligible. I think codification of the rules came in the late '50s or maybe very early '60s. (Though of course they keep changing.)

Telepaths, Murder, and Typographical Tricks: Alfred Bester's *The Demolished Man*

I hadn't reread *The Demolished Man* for a long time, perhaps twenty years. It's a great idea book, but it's also tense all the way through, and none of the characters are people I care to spend time with.

Sometimes I read old books and they feel clunky, but I can enjoy them despite that. This isn't one of those. This is a surprisingly modern-feeling novel—though, of course, very short. It reads like cyberpunk—apart from the cyber bit. It has everything I don't like about cyberpunk: unpleasant immoral characters, bribery, an underworld, a fast pace, lots of glitz, a metropolitan feel, chases, and a noir narrative voice that doesn't want you to get too close.

This is a good book, certainly a classic, unquestionably influential, but I don't warm to it. There are excellent reasons for reading it, and if you like William Gibson, you might well like this too, but while I love *The Stars My Destination* and Bester's short stories, I don't like this one.

This is a future world where humanity is inhabiting three planets and three moons—and a rich man's clock gives him the time on the meridian of all six of them, but he has to do sums to know what time it is in New York, where he happens to be. It's a future that's had some considerable technological advances on 1953, not just in one area but in many. It's a New York that has different classes, and people of both genders, though they all seem to be white. Most of the story takes place in Manhattan, with one excursion to a space habitat.

Society is full of Espers, called "peepers"—telepaths. Not even your thoughts are private, and there's not much significant crime, though there's still an underworld. We're told there hasn't been a premeditated murder in seventy years, because some peeper would see the intent and prevent the crime. The Espers are organized into a Guild with an Oath, they're very moral, but they're also trying eugenic breeding to produce more Espers with a goal of a totally telepathic world. They require intermarriage and children, they classify themselves into rigid classes, and they earn a lot seeing through people's secrets. Their punishment for breaking their oath is total ostracism from Esper society—and we see poor ostracized Jerry Church pressing up against the outside of a telepath party just to be able to overhear mental communication.

Bester describes the mental communication as making patterns impossible in speech, and represents this with typographical trickery. There's quite a lot of "@kins" and "Weyg&" kind of thing, which must have seemed very innovative in 1953, which is sufficiently ahead of 133tspeak that Bester can reasonably be considered to have either predicted or invented it. It seems a little precious now.

The patterns made by telepathy are also slightly too clever for my tastes—an eye in a stein, meaning "Einstein." I generally like them better when he describes them than when he attempts to convey them on the page. However, this was clearly the precedent for Walter Jon Williams's *Aristoi*. Generally, the telepathic communications are clear and well conveyed. Bester actually does succeed in making the Espers seem as if they have another channel of communication that isn't just silent speech—except when it is.

There's a computer justice system that can analyze very complex things, but on punch cards. There's a brief interlude among the decadent rich. (I am unaware of decadent rich people like this, but since they appear here, in James Blish's *A Case of Conscience* and Dorothy L. Sayers's *Murder Must Advertise,* then I have to believe that if three people satirize what is recognizably the same thing, they're probably working from a common original.) We see these decadent rich and the lowlifes at the fortune-tellers and the pawnshop, and much more unusually, the middle classes in the person of the girl who writes the earworm and the scientist who invents the rhodopsin capsule and others of Reich's subordinates.

The plot concerns a murder, first finding a way to commit it and then finding a way to prove the murderer did it. A murder mystery in a science fiction society isn't unusual now, but it was innovative in 1953. We begin in Reich's point of view as he plans the murder, finding ways to get around telepathic surveillance with an earworm, and then afterwards we switch to Lincoln Powell, Esper 1st, detective.

The best and the worst things about the book are closely allied. The whole thing is as Freudian as *The Last Battle* is Christian, and it causes the same kind of issues. First, it gives it some extra and interesting depth. We begin with a nightmare, and the absolutely best part of the book is another long nightmare toward the end that does the kind of sense-of-wonder things that only SF can do. But the adherence to the Freudian view of people also limits it unrealistically.

This is especially a problem with the female characters—not so much the dames, who are sufficiently stylized that it doesn't matter, but the actual characters Mary and Barbara really suffer. Indeed, the whole plot needs the Freudian thing to work, but while it's quite clever, it's a cheat. We've been in Reich's head, but Reich himself doesn't consciously know why he killed D'Courtney, or that D'Courtney is his father; he's just reenacting primal oedipal urges.

I feel as if I've spent this whole time tearing the book to shreds, and yet I do admire it. It contains images that I've remembered for decades—especially the nightmare image of Reich thinking he has everything he wants and then realizing the world has no stars and when he mentions stars nobody else knows what he's talking about.

1954

There were no Hugo Awards in 1954.

The 1954 International Fantasy Awards considered *The Demolished Man* and Theodore Sturgeon's *More Than Human*. *More Than Human* should definitely have been a Hugo nominee if it was eligible. It's another enduring classic, Sturgeon at his best and on his favorite topic.

COMMENTS ON 1954

6. RICH HORTON

The list for the awards that might have been, in 1954, is REALLY REALLY impressive, as the Retro Hugo nominees from a few years ago show: *The Caves of Steel*, by Isaac Asimov; *Fahrenheit 451*, by Ray Bradbury; *Childhood's End*, by Arthur C. Clarke; *Mission of Gravity*, by Hal Clement; and *More Than Human*, by Theodore Sturgeon. (Other potential choices, not as good but still quite good: Robert A. Heinlein's *Revolt in 2100* and *Starman Jones*, Fritz Leiber's *The Sinful Ones* and *The Green Millennium*, John Wyndham's *The Kraken Wakes* aka *Out of the Deeps*, Ward Moore's *Bring the Jubilee*, and Wilmar Shiras's *Children of the Atom*.)

1955

Winner: *They'd Rather Be Right,* by Mark Clifton and Frank Riley

Nominees:
None

There's kind of a trick fannish trivial pursuit question, which is, "Which is the worst book ever to win the Hugo?" The answer is *They'd Rather Be Right,* by Mark Clifton and Frank Riley, 1955's winner.

I don't know if the book deserves this reputation, because I have not read it, because when absolutely everybody tells me that the jar contains marmalade all the way down, I don't feel compelled to take the lid off. I have never heard a good word for this book. Sometimes these things worked and sometimes they didn't. This one didn't. The book is generally believed to be so awful that there are conspiracy theories about why it won. Goodness knows what the voters at Clevention in Cleveland in 1955 were thinking. The most sensible suggestion I've heard is Dave Langford's—Clifton had written good short stories, the voters hadn't read the novel and were going on past performance. In which case, oops. It isn't in print. It isn't in the library. It is barely in the memory of having been in print. It's quite clear that this has not stood the test of time.

Nineteen fifty-five, like 1953, did not release a list of nominees, so any guess as to what was in the voters' minds is just a guess.

The International Fantasy Award that year went to Edgar Pangborn's *A Mirror for Observers.* This is a brilliant, indescribable book that would have been a solid Hugo winner—one of the best five books of any year. It's in print in a gorgeous small-press edition from Old Earth Books.

The runner-up was Hal Clement's *Mission of Gravity*! How could the Hugo voters not have voted for *Mission of Gravity*—sometimes described as the only genuine hard science fiction novel? It's in print in an Orb edition, along with some stories set on the same planet.

Looking at 1954 novels, I am instantly struck dumb with amazement. Poul Anderson's *Brain Wave* and *The Broken Sword*! Asimov's *The Caves of Steel*! *The Fellowship of the Ring*! Richard Matheson's *I Am Legend*. Pohl and Kornbluth's *Search the Sky*!

In young adult, I see Heinlein's *The Star Beast,* Andre Norton's *The Stars Are Ours,* Eleanor Cameron's *The Wonderful Flight to the Mushroom Planet,* and C. S. Lewis's *The Horse and His Boy.*

Also in SF I haven't read but wouldn't be surprised to see on a Hugo short list, E. E. "Doc" Smith's *Children of the Lens* and L. Ron Hubbard's *To the Stars.*

I could easily compile a Hugo short list out of these books—either a "Jo's favorite five books published in 1954" or "What I imagine other people would have preferred," but in fact, any five of the books listed here would seem to me to be a pretty decent Hugo ballot that had stood the test of time. I'd somehow imagined that 1954 must have been a poor year, but it wasn't; it was a vintage year. Wow. The actual voters at Clevention inexplicably turned away from all these great things and chose *They'd Rather Be Right.*

But the good news is, nobody has to argue about what the worst book to win the Hugo is. Ever. I've been at Hugo loser parties where people aren't happy with what's won, and then somebody mentions *They'd Rather Be Right* and we all cheer up, because at least it's better than that.

Incidentally, the existence of this winner and my reluctance to read a book everyone says is awful also saved me from the thought that I would actually read all the Hugo winners in order to revisit them.

OTHER CATEGORIES

BEST NOVELETTE

Winner: "The Darfsteller," by Walter M. Miller Jr.

This is an absolutely brilliant short story from a writer on top of his form. Great choice. And hey, introduction of short fiction categories, what a good idea!

BEST SHORT STORY

Winner: "Allamagoosa," by Eric Frank Russell

Absolute classic, one of the best short stories of all time. Does the excellence of the short fiction winners make the novel choice better or worse?

BEST PROFESSIONAL MAGAZINE

Winner: *Astounding*, edited by John W. Campbell

Astounding published both short fiction winners . . . and the novel winner.

BEST PROFESSIONAL ARTIST

Winner: Frank Kelly Freas

BEST FANZINE

Winner: *Fantasy Times*, edited by James V. Taurasi Sr. and Ray Van Houten

The categories are getting to look a bit more like the categories we still know and love!

Comments on 1955

....

3. DD-B

The excellent short fiction choices don't make the novel choice better, but they do provide some evidence that the voters had a modicum of taste (or agreement with us). What voting system was used that year? If it was a simple single nontransferable vote, possibly the large number of excellent choices split the vote so widely that a dark horse slipped through. Ah, several comments online give the attendance of the convention as 38. That makes vote-splitting theories much easier to believe (though there could have been MORE voters than that, if they had supporting memberships back then, or even just if balloting by full members was done by mail in advance).

4. JO

DD-B: I'm not sure what voting system was used. I heard a rumor that it was done at the Worldcon by a show of hands! Very much not like today.

1956

Winner: *Double Star,* by Robert A. Heinlein

Nominees:
None

In 1956, Worldcon, NyCon II, was held in New York, and they chose a truly great set of Hugo winners, all of which have stood the test of time and all of which I unreservedly approve.

The Best Novel award went to Robert A. Heinlein's *Double Star,* one of my favorite books. It's one of Heinlein's best novels, a future with a colonized solar system in which one down-and-out actor gets the chance to play the role of a lifetime—impersonating an important politician. It's short, it's engaging, it has Martians—it's unquestionably Hugo-worthy.

We don't yet have a list of nominees. There were no other awards that year, so it's hard to know what else people at the time thought was outstanding. Plausible nominees: Isaac Asimov's *The End of Eternity,* Fredric Brown's *Martians Go Home,* Arthur C. Clarke's *Earthlight,* Frederik Pohl and Cyril Kornbluth's *Gladiator-At-Law,* C. M. Kornbluth's *Not This August,* Naomi Mitchison's *To the Chapel Perilous,* J. R. R. Tolkien's *The Return of the King,* and John Wyndham's *The Chrysalids.* All of these have since become classics, but I don't think any of them are likely to have been more popular than *Double Star.*

In YA, there was C. S. Lewis's *The Magician's Nephew;* two Andre Norton books, *Sargasso of Space* (under the name Andrew North) and *Star Guard;* and Heinlein's *Tunnel in the Sky.*

I think a very good book won, and in my judgment likely the best book* of that year.

Other Categories†

Best Novelette

Winner: "Exploration Team," by Murray Leinster

This was one of the first science fiction stories I read, in Amabel Williams-Ellis's (ed.) *Tales from the Galaxies* when I was a little kid, before I knew what science fiction was. I remember it well. Great story, but I haven't read it lately and I haven't heard other people talk about it much.

Best Short Story

Winner: "The Star," by Arthur C. Clarke

I think there's a wide consensus that this is one of the best short stories ever.

Best Professional Magazine

Winner: *Astounding,* edited by John W. Campbell Jr.

Again! *Astounding. Double Star* and "Exploration Team" appeared in it, but "The Star" appeared in *Infinity.*

---

*The Return of the King isn't a book; it's a third of a book. If we had a category for Best Completed Series, then *LOTR* would certainly have deserved it in 1956. I don't know whether it would have won, as it hadn't yet had US publication.
†In 2017, the nominees were rediscovered by Olav Rokne and they were *Call Him Dead* by Eric Frank Russell, *The End of Eternity* by Isaac Asimov, *Not This August* by Cyril Kornbluth, *The Long Tomorrow* by Leigh Brackett. This is the first woman on the short list, and also, wow I was wrong!

BEST PROFESSIONAL ARTIST

Winner: Frank Kelly Freas

BEST FAN MAGAZINE

Winner: *Inside and Science Fiction Advertiser,* edited by Ron Smith

MOST PROMISING NEW AUTHOR

Winner: Robert Silverberg

And he's absolutely gone on to fulfill that promise, continuing to write excellent science fiction in all the decades since.

BEST FEATURE WRITER

Winner: Willy Ley

BEST BOOK REVIEWER

Winner: Damon Knight

New category, and what an interesting one. I had no idea. I wonder why that died out—were not enough people reviewing books? I'd suggest reviving it. (But then, I would. . . .) Knight was an excellent choice; his criticism is still read.

COMMENTS ON 1956

1. DEMETRIOSX

Murray Leinster just tends to be forgotten, period. I started reading SF in the seventies and went pretty in depth, yet I hadn't really heard of him until they started doing some reprints in the eighties. Unfortunately, he just didn't seem to catch on again the way, say, Piper did.

4. MATT McIRVIN

Leinster's gotten some belated attention as the author of "A Logic Named Joe," a 1946 story that somehow got dozens of details of today's internet-connected, ubiquitous-computing world amazingly right— not just how they work but also how we use them and the opportunities and problems they create.

It's not spot-on, since it's basically a rogue-AI story, and some of the society's details are very much of the story's time, but Leinster somehow managed to figure out what a world full of networked personal computers would be like in ways that many SF writers didn't realize until it happened.

PARLIAMENTARY DEMOCRACY WITH MARTIANS: ROBERT A. HEINLEIN'S *DOUBLE STAR*

Double Star may well be Heinlein's best novel. It's generally a useless argument to try to determine what is the very best, but I think even people with different favorites would have to agree that this one is certainly a contender. It dates from when a book could be short and still be respected—it's barely an afternoon's read. I have always loved it because it does everything right.

There's a first-person narrator, Lawrence Smith, aka the Great Lorenzo, a vain, out-of-work actor who is hired to go to Mars to impersonate a politician, Bonforte, in a complicated act of interplanetary diplomacy. Lorenzo writes in Heinlein's confidential, confident voice, beginning with this pronouncement: "If a man walks in dressed like a hick and acting as if he owned the place, he's a spaceman." But the beauty of it is that Lorenzo is an unreliable narrator, he changes his mind as the story goes on, he is conned, he becomes not only the simulacrum but the reality of Bonforte. Within the 140 pages of the novel, Lorenzo changes his mind about everything from Martians to royalty, all in that confident tone and without ever noticing that he has really changed. Everything in him changes except that most important maxim: "The show must go on."

Double Star has a tight, exciting plot that never stops moving; an interesting future solar system with aliens and intrigue; and down-and-dirty parliamentary politics that actually make sense. But it is as a character study that it excels. I always say that a good character brings everything else along with them—their world, because only their world could have made them, and plot, because they have to be doing something. *Double Star* illustrates this perfectly. I also especially like the title. I have a weakness for titles that sound one kind of science-fictional and turn out to be another kind. (*When Gravity Fails* is another favorite example.) "Double Star" refers, of course, to Lorenzo and Bonforte, not to astronomy.

The technology is interesting—as so often in 1950s books, the spaceships are far ahead of the computers. The thing that made me blink was the tape spools small enough to slip into your handbag that could hold ten thousand words. How writers must have longed for them in 1955! How quaint they seem now, when last week a writer friend handed me a whole novel on a flash drive small enough to get lost in the fluff at the bottom of a handbag! But as is usual for Heinlein, the explanation of what's important about the "Farleyfile" still holds good, even though the technical details may have become obsolete. The same goes for the Martians—there are no Martians, but tolerance of diversity remains a good thing.

I also especially commend Heinlein for seeing and noting the virtues and advantages of a parliamentary democracy with a constitutional monarchy—Heinlein was a proud American, but you can see here that he wasn't blinkered by that.

I sometimes run across people who have read some random Heinlein book and can't understand why he dominated the genre for so long. *Double Star* is what I always suggest they read if they want to understand it. Writers can sigh at the smooth incluing, the beautiful pacing, the subtlety of voice—if they can get the necessary distance to admire it without being drawn right into it. If I don't enjoy reading it now as much as when I was a kid, that's only because it doesn't hold any surprises anymore.

1957

Best Novel

Winner: None

Nominees:
None

After 1955 and 1956 lulled me into a false sense of complacency—with me thinking that I could see in the Hugo Awards of those years the beginnings of the award I know today—1957 took me by surprise. The Worldcon that year was in London, Loncon I, the first overseas Worldcon. And British fans clearly decided to do something different with the Hugos. Something really different. Something indeed that makes no sense to me.

There were three categories for the Hugos of 1957, and none of them was fiction. They were Best US Magazine, Best British Magazine, and best Fan Magazine. I suppose this might reflect the prevailing view that magazines were where it was at, as well as British fans being unable to get hold of US books easily—which was a problem until 1994. But it must also reflect a belief that it isn't the stories that matter; it's where you read them. However, they did have nominees, so that's a good sign.

OTHER CATEGORIES

BEST AMERICAN PROFESSIONAL MAGAZINE

Winner: *Astounding*, edited by John W. Campbell Jr.

Anybody surprised? But this streak was about to be broken.

Nominees:
F&SF, edited by Anthony Boucher
Galaxy, edited by H. L. Gold
Infinity, edited by Larry T. Shaw

F&SF is the only magazine on the list still going under its original name. *Galaxy* was also a great magazine. *Infinity* is not such a well-known magazine, at least now, but it published Clarke's "The Star" the year before, so they were doing something right.

BEST BRITISH PROFESSIONAL MAGAZINE

Winner: *New Worlds*, edited by John Carnell

Nominee:
Nebula, edited by Peter Hamilton

Wait, Britain had two science fiction magazines? Why didn't I know this? Perhaps because it was before I was born.

BEST FAN MAGAZINE

Winner: *Science-Fiction Times*, edited by James V. Taurasi, Ray Van Houten, and Frank R. Prieto Jr.

Nominees:
Inside, edited by Ron Smith

Hyphen, edited by Walt Willis and Chuck Harris

Hyphen was robbed, I tell you, those old *Hyphen*s were golden.

Other categories they might have had? Well, they could have thought about novels, you know. Short fiction? But it's interesting that they were all reading the same fanzines but not the same novels and magazines.

The International Fantasy Award went to *The Lord of the Rings,* presumably considered as one thing. The International Fantasy Award then expired, presumably considering that with the publication of *The Lord of the Rings,* fantasy was now over.

Plausible nominees: Arthur C. Clarke's *The City and the Stars,* John Christopher's *The Death of Grass* (a cozy catastrophe), Frank Herbert's *The Dragon in the Sea* (claustrophobic futuristic undersea adventure), Philip Dick's *The Man Who Japed* and *The World Jones Made* (I don't like Dick, but lots of people do), Isaac Asimov's *The Naked Sun* (sequel to *The Caves of Steel,* one of Asimov's best), A. E. van Vogt's *The Players of Null-A* (aka *The Pawns of Null-A*), Frederik Pohl's *Slave Ship,* Alfred Bester's *The Stars My Destination* (aka *Tiger! Tiger!*), C. S. Lewis's *Till We Have Faces* (a weird fantasy based on Cupid and Psyche).

Or in YA: C. S. Lewis's *The Last Battle,* Asimov's *Lucky Starr* and *The Big Sun of Mercury,* Eleanor Cameron's *Stowaway to the Mushroom Planet,* and Heinlein's *Time for the Stars.*

I think out of all that, they might have been able to find something Hugo-worthy, don't you? There were some great books published in 1956, even if it wasn't quite so vintage a year as 1955. I think I'd have been torn between *The City and the Stars* and *The Stars My Destination,* but *The Naked Sun* is also terrific, and I'm very fond of *Time for the Stars.* What an odd year. What a relief it will be to get to 1958!

COMMENTS ON 1957

6. MARCUS ROWLAND

Nebula was a Scottish magazine, edited by Peter Hamilton (not the author, who was born a year after it folded), in print from 1952 to 1959.

7. RICH HORTON

The story I have heard—though, having been two years old at the time, I can't vouch for it—is that the reason no fiction categories were included was to protect the (British-administered) International Fantasy Award from competition. As you note, it was protected so well that it died immediately after!

I would certainly consider *The Stars My Destination* the proper Hugo winner for 1957, myself.

How about short fiction? Possible nominees, from a quick scan of the ISFB short fiction list for 1957: "Bodyguard," by "Christopher Grimm" (really Evelyn E. Smith); "Brightside Crossing," by Alan E. Nourse; "Horrer Howce," by Margaret St. Clair; "Margin of Profit," by Poul Anderson; "Fair," by "Keith Woodcott" (really John Brunner); "Plus X," by Eric Frank Russell; "Stranger Station," by Damon Knight; "The Country of the Kind," by Damon Knight; "The Anything Box," by Zenna Henderson; "The Dead Past," by Isaac Asimov; "The Man Who Came Early," by Poul Anderson; "The Man Who Ate the World," by Frederik Pohl; "The Skills of Xanadu," by Theodore Sturgeon.

I have a feeling I've forgotten some. My five-story nomination list would be "The Country of the Kind," "The Man Who Came Early," "The Dead Past," "Horrer Howce," and maybe "Stranger Station" or "The Skills of Xanadu."

I'd pick "The Dead Past" or "The Man Who Came Early" as the winners (maybe the first is "Best Novella" and the second "Best Short Story"), though I think "The Country of the Kind" is right up there too.

10. BOB

Weird year, all right. In the short fiction category, I would also include the prescient "And Now the News . . ." by Sturgeon, and as novella the last collaboration of Kuttner and Moore—*Rite of Passage*; and one of Asimov's most liked stories was also published—"The Last Answer."

12. RICH HORTON

Bob—good catch of "And Now the News . . ."—definitely one of the best stories of 1956, and now I can't decide whether I'd vote for it or the Asimov or the Anderson.

14. Rob Hansen

Interestingly, they used the same rockets for the Hugo in 1957 that had always been used for the IFAs. So while the bases were different, the actual trophies were identical.

16. David G. Hartwell

Someone did in fact give International Fantasy Awards in 1956, to Frank Herbert's *The Dragon in the Sea,* tied with William Golding's *Lord of the Flies.* I have a copy of the Gollancz first UK edition of the Herbert, with a band around it announcing the awards. And Frank showed me a picture of him accepting the award. Best I can figure, the American meeting on the IFA did not take place, but the UK one did, and the Brits unilaterally gave the awards. And the US fans refused to record them (to this day).

1958

Winner: *The Big Time*, by Fritz Leiber

Nominees:
None

The 1958 Hugo Awards were awarded at Solacon in South Gate (Los Angeles), and they still didn't announce nominees.

The Best Novel Hugo was Fritz Leiber's *The Big Time*, which was an interesting choice. It's in print, it has an ebook edition and an audio edition, and it's available in the library but only in French. It's a very short book about a time travelers' war, and it introduced many of the tropes of time travel. It's a very good book, and I like it, but although it's in print, I don't hear it talked about much, and I think Leiber isn't such a big name as he once was. He's best known now for his sword and sorcery, though he was prolific and wrote in almost every subgenre.

The Hugo was the only genre award given in 1958—in our award-filled times, it's a little hard to imagine. It's also hard to be sure what else the fans of 1958 might have been considering.

Plausible nominees: Ayn Rand's *Atlas Shrugged*, Jack Vance's *Big Planet*, Philip K. Dick's *The Cosmic Puppets* and *Eye in the Sky*, Ray Bradbury's *Dandelion Wine*, Arthur C. Clarke's *The Deep Range*, Robert Heinlein's *The Door into Summer* and *Citizen of the Galaxy*, Fred Hoyle's *The Black Cloud*, Van Vogt's *Empire of the Atom*, Philip José Farmer's *The Green Odyssey*, Wyndham's *The Midwich Cuckoos*, Nevil Shute's *On the Beach*, Frederic Brown's *Rogue in Space*, and Eric Frank Russell's *Wasp*.

Again, I could make "Jo's top five books of 1957" or "what I think would have been likely to be on the list" (and they'd be very different), but that's fairly useless. I think it would be possible to make a case for any of this list as five likely nominees. Lots of these books are still read and widely debated—perhaps more so than *The Big Time*.

OTHER CATEGORIES

BEST SHORT STORY

Winner: "Or All the Seas with Oysters," by Avram Davidson (*Galaxy*, May 1958)

Great choice, terrific classic unforgettable story. And from *Galaxy*. But from 1958, what's going on here? What's going on is that eligibility wasn't by calendar year but from Worldcon to Worldcon, or something of the kind. They didn't get this sorted for some time.

OUTSTANDING MOVIE

Winner: *The Incredible Shrinking Man*

BEST PROFESSIONAL MAGAZINE

Winner: *F&SF*, edited by Anthony Boucher

My goodness. Was Campbell surprised?

OUTSTANDING ARTIST

Winner: Frank Kelly Freas

. . . again. We've had only six years of Hugos, and already we're seeing repetition.

OUTSTANDING ACTIFAN

Winner: Walter A. Willis

Yay! But note that this is a person award, not a fanzine award. These categories may look a lot more normal, but they are still in flux.

COMMENTS ON 1958

15. ROB T.

Leiber's impact as a writer is somewhat diffuse not only because it was spread over several genres but also because this impact often came ahead of its time. Not only did the first Fafhrd and the Gray Mouser stories appear long before adventure fantasy became a marketable genre, but Leiber's seminal urban horror stories "The Automatic Pistol" and "Smoke Ghost"—which speculated on how supernatural or uncanny forces might manifest themselves in a modern technological setting—appeared decades before horror became a marketable genre, as well. Leiber was also one of the first writers in American SF to propose (in "Coming Attraction" and later stories) that high technology and cultural decadence weren't necessarily incompatible—that being surrounded by monuments of human rationality didn't mean human irrationality was just going to disappear. (Alfred Bester and Cyril Kornbluth made similar breakthroughs around the same time.)

Another factor that makes Leiber difficult to market is that not one of his novels is very much like any of the others, and most of the best are culminations or reworkings of themes from his short fiction. Thus we have *The Big Time* from the Changewar series and *The Swords of Lankhmar* from the F&M series; *Conjure Wife* fits in with Leiber's early horror stories, *The Green Millennium* among his early stories of technological decadence, and *Our Lady of Darkness* among Leiber's remarkable late series of autobiographical/roman à clef fantasies. (Shorter examples include "Catch That Zeppelin!," "Horrible Imaginings," and my personal favorite, "The Button Molder.")

The uniqueness of each of Leiber's novels means they don't play off one another as readily as those of novelists more inclined to stick to particular themes or types of stories. Leiber would probably benefit as much as Theodore Sturgeon from a comprehensive, chronological series of his short fiction (perhaps leaving out the F&M stories, which don't need the help).

1959

Winner: *A Case of Conscience*, by James Blish

Nominees:
The Enemy Stars, by Poul Anderson
Who?, by Algis Budrys
Have Space Suit—Will Travel, by Robert A. Heinlein
Immortality, Inc., by Robert Sheckley

The 1959 Hugo Awards were awarded at Detention, Detroit. The winning novel was James Blish's *A Case of Conscience*. It's religious science fiction. It posits a planet that has been arranged by the devil, along with aliens, especially as a trap for humanity. It's good to see the Hugo going to a philosophic adventure story like this. It's in print and in the library in French and English.

And we have nominees at last! There are four, and I have read all of them!

Robert A. Heinlein's *Have Space Suit—Will Travel* is a YA adventure with aliens and the fate of humanity. It's in print and in the library in English.

Poul Anderson's *The Enemy Stars* (aka "We Have Fed Our Sea") is a space opera adventure about survival on a spaceship when the teleporter breaks down. It's not in print, and it's not in the library. It's pretty good vintage Anderson.

Robert Sheckley's *Immortality, Inc.* (aka *Time Killer*), is near-future

SF about transferring consciousness into a dead body. It's not in print or in the library either.

Algis Budrys's *Who?* is a future Cold War novel—a scientist is patched up by the Soviets and sent home, or is he? It's in the library in French and English, but it's not in print.

So, five men, four American and one Free Lithuanian living in the United States. Heinlein had won before, but the others are all new on the ballot. Five very different books, all SF: a religious conundrum with aliens, a YA adventure (also with aliens), a space opera (without aliens), a near-future thriller, and a novel of identity. They're all good nominees, and any one of them would have been a worthy winner. Excellent!

What else might they have chosen? There are several things that could have been contenders—T. H. White's *The Once and Future King,* though only the last part was new in 1958, so it might not have been eligible. There's also Theodore Sturgeon's *To Marry Medusa* and Andre Norton's *The Time Traders.* I wouldn't have been surprised to see any of those on the short list, but I don't think they're better or more representative than what the voters nominated. So taking the five nominees as a whole, I think they do pretty well at representing the best of science fiction as it was in 1959.

OTHER CATEGORIES

BEST NOVELETTE

Winner: "The Big Front Yard," by Clifford D. Simak (*Astounding,* October 1958)

Nominees:
"Captivity," by Zenna Henderson (*F&SF,* June 1958)
"A Deskful of Girls," by Fritz Leiber (*F&SF,* April 1958)
"The Miracle-Workers," by Jack Vance (*Astounding,* July 1958)
"Rat in the Skull," by Rog Phillips (*If,* December 1958)

"Second Game," by Katherine MacLean and Charles V. De Vet
(*Astounding*, March 1958)
"Shark Ship," (aka "Reap the Dark Tide") by C. M. Kornbluth
(*Vanguard*, June 1958)
"Unwillingly to School," by Pauline Ashwell (*Astounding*, January
1958)

What a lot of nominees. The winner is excellent and memorable,
and I've read and remember several of the others—this looks like a
strong field. It's also nice to see three women here—these are the first
female Hugo contenders, and we get them the first year we have
nominees.

Best Short Story

Winner: "That Hell-Bound Train," by Robert Bloch (*F&SF*, September 1958)

Nominees:
"The Advent on Channel Twelve," by C. M. Kornbluth (*Star Science
Fiction Stories No. 4*)
"The Edge of the Sea," by Algis Budrys (*Venture*, March 1958)
"The Men Who Murdered Mohammed," by Alfred Bester (*F&SF*,
October 1958)
"Nine Yards of Other Cloth," by Manly Wade Wellman (*F&SF*, November 1958)
"Rump-Titty-Titty-Tum-Tah-Tee," by Fritz Leiber (*F&SF*, May
1958)
"Space to Swing a Cat," by Stanley Mullen (*Astounding*, June 1958)
"Theory of Rocketry," by C. M. Kornbluth (*F&SF*, July 1958)
"They've Been Working On . . . ," by Anton Lee Baker (*Astounding*,
August 1958)
"Triggerman," by J. F. Bone (*Astounding*, December 1958)

How could they not have given it to "The Men Who Murdered Mohammed"? It's one of my favorite short stories of all time! I haven't read (or don't remember) the Bloch, but there are some other good short stories here that have lasted. But "The Men Who Murdered Mohammed"! Come on!

BEST SF OR FANTASY MOVIE

Winner: No Award

Nominees:
The Fly (1958)
Horror of Dracula
The 7th Voyage of Sinbad

BEST PROFESSIONAL MAGAZINE

Winner: *F&SF*, edited by Anthony Boucher and Robert P. Mills

Nominees:
Astounding, edited by John W. Campbell Jr.
Galaxy, edited by H. L. Gold
Infinity, edited by Larry T. Shaw
New Worlds, edited by John Carnell

BEST PROFESSIONAL ARTIST

Winner: Frank Kelly Freas

Nominees:
Ed Emshwiller
Virgil Finlay
H. R. Van Dongen
Wally Wood

BEST AMATEUR MAGAZINE

Winner: *Fanac*, edited by Terry Carr and Ron Ellik

Nominees:

Cry of the Nameless, edited by F. M. and Elinor Busby, Burnett Toskey, and Wally Weber

Hyphen, edited by Walt Willis and Chuck Harris

JD-Argassy, edited by Lynn A. Hickman

Science-Fiction Times, edited by James V. Taurasi Sr., Ray Van Houten, and Frank R. Prieto Jr.

Yandro, edited by Robert Coulson and Juanita Coulson

BEST NEW AUTHOR OF 1958

Winner: No Award

Nominees:

Brian W. Aldiss (ran highest but lost to No Award)

Paul Ash

Pauline Ashwell

Rosel George Brown

Louis Charbonneau

Kit Reed

On this, it seems the voters might have been a bit too quick to vote for No Award. I think it's pretty clear that Brian Aldiss would have deserved the honor if it had been given—he's gone on to edit major anthologies and works of science fiction criticism, as well as writing major novels and short stories. But I don't know what the basis for this vote was, I don't know what he'd published by 1959, and maybe it wasn't all that impressive. As for the other contenders—Ashwell had a Hugo-nominated novelette that year and the next, but I'm not aware of any future work, and the others are minor writers or people who did not stay in the field.

COMMENTS ON 1959

4. RICH HORTON

A quick note on the new writer list. Obviously, Aldiss deserved to win; it's something of a shame there was a No Award, though I suspect voters were being honest and not voting when they didn't know.

But what's interesting is "Paul Ash"/Pauline Ashwell are the same person. She had two notable stories in 1958—the delightful Hugo nominee "Unwillingly to School" and the Paul Ash story, "Big Sword," which I haven't read but which gets admiring comment from some who have read it.

She has continued to write, intermittently, for decades, under both names. (Her real name is given as Pauline Whitby at the ISFDB—I assume that's her married name, though I'm not sure.) According to an article at *io9*, her actual first publication came at the age of fourteen, under the name "Paul Ashwell," in a very obscure magazine called *Yankee Science Fiction*.

Notable stories as Ash include a 1993 *Analog* serial, *The Man Who Stayed Behind*, as well as stories in 1966 (including the well-regarded "The Wings of a Bat") and 1988 to 1991, all in *Analog*.

Notable stories by Ashwell include several sequels to "Unwillingly to School" ("The Lost Kafoozalum" in 1960, "Rats in the Moon" in 1982, and eventually a fix-up novel, *Unwillingly to Earth* [1992]) and an unrelated novel, *Project FarCry*. Her most recent story credit at the ISFDB is "Elsewhere," in *Analog* in 2001.

She's still alive as far as I know, and she'd be eighty-two, so she may well be retired from writing.

Her best stories are the Lizzie Lee pieces, beginning with "Unwillingly to Earth." But in general, I found her work entertaining, though by no means a patch on Aldiss.

I wonder if the voting results would have changed if the votes for "Paul Ash" and "Pauline Ashwell" were combined.

Of the other new writer nominees, Rosel George Brown had a brief career, but did some interesting stuff before her untimely death in 1967, and Kit Reed has had a long, often brilliant career—she's a major

SF writer, though again not quite at Aldiss's level. On the whole, that's a pretty good Best New Writer nomination list.

11. DemetriosX

I just looked more closely at the amateur mag list. There are a lot of names that would become prominent. Terry Carr won, and we also see F. M. Busby and the Coulsons. How many people still come out of active fandom and the zines?

14. Rene Walling

@DemetriosX: There are still new writers coming up through fandom. Among those nominated for a Campbell in the last ten years or so are David Levine, John Scalzi, Lawrence Schoen, and Jo Walton. (There's more, I'm sure, but I know all of these folks either attended/organized conventions or published zines/blogs before being professional writers.)

Ever Outward: Robert A. Heinlein's *Have Space Suit—Will Travel*

Have Space Suit—Will Travel is the last of Heinlein's juveniles but for *Podkayne of Mars,* and it seems to me quite different from the others, and from Heinlein's other work. It starts traditionally in near-future America with a teenage boy who wants to go to the moon. It then opens out and out, to the moon, to Pluto, to Vega, to the Lesser Magellanic Cloud. It does the same opening out as far as stakes are concerned—there's a boy repairing a space suit and hoping to go to the moon one day, then he's kidnapped by flying-saucer aliens and trying to escape, then he's rescued by another set of aliens and hoping to get home, then he's surrounded by a league of aliens and the future of the human race is at stake.

Have Space Suit gets away with all of this in two ways—first, the first-person voice of Kip, who is very practical, very determined, and with no intention of giving up on anything ever. We accept the most amazing things happening because Kip is amazed and trying to figure out his options. Second, the book varies between extreme detail on things Heinlein knew about and could have Kip know about—space suit design, oxygen bottles, what soda jerks have in their pockets—and Clarke's Law magic baffled hand waves on the things he doesn't. If Kip knows how it works, he tells us; if he doesn't, he tells us that.

The oddest thing about *Have Space Suit* is that the protagonists, Kip and the little girl genius Peewee, are mostly passengers in the plot. If the book has a message, it's that you have to try your best even though you will fail sometimes. This is not like other Heinlein juveniles. When I was a kid, this was one of my least favorites of them, because of this. It wasn't the message I wanted. The message has grown on me somewhat, but the book hasn't, really.

Kip is a very passive protagonist, and he often does not achieve what he tries to do. I think this may have been Heinlein's deliberate intention, having noticed how little of this there is in fiction. But it disappointed me as an immature reader, and even now my favorite part of this book is the very beginning, when Kip is working as a soda jerk and educating himself and fixing his space suit.

The book begins like many Heinlein juveniles, with our teenage hero on near-future Earth with his eccentric family. *Time for the Stars*, *Farmer in the Sky*, *Starman Jones*, and *Tunnel in the Sky* all start that way. This Earth, in strong contrast to all of those, isn't dystopic. It's America of the 1950s, plus a moonbase. Centerville might as well be Pleasantville. The one thing wrong with it is that school is too much fun and not enough education, so Kip's father persuades Kip to study the important stuff—math and science and Latin—on his own.

Kip wants to go to the moon, so he enters a competition to win a trip there, by writing slogans on soap wrappers. You wouldn't believe how science-fictional I found this when I was twelve, so I won't tell you. But I thought it just as made up as the aliens.

Kip's also working as a soda jerk in a drugstore—this actually does mean he was serving soft drinks to people in a pharmacy, which, well, again with the science fiction, astonishing-future stuff. What an imagination I thought Heinlein had! Instead of cafés or restaurants, people are drinking cold Horlicks in chemist shops and calling it a "fountain"—what could be more futuristic? And Heinlein makes us feel Kip's pride in his work—his shakes are the thickest. And it's an actual pharmacy, the owner makes up prescriptions while Kip serves the drinks! It's up there with food pills.

Heinlein needed this as a plot device, so that Kip could be socializing with the horrible bully Ace Quigley while also selling soap, but he really made it work and seem almost plausible because Kip takes it so for granted. When I found out this was a real American thing, I was extremely taken aback.

Kip sells a lot of soap and makes a lot of entries to the competition. He doesn't win the trip, but he wins a used space suit, which he repairs and makes functional for fun. The description of him fixing the space suit is the best part of the book—and it seems that Heinlein may have worked on the development of early space suits and been talking from experience. (Bill Higgins has been giving talks about this connection, which I recommend if you can catch him.)

But even here we have the theme: "Microwave circuitry is never easy. It takes precision machining and a slip of a tool can foul up the impedance and ruin a mathematically calculated resonance. Well, I tried. Synthetic precision crystals are cheap from surplus houses and some transistors and other components I could vandalize from my own gear. And I made it work, after the fussiest pray-and-try-again I have ever done. But the consarned thing simply would not fit in my helmet. Call it a moral victory—I've never done better work. I finally bought one, precision made and embedded in plastic, from the same firm that sold me the crystal."

Thematically, we have: "Sometimes you can try your hardest and it won't work, but don't give up, try something else." And also we have the message Heinlein couldn't know he was writing: "It was 1959, and the day of teenagers being able to take the covers off everything and rejig it was almost over." I find that word "transistor" almost poignant there. Kids in Heinlein juveniles knew how things worked because they lived in a macroworld, with things big enough to tweak. Sure, computers are great and I shudder at the loneliness of the world without them, but that microwave transistor radio, "precision made and embedded in plastic," marks the beginning of the end of the possibilities of building a spaceship in your barn.

With a working space suit and summer almost over (and without his college plans sorted), Kip goes for a melancholy walk in the suit, nicknamed Oscar, and adventure hits him. Before he knows where he is, he's on a flying saucer headed for the moon, with two kinds of aliens and a little girl. Peewee's an odd character. She's eleven, she carries a rag doll, she's a genius and a brat. She persuaded her parents to let her go to the moon alone, and once on the moon, she was kidnapped by aliens who want to trade her for her father, a physicist. She escaped and stole a spaceship, then was recaptured with Kip.

Even when I was myself a twelve-year-old girl, I never identified with Peewee or found her remotely plausible. This wasn't a problem, because I had no trouble whatsoever identifying with Kip. Fortunately, nobody told me that I was supposed to identify with Peewee, and I only thought of it on this reading.

On the moon, after a brief and delightful interlude of Kip's being thrilled to be on the moon and in low gravity for the first time, they escape and try to walk forty miles to Tombaugh Base, through Lunar mountains and with Peewee's oxygen constantly running out because the connectors on her bottles are incompatible with Kip's. This is another wonderful passage—it's very hard. They almost die. And they almost make it, only to be picked up again by the bad guys in sight of the base. "Call it a moral victory" again. I can remember being furious at this on first reading. It's not what I expected from the kind of book it was. It's more than a setback. I remember comparing it to Caradhras, but from Caradhras, the Fellowship keep going on their quest, through Moria, but Kip and Peewee never get to Tombaugh Base, they get shanghaied farther and farther off, and they never rescue themselves.

Kip has met two kinds of aliens by this point. The first is the "Mother Thing," who is a Vegan. She is described as being somewhat lemurlike, with a pouch, and small enough to fit inside Kip's space suit with Kip. She's loving and nurturing and I have never liked her, not when I was twelve and not now either. She isn't developed enough to feel real. Heinlein had some great alien characters in other books—Sir Isaac Newton the Venusian dragon, and Willis the Martian. But generally, aliens are not his strong point—they tend to exist to be threats, in *Starman Jones* and *Methuselah's Children* and here with the Wormfaces. This is his one attempt at a benevolent League of Aliens who are more advanced and powerful than us, and it leaves me cold.

The Wormfaces, on the other hand, are great villain-aliens. They have three scanning eyes, and they have wormy faces, and they totally dominate humans the way humans dominate horses—that's a great description, and Kip can't resist them. When we get to the trial and the Wormfaces' justifying themselves at the end, they say Earth is empty but for animals, and I'd be sure they meant that, except for the way they want to kidnap Peewee's father. Their next stop is Pluto, where the two quisling humans who have been helping the Wormfaces get eaten by them, and Kip gets helplessly imprisoned for a long time. While imprisoned, he works out in great detail how far away Pluto is, and how far away the nearest stars are. One thing this book is great on is sense of scale, as it keeps expanding. It's odd how the loss of Pluto as a planet and the existence of the Kuiper belt have made the solid nine-planet solar system of older SF seem so dated.

The Mother Thing engineers an escape, killing the Wormfaces, and Kip has to go outside on Pluto in his space suit and place a beacon. This almost kills him, and is another passage of great difficulty that ends in failure—he sets off the beacon but doesn't make it back and has to be rescued by Peewee. He has successfully set off the beacon, however, because they are all rescued by the Vegans and taken to Vega, where Kip spends a long time recovering in bed in a simulacrum of his own room. Peewee gets a Clarke's Law magic space suit, but Kip decides to stick with Oscar. While in bed, he calculates, with Peewee's help, how far away Vega is from the sun.

As soon as Kip is well, and before we've seen half enough of Vega, the kids are whisked off to the Lesser Magellanic Cloud, where they see the Milky Way galaxy looking lovely. They work out how far it is to Vega, and really the distance between Vega and the sun doesn't matter at that scale.

The Wormfaces are on trial, and are condemned to have their planet rotated into another dimension, without their sun. I've always wondered about this, as the Wormfaces demonstrably have interstellar travel— did they have only one planet plus the base on Pluto and long-term complex designs on Earth? Seems odd when you think about it. Then the humans are tried, essentially for barbarism and aggressive tendencies, and the aliens decide to help Earth. But it isn't because of anything the kids do or don't do; they decide for inexplicable alien reasons, just as they have decided to judge the human race on two kidnapped children, a Roman, and a Neanderthal for inexplicable alien reasons. I would like to be swayed by Kip's speech to the assembled aliens of three galaxies, but it all seems pointless. It's aliens ex machina.

After that, we get a great postscript end, the kind of end you don't normally get on juveniles, when the kid goes home with the treasure—alien knowledge, in this case—and the grown-ups believe them and treat them as grown-ups. We also discover that Kip's eccentric father had, ha-ha, actually had a college fund all the time and hadn't told him, so he'd develop self-reliance, which seems bizarrely negligent when you consider it's Labor Day of the year Kip wants to go to college. But it's all okay anyway, because Peewee's father has arranged for Kip to have a scholarship to MIT, in exchange for sharing alien secrets with them.

What I like, though, is that the kids come back from their adventure and it doesn't all turn to leaves and nothing gained, as these things so often do. It's a very odd book, really. I keep rereading it periodically to see if I'll warm to it this time, but I never do. It's Heinlein, which naturally means every sentence is compulsively readable and leads to the next sentence inevitably, so even though I don't much like this book, I can't stop reading it once I start.

1960

Winner: *Starship Troopers,* by Robert A. Heinlein

Nominees:
Dorsai!, by Gordon R. Dickson
The Pirates of Zan, by Murray Leinster
That Sweet Little Old Lady, by Mark Phillips
The Sirens of Titan, by Kurt Vonnegut

The 1960 Hugo Awards were given at Pittcon, Pittsburgh, and they look comparatively normal. They have categories that are recognizably what the present categories grew out of.

The Best Novel Hugo was won by Robert A. Heinlein's *Starship Troopers,* a military science fiction [MilSF] novel that remains both popular and controversial today. It's in print, it's in the library in both languages, it's easily available, and has been since 1959. I think it's practically the definition of a lasting Hugo winner, even though some people hate it—it's a book people are still reading and talking about fifty years later.

There are four other nominees, of which I have read two. I read and enjoyed Gordon R. Dickson's *Dorsai!* It's in print, and it's in the library in French. It's also MilSF, with mercenaries on other planets, and I loved it when I was twelve but don't feel all that much urge to go back to it.

I haven't read Murray Leinster's *The Pirates of Zan,* aka *The Pirates of Ersatz.* I haven't read it, because while Leinster wrote good solid SF, he was never a favorite. I didn't come across this when I was reading everything indiscriminately. It may well be very good; I am entirely open to the possibility. It seems to be in print in various small-press editions, implying that it is out of copyright and people are still interested in it. It isn't in the library.

I have read Kurt Vonnegut's *The Sirens of Titan*, and this is one I loved when I was fourteen. It's a Vonnegut tall tale, written in first-person-asshole style, and full of Tralfalmadorian aliens manipulating Earth history to rescue a lost alien from Titan. It's the kind of thing that looks cool and sophisticated to teenagers, and I don't know whether it's embarrassment at my own self or at the book that makes it unreadable to me now. It is in print from Gollancz, and in the library in English. I think it has therefore stood the test of time, whatever I personally feel about it.

Mark Phillips was a pseudonym for Randall Garrett and Laurence M. Janifer, and their novel *That Sweet Little Old Lady* (aka *Brain Twister*) is the last thing on the 1960 ballot. I haven't read it, or even heard of it. It seems to be in print in small-press editions; it isn't in the library.

So, five nominees written by six men, all American. Heinlein is a prior winner. Leinster had been nominated for short work, but this is his first novel nomination. All the others are new to the Hugos. We have one military adventure, one space opera, one surreal adventure with aliens, and one gonzo near-future story about spies.

Other plausible nominees: Eric Frank Russell's *Next of Kin*. Andre Norton's *Beast Master*. Robert Bloch's *Psycho*. Pohl and Kornbluth's *Wolfsbane*. Shirley Jackson's *The Haunting of Hill House*. I'd put *Next of Kin* above *Dorsai!* or *The Sirens of Titan*. *The Haunting of Hill House* is undoubtedly a classic of its genre.

I think this is a year where you can argue a lot about whether these are the five best books, but where *Starship Troopers* would have won whatever the other four were.

Other Categories

Best Short Fiction

Winner: "Flowers for Algernon," by Daniel Keyes (*F&SF*, April 1959)

Nominees:
"The Alley Man," by Philip José Farmer (*F&SF*, June 1959)
"Cat and Mouse," by Ralph Williams (*Astounding*, June 1959)
"The Man Who Lost the Sea," by Theodore Sturgeon (*F&SF*, October 1959)
"The Pi Man," by Alfred Bester (*F&SF*, October 1959)

Well, I absolutely can't argue with the winner, as "Flowers for Algernon" is one of the best novellas ever written, but what happened to having separate categories for short story and novelette?

Best Dramatic Presentation

Winner: *The Twilight Zone* (TV series)

Nominees:
Men into Space
"Murder and the Android"
The Turn of the Screw (TV)
The World, the Flesh and the Devil

Best Professional Magazine

Winner: *F&SF*, edited by Robert P. Mills

Nominees:
Amazing Stories, edited by Cele Goldsmith
Astounding, edited by John W. Campbell Jr.

Fantastic Universe, edited by Hans Stefan Santesson
Galaxy, edited by H. L. Gold

BEST PROFESSIONAL ARTIST

Winner: Ed Emshwiller

Nominees:
Virgil Finlay
Frank Kelly Freas
Mel Hunter
Wally Wood

BEST FANZINE

Winner: *Cry of the Nameless*, edited by F. M. and Elinor Busby, Burnett Toskey, and Wally Weber

Nominees:
Fanac, edited by Terry Carr and Ron Ellik
JD-Argassy, edited by Lynn A. Hickman
Science-Fiction Times, edited by James V. Taurasi Sr., Ray Van Houten, and Frank R. Prieto Jr.
Yandro, Robert Coulson and Juanita Coulson

COMMENTS ON 1960

13. GARDNER DOZOIS

"Flowers for Algernon" probably still wins, but "The Man Who Lost the Sea" is an amazing story, and I know many writers who were deeply influenced by it.

26. RICH HORTON

As for "That Sweet Little Old Lady," I read it a few years ago, along with its sequels. (I was trying to read as much Janifer [or Larry M. Harris, as he was known then] as I could find, for perhaps obscure reasons.) It's a breezy-enough read (and better than its sequels, I think), but it's a very, very minor work, and actually quite silly. I was flabberghasted (i.e., surprised + aghast) to learn it had been short-listed for the Hugo.

27. RICH HORTON

For the short fiction, I really can't argue seriously with the win for "Flowers for Algernon," a truly wonderful story. But "The Man Who Lost the Sea" is even better. (One of my favorite short stories of all time.)

"The Alley Man" and "The Pi Man" are also quite good. (I prefer "The Pi Man" between those two.) I don't recall the Williams story.

Other potential short fiction nominees include one famous story that I'm surprised wasn't nominated: "'—All You Zombies—'," by Heinlein. Also, Anderson's "A Man to My Wounding," Chan Davis's "Adrift on the Policy Level," Avram Davidson's "Dagon" and "Take Wooden Indians," Randall Garrett's "Despoilers of the Golden Empire" (written as "David Gordon") (even if it's not really SF!), Cordwainer Smith's "Golden the Ship Was—Oh! Oh! Oh!," J. G. Ballard's "The Sound-Sweep" and "The Waiting Grounds," and Damon Knight's "What Rough Beast."

Also, the ISFDB suggests that 1959 saw the first publication in English of Jorge Luis Borges's "The Lottery in Babylon."

OVER THE HUMP: ROBERT A. HEINLEIN'S *STARSHIP TROOPERS*

I've read or participated in a zillion threads online about *Starship Troopers,* and practically all of them are arguments over the earned franchise issue with side arguments about Juan Rico's Filipino ancestry. I've seen people quoting "counting the fuzz on caterpillars" from both directions hundreds of times, but there's a lot more to it than that, and people very seldom talk about what a clever story it is.

It's a good story with a lot more to it! It isn't my favorite Heinlein—indeed, it's probably somewhere about fifteenth (he wrote a lot of books)—but it's a good, readable story and just so stylistically clever.

There's a standard way of telling a story, where you start off with incidents and information that slowly builds up to the point where the reader has learned enough about the world and the background that they can follow a fast-paced climactic sequence without needing to slow down to explain anything. This is the pacing of *Moby-Dick*, for instance, and it's a very common way to do SF, where you have to introduce and inclue a whole lot of world and background so as to make sense at all. It's a technique Heinlein knew intimately and used many times. In *Starship Troopers*, he does this backwards. And it isn't only the tech and world that he does this backwards with; he also does it with the emotional arc of the novel—the bit where you're supposed to start to care about characters before you see them killed. He does that backwards too; he does it "backwards and in high heels," like Ginger Rogers.

The book begins with a battle sequence in which troopers are bouncing around the landscape, exploding atomics and destroying everything in sight, and with the sergeant, Jelly, not taking the place of the dead lieutenant even though he's doing his job. Then it backs up to go through Juan's recruitment, boot camp, and early war experiences and acquaintance with these people, with frequent flashbacks to History and Moral Philosophy high school classes. Then when it's caught up to the beginning, it goes on to do Juan's officer training. And it does this all in the confiding, compelling, but unreliable first-person narration of Juan Rico himself. Anybody can call voices from the vast deep, but Heinlein was definitely one of those who got them to answer. Instead of giving you the information you will want, he gives you the information so you can slot it in afterwards.

Heinlein was absolutely at his peak when he wrote this in 1959. He had so much technical stylistic mastery of the craft of writing science fiction that he could do something like this and get away with it. I'm tempted to say "don't try this at home."

Starship Troopers is best viewed with Heinlein's juveniles, because it's definitely the story of a boy becoming a man. More than that, it's a story of a boy being transformed into a soldier, going through the military training that redefines his identity and loyalty and motivation. Heinlein had been through this himself, at a different tech level—I have no doubt that the boot camp sections and the bull sessions where they're talking about the expurgated Bugs and the blankety-blank civilians are as authentic as it is possible to write them, given the constraints of the time.

It's a juvenile; it's about going into the world of work. It has no whiff of sex, and the violence is at a level perfectly acceptable for twelve-year-olds. The reason it's an adult novel is the (much argued-over) politics, which I strongly suspect Heinlein put in far more to make people think than as firmly held beliefs intended to convince people. Anyone who wants to argue that it reflects Heinlein's own opinions should look at the beautiful reference to the War of 1812 as "one of the brush-fire wars on the sidelines of the Napoleonic Conflict." Heinlein was a patriotic American who could see over the hump of his own prejudices, but I feel sure that wasn't his own opinion of the War of 1812! Also, throwing in arguments about who ought to get the franchise was one of his favorite ways of being stimulating. In *Expanded Universe,* he suggested only women should have it. I doubt he any more meant that only veterans should have it than he meant that. Probably he'd have been delighted at how much the book has made people think and argue. It's astonishing that it's still controversial now, after fifty years.

I was surprised how early it was. I'd somehow gathered the impression that it was in some way a Vietnam protest book, but it isn't. (I also thought "The Liberation of Earth" was a Vietnam protest story. The Korean conflict had somehow vanished from the mythologically significant history of the twentieth century by the time I was a teenager.) And was juvenile delinquency terrible in the fifties in the United States? It's not the way the era is remembered, but there's that discussion about parks you can't go into and how corporal punishment isn't allowed—it sounds more like the stereotypical seventies.

The one point where it really feels of its time is the gender politics—Heinlein was well ahead of the curve for 1959 in having women fight as pilots, but . . . Juan's thoughts about women being "why we fight" are just weird now. I don't know how many women read it in 1959 and wanted to have a powered suit (talk about a great equalizer!) or what Heinlein would have made of women's desire to serve loyally in the front lines, putting their bodies between home and war's desolation. As a kid, I didn't find it problematic; I just rolled my eyes and went right on identifying with Juan Rico. Now, well, I can see the points where Juan isn't a reliable narrator, in part because what Heinlein's writing about is the way he's being absorbed into the MI in much the same way that the bacon I ate for breakfast is being absorbed into me, and in part because he isn't all that bright and is happy to take simple answers that are handed to him. (Heinlein palms the card of their "philosophy" having mathematical logic underlying it. Show your work. . . .) And the "women smell nice" is part of Juan's worldview and not a problem, but the segregated service and the chaperonage are part of the fifties' worldview and rub like grit in an oyster.

More than anything, this is military SF done extremely well. One of the advantages of SF is that you can have an enemy who is unquestionably wrong. The Bugs are interstellar-traveling hive minds, and humanity can't communicate with them, and also they attacked first. There's no moral issue fighting them. (Joe Haldeman has a brilliant reply to this in his novel *1968*.) But meanwhile, you can just enjoy them being sentimental in the way old soldiers are and getting out there and blasting bugs.

1961

Best Novel

Winner: *A Canticle for Leibowitz*, by Walter M. Miller

Nominees:
The High Crusade, by Poul Anderson
Rogue Moon, by Algis Budrys
Deathworld, by Harry Harrison
Venus Plus X, by Theodore Sturgeon

The 1961 Hugo Awards were held in Seacon in Seattle.

The Best Novel winner was Walter M. Miller's *A Canticle for Leibowitz*. It's a book about a postapocalyptic order of monks who preserve knowledge of science through a new dark age and toward a new apocalypse. It's definitely a classic and a book that has lasted—it's in print from a major publisher, it's in the library in French and English, and I frequently hear it mentioned in discussion. I think it's a very worthy Hugo winner.

Harry Harrison's *Deathworld* is the only one of the five I haven't read. I'm not sure why I haven't—I have read quite a bit of other Harrison and enjoyed most of it. It's in print from a small press, Wildside. It seems to be an exciting adventure of planetary exploration. It's in the library in French only.

Poul Anderson's *The High Crusade* has long been a favorite of mine. It has recently been republished by Baen in a fiftieth-anniversary edition. It's in the library in French and English.

Algis Budrys's *Rogue Moon* is not in print, and not in the library either, so I have to conclude that it hasn't stood the test of time. I remember it as a very pulpy adventure with people exploring an alien base on the moon—not as memorable as *Who?*

Theodore Sturgeon's *Venus Plus X* is a thought-provoking novel about gender issues—it's a tale of androgynes living in utopia, and if it had been published more recently, it would have won a Tiptree Award. It's a clever, thought-provoking book that's both weirdly ahead of its time and yet could not have been written in any other. It's in print from Vintage, and in the library in English only.

Of the four I have read, I'd say we have three really memorable SF novels that have lasted. Do these five books show where the genre was in 1960? Yes, if the genre was half thought-provoking stories and half exciting romps on other planets—and that feels about right.

What else was there that year? Again using Wikipedia's list, I find a whole lot of things. There's Philip K. Dick's *Dr. Futurity*, Frederik Pohl's *Drunkard's Walk*, Peter S. Beagle's *A Fine and Private Place*, L. Sprague de Camp's *The Glory That Was*, Nikos Kazantzakis's *The Last Temptation of Christ* (published as mainstream), Poul Anderson's *Tau Zero* (a much more serious book than *The High Crusade*), Judith Merril's *The Tomorrow People*, John Wyndham's *Trouble with Lichen*, Alan Garner's *The Weirdstone of Brisingamen*, and James H. Schmitz's *Agent of Vega*.

It wouldn't be hard to argue that one or two of those ought to be on the list in place of one or two of the others, but I think *A Canticle for Leibowitz* is the standout book of the year, in any case. So were the voters at Seacon doing a good job of picking the five best books? Not a perfect job, but a pretty good job, yes, I think so.

OTHER CATEGORIES

BEST SHORT FICTION

Winner: "The Longest Voyage," by Poul Anderson (*Analog*, December 1960)

Nominees:
"The Lost Kafoozalum," by Pauline Ashwell (*Analog,* October 1960)
"Need," by Theodore Sturgeon (*Beyond*)
"Open to Me, My Sister," by Philip José Farmer (*F&SF,* May 1960)

Poul Anderson and Theodore Sturgeon were having good years! And there's Pauline Ashwell again too.

Best Dramatic Presentation

Winner: *The Twilight Zone* (TV series)

Nominees:
The Time Machine
Village of the Damned

Best Professional Magazine

Winner: *Astounding/Analog,* edited by John W. Campbell Jr.

Nominees:
Amazing Stories, edited by Cele Goldsmith
F&SF, edited by Robert P. Mills

Best Professional Artist

Winner: Ed Emshwiller

Nominees:
Virgil Finlay
Frank Kelly Freas
Mel Hunter

Best Fanzine

Winner: *Who Killed Science Fiction?,* edited by Earl Kemp

Nominees:
Discord, edited by Redd Boggs
Fanac, edited by Terry Carr and Ron Ellik
Habakkuk, edited by Bill Donaho
Shangri L'Affaires, edited by Bjo Trimble and John Trimble
Yandro, edited by Robert Coulson and Juanita Coulson

COMMENTS ON 1961

9. CLARKEMYERS

Rogue Moon may not be what many people read SF for—in many ways, the book is more character study than world-building—though the MacGuffin raises all the philosophical questions any book could stand—*Rogue Moon* lacks the SF pattern incluing, the super science is taken for granted though the Super Scientist is very well drawn. *Rogue Moon* doesn't much need the skills of SF reading (no more than, say, Nevil Shute—which often isn't SF, for all the engineering included), but perhaps the reader should be informed or perhaps deformed by some experiences. Likely the reader who couldn't stand some other writers—David Drake or *Starship Troopers*—wouldn't finish *Rogue Moon*. Chatting with AJ about *Rogue Moon* and some folks from Chicago, I was amused at the author's comment that all the characters were drawn from life—though he hadn't yet met all of them when he wrote *Rogue Moon*, he recognized them when he did meet them.

Someplace around here, I've already given my take on the Death-world Trilogy—which was, I think, very much a Vietnam War–influenced tale of the nature of history and human progress in the interaction of different cultures and technology. The first book is in some part an adventure story and learning, much like the Leinstar/Jenkins Exploration Party, but also a tale of cultural interaction—maybe *The Ugly American*? The second book could be seen as not only *A Connecticut Yankee in King Arthur's Court* with more lasting effects but also equally tragic, and the third book is a treatise on what it really takes to do well-meaning nation-building and what it costs. More pages and so demanding more time than some will give to extract the message, but a very good sugar coating on the message just the same.

13. RICH HORTON
Other potential Hugo nominees:
"Old Hundredth," by Brian W. Aldiss
"Something Bright," by Zenna Henderson
"The Lady Who Sailed the Soul," by Cordwainer Smith
"The Voices of Time," by J. G. Ballard

On balance, I'd say the actual Hugo nominee list is pretty good, but any of those listed above could surely have been added. When I first read it, I'd have eagerly endorsed the Hugo for "The Longest Voyage." While I still like it, on rereading it a couple of years ago, it seemed diminished. "The Lost Kafoozalum" (sequel to "Unwillingly to Earth") is plenty of fun. I don't remember "Need" all that well, but I think it was pretty good. The Farmer has a good reputation, but I've never read it, and I don't usually like Farmer as much as others do. If I were to give a Retro Hugo, it would probably be to Smith's "The Lady Who Sailed the Soul" or Ballard's "The Voices of Time" (that last, one of my favorite early Ballard stories).

16. GARDNER DOZOIS
A Canticle for Leibowitz deserved its Hugo, but you're seriously underestimating *Rogue Moon*, a book almost as influential on later work as *Canticle*, if not more so.

For short stuff, Anderson's "The Longest Voyage," perhaps my favorite story by him, deserved its Hugo out of that list of finalists, although "Old Hundreth" and "The Lady Who Sailed the Soul" have their virtues too.

18. DAVID G. HARTWELL
A word or two on Harry Harrison—at that time, Harrison was very much an ambitious SF writer in the literary sense. He and Brian Aldiss were about to start the first critical journal of SF, and by four years later, he was seen as one of the four people behind the New Wave in

the UK: Aldiss, Ballard, Harrison, Moorcock. *Deathworld* is a good book and not a piece of pulp fiction, a harbinger of Harrison's best work to follow in the next few years.

And if you are interested, I knew Algis Budrys fairly well, and he never got over losing the Hugo to Miller.

22. RICH HORTON

The Death Machine was Budrys's first choice for a title. (I think it did have at least one paperback edition under that title.) There is a nice thread in the wonderful book *Proceedings of the Institute for Twenty-First Century Studies* (*PITFCS*), a fanzine for SF writers from (mostly) the early sixties, edited by Theodore Cogswell, in which Budrys and others (including Kingsley Amis) discuss *Rogue Moon* at length, including how Budrys cut it for the *F&SF* publication. Several other titles are suggested, including *The Armiger* and *The Bend in the Driveway* (or something, memory perhaps fails me).

PITFCS is truly a fascinating book. To hark back to the previous Hugo thread, it also includes some discussion of *Starship Troopers*. Blish (who objected to the novel in part because it was originally intended to be a juvenile) promised to write a juvenile novel of his own as a counter. The result was *Mission to the Heart Stars,* which in my opinion is one of Blish's worst novels (and he was an unusual writer with a really wide range of quality, from excellent all the way down to unpublishably bad)—one might possibly endorse the ideas behind the Blish novel in place of those behind *Starship Troopers,* but the novel itself is dreadful.

DARK AGES AND DOUBT: WALTER M. MILLER'S
A CANTICLE FOR LEIBOWITZ

A Canticle for Leibowitz is about a world that has been through a flood of fire—a nuclear war that has left survivors to grope through a new dark age. It's set in the barbarous ruins of the United States, and it's explicitly reminiscent of the period after the fall of Rome, when the

Church kept learning alive. It's a clearly cyclic history, with civilization rising and destroying itself again. You'd think this would be a terrible downer, but in fact, it's light and funny and clever as well as moving and effective and having a message.

It treads some very strange ground—between fantasy and science fiction (the Wandering Jew wanders through), between science and religion, between faith and reason, between humor and pathos. It's an amazing book, covering a thousand years of future history, making me laugh and making me care. It's hard to think of anything with the same kind of scope and scale.

Walter M. Miller was an absolutely wonderful short story writer. In short form, he managed to produce a lot of poignant, memorable, clever science fiction. *A Canticle for Leibowitz* is a fix-up of three shorter works, and he never wrote another novel. There's a sequel of sorts, *Saint Leibowitz and the Wild Horse Woman,* which he worked at for years and which was finished for him by Terry Bisson. Despite loving Bisson, I haven't been able to bring myself to read it. For me, *A Canticle for Leibowitz* is complete and perfect and doesn't need any supplementary material, sequels or prequels or inquels.

The three sections of *A Canticle for Leibowitz* were published in SF magazines in the late fifties, and then the novel came out in 1960. The concerns about nuclear war, and the particular form of nuclear war, are very much of that time. This is a rain of fire that destroys civilization and leaves mutants but doesn't destroy the planet—that waits for the end of the book and the final destruction.

This is the survivable nuclear war of the fifties and sixties, the war of *The Chrysalids* and *Farnham's Freehold.* But this isn't a survivalist novel, or a mutant novel—although there are mutants. This is a novel about a monastery preserving science through a dark age. Almost all the characters are monks. The central question is that of knowledge—both the knowledge the monks preserve, hiding the books, and then copying and recopying them without comprehension, and the question of what knowledge is and what it is for. There's the irony that Leibowitz, the sainted founder of their order, was himself Jewish, which the reader knows but the monks do not.

There's the Wandering Jew—and the question of whether he's really the Wandering Jew. When I think about the book, I keep coming back to the illuminated blueprint, done in gold leaf with beautiful lettering and absolutely no idea what it is that it describes and decorates. We see three time periods of the monastery of Saint Leibowitz, and we can deduce a fourth, the foundation, from what we know and what they know. There's a nuclear war, with awful consequences, followed by a hysterical turning on scientists, who are considered responsible, and on anyone educated—the "simpleton" movement. In response, Leibowitz and others became bookleggers and memorizers, using the church as a means of preserving science.

The story starts several generations later, when "simpleton" is a polite form of address to a stranger, like "sport" to a mutant. The first section is about Brother Francis and the canonization of Saint Leibowitz. The middle section is set at a time secular civilization is just beginning to get science organized, a new renaissance. And the third section is set just before the new apocalypse, with a few monks escaping to the stars and God's new promise. I want to repeat: It's delightful to read. It's easy to forget just how much sheer fun it is. I thoroughly enjoyed it—even the perspective of the buzzards and the hungry shark.

It's a surprisingly positive book. The details of the monastery are pretty good. The Catholic Church was in the process of abandoning Latin at the time he was writing, and had renounced it entirely by the time the novel was published in book form, but he has them using it. (I have no problem with this. Of course, they'd have gone back to Latin in the event of a global catastrophe. I mean, it's obvious. I'd do the same myself.) The preservation of science and knowledge generally is very well done. I love the scientist reading a fragment of *R.U.R.* and deducing from it that humanity as he knew it was a created servant race of the original masters who destroyed themselves.

There's no dark-age direct equivalent of bookleggers, but that doesn't matter. Theologically, though, looking at the fantasy aspects, I find it odd. To start with, there's the Wandering Jew, who appears in the first and second parts but not in the third. In the first part, he leads

Brother Francis to the hidden fallout chamber. In the second, he's known as Benjamin and claims to be Lazarus, explicitly waiting for the Second Coming. He doesn't appear in the third part, and there's no reference to him—has he gone to the stars? If Rachel is the Messiah, he misses her. And is she? I think we're supposed to believe she is—and I like the weirdness of it, the science-fictionality. I don't know that it's orthodox Catholicism—and I gather from Wikipedia that Miller was a Catholic, and was involved in bombing Monte Cassino in WWII and then thought better of it. If this is true, he certainly made something to set against that destruction.

Teresa Nielsen Hayden says that if something contains spaceships, it's SF, unless it contains the Holy Grail, which makes it fantasy. I don't know whether the Wandering Jew (and potentially a new female mutant Messiah) counts as the Holy Grail or not in this context. There are spaceships, the monks are taking off in them as the new flood of fire falls at the end of the book. It doesn't really matter whether it's science fiction or fantasy or both. Hugo votes have never had much problem with mysticism, and they definitely noticed that this really is a brilliant book.

REALLY GOOD FUN: POUL ANDERSON'S
THE HIGH CRUSADE

Poul Anderson was the first science fiction writer I read once I'd discovered science fiction was a genre. (This was because I was starting in alphabetical order.) I have been fond of his work for decades, and I sometimes think that it's possible to define all of SF as variations on themes from Poul Anderson. *The High Crusade* is a short novel, and it's funny and clever and it works. It's a quick read, which is good because it's the kind of book that's hard to put down.

I always think of it as being in the same category as *Lord Kalvan of Otherwhen* or *Lest Darkness Fall*, though it's not really like that at all. The premise of *The High Crusade* is that in 1345, just as Sir Roger de Tourneville is getting ready to go to France to fight for the king, an alien spaceship lands in a little Lincolnshire village. The medieval army quickly overruns the spaceship and eventually the alien empire, by a mixture of bluff, combining medieval and futuristic tech, fast talk, and deceit, as you would, really. It may not be plausible, but it's fun, and anyway, it's more plausible than you might imagine. There's a scene, for instance, when they use alien bombs in a wooden trebuchet that naturally doesn't show up on radar.

One of the things that's so great about this book is the voice of Brother Parvus, a monk with a gift for languages, who is rather out of his depth. The book is his first-person chronicle of the events, and the voice is just right. The way he slowly comes to understand the alien view of the universe and reconcile it with his own worldview is lovely. At one point, he decides that the biblical "four corners of the world" actually imply a cubical universe, with lots of stars and planets in it.

He teaches the alien Latin, which means it can communicate only with the clergy—but, hey, it obviously makes sense. (Latin seems to have been much on the minds of the Hugo nominees of 1961.) The best thing of all is that they lose Earth. Their first thought on capturing the spaceship is how much destruction they can do with it in France, but they are betrayed by their alien prisoner and end up on an alien planet—with no way of getting back. So it's a secret history—humanity takes over the alien empire and imposes feudalism on the aliens, and they're still out there. Indeed, the frame story is about people in our future discovering them to everyone's amazement.

The medieval tech is very well done, and I'm absolutely sure Anderson knew exactly how much weight an English cavalry charge could knock down, and how much airplane skin an arrow from a longbow could pierce. The alien tech is weird. It's 1960s tech plus FTL and force shields. The navigation notes that tell where to find Earth that get destroyed were written on paper. The spaceship had an autopilot, but no computer. This makes it much easier for the knights to figure things out—I kept thinking they're figuring it out more easily than they could if they had our tech, which shows what a long way we've come since 1960. This isn't a problem with reading the book now; it's just how it is.

This is a fun, fast read, and just what you want as a palate cleanser. The new Baen cover is great—it's an illustration of the novel, and it tells you what you're going to get, knights on horseback going after green aliens in spaceships. There's also treachery, intrigue, and courtly love, all packed into a mere 181 pages. I'm an absolute sucker for this kind of thing, and it doesn't get any better than this.

1962

Winner: *Stranger in a Strange Land*, by Robert A. Heinlein

Nominees:
Dark Universe, by Daniel Galouye
Time Is the Simplest Thing, by Clifford D. Simak
Second Ending, by James White
Planet of the Damned, by Harry Harrison

The 1962 Hugo Awards were given at Chicon III in Chicago. The Best Novel Hugo went to Robert A. Heinlein for *Stranger in a Strange Land*. *Stranger in a Strange Land* was an amazing phenomenon, becoming popular way outside normal science fiction reading circles. Some say it was one of the precipitating influences on the counterculture of the sixties; it founded a religion and did a lot to popularize polyamory. It has never been out of print, it has been a bestseller for decades. It's in my library. It's my perception that the critical reputation of the book isn't so high as it used to be, but I could be mistaken.

There were four other nominees, of which I've read two: I've read Daniel Galouye's *Dark Universe*. It's a fun story of people living underground, originally to escape a nuclear disaster, but subsequently out of habit. It's the story of one boy who wants more and finds a new world outside, one where having eyes is useful, as it hasn't been down in the darkness. It wasn't published as YA, but it reads as one now. It's not in print. It's in the library in French.

Clifford Simak's *Time Is the Simplest Thing* (*The Fisherman*) is a story about a man who has telepathically contacted aliens and is consequently on the run. I read this a very long time ago and don't remember it well. It isn't in print, but it is also in the library in French.

James White's *Second Ending:* I couldn't remember whether I'd read this or not—I've read some White, and it's a fairly bland title. It's described as "the last man in a universe of robots," which I think I would remember. It isn't in print, and it isn't in the library.

Harry Harrison's *Planet of the Damned* (*A Sense of Obligation*). I definitely haven't read it; it isn't in print or in the library. It seems to be about a man who must leave Earth and save a hellish planet called Dis.

So five nominees, all men, four American and one Northern Irish. Heinlein is a previous winner, Harrison is a previous nominee, Simak had a previous short-form nomination, the other two are Hugo newcomers. We have one near-future novel of religions and Martians, one postapocalyptic, one telepathic alien novel, a survivalist novel, and a space opera. Looking at these five, I'd say we have one enduring classic that I do not like very much, two minor fun novels I have read and enjoyed but that have not lasted well, and two minor novels I haven't read and that also haven't lasted well. So surely this couldn't be the best possible short list out of what was available?

Other possibilities: Marion Zimmer Bradley's *The Door Through Space*, Arthur C. Clarke's *A Fall of Moondust*, Stanislaw Lem's *Memoirs Found in a Bathtub*, *Return from the Stars*, and *Solaris*, Lester del Rey's *Moon of Mutiny*, Kurt Vonnegut's *Mother Night*, Poul Anderson's *Orbit Unlimited* and *Three Hearts and Three Lions*, Norton Juster's *The Phantom Tollbooth*, Theodore Sturgeon's *Some of Your Blood*, and Harry Harrison's *The Stainless Steel Rat*. It's very hard to look at that list and not think that at the very least, *Solaris* and *A Fall of Moondust* should have been on the Hugo ballot.

I think the nominators dropped the ball here; I don't think they picked the five best books that showed what the field was doing. As with the previous year, I think *Stranger*'s a good winner and might well have won against any competition available. But with all the benefit of hindsight, this strikes me as a disappointing short list.

OTHER CATEGORIES

BEST SHORT FICTION

Winner: Hothouse series (collected as *The Long Afternoon of Earth*), by Brian W. Aldiss (*F&SF*, February, April, July, September, and December 1961)

Nominees:
"Lion Loose," by James H. Schmitz (*Analog*, October 1961)
"Monument," by Lloyd Biggle Jr. (*Analog*, June 1961)
"Scylla's Daughter," by Fritz Leiber (*Fantastic*, May 1961)
"Status Quo," by Mack Reynolds (*Analog*, August 1961)

This strikes me as a very good list of short fiction, much of which has lasted. I'd have given it to Biggle, but maybe the voters felt sorry they'd slighted Aldiss as Best New Writer.

BEST DRAMATIC PRESENTATION

Winner: *The Twilight Zone* (TV series)

Nominees:
The Fabulous World of Jules Verne
Thriller (TV series)
The Two Worlds of Charlie Gordon
Village of the Damned

What was "The Two Worlds of Charlie Gordon?" Was it some kind of adaptation of "Flowers for Algernon"?

BEST PROFESSIONAL MAGAZINE

Winner: *Analog*, edited by John W. Campbell Jr.

Nominees:
Amazing Stories, edited by Cele Goldsmith
F&SF, edited by Robert P. Mills
Galaxy, edited by H. L. Gold
Science Fantasy, edited by John Carnell

BEST PROFESSIONAL ARTIST

Winner: Ed Emshwiller

Nominees:
Virgil Finlay
Mel Hunter
John Schoenherr
Alex Schomburg

BEST FANZINE

Winner: *Warhoon,* edited by Richard Bergeron

Nominees:
Amra, edited by George Scithers
Axe, edited by Larry Shaw and Noreen Shaw
Cry, edited by F. M. Busby and Elinor Busby and Wally Weber
Yandro, edited by Robert Coulson and Juanita Coulson

Chicon III also gave three special awards.

Special Award: Cele Goldsmith for editing *Amazing* and *Fantastic*
Special Award: Donald H. Tuck for *The Handbook of Science Fiction
and Fantasy*
Special Award: Fritz Leiber and the Hoffman Electronic Corporation
for the use of science fiction in advertisements

The first of these seems particularly odd because *Amazing,* with Goldsmith as editor, was nominated for a Hugo and did not win. The other

two are clearly things for which the Hugos did not have categories at the time—the last one still doesn't. Having a Hugo for Best Ad seems like something from a Frederik Pohl story. I don't know what those SF advertisements were, and a cursory Google search isn't finding much. Anyone?

COMMENTS ON 1962

1. PHIALA

It's got to be this:

> *Hoffman Electronics, a firm that contracted for the Defense Department, commissioned six short-short stories by various well-known SF authors. These stories appeared throughout 1962 as part of advertisements for Hoffman which originally appeared in the pages of* Scientific American.
> *Authors: van Vogt, Asimov (2), Leiber, Riley, Heinlein.*

I hadn't known anything about these ads either. That's fascinating. I wish SF had that kind of place in modern innovation.

12. JAMES DAVIS NICOLL

Americans tend to ignore works outside the United States and United Kingdom, and, hey, I'm an American too. Donald Wollheim tried to address this in the 1970s after he got his own imprint (DAW Books), importing and translating SF books from other languages. (Generally European, as I recall, or at least if DAW had a Japanese author, I missed it.) My impression is that sales were generally dismal.

As an indication of the nightmarish future toward which we careen, I think it's easier for Yank publishers to find, acquire, and successfully market foreign-landish fiction in North America than it was thirty years ago. Where an American author in the 1980s might feel the need to adopt a more mainstream name to avoid the Soviet taint of their birth surname, these days, Ogawas, Lukyanenkos, Sapkowskis, Sakurazakas, and so on seem not to be driving readers away with their flagrantly non-Anglo-Celt names.

Of course, J. K. Rowling had to be translated into American to sell in the United States. I blame lingering resentments from the Monroe administration.

Asimov got to stay Asimov because he got published first by someone who wasn't John W. Campbell Jr., IIRC Asimov's comments.

13. KEVIN STANDLEE

If the Special Awards were the same way they are today, they weren't Hugo Awards. Special Awards are given by the committee, not by the voter-selection process. (A Special Hugo category is not the same thing: that's a category added by the committee to the nominating ballot, after which it behaves like the other categories.)

Solaris would have been eligible—first publication in any language counts—but it's unlikely enough voters would have seen it. First English publication gives another shot. (This assumes the rules were the same back then as they are now. I'm too lazy right now to go look through the historical versions of the WSFS constitution to find out when the English-publication rule was added.)

As far as I know, the Hugo Award has never actually been explicitly only for English-language SF, although it appears many people assume that it always has been and currently is. Indeed, a fair number of people appear to assume that the Hugo is exclusively for American science fiction, the number of counterexamples notwithstanding. They never read the rules, since they already know the Truth and facts are irrelevant.

14. DEMETRIOSX

James @12/10: To be fair, Rowling didn't get translated much, and that is largely because they were initially sold as children's books. Yes, the marketeers at the publisher insisted on changing the first title, but I bet these days she has the clout to insist otherwise. Terry Pratchett is quite adamant about his books not being Americanized, and he gets away with it.

15. James Davis Nicoll

Terry Pratchett has his own sword forged by his own hands from meteoric iron, which must be of considerable utility when negotiating contracts.

25. Gardner Dozois

The Hothouse stories probably deserved to win, but don't overlook "Scylla's Daughter," one of the best of the Fafhrd and Gray Mouser stories, and perhaps the one that blurs the genre boundaries the most—a time traveler pops up in the middle of it! Most of the other stories are pretty much forgotten by this point.

30. Rich Horton

I quite like the Hothouse stories, and of the nominees listed, I think they're the best choice for the award (much as part of me wishes James Schmitz had won a Hugo sometime!) But we should remember that their award was highly controversial—because it was not for a single story, but for a linked group of stories. I believe the rules were clarified after that to make sure that future awards went only to single stories.

There were several other short stories worthy of nomination, however. My list:

"A Planet Named Shayol," by Cordwainer Smith
"Alpha Ralpha Boulevard," by Cordwainer Smith
"An Old-Fashioned Bird Christmas," by Margaret St. Clair
"Billennium," by J. G. Ballard
"Harrison Bergeron," by Kurt Vonnegut
"The Beat Cluster," by Fritz Leiber
"The Deep Down Dragon," by Judith Merril
"Wall of Crystal, Eye of Night," by Algis Budrys

I think that's an impressive list. I particularly like the two Smith stories, and the Vonnegut—and perhaps most of all, the Budrys. I love "Wall of Crystal, Eye of Night." But, do I think "Wall of Crystal, Eye of Night" should have won the Hugo? No. Do I think the Hothouse stories should have won the Hugo? No.

In fact, one of the great SF stories of all time was published in the January 1961 issue of *F&SF*. One of my favorite stories ever. I think the clear-cut choice for the 1962 Hugo for Best Short Fiction should have been Avram Davidson's "The Sources of the Nile," a very funny, and also oddly heartbreaking, story of a family that anticipates fashion, and a man's obsession with them.

53. Michael F. Flynn

The story I heard about the live TV version of "Flowers for Algernon" was this (from Stan Schmidt, who had it from fellow Ohioan Daniel Keyes). Cliff Robertson really loved the story and brought it to TV. During rehearsals, the Sponsor became distraught. "Charly regresses at the end!" That might be okay for a movie, but TV is inside people's homes, and happy endings are preferred. The last scene had Charly reading a physics book with despair—he could no longer understand it, but knew that he once could. So, just add a final final scene, they told him: have it all suddenly come back to him.

Now it was Robertson's turn to be appalled. That would ruin the whole point of the story! The Sponsor said, People don't like to feel unhappy inside their own homes. Have him reading the book, then his eyes brighten, and he starts to flip the pages with more excitement, and we fade to black. Robertson was stuck.

But they forgot it was live TV and Robertson was an actor. He timed the show perfectly . . . to run a little long. And he did let his eyes go wide and he did flip the pages with gathering excitement—after the cameras had gone dark.

As a result, he couldn't get a TV gig for quite a few years.

Smug Messiah: Robert A. Heinlein's *Stranger in a Strange Land*

....

Stranger in a Strange Land was a publishing phenomenon. When it was published in 1961, it didn't sell only to science fiction readers—it sold widely to everyone, even people who didn't normally read at all. People claim it was one of the things that founded the counterculture of the sixties in the United States. It's Heinlein's best-known book and it has been in print continuously ever since first publication. Sitting reading it in the metro, a total stranger assured me that it was a good book. It was a zeitgeist book that captured imaginations. It's undoubtedly a science fiction classic. But I don't like it. I have never liked it.

My husband, seeing me reading this at the breakfast table, asked if I was continuing my theme of religious SF. I said I was continuing my theme of Hugo-winning SF—but that comes to the same thing. Hugo voters definitely did give Hugos to a lot of religious SF in the early sixties. I hadn't noticed this, but it's inarguable.

Every time I read *Stranger*, I start off thinking, "No, I do like it! This is great!" The beginning is terrific. There was an expedition to Mars, and they all died except for a baby. The baby was brought up by Martians. Now that baby, grown up, is back on Earth, and he's the center of political intrigue. A journalist and a nurse are trying to rescue him. Everything on Earth is beyond his comprehension, but he's trying to understand. It's all terrific, and Heinlein couldn't write a dull sentence to save his life. Then they escape, and we get to Jubal Harshaw, a marvelous old writer with hot and cold running beautiful secretaries, and I get turned off.

I don't stop reading. These are Heinlein sentences, after all. But I do stop enjoying it. My problem with this book is that everybody is revoltingly smug. It's not just Jubal; it's all of them. Even Mike the Martian becomes smug once he gets Earth figured out. And smug is boring. They all now lecture each other about how the world works at great length, and their conclusions are smug. I also mostly don't agree with them, but that doesn't bother me so much—I find it more annoying when I do. I mean, I think Rodin was the greatest sculptor since Bernini, but when Jubal starts touching the cheek of the caryatid fallen under her load and patronizing her, you can hear my teeth grinding in Poughkeepsie.

Beyond that, there isn't really a plot. It starts out looking as if it's going to have a plot—politicians scheming against Mike—but that gets defanged, politicians are co-opted. The rest of the book is Mike wandering about the United States, looking at things and then starting a religion where everybody gets to have lots of sex and no jealousy and learns to speak Martian. Everything is too easy. Barriers go down when you lean on them. Mike can make people disappear, he can do magic, he has near infinite wealth, he can change what he looks like, he's great in bed. . . .

Then out of nowhere, he gets killed in a much-too-parallel messianic martyrdom, and his friends eat his body. Yuck, I thought when I was twelve, and yuck I still think. Oh, cannibalism is a silly taboo that I should get over, eh? Heinlein made the point about cultural expectations better elsewhere—and really, he made all these points better elsewhere. This is supposed to be his great book? The man from Mars wanders around for a bit and gets conveniently martyred? And it's literally a deus ex machina—Mike was protected by the Martian Old Ones and then when they're done with him, he's destroyed by an archangel, according to plan.

The big other thing I don't like about it isn't fair—it isn't the book's fault it sold so well and was a cultural phenomenon and so it's the only Heinlein book a lot of people have read. But this is the case, and it means that I am constantly hearing people say, "Heinlein was boring, Heinlein was smug, Heinlein had an 'old man who knows everything' character, Heinlein's portrayals of women are problematic, Heinlein thought gay people have a wrongness, Heinlein was obsessed with sex in a creepy way," when these things either apply only to this one book or are far worse in this book than elsewhere.

The things I do like would be a much shorter list. I like the beginning, and I regret the book it might have grown into from that starting point. My son once had to write a book report on it for school, and without lying at all, he managed to make it sound like the Heinlein juvenile it might have been. I like the bits in heaven. They are actually clever and tell me things about the universe, and they are funny. I think the satire about the church-sponsored brands of beer and bread and so on, the whole ridiculous Fosterite Church, deserves to be in a better book. I like the world-building—the way what we have here is 1950s America exaggerated out to the edge and gone crazy. And I like Dr. Mahmoud—a Muslim scientist.

I like the ad for Malthusian lozenges, and I think it's worth looking

at for a moment because it's a good way in to talking about sex. Ben
and Jill watch the ad on a date. The ad is for a contraceptive pill—
Malthusian lozenges is a charmingly science-fictional name for them,
simultaneously old-fashioned and futuristic. They claim to be modern
and better than the other methods—which is exactly the way ads like
that do make their claims. Ben asks Jill if she uses them. She says they
are a quack nostrum. Really? They advertise quack nostrums on TV?
There could be quack nostrum contraceptives? No FDA or equivalent?
Then she quickly says he's assuming she needs them—because while
we have contraceptives, we also have the assumption of 1950s legs-
crossed "no sex before marriage" hypocrisy.

Now, demonstrating how silly this is as a sexual ethical system is
partly what the book's trying to do later with all the Martian guilt-free
sex stuff. And in 1961, this stuff was in free fall—until well into the
seventies and second-wave feminism. Even now there's a lot of weird
hypocrisy about female sexuality. This isn't an easy problem, and I suppose I should give Heinlein points for trying it. But . . . okay, it was a
different time.

But Heinlein throughout this book has the implicit and explicit
attitude that sex is something men want and women own. When he
talks about women enjoying sex, he means women enjoying sex with
any and all partners. Never mind Jill's comment that nine times out of
ten, rape is partly the woman's fault—which is unpardonable, but this
is Jill's in-character dialogue, and before her enlightenment and subsequent conversion to smug know-it-all. And I'm also not talking about
the "grokking a wrongness" in "poor inbetweeners" of gay men, or Ben's
squeamishness. These things are arguably pre-enlightenment characters. I'm talking here about attitudes implicit in the text, and explicit
statements by Jubal, Mike, and post-conversion women. And that is
quite directly that all men are straight, and once women get rid of their
inhibitions, they will want sex with everybody, all the time, just like in
porn. Eskimo wife-sharing is explicitly and approvingly mentioned—
without discussion of whether the wives had a choice. You're not going
to have this blissful sharing of sex with all if you do allow women a
choice—and women do indeed like sex, Heinlein was right, but in reality, unlike in this book . . . we are picky. And come to that, men are

also picky. And sex is something people do together. Even in a paradise the way it's described, when people can grow magically younger
and don't need to sleep, some people are going to say no sometimes to
other people, and the other people will be disappointed and grumpy. It
won't all perfectly overlap so that nobody is ever attracted to anyone
who isn't attracted to them. So you will have friction, and that opens
the door to entropy. Also, what's with everybody having babies? I appreciate that sexual attitudes were in free fall, I appreciate that the traditional cultural ones sucked and nobody had worked out how it was
going to be when women had equal pay and did not have to sell themselves in marriage or prostitution and could be equal people, I appreciate
that we need babies to have more people. I even had a baby myself. But
even so there's something creepy about that.

Generally, when I talk about women in Heinlein, I don't think about
this book, because I manage to forget about it. In general, excluding
Stranger, I think Heinlein did a much better job at writing women than
his contemporaries. But here—gah. All the women are identical. They're
all young and beautiful and interchangeable. If they're older (Patty,
Allie, Ruth), they think themselves magically younger, to be attractive, so men can like looking at them, but smug old Jubal doesn't need
to do that to attract women. There's only one actually old woman in the
book: Alice Douglas, the horrible wife of the Secretary General, who
is described by Archangel Foster as "essentially virginal," who sleeps
apart from her husband, and who appears as a shrew obsessed with
astrological advice.

One point, however, for Mike's mother's having (offstage and before
the book starts) invented the Lyle drive for spaceships. It's perfectly possible that I'd be prepared to forgive everything else if the characters
weren't so smug and if there were a plot arising from their actions. But
Hugo-winning classic though it is, I do not like this book and cannot
recommend it.

1963

Winner: *The Man in the High Castle,* by Philip K. Dick

Nominees:
A Fall of Moondust, by Arthur C. Clarke
Little Fuzzy, by H. Beam Piper
Sylva, by Vercors
The Sword of Aldones, by Marion Zimmer Bradley

The 1963 Hugo Awards were given at Discon I in Washington, D.C.

The Best Novel winner was Philip K. Dick's *The Man in the High Castle,* an alternate history novel considered by many to be Dick's masterpiece. It's in print, it's in the library in English and French, it's certainly a classic seminal work of science fiction. I haven't read it.

There's a game people play in David Lodge's novel *Changing Places* (perhaps the canonical university-professor-contemplating-adultery novel), where everyone announces something they haven't read. A literature professor announces that he hasn't read *Hamlet* and wins the game but loses his job. I feel a little like that, admitting that I haven't read *The Man in the High Castle.* Like the guy who hadn't read *Hamlet,* I know a lot about it anyway just by cultural osmosis. I know the plot was done using the *I Ching.* I know it's set in a Hitler-wins world, and somebody writes a book in it where Hitler loses, but the other world is very different from our world. I know enough about it that I could have faked my way through a paragraph about it without admitting I haven't read it—but I said I was going to admit it when I hadn't read things and say why. I haven't read it, because I have read half a dozen assorted Dick novels and hated all of them. I can see that he's a very good writer, but I can't stand the way his mind works. I gave up on him before reading this book, but I have so consistently a negative response to his books that I doubt it would change my mind.

There are four other nominees, three of which I have read and one of which I have neither read nor previously heard of. I complained, talking about 1962, that Arthur C. Clarke's *A Fall of Moondust* was unfairly neglected in 1962's ballot. Clearly the fans at Discon agreed with me, because they put it on the ballot for 1963, despite 1961 publication. Great book. Great choice. It's neither in print nor in the library, but it has been in print recently in the Gollancz SF Masterworks series.

Next is a book I love, H. Beam Piper's *Little Fuzzy*. It's out of copyright and downloadable for free, so being in print isn't an issue. It's about a planet with aliens who almost qualify as sapient. It's in the library in English. Another enduring classic and great choice.

Now we have Marion Zimmer Bradley's *The Sword of Aldones*—first woman on the novel short list! *The Sword of Aldones* is the first Darkover book—it's on the edge of SF and fantasy. It introduces Bradley's most popular and complex world. It's melodramatic and stirring. I read it rather recently—I'd read the rewritten version, *Sharra's Exile*, and happened to come across a copy of the original. I wouldn't say it's an enduring classic, though the world it introduces is definitely still alive.

Last is *Sylva* by "Vercors" (a pseudonym for Jean Bruller), a novel translated from French.* I am astonished. I mean, okay, this happened the year before I was born and things were different then, but can you imagine seeing a translated novel on the Hugo ballot today?† Wow. I hadn't heard of it. Wikipedia says it's about a fox who turns into a woman. Fantastic Fiction says it's about time travelers, Jimi Hendrix, and Jesus. It sounds fascinating. Vercors appears to have been a prolific

---

*This remains the only translation ever to appear on the Hugo ballot.
†2018, we have had 2 translated novels on the ballot since, and Cixin Liu's *The Three-Body Problem* won in 2015. Huzzah!

and well-known French writer—he adopted the pseudonym when he was in the Resistance. *Sylva* isn't in print in English, nor is it in the library in either language, though several of his other books are. Fascinating!

So, five nominees, and for the first time some diversity! Four men and one woman, three Americans, an Englishman living in Sri Lanka, and a Frenchman. Clarke had won a short fiction Hugo, but the other four were all new to the Hugo ballot. As for the books, we have one alternate history, one really hard SF novel, one anthropological SF novel, one planetary romance, and one very odd translation. I'd say all of them but *Sylva* have stood the test of time, so this is a pretty good list.

What else might they have considered? Possibly J. G. Ballard's *The Drowned World*, Ray Bradbury's *Something Wicked This Way Comes*, Anthony Burgess's *A Clockwork Orange* (published as mainstream), Aldous Huxley's *Island* (also published as mainstream), and Madeleine L'Engle's *A Wrinkle in Time*. I think any of these would have been good nominees, but none of them really screams out that it was omitted. So 1963 looks as if it's doing okay overall—this is a varied set of books that are all pretty good and don't overlook very much.

OTHER CATEGORIES

BEST SHORT FICTION

Winner: "The Dragon Masters," by Jack Vance (*Galaxy*, August 1962)

Nominees:
"Myrrha," by Gary Jennings (*F&SF*, September 1962)
"The Unholy Grail," by Fritz Leiber (*Fantastic*, October 1962)
"When You Care, When You Love," by Theodore Sturgeon (*F&SF*, September 1962)
"Where Is the Bird of Fire?," by Thomas Burnett Swann (*Science Fantasy*, April 1962)

It's hard to imagine a year so strong that there was something good enough to beat "When You Care, When You Love," but there it is.

Best Dramatic Presentation

Winner: No Award

Nominees:
Burn, Witch, Burn
The Day the Earth Caught Fire
Last Year at Marienbad
The Twilight Zone (TV series)

Best Professional Magazine

Winner: *F&SF*, edited by Robert P. Mills and Avram Davidson

Nominees:
Analog, edited by John W. Campbell Jr.
Fantastic, edited by Cele Goldsmith
Galaxy, edited by Frederik Pohl
Science Fantasy, edited by John Carnell

Oh, look—Pohl had taken over *Galaxy*!

Best Professional Artist

Winner: Roy Krenkel

Nominees:
Ed Emshwiller
Virgil Finlay
Jack Gaughan
John Schoenherr

Best Amateur Magazine

Winner: *Xero,* edited by Pat Lupoff and Richard A. Lupoff

Nominees:
Mirage, edited by Jack L. Chalker
Shangri L'Affaires, edited by Fred Patten, Albert Lewis, Bjo Trimble, and John Trimble
Warhoon, edited by Richard Bergeron
Yandro, edited by Robert Coulson and Juanita Coulson

Discon 1 also gave out two Special Awards:

Special Award: P. Schuyler Miller for book reviews in *Analog*
Special Award: Isaac Asimov for science articles in *Fantasy & Science Fiction*

Both of these strike me as excellent choices, both as Special Award categories and as actual things. Asimov's science essays in particular were a joy to read and well deserving of a Hugo.

Comments on 1963

2. Rich Horton

Let me be the first of a bazillion people who will suggest that *The Man in the High Castle* is not entirely characteristic of many of Dick's novels—so if you WERE ever going to try him, that might be the one to try. That said, in all honesty, it probably wouldn't change your mind.

This is the first year I have a chance to knowledgeably comment on the fanzine, because I have read *The Best of Xero.* It was excellent, and thus I am happy to endorse *Xero*'s Hugo. By the way, I believe Pat Lupoff may have been the first woman to win or share a Hugo. (One of *Xero*'s regular contributors was Roger Ebert, incidentally.)

15. Jo

I'm not going to read it. Dick is one of those writers where I feel I had to gnaw off a paw to escape the last time, you can't get me back into that trap. I have no hesitation saying he's a good writer, as opposed to a bad writer; I'm just not sure he's a good writer as opposed to an evil writer. The way he thinks—the kind of characters he writes about, the kind of stories he tells, the kind of worlds he builds—repel me.

25. Rich Horton

Of course, "The Dragon Masters" is prime Vance, and a worthy Hugo winner.

"The Moon Moth" was actually published in 1961, and we should have mentioned it as a worthy potential nominee for the 1962 Hugos.

I liked "When You Care, When You Love," but it's not my very favorite Sturgeon. And I must confess that I have not read "The Unholy Grail" nor "Myrhha." "Where Is the Bird of Fire?" is impressive work by a sadly much neglected writer these days, Thomas Burnett Swann. But even with all these, I'd stick with one or the other Vance for the Hugo.

Other stories worth remembering:

Ursula Le Guin's first genre sale, "April in Paris," which is delightful
"The Cage of Sand" and "The Garden of Time," by J. G. Ballard
"Epilogue," by Poul Anderson
"For Love," another of my favorite Algis Budrys stories
"Hop-Friend," by Terry Carr
"Sail 25," by Jack Vance
"The 64-Square Madhouse," by Fritz Leiber
"The Ballad of Lost C'Mell," by Cordwainer Smith
"The Circuit Riders," by R. C. FitzPatrick
"The Place Where Chicago Was," by Jim Harmon
"The Streets of Ashkelon," by Harry Harrison

Of those, I would say that "The Ballad of Lost C'Mell" surely should have been on the ballot.

31. RUSH-THAT-SPEAKS

Mitchison's *Memoirs of a Spacewoman* really should have been nominated. It is amazingly ahead of its time; the first time I read it, I assumed it had been written in the late 1970s for the sexual politics alone.

32. BOB

Sylva is a lovely short novel about a man in love with a woman who is in reality a fox. There is no mention of Jimi Hendrix! It was the final novel I collected to complete my reading of the Hugo-nominated works. I finally found a paperback copy of it in the 1980s at the wonderful and hugely lamented A Change of Hobbit bookstore in Santa Monica. That was a haven for the SF/F reader.

Of the short fiction, I agree with Rich Horton's list but have to include: "The Man Who Made Friends with Electricity" by Fritz Leiber and "Seven-Day Terror" by the inimitable R. A. Lafferty.

How they consistently overlooked Cordwainer Smith's short fiction boggles the mind. For me, it would be a three-way tie for the Sturgeon, the Vance, and "The Ballad of Lost C'Mell," with Lafferty and either "The Man Who Made Friends with Electricity" or "The 64-Square Madhouse" by Leiber to fill up a superb short fiction ballot.

36. GARDNER DOZOIS

I think the fans got it right this year. As I said earlier, I have a sneaking fondness for *A Fall of Moondust,* but it doesn't win over *The Man in the High Castle.* In fact (sorry, Jo), nothing else in the novel category even comes close for quality.

"The Dragon Masters" is an even clearer winner in short fiction. "When You Care, When You Love" is not my favorite Sturgeon, and even the Fritz Leiber story is weak. "The Moon Moth" is a terrific story, but "The Dragon Masters," which is still wonderful today, gets the nod by a slight edge from me.

37. NEIL IN CHICAGO

I think I mentioned "last year" that you're getting into my own experience. My freshman high school English teacher confiscated the

Galaxy with the wonderful orange and green Gaughan cover because we were supposed to be reading *Kidnapped*. And that Sturgeon was in the Sturgeon issue of *F&SF*, with a wonderful Emsh cover.

41. RICH HORTON

Two fine pieces of short fiction I forgot: Brian W. Aldiss's "Basis for Negotiation" (which presciently anticipated the political arguments about SDI two decades in advance) and Avram Davidson's "The Singular Events Which Occurred in the Hovel Off the Alley Off Eye Street."

Neither would be my Hugo pick, but both are good stories that deserve remembering.

44. RICH HORTON

At the risk of coming in WAY TOO LATE on the discussion—not that I haven't posted before!—I should add one novella from 1962 that I forgot, one which probably is my favorite story from 1962, and which I would argue should have won the Hugo. I missed it because it's usually regarded as part of a novel, but it works great as a stand-alone story, and it was first published alone, in the UK magazine *Science Fiction Adventures*.

So: "The Fullness of Time," by John Brunner. One of the great time travel stories ever. It's the concluding part to Brunner's novel *Times Without Number* (1962, revised 1969), which would have been a worthy nominee.

The SFA publication was probably missed by most American fans, and the Ace publication of the novel meant that folks wouldn't have thought of the last part as a separate story.

A FUTURE THAT NEVER CAME: ARTHUR C. CLARKE'S *A FALL OF MOONDUST*

I remembered this book as an exciting technical story about a rescue on the moon—and my goodness, that's what it still is. *A Fall of Moon-*

dust remains an edge-of-the-seat exciting technical story of a rescue on the moon. It's the 2050s. The solar system is being colonized. On the moon, they want to make some money from tourism. They have a boat that skims over the dust in the "Sea of Thirst," just a tour bus, really, out there to give the tourists a show—until the day when there's a moon-quake and the boat slips down into the dust. The rest of the book is the story of the passengers and crew trapped under the dust, and the attempts of the people on the surface to rescue them. It's as unputdownable today as when I first read it.

I never get tired of laughing at computers in old SF. The computers here are ballistic calculators! They don't have screens and are huge and aren't connected together! People dictate memos and then correct print-outs! On the other hand, before I laugh too much, where is my moon-base? (You wait until you're uploaded into cyberimmortality, the first thing you'll hear there will be, "This is what you call the future? Where's my flying car already?")

There's one lovely bit that is entirely dictated by this weirdness of tech level. When they try to pool their entertainment options under the dust, they have only two novels and no games. Imagine the options a group of twenty people would be able to offer today . . . at least until their batteries ran down. They make cards from fifty-two pieces of notepaper and play poker, and read aloud from their fiction. What they have is magnificent—the classic Western *Shane*, in a university-press edition with footnotes, and a current bestseller, *The Orange and the Apple*, the romance between Isaac Newton and Nell Gwynne. (Neal Stephenson should write it.) The humor of this is done lightly but wonderfully. The thing that makes it even funnier now is that I wouldn't be at all surprised by a university-press *Shane*, even though Clarke's joking.

The other very old-fashioned thing is the gender politics, which can best be summed up as "awful." Hello, sexism fairy! The main characters are all men—the pilot, the guy in charge of the rescue, the grumpy astronomer, the reporter. The women who do exist—the ones on the ship—don't have jobs if they are married. (This is particularly notable because there's a comment that Earth educates everyone because they have so many technical jobs, they can't afford to waste men. . . . Quite.)

There's a stewardess who is the nominal love interest—and I thought this romance was perfunctory even when I was a kid. There's a female journalist who's a shrew and who is said to suffer from "impacted virginity." This is well over the line into offensive. There's a fat wife who used to be a dancer. (She is said to have lost "a couple of kilogrammes" in two days on short rations. I think this is Clarke trying to use scientific units while not being comfortable with them. One kilo, or a couple of pounds, sure.) She's a caricature but generally as characterized as most of the passengers. Apart from that, there are no women appearing in this novel—all the engineers, pilots, astronomers, et cetera are male. Women get to be support staff and naughty dancers and wives. It's this sort of thing you have to measure "Delilah and the Space Rigger" against.

Before I put all of that firmly behind me in the box marked "it was 1961," I shall also mention that hotels on the moon all have stairs because you don't need elevators at that gravity—with the unwritten corollary that nobody would ever be in a wheelchair or have a baby in a stroller, or have trouble with stairs even in low gravity. Race politics does slightly better. There is a wholly admirable engineer called McKenzie who is 100 percent Australian Aborigine, and 100 percent culturally assimilated. This isn't the level of multiculturalism one would want today, but for 1961, it's really good. (I wonder if Clarke once met a memorably cool black engineer called McKenzie, because that's also the name of the family in *Imperial Earth*, with a slightly different spelling.)

The characters are all fairly lightly sketched, but it doesn't matter, because the dilemma and the lunar landscape are the real characters here, and they're utterly three-dimensional. The tension never lets up. The ship goes under the surface, and time is ticking and heat is rising and oxygen is running out and more things keep happening—it's riveting. You can never forget you're on the moon. In the worst shipwreck on Earth, there was at least air to breathe! Earth here is a distant crescent hanging in the sky. The farthest away help comes is from L2. All Earth can do is watch. Some of the passengers are comic relief, but the vast majority of the characters in this book are competent men doing their jobs. Even the grumpy astronomer is a competent man doing his job with a bit of sarcasm.

This is the future that didn't happen, the future where the boffins of the 1950s rose up and colonized the solar system with slide rules and general cooperative intellectual competence. This moon was first reached in 1967 by the Soviets—and this was published after Kennedy announced the space race, so Clarke was putting his money on the other side. The hotels have notices in English, Russian, and Chinese, but there's no indication that the Cold War is still a problem. *A Fall of Moondust* is a classic of science fiction—a "man against nature" story, at one-sixth gravity and in a sea of dust that's halfway to being a liquid. The characters are thin, but the prose is full of the poetry of science. We have come a long way since 1961, but this is readable, exciting, and chock-full of sense of wonder.

1964

Winner: *Way Station,* by Clifford D. Simak

Nominees:
Cat's Cradle, by Kurt Vonnegut Jr.
Dune World, by Frank Herbert
Glory Road, by Robert A. Heinlein
Witch World, by Andre Norton

The 1964 Hugo Awards were given in Pacificon II in Oakland, California.

It's lovely to think that I was born in the year when *Way Station* (aka *Here Gather the Stars*) won the Best Novel Hugo. I didn't know anything about it at the time, obviously, but it makes me happy now. *Way Station* is a gentle pastoral hard science fiction novel with aliens and ideas and a quiet man going for walks and thinking. It isn't really like anything much else, and I applaud the Pacificon voters for selecting such an excellent book. It's in print in a gorgeous hardcover from Old Earth Books, and it's in my library.

We have four other nominees, and I've read them all. *Cat's Cradle,* by Kurt Vonnegut Jr., is a better book than *The Sirens of Titan.* It's almost a cozy catastrophe, it's about the world ending because of a form of water that freezes at room temperature, but it's a weird comedy. I loved it to bits when I was fourteen. It's widely in print, but it's not in the library.

Dune World by Frank Herbert, is the serialization of the first chunk of Dune, I'm not sure how much. *Dune* itself won later, so let's leave it for now. It's in print and in the library in French and English.

Glory Road, by Robert A. Heinlein, is one of my least favorite Heinleins. It's a transdimensional romp, and it doesn't work for me. I think it's one of Heinlein's weakest books—it's as if he's trying to do sword and sorcery but making it SF and not taking any joy in it. It's in print in an Orb edition, and it's in the library, so despite the fact that I don't like it, I have to admit it's lasted well.

Witch World, by Andre Norton, is another case of fantasy thinly disguised as SF. A man from our world finds his way through a gate to another world, where magic works. It's much more fun than *Glory Road,* though very light and far from Norton's best. Another female novel nominee, for anyone counting. (I think people knew Norton was a woman, despite the faintly male name?) It's in print, in an audio edition, and in the library.

So, four men and one woman, all American. Heinlein's a previous winner, Vonnegut and Simak were prior nominees, Norton and Herbert were newcomers. We have one pastoral SF with aliens, one twisted cozy catastrophe, one wide-screen baroque space opera, and two transdimensional-gate fantasies. What else might they have chosen?

Other possibilities: John Brunner's *The Stardroppers,* a very minor novel, but I like it; Walter Tevis's *The Man Who Fell to Earth;* Pierre Boulle's *Planet of the Apes;* H. Beam Piper's *Space Viking;* Samuel R. Delany's *Captives of the Flame;* Philip K. Dick's *The Game-Players of Titan.* In YA, there's Alan Garner's *The Moon of Gomrath;* Robert Heinlein's *Podkayne of Mars;* Joan Aiken's *The Wolves of Willoughby Chase,* and Arthur C. Clarke's *Dolphin Island.*

It's clearly a strong year, with all kinds of SF being written. I'd put the Piper above the Norton and the Heinlein, and I do feel *Dune*'s being eligible twice (and thus taking two slots) is annoying. If I were making a list of "Jo's favorite SF from the year she was born," it wouldn't be this short list. But *Way Station* is an excellent winner, and the five nominees do give a good snapshot of the field.

OTHER CATEGORIES

....

BEST SHORT FICTION

Winner: "No Truce with Kings," Poul Anderson (*F&SF,* June 1963)

Nominees:
"Code Three," Rick Raphael (*Analog,* February 1963)
"A Rose for Ecclesiastes," Roger Zelazny (*F&SF,* November 1963)
"Savage Pellucidar," Edgar Rice Burroughs (*Amazing Stories,* November 1963)

Now, that's an odd result. "No Truce with Kings" is a pretty good Anderson novella, but "A Rose for Ecclesiastes" is one of the best short pieces ever written.

There was a movement within SF at this time that we usually call the New Wave, and which was associated with the British magazine *New Worlds* under the editorship of Michael Moorcock and with a group of writers, UK and US, who all emerged around the mid-sixties: Ballard, Brunner, Zelazny, Ellison, Delany, Spinrad, and others. New Wave was more of a sensibility than anything else—a move away from Campbellian SF toward more focus on style and character. Many people were very excited by this, in both directions—there were fans who passionately loved New Wave and fans equally passionately opposed to it. When looking at these nominations and results over the next few years, it's useful to be aware that this was going on and that it was a time of ferment. I think "A Rose for Ecclesiastes" is the first New Wave nomination.

BEST SF BOOK PUBLISHER

Winner: Ace

Nominees:
Ballantine

Doubleday
Pyramid

Interestingly, by 1964, we have enough publishers publishing SF that they could start a category. The Locus Awards still have this category, won annually for the last eleven thousand years by Tor, but the Hugos have given up on it. Well, I'd have given it to Ace in 1964, too. Think of those lovely Ace Doubles!

Best Professional Magazine

Winner: *Analog,* edited by John W. Campbell Jr.

Nominees:
Amazing Stories, edited by Cele Goldsmith
F&SF, edited by Avram Davidson
Galaxy, edited by Frederik Pohl
Science Fantasy, edited by John Carnell

Best Professional Artist

Winner: Ed Emshwiller

Nominees:
Virgil Finlay
Frank Frazetta
Roy Krenkel
John Schoenherr

Best Amateur Magazine

Winner: *Amra,* edited by George Scithers

Nominees:
ERB-dom, edited by Camille Cazedessus Jr.
Starspinkle, edited by Ron Ellik

Yandro, edited by Robert Coulson and Juanita Coulson

Look what there isn't! Not just No Award, no Best Dramatic Presentation category at all! I expect the oracles told them that somebody was about to be born who would be pleased to hear it.

COMMENTS ON 1964

10. RICH HORTON

Jo's list of plausible novel nominees seems about right to me, though I wonder how she could ever have left off the eternal classic *Galaxy 666,* by "Pel Torro" (Lionel Fanthorpe). Other enjoyable novels (though mostly not really Hugo-nominee potential) include Daniel F. Galouye's *Lords of the Psychon;* two by H. Beam Piper: *Junkyard Planet* aka *The Cosmic Computer* and *Space Viking; Sign of the Labrys,* by Margaret St. Clair (famous for the horrendous original blurb); and *The Million Cities,* by J. T. McIntosh.

11. RICH HORTON

Now for the short fiction. Not a bad nomination list, except for the odd inclusion of the *ERB* piece. "Code Three" is little remembered now, but it was decent *Analog* stuff of its time. Not on a par with the other two, though.

"No Truce with Kings" is very good, but "A Rose for Ecclesiastes" is magnificent, one of my very favorite SF stories ever. It clearly should have won, and I assume Anderson's familiarity with readers—Zelazny was still a new writer—carried the day. By the way, I would NOT call "A Rose for Ecclesiastes" New Wave.

Other potential short fiction nominees:

Another Anderson story, "What'll You Give?" published under his pseudonym "Winston P. Sanders" (and also known, when reprinted in his fix-up novel *Tales of the Flying Mountains,* under the French version of the title, "Que Donn'rez Vous?")

And one more Anderson piece, "The Three-Cornered Wheel"

"The Totally Rich," by Brunner

Peter S. Beagle's "Come Lady Death," though that appeared in 1963 in the *Atlantic Monthly*, and probably wasn't seen by many SF readers until its 1966 reprint in *F&SF*

"Die, Shadow!," by Algis Budrys

"Drunkboat," "On the Gem Planet," and "Think Blue, Count Two," by Cordwainer Smith

"Green Magic," by Jack Vance (a favorite Vance story for me)

"The Great Nebraska Sea," by Allen Danzig

"What Strange Stars and Skies," by Avram Davidson

"The Time Tombs," by J. G. Ballard

"They Don't Make Life Like They Used To," by Alfred Bester, one of his best stories, and not well-enough known

"Thin Edge," by "Jonathan Blake Mackenzie"—Randall Garrett

"Bazaar of the Bizarre" and "X Marks the Pedwalk," by Fritz Leiber

If I were making a nomination list, I'd keep "No Truce with Kings" and "A Rose for Ecclesiastes," and add Bester's "They Don't Make Life Like They Used To," Vance's "Green Magic," and either Davidson's "What Strange Stars and Skies" or Leiber's "Bazaar of the Bizarre," or maybe Beagle's "Come Lady Death."

But no matter what, "A Rose for Ecclesiastes" is my choice for Best Short Fiction of 1963.

13. BOB

The short fiction possibilities that haven't been mentioned but should be included in the mix are: "Bernie the Faust," by William Tenn—brilliant story; "New Folks' Home," by Clifford Simak—these were his best writing years, I think; "Fortress Ship," by Fred Saberhagen—first of the Berserker series; "The Faces Outside," by Bruce McAllister; "The Pain Peddlers," by Robert Silverberg (the basis for *Thorns* in 1967); and "If There Were No Benny Cemoli," by Philip K. Dick.

Hard year to pick my favorite nominations, but "A Rose for Ecclesiastes" is what I consider the best one as well. Beautiful and haunting.

30. Neil in Chicago

The cover of the issue of *F&SF* for "A Rose for Ecclesiastes" was the last piece Hannes Bok ever did, and it's a treasure.

The permeation of the "hippie movement" by science fiction is mostly lost in the mythologization. (The lyrics of Jefferson Airplane's "Crown of Creation" are a paragraph from John Wyndham's *The Chrysalids*.) The corporate holding entity that owns rights to all the Grateful Dead's music is Ice Nine Publishing.

Rich Horton has picked out some more great stories. "Totally Rich" is tremendous; and to the best of my knowledge, the least great Cordwainer Smith is wonderful; and "They Don't Make Life Like They Used To"? Wow.

You are entering the apogee of *Playboy*. It was a lifestyle magazine, not just a skin mag, and Hefner's liking for science fiction paid Sheckley, Vonnegut, Bradbury, and Clarke, among others. The "U. K. Le Guin" anecdote is well known too. If you find a link to a list of *Playboy*'s science fiction, follow it. You'll be impressed.

I Think I'll Go for a Walk and Think About Aliens: Clifford Simak's *Way Station*

I don't know how long it is since I first read *Way Station*, maybe thirty years. It's a strangely pastoral hard SF story. The CIA investigate a man who is more than a hundred years old, but looks thirty. They can't get into his house, but there's an alien buried behind it. After this beginning, the book closes in on Enoch, the contemplative keeper of the alien way station and his quiet unchanging life.

It's a character study of a man who has for years been an observer. He observes Earth, going for a brief walk each day and reading papers and magazines to keep him connected to his planet. He observes the aliens who pass through his station—the aliens teleport about the galaxy but need to stop regularly and re-collect themselves lest they become scattered by their passage. He collects the toys and gifts they leave him, often without comprehending them. He makes notes in his journal about the aliens he meets and what he can glean about galactic society.

He goes for walks through the beautiful Wisconsin countryside. He thinks about weird aliens he has met and chatted with and made friends with or never seen again. He frets vaguely about the ongoing Cold War and humanity's ability to blow themselves up. He contemplates a truly chilling alien option for saving the world by making everyone stupid for a few generations—a catastrophic Babel event that would be better than destroying humanity and the planet. He sends aliens on to the next stage of their incomprehensible journeys, he plays with creating artificial intelligences, he tries to figure out alien mathematical systems, he goes for a walk.

> *For years I've tried to understand and to conform to all the ethics and ideas of all the people who have come through this station. I've pushed my own human instincts and training to one side. I've tried to understand other viewpoints and to evaluate other ways of thinking, many of which did violence to my own. I'm glad of it, for it had given me a chance to go beyond the narrowness of Earth.*

There is in fact a plot, but I had completely forgotten it and wasn't all that impressed to rediscover it. What I remembered about the book was Enoch tending the alien visitors and aging only while he was outside the station. That character study is what's interesting and memorable about this book, and on this reread, it's still what I liked about it.

Rereading it now, I was surprised. It seems like a really unrepresentative science fiction book, and I'm amazed people liked it enough for it to win a Hugo, but I also really enjoyed it. I'm glad I read it, but I'm also a little bemused. Nothing happened! But there were aliens! So I guess that's okay, then. Also it was lyrical and lovely, and there's a high density of ideas I associate with classic SF. Maybe I'll read it again in another thirty years and see what I think of it then.

1965

BEST NOVEL

Winner: *The Wanderer*, by Fritz Leiber

Nominees:
Davy, by Edgar Pangborn
The Planet Buyer, by Cordwainer Smith
The Whole Man/Telepathist, by John Brunner

The Hugo Awards for 1965 were given at Loncon II, in London. Unlike the previous British convention, they gave awards in the previously established categories—I don't know how they managed with publication and eligibility issues.

The Best Novel winner was Fritz Leiber's *The Wanderer*. It's a disaster novel about a traveling planet that comes into the solar system to refuel and causes chaos. It's in print as an ebook and was recently in print from Gollancz in the United Kingdom It's in the library in English. I haven't read it—I thought I had, but when I got it out of the library, it was clear I had confused it with a different Leiber book. I have no opinion as to whether or not it was a good Hugo winner.

There are three other novel nominees, and making up for my lapse over the Leiber, I've read all of them. Edgar Pangborn's *Davy* is in print from Old Earth Books. It's a story of a boy having an adventure in a postapocalyptic world, and it's more like Kim Stanley Robinson's *The Wild Shore* than anything else. Like most of Pangborn, it's gentle and clever. I was lucky enough to discover Pangborn when I was a teenager, and I loved him. It's in the library in English.

Cordwainer Smith's *The Planet Buyer* is the first half of *Norstrilia*. It's a classic, and it's brilliant, and I can't believe it didn't win. It's in print from NESFA, and it's in the library in both languages. Like most of Cordwainer Smith, it's hard to describe. It's beautifully written and weird, and it's about genetically engineered animal people and longevity drugs, and the only problem with it is that your eyes keep getting wider and wider as you go, and it's hard to read like that.

The last nominee is John Brunner's *The Whole Man* (UK title: *Telepathist*). It isn't in print, it hasn't been in print since 1990, and maybe I am the only person who loves it. It was one of the first science fiction books I read, and it's about this guy who is a mutant telepath in the near future, and it doesn't make him happy. It isn't Brunner's best, but it's a very good book and it would have been a worthy Hugo winner. (Also, first time something nominated is by a friend of mine, though of course John wasn't my friend in 1965, when I could barely talk.)

So, four nominees, all men, three American and one English. Leiber's a previous winner, but all the rest are newcomers. We have a near-future telepath, a far-future revolt over geriatric drugs and freedom, a post-apocalyptic odyssey, and a disaster novel about a wandering planet—all solidly science-fictional, all pretty good books, all worthy nominees. I'd have been happy with any of the three I've read as winners, and I'm reserving judgment on the Leiber.

What did they miss? Quite a lot. One can only applaud Hugo nominees for not selecting Heinlein's *Farnham's Freehold,* and I think this demonstrates that people do not blindly nominate favorite writers no matter how bad the book. But Marion Zimmer Bradley's *The Bloody Sun* is a better novel than *The Sword of Aldones,* which was nominated the year before. Previous winner Philip Dick had a bumper year, with *Clans of the Alphane Moon, The Simulacra,* and *Martian-Time Slip,* and none of them were noticed. Also ignored were Keith Laumer's *The Great Time Machine Hoax,* Arkady and Boris Strugatsky's *Hard to Be a God,* Jack Vance's *The Killing Machine* and *The Star King,* Daniel Galouye's *Simulacron-3* (aka *Counterfeit World*) Samuel Delany's *The Towers of Toron*, J. G. Ballard's *The Burning World,* and Brian Aldiss's *Greybeard. Greybeard* in particular is a classic. In YA fantasy, there's Lloyd Alexander's *The Book of Three* and Roald Dahl's *Charlie and the Chocolate Factory.*

In the face of all this, it's hard to feel confident that the nominees were the four best novels of 1964. If we were going to select something to fill the empty fifth slot, we'd have a hard time choosing, I think.

OTHER CATEGORIES

BEST SHORT FICTION

Winner: "Soldier, Ask Not," by Gordon R. Dickson (*Galaxy*, October 1964)

Nominees:
"Little Dog Gone," by Robert F. Young (*Worlds of Tomorrow*, February 1964)
"Once a Cop," by Rick Raphael (*Analog*, May 1964)

I'm surprised at such a short short list, but the winner is a good story, and the Young is pretty good too.

BEST DRAMATIC PRESENTATION

Winner: *Dr. Strangelove*

Nominee:
7 Faces of Dr. Lao

I'm actually not going to complain, for once, as I think *Dr. Strangelove* is actually a good movie and SF at the same time. I don't think it's worth having a category with so few possible entrants, but at least in 1965 they gave it to a worthy winner.

BEST SF BOOK PUBLISHER

Winner: Ballantine

Nominees:
Ace
Gollancz
Pyramid

I guess Gollancz got on there because it was a British Worldcon. Dear old Gollancz with their yellow covers. I loved them when I was a teenager. Even now, a yellow spine on a hardback lifts my heart, the same as an orange spine on a paperback.

Best Professional Magazine

Winner: *Analog*, edited by John W. Campbell Jr.

Nominees:
F&SF, edited by Avram Davidson
Galaxy, edited by Frederik Pohl
If, edited by Frederik Pohl

Talk about competing against yourself! Two nominations for Pohl for different magazines. No nomination for Moorcock, who took over *New Worlds* the year before.

Best Professional Artist

Winner: John Schoenherr

Nominees:
Ed Emshwiller
Frank Frazetta
Jack Gaughan

Best Fanzine

Winner: *Yandro*, edited by Robert Coulson and Juanita Coulson

Nominees:
Double: Bill, edited by Bill Bowers and Bill Mallardi
Zenith, edited by Peter R. Weston

COMMENTS ON 1965

9. KEVIN STANDLEE

Regarding the short nominating lists: I don't know if this had made it into the rules by 1965, but currently there are rules that can reduce the number of nominations in a category down to three if the fourth- and fifth-place nominees don't receive a specified minimum percentage of the total nominating ballots cast in a category. This has happened a couple of times in the past ten or fifteen years, but it's rare. The last time I remember it happening (and I may be wrong about this) was in 1995, in the short-lived Best Original Artwork category, where it was a clear sign of lack of interest in the category and of an excessively broad category in the sense that the voters' preferences wouldn't converge on a short list. You can't administer a category where there are fifty nominees all with two or three votes each.

10. DEMETRIOSX

Something else that jumped out at me. This is the second year in a row where the MacGuffin of one of the nominees involves an organic compound crucial for the functioning of civilization, but which grows only on one world and cannot be synthesized. Was this some idea that was being bandied about or reflected some aspect of what was going on at the time?

11. JO

DemetriosX: Good question. And while you were thinking about that, Rene mentioned that two of the nominees for 1965 have catgirls—the Leiber and the Smith. I think odd things like that tend to make interesting patterns that aren't always a reflection of anything—I can't think of any 1960s organic shortages, or catgirl invasions either.

20. Rich Horton

Of the three short fiction nominees, the only one I've read is the winner, which I do think a very strong story, and a worthy Hugo winner.

Other potential nominees:

"Mary" aka "An Ancient Madness," by Damon Knight
"The Sea's Furthest End," by Damien Broderick
"Father of the Stars," by Frederik Pohl
"Man on Bridge," by Brian W. Aldiss
"Sea Wrack," by Edward Jesby (reprinted in *F&SF* in 2009 as part of its sixtieth-anniversary celebration)
"The Dowry of the Angyar" aka "Semley's Necklace," by Ursula K. Le Guin
Two others by Le Guin: "The Word of Unbinding" and "The Rule of Names," our first introductions to Earthsea
"The Crime and the Glory of Commander Suzdal" and "The Dead Lady of Clown Town," by Cordwainer Smith
"The Drowned Giant" and "The Terminal Beach," by J. G. Ballard
"The Graveyard Heart," by Roger Zelazny

Were I to construct a short list of five, I think I'd keep the Dickson, and add one of the Smith stories, plus "The Terminal Beach," perhaps "Man on Bridge," perhaps "Semley's Necklace."

29. Gardner Dozois

Was not as impressed as everyone else with the Dickson. Out of the stuff mentioned so far, my vote would have gone to Zelazny's "The Graveyard Heart" or Smith's "The Dead Lady of Clown Town," although Knight's "Mary" is a good story too. (As is "The Rule of Names.")

Telepathy and Healing: John Brunner's
The Whole Man (aka *Telepathist*)

....

Telepathist (UK title) or *The Whole Man* (better US title) was one of the first science fiction books I read, one of the things that defined the edges of the genre for me early on. I've always liked it. It was also one of the first adult books I bought—I own the Fontana 1978 reprint. Reading it now, there are all those echoes of the times I read it before.

It's a strange book. It's a fix-up, very episodic. All the sections appeared in magazines before being put together as a book, and the seams show. It's not as wonderful as I thought it was when I was twelve, and it's not as good as Brunner's best work, like *Stand on Zanzibar*. But it's still an enjoyable read, and a thoughtful book about a crippled telepath in a near future. It has flashes of genuine brilliance, which were I think what always attracted me to it.

Gerry Howson is born in a time of troubles in a near-future Britain to a selfish stupid mother and a dead terrorist father. The stigma of having unmarried parents has vanished so completely that I almost didn't mention it, but it was real in 1964 and real to Gerry. But more than that, he's born crippled, he lurches when he walks and never goes through puberty—we later learn that his telepathic organ is taking up room in his brain where people normally have their body image, so he can't be helped. He is the most powerful telepath ever discovered. The book is his life story from birth to finding fulfillment.

Most science fiction novels are shaped as adventures. This is still the case, and it was even more the case in 1964. Brunner chose to shape this instead as a psychological story. Gerry Howson has an amazing talent that makes him special, but the price of that talent is not only physical discomfort but isolation from society as well. People recoil from him; he repels them. He's better than normal, but he can't ever be normal. Humanity needs him, but it finds him hard to love. The novel is his slow journey to finding a way to share his gifts and have friends.

Where it's best is in the world-building. This is a future world that didn't happen, but it's surprisingly close to the world that did—a world without a Cold War, with UN intervention in troubled countries, with economic depressions and terrorist insurgencies. It's also an impressively international world—Gerry's British, and white, but we have major characters who are Indian and Israeli, minor characters from other countries, and the telepathists' center is in Ulan Bator. This isn't the generic future of 1964, and it feels grittily real. There isn't much new technology, but Brunner has thought about what there is, and the uses of "computers" in graphics and for art before there were computers.

Telepathy is used by the peacekeepers, but what we see Gerry using it for is therapy—much like Zelazny's *The Dream Master/He Who Shapes*. ("City of the Tiger," that section of the novel, appeared first in 1958, and *He Who Shapes* in 1965, so Zelazny may have been influenced by Brunner, or it may just have been a zeitgeist thing.) Gerry goes into the dreams of telepaths who have caught others up in their fantasies and frees them. This is done vividly and effectively, and the strongest images of the book come from these sections. There's also a wonderful passage where he befriends a deaf-and-mute girl—in fact, she rescues him—and is literally the first person who can truly communicate with her.

The last section is the weakest, with Gerry finding friends and acceptance among counterculture students and discovering a way to use his talents to share his imagination as art. It's emotionally thin and unsatisfying—and even as a teenager, I wanted to like it more than I did like it. Gerry is more plausible miserable.

But this isn't the story most people would write—yes, there's the crippled boy who nobody loves, who turns out to be the one with the amazing talent. It's a good book because it goes on after that, it takes it further, what happens when you have the superhuman talent and you're still unlovable and unloved and uncomfortable all the time? Where do you get your dreams from? I admire Brunner for trying this end even if he didn't entirely make it work. You can see him stretching himself, getting less pulpy, becoming the mature writer he would be at the peak of his skills.

1966

Winner: *Dune*, by Frank Herbert
This Immortal, by Roger Zelazny

Nominees:
The Moon Is a Harsh Mistress, by Robert A. Heinlein
Skylark DuQuesne, by E. E. "Doc" Smith
The Squares of the City, by John Brunner

The Hugo Awards for 1966 were handed out in Tricon, in Cleveland. The Best Novel Award was a tie, for the first time ever, and one of only three novel ties in the history of the award. The two winners were Frank Herbert's *Dune* and Roger Zelazny's . . . *And Call Me Conrad* aka *This Immortal*. They are both wonderful books, and I've just re-read them back to back, and if I'd had the deciding vote, I'm not sure which I'd have given it to. *Dune* is a huge book, an overwhelming experience, clever, full of ideas, baroque. It has factions plotting over spice that makes people prescient and able to travel FTL, it has a messiah, and it has a really good description and experience of being prescient. It's written in a notably ornate and baroque style.

And Call Me Conrad is a short, funny book about a wisecracking mutant immortal in a postapocalyptic future Earth that wants to be free of alien domination. It uses Greek mythology for resonance. It sets a pattern for what Zelazny was going to do later. It's accomplished and stylish and fast paced in a way *Dune* just isn't. You could compare them to a bludgeon and a stiletto. But they are both great books, and great classics of science fiction, and they both deserve their Hugo. I've read both of them a million times.

Dune is thoroughly in print, and is in the library in both languages. *This Immortal* doesn't seem to be in print—please tell me I'm wrong. There was a Gollancz SF Masterworks edition in 2000, and an iBooks edition. It's in the library in French only. By the measures I'm using, then, *Dune* has lasted better. There have also been two films of *Dune*, and lots of sequels, and no films or sequels to *This Immortal*. It would make a great film. But thank you, Zelazny, for writing *Lord of Light* and the Amber books and not giving us *This Immortal Messiah, Children of This Immortal, God Emperor of This Immortal* . . . no. There should be more books complete as they are. And *This Immortal* should be in print, dammit.

In some ways, we have one traditional winner and one New Wave winner—but then again, for all that it was published in *Analog*, *Dune* isn't that traditional. *Dune* was published over two years in *Analog*, and then as a book, and so was eligible in 1964, when first nominated, and still eligible to win in 1966. I'm glad these rules have been tightened up since, because it gave some books more than a fair chance.

There were three other nominees, and I've read two of them. First, Robert Heinlein's *The Moon Is a Harsh Mistress*. This was also eligible twice, in magazine and book form, and it won the year after, so let's leave it for then.

Next, E. E. Doc Smith's *Skylark DuQuesne*—the conclusion of the Skylark series. I haven't read it, but I have every reason to believe it's slightly old-fashioned top-class pulpy adventure like the rest of Doc Smith. It's not in print, and it's not in the library.

John Brunner's *The Squares of the City*—this isn't in print or in the library either. This is a book about a revolution in a third-world country where the two leaders are doing it as a game of chess played with real people in a real city without the real people knowing. It's perhaps a little too clever, and I don't much care for the main character, but it was an ambitious book that helped get Brunner into position for writing his truly great books later.

So, five books, two winners. All five nominees are male, one English and four American. Heinlein's a previous winner, Brunner and

Herbert are previous nominees, Zelazny is a previous short-form nominee, Doc Smith is new to the ballot. We have an ecological messianic novel, a mythologically resonant novel of a devastated future Earth, a revolution on the moon, a pulp adventure in space, and a low-key revolution in a third-world country. Not quite what you would expect, and an interesting set of books that show how diverse and exciting SF was at that moment.

What else might they have considered, and was there anything they missed? Well, for the first time for a long time, there were other awards.

The Nebulas, the awards given by the professional association, the Science Fiction Writers of America, were given for the first time in 1966. The Nebulas are SF's other prestigious award. The Hugos are awarded by fans, and the Nebulas by writers, so some people say the Nebulas are professional and literary and the Hugos demotic and popular—we will examine this view as we look at the actual nominees. Nebula rules have changed a lot over time. Currently, they cover calendar years, accept nominations from all SFWA members, and then produce a short list of works with the highest number of nominations, much like the Hugos. At other times, eligibility has extended for two years, bringing the award out of sync with other awards, and there has been a jury that can add works to the ballot. Because the nomination process was visible to other SFWA members, the Nebulas have always been open to accusations of logrolling and internal campaigning, and I think SFWA was very wise to revise its process on this in recent years.

The award itself is a clear plastic monolith containing a nebula and, more recently, some planets that make each trophy individual.

The 1966 Nebula ballot is extremely long. As for the "more literary" element of the award, this year certainly doesn't show that. In a year in which the Hugos were won by Zelazny and Herbert, the Nebula was won by *Dune* alone, and *This Immortal* wasn't even on the ballot. Indeed, apart from *Dune,* there's no overlap at all. The Nebula ballot consisted of

Dune, by Frank Herbert
All Flesh Is Grass, by Clifford D. Simak
The Clone, by Ted Thomas and Kate Wilhelm

Dr. Bloodmoney, by Philip K. Dick
The Escape Orbit, by James White
The Genocides, by Thomas M. Disch
Nova Express, by William S. Burroughs
A Plague of Demons, by Keith Laumer
Rogue Dragon, by Avram Davidson
The Ship That Sailed the Time Stream, by G. C. Edmondson
The Star Fox, by Poul Anderson
The Three Stigmata of Palmer Eldritch, by Philip K. Dick

A short list of twelve titles! Most of these seem like they'd have been reasonable additions to the Hugo ballot; none of them seems as if it's screaming to be on there in place of the actual nominees. And it's interesting that there's so little overlap—did fan and pro tastes diverse so much? Yet pro writers are frequently fans, too, and vote for the Hugos. Why did fans prefer Heinlein and Brunner and Zelazny and pros Laumer and Edmondson and Simak? It's not really what you'd expect. But it was the first year.

And what else was there? Potentially Harry Harrison's *Bill, the Galactic Hero,* Samuel Delany's *City of a Thousand Suns,* Philip José Farmer's *Dare,* H. Beam Piper's *Gunpowder God,* and Poul Anderson's *The Corridors of Time.* Nothing there that seems egregiously overlooked.

OTHER CATEGORIES

BEST ALL-TIME SERIES

Winner: Foundation, by Isaac Asimov

Nominees:
Barsoom, by Edgar Rice Burroughs
Future History, by Robert A. Heinlein
Lensman, by Edward E. Smith
The Lord of the Rings, by J. R. R. Tolkien

Well, that's a very odd category with some extremely odd nominees, and some of those things are not like the others. I'm somewhat surprised that Foundation won, even though I like the Foundation books. There is a problem with series and awards, and maybe an award for series (to be given maybe every five years, with series eligible in the year the last volume comes out?) would be a good idea, because they are different from a novel in the same way a novel is different from a short story. But "Best All-Time Series" is a little silly.*

Best Short Fiction

Winner: "'Repent, Harlequin!' Said the Ticktockman," by Harlan Ellison (*Galaxy*, December 1965)

Nominees:
"Day of the Great Shout," by Philip José Farmer (*Worlds of Tomorrow*, January 1965)
"The Doors of His Face, the Lamps of His Mouth," by Roger Zelazny (*F&SF*, March 1965)
"Marque and Reprisal," by Poul Anderson (*F&SF*, February 1965)
"Stardock," by Fritz Leiber (*Fantastic*, September 1965)

Great selection, good choice.

Best Professional Magazine

Winner: *If*, edited by Frederik Pohl

Nominees:
Amazing Stories, edited by Cele Goldsmith
Analog, edited by John W. Campbell Jr.
F&SF, edited by Ed Ferman
Galaxy, edited by Frederik Pohl

---

*A Best Series Hugo was introduced in 2017 with very complete eligibility notes.

I can see that Pohl was one of the best editors that year, but *If,* rather than *Galaxy?*

BEST PROFESSIONAL ARTIST

Winner: Frank Frazetta

Nominees:
Frank Kelly Freas
Jack Gaughan
Gray Morrow
John Schoenherr

BEST AMATEUR MAGAZINE

Winner: *ERB-dom,* edited by Camille Cazedessus Jr.

Nominees:
Double: Bill, edited by Bill Bowers and Bill Mallardi
Niekas, edited by Edmund R. Meskys and Felice Rolfe
Yandro, edited by Robert Coulson and Juanita Coulson
Zenith Speculation, edited by Peter R. Weston

COMMENTS ON 1966

11. GARDNER DOZOIS

My heart belongs to *This Immortal,* one of my favorite books, and that's almost certainly what I would have voted for, probably still would, but to be honest, *Dune* has had a far greater and more sustained impact on subsequent SF than *This Immortal* did.

"The Doors of His Face, the Lamps of His Mouth" is exquisitely written, one of the best-written SF stories of the decade if not of all times, but it's calorie-light on content, being (as Alex Eisenstein pointed out at the time) basically the familiar story of the Great White Hunter who loses his nerve, becomes a burnt-out drunk, and has to face his fears before he can put his life back on track again. I like "Stardock," but what SHOULD have won in this category, in my opinion, was Zelazny's other 1966 story, the novella *He Who Shapes*, which is much better at that length than it was padded out to the novel *The Dream Master*.

Fred Pohl considered *Galaxy* to be his major, prestigious magazine and *If* the "remainder outlet" where he dumped stuff he didn't have room for in *Galaxy*, and it annoyed him that *If* kept winning the Hugo instead of *Galaxy*, as it did several times in a row. *If* was more fun, though, a loosier, jazzier magazine than the somewhat stuffy *Galaxy*, more full of colorful adventure fiction, and I'd have voted for it myself.

21. RICH HORTON

"'Repent, Harlequin!' Said the Ticktockman" made a great impression on me when I first read it, and I don't think it's a bad choice for the Hugo. That said, from this remove, my favorite among the nominees is "The Doors of His Face, the Lamps of His Mouth." Let's take a quick look at the Nebula winners in short fiction. The Nebulas introduced the concept of three separate short fiction categories, which the Hugos eventually, after some fits and starts, adopted. So,

Nebula, Best Novella:

He Who Shapes, by Roger Zelazny (*Amazing Stories*, January, February 1965)
The Saliva Tree, by Brian W. Aldiss (*F&SF*, September 1965)
The Ballad of Beta-2, by Samuel R. Delany (Ace)
The Mercurymen, by C. C. MacApp (*Galaxy*, December 1965)
On the Storm Planet, by Cordwainer Smith (*Galaxy*, February 1965)
Research Alpha, by A. E. van Vogt and James H. Schmitz (*If*, July 1965)
Rogue Dragon, by Avram Davidson (*F&SF*, July 1965)
Under Two Moons, by Frederik Pohl (*If*, September 1965)

An interesting list. Note the Ace Double half from Delany— normally in those days, these were called novels. But "The Ballad of Beta-2" is only 29,000 words long, so it is correctly called a novella.

I'd say the voters unerrantly picked the two best novellas of the nominees—I like them both. Note that Zelazny's novella was also an Ace Double, under the title *The Dream Master*.

Novelette:

"The Doors of His Face, the Lamps of His Mouth," by Roger Zelazny (*F&SF*, March 1965)

"102 H-Bombs," by Thomas M. Disch (*Fantastic*, March 1965)

"The Adventure of the Extraterrestrial," by Mack Reynolds (*Analog*, July 1965)

"At the Institute," by Norman Kagan (*Worlds of Tomorrow*, September 1965)

"The Decision Makers," by Joseph Green (*Galaxy*, April 1965)

"The Earth Merchants," by Norman Kagan (*F&SF*, May 1965)

"Four Ghosts in Hamlet," by Fritz Leiber (*F&SF*, January 1965)

"Goblin Night," by James H. Schmitz (*Analog*, April 1965)

"Half a Loaf," by R. C. Fitzpatrick (*Analog*, August 1965)

"Laugh Along with Franz," by Norman Kagan (*Galaxy*, December 1965)

"The Life of Your Time," by Michael Karageorge (*Analog*, September 1965) (Karageorge is a pseudonym for Poul Anderson)

"Maiden Voyage," by J. W. Schutz (*F&SF*, March 1965)

"The Masculinist Revolt," by William Tenn (*F&SF*, August 1965)

"Masque of the Red Shift," by Fred Saberhagen (*If*, November 1965)

"Planet of Forgetting," by James H. Schmitz (*Galaxy*, February 1965)

"Shall We Have a Little Talk?," by Robert Sheckley (*Galaxy*, October 1965)

"The Shipwrecked Hotel," by James Blish and Norman L. Knight (*Galaxy*, August 1965)

"Small One," by E. Clayton McCarty (*If*, February 1965)

"Vanishing Point," by Jonathan Brand (*If*, January 1965)

Boy, the Nebula nomination lists were long in the early years! According to my source for these lists, Mark Kelly's *Locus* Index to SF Awards, any story that got even one nomination made the final ballot.

For me there are two great stories here: "The Doors of His Face, the Lamps of His Mouth," and "Four Ghosts in Hamlet." My clear choice lies with the actual winner, Zelazny's story.

Short Story:

"'Repent, Harlequin!' Said the Ticktockman," by Harlan Ellison (*Galaxy*, December 1965)

"Balanced Ecology," by James H. Schmitz (*Analog*, March 1965)

"Becalmed in Hell," by Larry Niven (*F&SF*, July 1965)

"A Better Mousehole," by Edgar Pangborn (*Galaxy*, October 1965)

"Better Than Ever," by Alex Kirs (*F&SF*, March 1965)

"Calling Dr. Clockwork," by Ron Goulart (*Amazing Stories*, March 1965)

"Come to Venus Melancholy," by Thomas M. Disch (*F&SF*, November 1965)

"Computers Don't Argue," by Gordon R. Dickson (*Analog*, September 1965)

"Cyclops," by Fritz Leiber (*Worlds of Tomorrow*, September 1965)

"Devil Car," by Roger Zelazny (*Galaxy*, June 1965)

"The Eight Billion," by Richard Wilson (*F&SF*, July 1965)

"Eyes Do More Than See," by Isaac Asimov (*F&SF*, April 1965)

"A Few Kindred Spirits," by John Christopher (*F&SF*, November 1965)

"Founding Father," by Isaac Asimov (*Galaxy*, October 1965)

"Game," by Donald Barthelme (*The New Yorker*, July 31, 1965)

"The Good New Days," by Fritz Leiber (*Galaxy*, October 1965)

"The House the Blakeneys Built," by Avram Davidson (*F&SF*, January 1965)

"In Our Block," by R. A. Lafferty (*If*, July 1965)

"Inside Man," by H. L. Gold (*Galaxy*, October 1965)

"Keep Them Happy," by Robert Rohrer (*F&SF*, April 1965)

"A Leader for Yesteryear," by Mack Reynolds (*If*, October 1965)

"Lord Moon," by Jane Beauclerk (*F&SF*, April 1965)

"The Mischief Maker," by Richard Olin (*Analog*, October 1965)

"Of One Mind," by James A. Durham (*If*, March 1965)

"Over the River and Through the Woods," by Clifford D. Simak
(*Amazing Stories*, May 1965)
"The Peacock King," by Larry McCombs and Ted White (*F&SF*, November 1965)
"Slow Tuesday Night," by R. A. Lafferty (*Galaxy*, April 1965)
"Souvenir," by J. G. Ballard (*Playboy*, May 1965)
"Though a Sparrow Fall," by Scott Nichols (*Analog*, July 1965)
"Uncollected Works," by Lin Carter (*F&SF*, March 1965)
"Wrong-Way Street," by Larry Niven (*Galaxy*, April 1965)

Ellison won here as well, and a worthy winner. I do like "Balanced Ecology" a good deal. I note the presence of two early Niven stories—clearly, he got instant notice. The other real contender, in my mind, is Lafferty's "Slow Tuesday Night."

22. RICH HORTON

Finally, I was able to find several really surprising omissions from the nomination lists. I'm not sure of their length, but any of these stories would have seemed at least worth a Nebula nomination:

"The Muddle of the Woad," by Randall Garrett
"Man in His Time," by Brian W. Aldiss
"Traveller's Rest," by David I. Masson

Of those, at least "Man in His Time" and "Traveller's Rest" are brilliant. However, they weren't actually eligible for the Nebula, as they both first appeared in the UK, the Aldiss story in *Science Fantasy*, and the Masson in *New Worlds*. That explains the lack of notice from the Hugo nominators too. In fact, "Man in His Time" did get nominations the following year for both Hugo and Nebula, and "Traveller's Rest" was picked for both Merril's Year's Best, and Wollheim/Carr's.

At any rate, my Best Short Fiction nomination list would have had the Ellison, Zelazny, Aldiss, and Masson stories for sure, plus either "Slow Tuesday Night" or "Four Ghosts in Hamlet." And to my mind, the clear best story of 1965, at this remove, is "Traveller's Rest," by David I. Masson, a truly amazing story.

24. GARDNER DOZOIS

In the Nebula short story ballot, my vote would probably go to "Slow Tuesday Night," although Davidson's "The House the Blakeneys Built" is good too.

Novella, I'd go for "He Who Shapes," followed by Smith's "On the Storm Planet."

Novelette, probably "The Doors of His Face," although "Four Ghosts in Hamlet" is very good too.

WISECRACKING, ALIENS, AND HOT PLACES: ROGER ZELAZNY'S *THIS IMMORTAL* (". . . AND CALL ME CONRAD")

This Immortal, or . . . *And Call Me Conrad* was Roger Zelazny's first novel, and it showcases a lot of the things that he typically did. It's unquestionably science fiction, but it uses mythic resonance in a way more familiar in fantasy. It has a first-person smart-ass hero wisecracking his way across the adventure. It's fast moving and builds the world up as a neat piece of juggling—and of course, it's poetic and beautifully written. I can see some people hating Zelazny for the very things I love about him—the style, the prose, the offhand world-building. It doesn't always work for me. But when it does, as here, it's lovely.

In *This Immortal,* Zelazny is using Greek mythology, and Greek folktales too. In the first line, Conrad is accused by his wife, Cassandra (who is, naturally, always right and never believed), of being a kallikanzaros—one of the demons who try to destroy the world and are scared away by the Easter bells. He's tall and hairy with one leg shorter than the other, and he somehow just doesn't seem to age. This is because there was a nuclear war on Earth, the "Three Days," and there are a whole lot of mutants around, especially near the "hot places" that are still radioactive. There are also a whole lot of alien tourists, and Conrad's job involves taking one of them on a tour of beautiful but devastated Earth, while other people, human, mutant, and alien, seem desperate to kill him.

There's a complicated backstory—after the nuclear war, the colonies on Mars and Titan had to manage on their own. They were rescued by blue-skinned humanoid aliens from Vega, who took them to their planets; even though the presence of humans detracts from the value of real estate, cheap sentient labor and entertainment make it worth it. Meanwhile, Earth has a lot of mutants, a civilization based on the less-damaged islands, and the only thing that's thriving is the tourist trade as bored Vegans visit to be entertained. Conrad's been trying to save the world, or possibly destroy it, for a long time now. The exiled human population are a problem, having their own agenda, and the Vegans want resorts and seem to see all humans as whores.

What we have here is a picaresque in the traditional old-fashioned sense—the characters go from place to place and encounter and overcome dangers while we learn about them and about the world. Zelazny gives us enough of all three things—the encounters, the characters, and the world—to keep us fascinated and tantalized. There could always be more. The end is something of a deus ex machina, but in a way that fits very well with everything that has gone before. There are moments in this book that are as good as anything Zelazny ever wrote—getting a telepathic flash of being in the alien's mind and seeing ultraviolet colors in a white flower, fighting a boadile and wondering how many legs it has, Hasan saying the devil has forgiven him.

In League with the Future: Frank Herbert's *Dune*

Dune is a book that sneaks up on you. It's an easy book to make fun of—ultra baroque, ridiculously complex plotting, long pauses while people assess each other—and yet when all's said and done, it sneaks up on you and sucks you in. It does a number of clever things, and it plays with some interesting ideas, and step by step it builds a very seductive world.

It's far from an Aristotelian plot—it's a weird cocktail, part messianic, part intrigue, part ecological, but it works. I loved it when I was a teenager, and I read the sequels, which are each half as good as the one before, and I didn't give up until they were homeopathically good.

I reread *Dune* frequently when I was young, but I hadn't read it for a long time, not since 1990 at least. I thought maybe I would have grown out of it. But picking it up now to consider it as 1966's Hugo winner, I was wrong. It got me again. I have reservations, of course I do. But I thoroughly enjoyed reading it, and I'd recommend it.

This is another one for the "religious SF" pile. But the religion in question is a distorted Islam. One of the things Herbert succeeds in doing here is making this seem like a far future that starts from here, and making the time between seem like history. He does it mainly by hinting and not explaining, and it works. It also has great names that plausibly come from different cultures—Duncan Idaho and Feyd-Rautha Harkonnen and Stilgar.

Paul Atreides is the heir to a Dukedom, and we are told unequivocably and right away in the chapter start quotes that he will become Muad'Dib, that he will be a phenomenon, somebody worth writing books about within his universe. Before we know what Muad'Dib is, we know that's Paul's destiny. The quotes come from books—*Arrakis Awakening, A Child's History of Muad'Dib, In My Father's House*, et cetera—all written in the future of the text we are reading. They do a number of clever things. First, they give information; second, they give information the characters don't yet know and hence foreshadow, sometimes more subtly and sometimes less. They therefore build up a sense of tragic inevitability, as with Yueh's betrayal and Leto's downfall. We know it's going to happen, we know it's going to have huge mythic significance, but we don't know exactly when, and we don't know how Paul and Jessica will survive. Thus the chapter start quotes set us up to be ready for Paul's weird prophetic abilities, how they show and hide events at the same time, they make us understand them as if they have happened to us.

This really is amazingly clever—chapter start quotes are an old device, but this is an astonishing use of them. It's giving us a prescient weighted experience and two layers of time at the same time, so that when Paul gets that, we understand it. The other clever thing the quotes do is that they come from a whole pile of books about Paul and written by "the Princess Irulan." When we finally meet Irulan as a character and hear she has literary aspirations, that's another and unexpected connection.

We have a universe that is balanced, Great Houses against Emperor against Guild—the Guild of pilots who are the only ones who can move ships between the stars. And moving across this balance, there's the all-female Bene Gesserit, a eugenic society with secret aims, and the Spice, which allows the Guild to see futures and therefore fly, and the Bene Gesserit to see futures and therefore plot. Spice comes only from Arrakis, the dune planet.

The balance falters when Arrakis is given to Paul's father, Duke Leto, and Leto has plans for the desert dwellers, the Fremen. Unknown to him, they have secret terraforming plans, and a strand of ecology has insinuated itself into their religion. Their religion has also been twisted in the past by the Bene Gesserit, who spread legends on planets to make it easier for any of their members who happen to get stuck there. In addition to this, there was a revolt in the past (the Butlerian Jihad, mentioned, not described) in which computers were destroyed, and now people trained to think like computers, mentats, are valuable members of society, though both the ones we see are also trained as assassins.

The whole plot is what happens after the balance is tipped, and how it comes into a new balance. Everybody has their own agenda, and all the agendas are twisted. The Harkonnens, enemies of the Atreides, the Emperor, the Bene Gesserit, the Fremen, everyone. A lot of what makes the book good is the depth of the world-building. Herbert takes all the time he needs to build his world, one funny word at a time. The book starts on Caledan, and moves slowly to Arrakis, and this is good, we need that time. It starts really slowly, establishing characters. Paul and Jessica aren't normal, but they come from a world much more like ours into a world where every drop of water is precious and the culture has been utterly shaped by that. And it really feels as if it has. Paul and Jessica are thrust out among the Fremen and have to learn to adjust, at the same time as Paul is learning to use his prescient powers. The different cultures build up drop by drop until they feel completely real.

So, caveats. It's incredibly overwritten and purple. At times it almost seems like self-parody. The plotting is unnecessarily baroque. There are some lovely set pieces, but there are also some ridiculous ones. The prescience is brilliant, but the race memory—if you had race memory of all your ancestors through your genes, that would give you their memory up to the time they conceived their child, not their wisdom in old age and experience, but a whole pile of twenty-year-olds. Agamemnon's children were all conceived before Troy, and Shakespeare's before he left Stratford. Their memories won't be that much use.

But all of that aside, it got me, I wanted to keep reading it, and by the end, I was utterly caught up in it and asking myself if the sequels really were as bad as I remember, because I wanted more. The sequels are not worth it. But if you haven't read *Dune* itself, do pick it up. It's entirely self-contained, it has a beginning and a satisfying end, it's a classic, it's a good story, and it's one of the things that helps define the edges of what science fiction can be.

1967

Winner: *The Moon Is a Harsh Mistress,* by Robert A. Heinlein

Nominees:
Babel-17, by Samuel R. Delany
Flowers for Algernon, by Daniel Keyes
Too Many Magicians, by Randall Garrett
Day of the Minotaur, by Thomas Burnett Swann
The Witches of Karres, by James H. Schmitz

The 1967 Worldcon was NyCon 3, in New York, and the Hugo Awards were presented there. The Best Novel award was given to Robert A. Heinlein's *The Moon Is a Harsh Mistress,* a story of a revolution on the moon and a computer becoming a person. It's definitely a classic, it's in print, and it's in my library in English and French.

There are five other nominees, of which I have read three. There's Samuel R. Delany's *Babel-17,* which is utterly brilliant and well ahead of its time. It's amazing, and I can't summarize it in a line. It's about war and linguistics and survival and poetry and identity, and it seems to me that if it were published today, we'd still be excited about it and nominate it for awards. It's in print and in the library in both languages, and I've had conversations about it recently, so it has plain lasted.

Then there's the novel version of *Flowers for Algernon,* by Daniel Keyes. I think it's slightly inferior to the novella version, which already won the Hugo. I wonder if people were reluctant to vote for it for that reason, because it had already won? It's about a man with the IQ of a small child who goes through a process that makes him more intelligent and then wears off. It's more thoroughly in print and in the library than anything else so far, and it now appears to be a set book for reading in high school.

Randall Garrett's *Too Many Magicians* is a Lord Darcy novel, and it doesn't seem to belong in the same list as the others—it's much more old-fashioned. It's also fantasy, and I think this is the first time an outright fantasy has been nominated. It's an alternate history where Richard I doesn't die on crusade and comes home and discovers the laws of magic, which are very scientific. The stories are all mysteries with the magic carefully integrated. *Too Many Magicians* is fun, but not really of the quality of the other nominees so far. It's in print in an omnibus. It's not in the library.

I haven't read *Day of the Minotaur*, by Thomas Burnett Swann. I've never come across it. It seems to be historical fantasy. It isn't in print, but it's in the library in French.

I also haven't read James H. Schmitz's *The Witches of Karres*, but I know more about it. It's science fiction adventure, and for many people it's a beloved classic. I tried to read it a few years ago when it was reissued and many people were talking about it, but it seemed to me one of those books where you had to be twelve; I just couldn't get into it. No doubt this is my failure. It's in print, in an edition edited by Eric Flint, but not in the library.

So six nominees, all American men. Heinlein's a previous winner; all the others are newcomers. Of the four I've read, we have three excellent novels and one good one. And we have a revolution on the moon, a complex future and alien languages, the nature of intelligence, a historical fantasy, a space opera adventure, and a magical mystery. What a lot of ground science fiction covers!

The Nebulas for 1967 were given to *Babel-17* and *Flowers for Algernon*, with *The Moon Is a Harsh Mistress* also nominated, and nothing else, as if making up for their enthusiasm the year before. This is a rare total overlap of nominees. I'm glad *Babel-17* won something.

What else might they have considered, and did they miss anything? Well, Delany also published *Empire Star*, one of my favorite books of all time, and well worthy of a nomination, in my opinion. Harry Harrison's *Make Room! Make Room!* is a significant book that's still being talked about. It's somewhat gonzo but also brilliant, so how about Robert Sheckley's *Mindswap*? Le Guin published *Planet of Exile* and *Rocannon's World.* Van Vogt published *The Players of Null-A,* and Larry Niven *World of Ptaavs.*

So were the six books on the short list the best and most lasting of 1967? Some of them definitely were. But there were also some odd choices and definite omissions, so I think on the whole for this year, I'd say not.

OTHER CATEGORIES

BEST NOVELETTE

Winner: "The Last Castle," by Jack Vance (*Galaxy,* April 1966)

Nominees:
"The Alchemist," by Charles L. Harness (*Analog,* May 1966)
"Apology to Inky," by Robert M. Green Jr. (*F&SF,* January 1966)
"Call Him Lord," by Gordon R. Dickson (*Analog,* May 1966)
"The Eskimo Invasion," by Hayden Howard (*Galaxy,* June 1966)
"For a Breath I Tarry," by Roger Zelazny (*Fantastic,* September 1966)
"The Manor of Roses," by Thomas Burnett Swann (*F&SF,* November 1966)
"An Ornament to His Profession," by Charles L. Harness (*Analog,* February 1966)
"This Moment of the Storm," by Roger Zelazny (*F&SF,* June 1966)

Look, two short fiction categories! And about time too. I'd have had a hard time choosing between the Zelaznys here. The Nebula also went to "The Last Castle," with the Harness and Avram Davidson's "Clash of Star-Kings" also nominated.

Best Short Story

Winner: "Neutron Star," by Larry Niven (*If,* October 1966)

Nominees:
"Comes Now the Power," by Roger Zelazny (*Magazine of Horror 14,* Winter 1966/67)
"Delusions for a Dragon Slayer," by Harlan Ellison (*Knight,* September 1966)
"Light of Other Days," by Bob Shaw (*Analog,* August 1966)
"Man in His Time," by Brian W. Aldiss (*Who Can Replace a Man?*)
"Mr. Jester," by Fred Saberhagen (*If,* January 1966)
"Rat Race," by Raymond F. Jones (*Analog,* April 1966)
"The Secret Place," by Richard McKenna (*Orbit 1*)

Wow. "Neutron Star" is a brilliant story, but both "Light of Other Days" and "Who Can Replace a Man?" are part of the furniture of my brain. That would have been a really hard choice. The Nebula went to "The Secret Place," with "Who Can Replace a Man" and "Light of Other Days" also listed.

Best Dramatic Presentation

Winner: *Star Trek:* "The Menagerie"

Nominees:
Fahrenheit 451
Fantastic Voyage
Star Trek: "The Corbomite Maneuver"
Star Trek: "The Naked Time"

Best Professional Magazine

Winner: *If,* edited by Frederik Pohl

Nominees:
Analog, edited by John W. Campbell Jr.
Galaxy, edited by Frederik Pohl
New Worlds, edited by Michael Moorcock

This shows the impression the New Wave was having already, even though none of the nominees are from *New Worlds*, what we see here for the first time is a British magazine being nominated as best magazine at an American Worldcon.

BEST PROFESSIONAL ARTIST

Winner: Jack Gaughan

Nominees:
Frank Kelly Freas
Gray Morrow
John Schoenherr

The fan categories have also burgeoned into the three categories we have today.

BEST FANZINE

Winner: *Niekas*, edited by Edmund R. Meskys and Felice Rolfe

Nominees:
Australian SF Review, edited by John Bangsund
Habakkuk, edited by Bill Donaho
Lighthouse, edited by Terry Carr
Riverside Quarterly, edited by Leland Sapiro
Trumpet, edited by Tom Reamy
Yandro, edited by Robert Coulson and Juanita Coulson

Best Fan Writer

Winner: Alexei Panshin

Nominees:
Norm Clarke
Bill Donaho
Harry Warner Jr.
Paul J. Willis

Best Fan Artist

Winner: Jack Gaughan

Nominees:
George Barr
Jeff Jones
Steve Stiles
Arthur Thomson

Comments on 1967

14. Rich Horton

The novellas/novelettes. (I suspect it was the Nebula addition of no-vella as a category that led to the widespread use of that as a category. Most older magazines that I've seen usually just listed "Novelettes" (often defined as stories over ten thousand words, though that varied); and sometimes "Short Novels" for stories over about twenty thousand words).

I think it's a pretty strong couple of nomination lists. Don't know why they were so long, perhaps a reaction to the long nomination lists for the Nebula the year before? (Oddly, the Nebula short lists were really short, only three deep in most cases.)

For novella/novelette, "The Last Castle" is perhaps my favorite Vance shorter work, and it's a good choice for the award. But my gosh, so too would have been either Zelazny story—both "For a Breath I Tarry" and "This Moment of the Storm" are wonderful. He also published "The Keys to December" in 1966, which is almost as good. And a similarly brilliant short story, "Divine Madness."

"Call Him Lord," the Nebula winner for Best Novelette, is very fine work, though I wouldn't have given it a Hugo over the other contenders. Hayden Howard's "The Eskimo Invasion" is also good stuff. I haven't read Green's story. I'm a big Charles Harness fan, and both of Harness's nominees are strong stories, though again not better than the Vance or Zelazny stories.

The one real contender, besides Vance and Zelazny, among the nominees, is Thomas Burnett Swann's "The Manor of Roses," which is just stunning. It's Swann's best story by far, great work, and not well enough remembered. (He later expanded it to a novel, not as good, *The Tournament of Thorns* [1976].)

There were some worthy novellas and novelettes not nominated for the Hugo. We've already mentioned "Empire Star," which is wonderful, of course, though I confess I'd not have given it the award over any of Vance, Zelazny, or Swann. There's also the Nebula nominee "Clash of Star-Kings," by Avram Davidson. It's good work, but not my favorite Davidson. It's best for its description of life in Mexico for an expatriate American. (Shockingly enough, at the time, Davidson was living in Mexico.) Davidson called it *Tlaloc*, but predicted that Don Wollheim would change the title to something like *Aztec Goddesses from Outer Space with Big Boobs*—Wollheim's eventual title wasn't that bad, but it certainly was going in that direction!

Some other novellas/novelettes worth a look (I'm guessing as to the length, in many cases):

"Bookworm, Run!," by Vernor Vinge
"Door to Anywhere," by Poul Anderson
"We Can Remember It for You Wholesale," by Philip K. Dick

16. RICH HORTON

Now to the short stories.

In the first place, while I love "Neutron Star," I do think there was another clear-cut choice, my definite favorite this year, and one of my favorite stories of all time, and that's "Light of Other Days." (And no, I don't care that it has a science error at least as egregious as Niven's screwup about the tides.)

Of the other nominees, I think "Man in His Time" by Aldiss is brilliant. And perhaps we should clear up some confusion. "Who Can Replace a Man?" aka "But Who Can Replace a Man?" is another short story by Aldiss, first published back in 1958. It's very good, mind you. It is the title story of the collection in which "Man in His Time" was first published in the United States.

I'm not that familiar with the other short story nominees. "The Secret Place," the Nebula winner, is good, but not nearly as good as "Light of Other Days," nor as good as the Aldiss or Niven stories.

There was one other 1966 story that is pretty much on that very top level, though, and it's perhaps the most influential of them all. This is "Day Million," by Frederik Pohl. It was published in *Rogue*, which may explain why the nominators ignored it. It should have gotten a nomination, though, and it should have won in most years (but not against "Light of Other Days.")

A few more potential nominees:

"A Man Must Die," by John Clute (Really, try it, it's great! Even you, James Nicoll!)

Three by R. A. Lafferty: "Among the Hairy Earthmen," "Nine Hundred Grandmothers," "Primary Education of the Camiroi"

"Be Merry," by Algis Budrys (He also published an excellent non-SF story, "The Master of the Hounds," a crime story with a great last line.)

"When I Was Miss Dow," by Sonya Dorman (who abandoned SF for poetry a few years later, and she was a damn good poet, too)

18. GARDNER DOZOIS

I have no problem with "The Last Castle" winning, although I like Zelazny's "This Moment of the Storm" almost as well (like it better, in fact, than the better-known "For a Breath I Tarry").

Short story is weaker. Of that list, I suppose "Light of Other Days" deserved to win, it being the only one of the list that still gets read and talked about much, although I never liked it as much as some people did. Like the suggestion that Lafferty's "Nine Hundred Grandmothers" or Budrys's "Be Merry" might have made good substitutes.

19. MICHAEL F. FLYNN

Too Many Magicians

It's not that the magic is psi. It isn't, though one must have the Talent to use it. It had an SFnal feel because the magic was material and lawful: you couldn't do just anything. In one of the short stories, Master Sean, the "forensic sorceror," uses magic to determine that a particular bullet came from a particular gun, but explains that the Law of Relevance means he can't likewise determine who fired the gun. It's relevant to the bullet which gun fired it, for it would not be the bullet it is (the wear and tear) if it had not been fired from that particular gun. But it is not relevant to the gun who pulled the trigger, since the wear and tear was mechanical. It was that sort of scientificating of the magic that made it charming.

25. GARDNER DOZOIS

Forgot about "Day Million," but I guess that would probably get my Hugo vote in the short story category. A clear precursor of all the Posthuman stories that came after it, years ahead of its time, and hugely influential on everything that came after it.

A Self-Aware Computer and a Revolution on the Moon: Robert A. Heinlein's *The Moon Is a Harsh Mistress*

The Moon Is a Harsh Mistress is a book with a lot in it. It's about a revolution on the moon. It's about a computer that has become self-aware and is slowly becoming a person. It's got polyamory and half a ton of gender issues and lots of very odd politics.

What I have always loved about it is the experimental style, and Mike, the computer who isn't meant to be alive. My fifteen-year-old self and my present-day self are united in thinking that Mike is the best character in the book. But on this reread, I found something problematic even with him. However, all problems aside, this is a significant book in the history of the genre, and even better, it has the Heinlein magic readability. It's amazingly engrossing from the first minute, and it drew me along as irresistibly now as when I was a teenager. It's a great story written in a great voice. I'm not saying it won't drive you nuts in several ways, but it's nevertheless important, fun, and good.

First, Mike. I think Mike is a wonderfully done portrait of a self-aware computer. He's convincingly alien, he's convincingly young, he's convincingly simultaneously naïve and well informed. Heinlein really makes him work as a character—and that's even more amazing when you consider the leaps in computer technology between 1967 and now mean that the actual descriptions of what he's designed for and what he does mean that he has less processing power than a set of car keys. Mannie is a hardware guy, he takes plates off to fix crashes, he finds (or pretends to find) literal bugs—a fly inside the case. He writes his own programs, you know, but he then prints them out. The admin people who work with him write their letters on typewriters. Mike's simultaneously a mixture of very old-fashioned and futuristically impossible—and I don't care. I totally believe in him. I am completely convinced. This is exactly how a self-aware computer would be—like a person with autism trying to logic his way through why other people act the way they do.

Having said that, I have two problems with Mike. One is the figuring the odds for the revolution. I'd have bought it if he did it once. It's the complex refiguring and odds changing and—no. People complain about the Dust hypothesis in *Permutation City* that you can't calculate things out of order, and this is worse. You can't work out odds of 7 to 1 against and then say they will keep getting worse until they get better. It makes no sense. The second problem is that he dies in the end. My problem with that when I was fifteen was that it made me cry and I missed him. It still makes me cry—it's a well-written and well-paced death—but this time I suddenly thought that he had to die. He had to die because otherwise, *quis custodiet?* It's very convenient for the revolution to have this corrupt near-omnipotent computer on their side, rigging elections, controlling the phone system. And it's incredibly convenient that he dies and thus doesn't become a dictator—because how could it have gone but trust the computer, the computer is your friend? Mike doesn't have morals or ideals; he's doing the revolution for company and human attention. He has an orgasm when he bombs Earth. He couldn't live without becoming a worse dictator than the Warden ever was. And Heinlein knew that, and killed him and furthermore made me cry for him. (Don't bother telling about the rescue attempt in *The Cat Who Walks Through Walls*. Does not exist, does not fit. Not true. Have forgotten about. Don't remind.)

During the discussions here and elsewhere about the Patterson biography, Farah Mendlesohn pointed out that Heinlein was trying to imagine women's liberation and getting it wrong. I think this is precisely it. We say "women's lib" without really thinking of the implication—that before second-wave feminism, even white women in the first world were not free. If you consider that all the women Heinlein had ever known were living in a system that had them pretty much enslaved, it's excellent that he wanted to imagine how we would be if we were free, and not all that surprising that he couldn't quite figure out what it would be like. I don't think the situation as described on the moon would lead to the situation we see—but I don't think any of it would. Also, surely the disproportionate lack of women transportees would disappear once people were having children—and they're having lots of children.

The division of labor in Luna is incredibly sexist (running a beauty shop, but never being a judge or an engineer . . .) and the Lysistrata corps is really annoying. There's also the pervasive thing of women being manipulative—well, I guess we'd all be manipulative if it was the only way to get by.

Following on from that, Mannie's line marriage is described in detail. I'd never heard of anything like it when I was fifteen—and I still never have. There isn't anything like it. This isn't how people do polyamory. The thing that makes it squicky is the age difference. This is enhanced by Mannie calling the oldest man "Grandpaw" and the oldest woman "Mum"—ick. And I almost gagged at the description of Ludmilla's death. She's fourteen, and she's married all these older people, and when she dies bravely in battle, Mannie describes her wound as "a bullet between her lovely little girl breasts." This is probably the thing that bothers me the most in all of Heinlein.

As far as people of color goes, the book does pretty well for now, or splendidly for the time when it was written. Mannie is mixed race with dark skin. There are a huge number of other people described as being dark-skinned, and Professor de la Paz is Hispanic. There's one heroic African transportee who dies. The description of Chinese people as "Chinee" isn't good, but the mention of Chinese babies being small is probably what was believed at the time. Hong Kong Luna is a thriving and free city—the most free city on the moon. What we see is a colony where people of many origins are beginning to define their own ethnicity as Loonies. I think Heinlein really wanted to get this right and tried hard.

It's also probably worth mentioning that our narrator and protagonist, Mannie, is disabled. He has only one arm. His other arm is a set of prostheses that are in some ways better than the original, but there's a memorable moment when he's going to Earth and he's been put in his pressure suit without an arm. This is exactly the kind of unthinking stupidity-intended-kindly that people do all the time. It really rings true. Of course, Heinlein spent a lot of time in and around hospitals. He'd have had plenty of chance to see this kind of thing.

Politics—the revolution is ostensibly anarchist-libertarian, but in fact, it's all being cynically manipulated. It's quite clear in the frame that apolitical Mannie preferred Luna before it was free. The ideology of the revolution is that of freeing Luna, against the status quo but not really for anything. There's so much waving of political sound bites that this almost gets obscured. And the sound bites are nifty—TANSTAFFL and so on. But this is really a coup. I've read people saying that this revolution is supposedly based on the American Revolution of 1776, but the social and economic conditions don't seem to me in any way parallel, nor was that engineered by cynical behind-the-scenes manipulators. Nor would the United States have been reduced to cannibalism in eight years—why, Canada still hasn't been reduced to cannibalism! But the whole economic setup of growing wheat on the moon to send to the starving people of India is nonsense anyway. The dice are so very loaded, you can hear them rattling. Well, I couldn't when I was fifteen, but at that point I was listening only to Mike.

The book is written in a very interesting futuristic style. A lot of the word choices are Australian rather than US or UK English—this is explained within the novel by the large proportion of Aussies forcibly emigrating when China conquered Australia. Also, the general fractured style—no articles, a dearth of possessives—is reminiscent of Russian. Some Russian words are sprinkled in as well. Since the whole book is written in Mannie's first person, this works very well. I'm not in a very good position to evaluate it—it blew me away when I first read it. I don't know what I'd think if I came across it for the first time now. But it flows; it genuinely feels like a possible future variant of English. Similarly the name selection feels like the way this works in an actual society.

I don't know how to sum this one up. It made me laugh, it made me cry, it made me grit my teeth, it made me gag, I couldn't put it down, but I probably won't read it again for a long time. So, that would be a mixed reaction, then.

1968

Winner: *Lord of Light*, by Roger Zelazny

Nominees:
The Butterfly Kid, by Chester Anderson
The Einstein Intersection, by Samuel R. Delany
Thorns, by Robert Silverberg
Chthon, by Piers Anthony

The 1968 Hugo Awards were presented at Baycon in Oakland, California. The novel winner was Roger Zelazny's *Lord of Light*. It's science fiction in which the crew of a starship have taken on the attributes of Hindu gods to rule the planet populated by the descendants of passengers of the ship, and one of the original crew starts a new Buddhist religion as a rebellion. Many people love it. It's in print in the SF Masterworks series, and it's in my library in English and French, so I think we can say it has lasted.

There are four other nominees, and I've read three of them, and I'm really sorry but 1968 seems to be a "books I don't like" year.

Let's start with the one I do like, but which should never have been a nominee—were the voters all stoned? Chester Anderson's *The Butterfly Kid* is that rare thing: hippie science fiction. It was 1968, and doubtless this was published right at the heart of the Summer of Love. It's a charming book about drugs that really change reality. It's part of the loose "Greenwich Village" trilogy with Michael Kurland's *The*

Unicorn Girl and T. A. Waters's (much weaker) *The Probability Pad*, and the characters have the names of the authors. I read *The Unicorn Girl* first—indeed, I read it very early, before I knew what SF was, and it's surprising it didn't warp me forever. *The Butterfly Kid* is very much of its time and I kind of like it, but it has all the depth of a Twinkie. It isn't in print and hasn't been republished since 1980. It isn't in the library, and I think it's fair to say that while some people remember it fondly, it's mostly forgotten.

The Einstein Intersection is my least favorite Samuel Delany science fiction novel. I tried rereading it last year after I suddenly loved *Nova*, but clearly I'm still not old enough for it, dammit. It's about far-future mutants, and it's about searching for love, and it uses mythological imagery in the same way Delany did so brilliantly in *Nova* and *Babel-17*, but I can't find anything to connect to, and it always slips away from me. It's another classic example of a story that doesn't have a surface for you to skitter over. But I'm quite ready to admit that my problem with it is a problem with me—indeed, I'm longing for this problem with me to be fixed, and fairly confident that if I keep trying, I'll like it sometime in the future. Delany's one of my favorite writers, after all! (But . . . this has been my stance with reference to this book for the last thirty years.) This probably is a worthy nominee that I just don't appreciate. It's in print from Wesleyan University Press, and it's in the library in English.

Robert Silverberg's *Thorns* is brilliant but terrible. It's the story of a future sadistic media tycoon getting two damaged people to fall in love for the entertainment of the masses. I read it in the early eighties and I've never reread it, because it's just too painful. Silverberg is a wonderful writer, but with a subject like this, that's not a plus. It's just too much. *Thorns* definitely deserved the nomination. It's not in print, though it was fairly recently reprinted in the Gollancz SF Masterworks series. It's in the library in French only.

Last comes the one I haven't read, Piers Anthony's *Chthon*. It's his first novel and apparently grim, about a prisoner in a horrific future—and also atypically cleverly structured. I have no opinion on it, and I'm unlikely to read it even though people say it's better than the Anthony I have read. It's neither in print nor in the library.

So five nominees, all American men. Zelazny's a previous winner, Delany's a previous nominee, Silverberg won for best new writer but this is his first novel nomination, Anthony and Anderson are new. And we have near-future hippies, a near-future prison, a near-future sadist, a postapocalyptic quest, and a far-future colony with gods.

Nineteen sixty-eight's nominees match my tastes least of any year yet! Was it just a year when everyone was writing books I don't like, or what else might they have chosen?

The Nebula went to *The Einstein Intersection,* and the nominees overlap except for the addition of *The Eskimo Invasion* by Hayden Howard instead of the Anderson. I know nothing about this book except that it's a fix-up of shorter work.

Books I'd have preferred to see on the ballot include: Ursula K. Le Guin's *City of Illusions;* Thomas M. Disch's *Echo Round His Bones;* Ira Levin's *Rosemary's Baby;* Robert Silverberg's *Gate of Worlds;* Angela Carter's *The Magic Toyshop;* Clifford Simak's *Why Call Them Back from Heaven?;* and Poul Anderson's *World Without Stars.*

Other possibilities: Norman Spinrad's *Agent of Chaos;* Philip K. Dick's *Counter-Clock World;* Brian Aldiss's *Report on Probability A;* Michael Moorcock's *The Jewel in the Skull;* E. C. Tubb's *The Winds of Gath* . . . oh, all right, not really Hugo material, but I did enjoy those Dumarest books and this is the first one. And in YA books, Nicholas Fisk's *Space Hostages,* and John Christopher's *The City of Gold and Lead,* both of which are solid SF and which I loved to pieces as a kid, and Alan Garner's *The Owl Service,* which is fantasy and probably his best book.

Do I think the five nominees are the best five books of the year? Not a chance. Do I think they give a good picture of where the field was? I think they probably do. And I also think that despite all its problems, *Lord of Light* was the best of them. There are people who say that the people who came into fandom via *Star Trek* shifted the balance of the Hugos. I don't see any evidence of that in this novel list. What I do see here is the victory of the New Wave.

OTHER CATEGORIES

BEST NOVELLA

Winner: (tie) *Riders of the Purple Wage*, by Philip José Farmer (*Dangerous Visions*)
Weyr Search, by Anne McCaffrey (*Analog*, October 1967)

Nominees:
Damnation Alley, by Roger Zelazny (*Galaxy*, October 1967)
Hawksbill Station, by Robert Silverberg (*Galaxy*, August 1967)
The Star Pit, by Samuel R. Delany (*Worlds of Tomorrow*, February 1967)

Look, a novella category! And what a terrific one! You couldn't ask for two more different winners, but they are both wonderful in their own ways . . . and I really love *Hawksbill Station* and *The Star Pit* too. The Nebulas gave their novella award to Moorcock's *Behold the Man*. Can't argue with that. And (as well as some overlap) they also nominated Sturgeon's *If All Men Were Brothers, Would You Let One Marry Your Sister?* So if this was a bad year for novels, it was one of the best years ever for novellas. I honestly would have had a hard time nominating just five, and I don't know how I would have voted.

BEST NOVELETTE

Winner: "Gonna Roll the Bones," by Fritz Leiber (*Dangerous Visions*)

Nominees:
"Faith of Our Fathers," by Philip K. Dick (*Dangerous Visions*)
"Pretty Maggie Moneyeyes," by Harlan Ellison (*Knight*, May 1967)
"Wizard's World," by Andre Norton (*If*, June 1967)

Dangerous Visions cleaning up in the awards, and not surprising. It really was an astonishing anthology. The Nebulas also have Niven's

"Flatlander," and Zelazny's "The Keys to December" and "This Mortal Mountain."

BEST SHORT STORY

Winner: "I Have No Mouth, and I Must Scream," by Harlan Ellison (*If,* March 1967)

Nominees:
"Aye, and Gomorrah . . . ," by Samuel R. Delany (*Dangerous Visions*)
"The Jigsaw Man," by Larry Niven (*Dangerous Visions*)

BEST DRAMATIC PRESENTATION

Winner: *Star Trek:* "The City on the Edge of Forever," by Harlan Ellison

Nominees:
Star Trek: "Mirror, Mirror," by Jerome Bixby
Star Trek: "The Trouble with Tribbles," by David Gerrold
Star Trek: "The Doomsday Machine," by Norman Spinrad
Star Trek: "Amok Time," by Theodore Sturgeon

All *Star Trek,* all the time. I don't think I've seen any of these episodes, but I know a surprising amount about them by fannish osmosis. I didn't, however, know that "Amok Time" was by Sturgeon. But of course it was. It all makes sense now. Who else could have put the sex in?

BEST PROFESSIONAL MAGAZINE

Winner: *If,* edited by Frederik Pohl

Nominees:
Analog, edited by John W. Campbell Jr.
F&SF, edited by Edward L. Ferman
Galaxy, edited by Frederik Pohl
New Worlds, edited by Michael Moorcock

BEST PROFESSIONAL ARTIST

Winner: Jack Gaughan

Nominees:
Chesley Bonestell
Frank Frazetta
Frank Kelly Freas
Gray Morrow
John Schoenherr

BEST FANZINE

Winner: *Amra*, edited by George Scithers

Nominees:
Australian SF Review, edited by John Bangsund
Lighthouse, edited by Terry Carr
Odd, edited by Raymond D. Fisher
Psychotic, edited by Richard E. Geis
Yandro, edited by Robert Coulson and Juanita Coulson

BEST FAN WRITER

Winner: Ted White

Nominees:
Ruth Berman
Harlan Ellison (nomination withdrawn)
Alexei Panshin (nomination withdrawn)
Harry Warner Jr.

Panshin said in *File 770* in 2010 that he withdrew because he had won the year before and hoped to set a precedent. Ellison reportedly withdrew because he had won a Hugo and Nebula in the past.

BEST FAN ARTIST

Winner: George Barr

Nominees:
Johnny Chambers
Jack Gaughan (nomination withdrawn)
Steve Stiles
Arthur Thomson
Bjo Trimble

COMMENTS ON 1968

18. GARDNER DOZOIS

It was a much stronger year for novella, although I never liked either the much-overhyped *Riders of the Purple Wage* or *Weyr Search*, and Zelazny's *Damnation Alley* is weak, although the novella version is stronger than the novel version (let alone the film). The clear winner here is Delany's *The Star Pit*, head and shoulders above everything else, which shows what Delany could do with space opera when he bothered to try, and which shares some of the same strengths as *Nova*. Runner-up would be Silverberg's *Hawksbill Station*, a tough-minded and rather stark story, also much better as a novella than in its expanded novel version.

In novelette, Leiber's "Gonna Roll the Bones" is overrated, and won mostly for nostalgia for better things Leiber had published in the past, I think. "Faith of Our Fathers" is brutal and hard-hitting, and is actually much more of a horror story (where God, or something that will pass for Him, is the supernatural menace) than an SF story. "Pretty Maggie Moneyeyes" is one of Ellison's best stories, although again, more a horror story than an SF story. "Wizard's World" is weak. The Hugo here should have gone to Zelazny's "The Keys to December," one of his strongest stories, much more so than his rather weak "This Mortal Mountain."

Although it's secured its place as a famous story and is probably read more than anything else here, I've never really liked "I Have No Mouth, and I Must Scream," which seems overheated to me. The Niven, the Wilhelm, the Thomas, the Leiber, and the Brentnor are all relatively minor. I liked "Aye, and Gomorrah . . . ," and it's certainly been influential (I saw its undeniable footprints on a Lavie Tidhar story just this year), but I would have given the Hugo to Delany's "Driftglass," which is less flashy but deeper and more humane.

Ellison wins the Best *Star Trek* episode race, although Gerrold isn't far behind him. *If* deserved its Best Magazine win.

20. RICH HORTON

I'd like to make a couple of suggestions among books I haven't read:

An Age, by Brian W. Aldiss—as I said, I haven't read it, but it's by Aldiss, so it ought to be in the hunt.

Ice, by Anna Kavan—seems to be held in EXTREMELY high regard by those who have read it. I really must try it.

And some recommendations of books I have read:

Algis Budrys's *The Iron Thorn* aka *The Amsirs and the Iron Thorn*—seems to be not much liked, but I loved it. Then again, I love most of Budrys's work.

The Magus, by John Fowles—a major novel, though to my mind, not really fantastical enough for this award. But you could make a case.

One Hundred Years of Solitude, by Gabriel García Márquez—one of the best novels I have ever read. But of course it had no chance of winning, having appeared only in Spanish at that time.

The Master and Margarita, by Mikhail Bulgakov—also one of the best novels I have ever read. I believe the 1967 version (of a book written in the thirties, of course) was censored, however.

The Third Policeman, by Flann O'Brien—like *The Master and Margarita,* a posthumous publication of a work finished decades earlier. And a great novel.

So, seriously, you could have had a great nomination list composed entirely of works published in the mainstream: the García Márquez, O'Brien, Bulgakov, Fowles, and Kavan novels.

22. SUPERGEE

The Butterfly Kid was a lot of fun at the time. "As you Earthlings say, if you cannot run your tongue along them, merge with them." I don't think I dare go back to it.

27. JAMES DAVIS NICOLL

I don't think I dare go back to it.

Oh, I think it still is fun. In fact, in general if you have to read just one book this year about futuristic hippies living in Greenwich Village who find themselves protecting Earth from malevolent space lobsters and their human quisling, read this one.

28. GARDNER DOZOIS

There's dozens of those! I get tired of them.

29. RICH HORTON

Okay, the short fiction.

Novellas first. I enjoyed the two novella winners in their way, *Weyr Search* probably more back then, and I don't think they are bad stories, but neither would get my vote. Of the other nominees, I'm not a big *Damnation Alley* fan, and *If All Men Were Brothers, Would You Let One Marry Your Sister?* is fine but not at all my favorite Sturgeon. *Hawksbill Station* is excellent. But the clear runaway best story of the nominees is *The Star Pit*, which is astonishingly good, and which has always seemed to me to get less notice than it deserved.

There was also a good Richard McKenna novella, *Fiddler's Green*.

But even *The Star Pit* might not get my vote for Best Novella of 1967—though it might. There was another story with star in the title that I totally love:

Starfog, by Poul Anderson—which is close to my favorite Poul Anderson story of all time. For me, it's between that and Delany's story for Best Novella.

The novelette list of nominees is decent. "The Keys to December" is probably the best, though it's really a 1966 story (in *New Worlds*, which is why it was only eligible for the Nebula for 1967, after its reprint in the Wollheim/Carr Best of the Year book). I do like "Gonna Roll the Bones," but I might agree that it's overrated.

However, a bunch of great novelettes were missed. Here's my list:

From Thomas Disch (who was at his SFnal peak): "Problems of Creativeness" (which became part of his novel *334*); and "Casablanca" (which the ISFDB credits to an Alfred Hitchcock anthology, *Stories That Scared Even Me*, which surprises me, as I hadn't known they featured originals).

Two really neat stories from Joanna Russ, the first two of her Alyx stories, both from *Orbit 2* (one of the truly great single issues of an original anthology series I know of): "The Adventuress" (later retitled "Bluestocking"); and "I Gave Her Sack and Sherry" (later retitled "I Thought She Was Afeard till She Stroked My Beard"). (I like all four of those titles.)

Another *Orbit 2* story, Gene Wolfe's first genre publication: "Trip, Trap."

Jack Vance's "The Narrow Land."

And one from Keith Roberts: "Coranda," his first story of a couple set in Michael Moorcock's Ice Schooner future.

I'm not really sure to which I'd give the Hugo were I to vote again now—one of the Disch or one of the Russ stories, perhaps.

And Short Story—odd that there were only three nominees in a pretty strong year, all Ellison-related stories. My favorite is "Aye, and Gomorrah . . . ," which I really think is amazing. (Yes, "Driftglass" is also very good, but I'd still say I prefer "Aye, and Gomorrah. . . .") I do like the Ellison story a lot, though (as with much Ellison) "overwrought" is indeed a fair description. And Niven's "The Jigsaw Man" is also very fine.

Besides the Nebula nominees (of which "Driftglass" and "Baby, You Were Great" are the only ones I really remember), I might suggest the following as potential nominees:

"Go, Go, Go, said the Bird," by Sonya Dorman
"Thus We Frustrate Charlemagne" and "Land of the Great Horses," by R. A. Lafferty
The ever-controversial "The Heat Death of the Universe," by Pamela Zoline

"The Winter Flies" aka "The Inner Circles," by Fritz Leiber
"The Power of Every Root," by Avram Davidson
"Full Sun," by Brian W. Aldiss

Of all the short stories, I'd stick with "Aye, and Gomorrah . . ." as the best short story of 1967.

30. GARDNER DOZOIS

Fiddler's Green—a very odd story, almost Lafferty-like in its conceptualization, and almost unknown today—and *Starfog* are both very good, but for me, they don't beat *The Star Pit*.

It's a tough call between "Problems of Creativity" and "The Keys to December." Think I'd go with the Zelazny, though.

"Thus We Frustrate Charlemagne," "Full Sun," and "Coranda" are all very good, but I think I'll stick with "Driftglass."

FANTASY DISGUISED AS SCIENCE FICTION DISGUISED AS FANTASY: ROGER ZELAZNY'S *LORD OF LIGHT*

I have never liked *Lord of Light*. If I've ever been in a conversation with you and you've mentioned how great it is and I've nodded and smiled, I apologize. The reason I'd have done that is because my dislike of the book is amorphous and hard to pin down, which makes it hard to defend when I know it's a much-loved classic. There's also the thing when I haven't read it for a while and I start believing that it must be the book everybody else seems to find, rather than the one I remember.

The story of *Lord of Light* is that a group of high-tech people with ineluctable European-origin names like Sam, Jan Olvegg, Candi, and Madeleine colonized a planet on which they are now pretending to be the Hindu pantheon.

The local population consists of their descendants and the descendants of the passengers on the ship they crewed. This situation, where the privileged crew rules the unprivileged passengers, isn't unusual, but having a story about it from the crew point of view is—though, actually, as *Lord of Light* is 1967, it predates *A Gift from Earth* and most of the other examples I can think of. There are demons who were the original inhabitants of the planet, who happen to be beings of pure energy. The colonists live at a low tech level and in a culture that seems to be somebody's approximation of ancient India. The "gods" enjoy a high tech level. There is technological reincarnation. Everybody, at the age of sixty unless they've been unfortunate enough to die earlier, goes to be judged by the gods, their past lives are seen in detail and they're given a karmically appropriate new body—age, gender, and species chosen by the gods.

Most of the gods are not the original settlers—war and attrition and elimination of the opposition—but younger demigods who have been promoted. One of the First, Sam, wants to bring technology to the ordinary people and opposes the gods, at first by starting up Buddhism in opposition to their imposed version of Hinduism, and later by war.

It's actually possible to argue about whether the book is science fiction or fantasy. It feels like fantasy, but there's the clear science-fictional and technological underpinnings of everything. But the "gods" have aspects and attributes—the attributes are high tech, the "aspects" are apparently psionic skills that work even in new bodies. There are things they do with technology and things they do with the sheer power of their mind—Yama has a death gaze, Sam can bind energy. The lines are blurry in more than one direction. This is one of my problems with it. I think Zelazny wanted it both ways, he wanted the mythic resonance, he wanted war in heaven, and he wanted it all to be grounded. I think he did this better elsewhere.

If someone wrote this book today, we'd probably call the use of Hindu mythology and Indian trappings cultural appropriation. In 1967, I think we call it getting points for being aware that the rest of the world existed. There's absolutely no explanation for why the First decided on that system of control in particular. It clearly isn't intended in any way as an authentic portrayal of India or Hindu religion, more a caricature set up deliberately to maximize the power of the "gods." Then there's the introduction of Buddhism. I'm not really comfortable with this—unlike the religions Zelazny used so well elsewhere, these are living religions.

My real problem with the book is that I don't care about the characters or what happens to them. Every time I've read this book, I've forced myself through it as a cold intellectual exercise. There are things about it that I can see are clever and were innovative when it was new. But none of the characters feels real. It's written in omniscient, not the first-wiseass that Zelazny did so brilliantly, and I think it suffers from that. Sam's motivations are obscure, the other characters' even more so. It's huge and mythic and it just doesn't ever warm up for me.

The first time I read it, I had the familiar sensation of thinking the book was too old for me and I should leave it for later. When I was a child, books were finite—the house was full of them, but new ones seldom came into it. I didn't discover the library until I was twelve. Books on the shelves got read and reread, and if I couldn't get into them, if they were too old for me, I'd keep nibbling at them. For the record, I eventually got old enough for *Lorna Doone,* George Eliot, and T. H. White, but I haven't reached that pinnacle with Thomas Hardy. I think I was right that *Lord of Light* was too old for me the first time—I couldn't figure out that most of the book is a massive flashback, and the fantastical science fiction fantasy thing confused me. I didn't like it, but I kept coming back to it. Now I do feel I understand it, but I still don't like it. Maybe it'll reveal itself to me as the masterpiece other people say it is when I'm sixty, but I'm not betting on it. Not throwing it out either, though.

1969

Winner: *Stand on Zanzibar,* by John Brunner

Nominees:
Nova, by Samuel R. Delany
Rite of Passage, by Alexei Panshin
The Goblin Reservation, by Clifford Simak
Past Master, by R. A. Lafferty

The 1969 Hugo Awards were presented at St. Louiscon in St. Louis, Missouri. The Best Novel award went to John Brunner's *Stand on Zanzibar,* one of my favorite books, and Brunner's absolute best. Brunner decided to write four books each set fifty years ahead and each extrapolating different trends of the present forward. *Stand on Zanzibar* is overpopulation and sexual freedom, *The Sheep Look Up* is environmental devastation and domestic terrorism, *The Jagged Orbit* is racial tensions and weapon enthusiasm, and *The Shockwave Rider* is computers and organized crime. *Stand on Zanzibar* is the best of them. It's a mosaic novel, using ads and music and news reports and different characters to build up the world and the story, in the style of Dos Passos. It's a really good story, absolutely full of cool stuff, a great world and interesting characters. It's in print from Orb, it's been pretty solidly in print ever since 1968, and it's definitely a classic. It's in the library in French only.

There are four other nominees, and I've read three of them. Samuel R. Delany's *Nova* is so wonderful that I've written about it on Tor.com twice. I love it. It's in print, and it's in the library in both languages. It's about work and resources and art and stealing fire from heaven and possible choices in a complex future world. As with *Babel-17*, not only a classic but still exciting too.

Alexei Panshin's *Rite of Passage* is another excellent book I've written about. It's a coming-of-age story about the balance of power between starships and planets. It won the Nebula. It's in print, but not in the library.

I've read Clifford Simak's *The Goblin Reservation*, but I don't own it and I haven't reread it in a long time. It has aliens and time travel and matter transmission, it's gently funny, and it's on an odd border between science fiction and fantasy. I remember it as being fairly slight. It's not in print, and it's in the library in French only.

I haven't read R. A. Lafferty's *Past Master*, despite having heard good things about it, because Lafferty's short stories tend to be things where I can't read more than one of them at a time, so a whole novel seems intimidating. It's not in print, but it's in the library in English.

Five nominees, four American and one English, all men. Brunner, Delany, and Simak had been nominated before, Panshin had won a fan writer Hugo, Lafferty is a newcomer. We have a novel of near-future Earth written in the style of Dos Passos; an elegant space adventure spanning three galaxies with an interest in class and art and economics; a juvenile set on a starship and distant planet about what growing up really means; a strange gentle story about aliens, technology, and goblins, and a tall tale. What a range, within genre! Again, we see that the fans were happy to embrace New Wave experimental works, and also keep on nominating traditional writers like Simak—and for that matter, like *Rite of Passage*. I think the voters made the right choice, but if *Nova* or *Rite of Passage* had won, I'd have been just as happy.

So, looking elsewhere, this seems to be the year of "How could they miss that?"

Non-overlapping Nebula nominees: James Blish's *Black Easter*, Philip K. Dick's *Do Androids Dream of Electric Sheep*, Robert Silverberg's *The Masks of Time*, and Joanna Russ's *Picnic on Paradise*.

Black Easter is brilliant but very strange and close to being horror; I wouldn't expect to see it on a Hugo ballot. I have read *Do Androids,* and I suspect it's better thought of now than it was then because of the Ridley Scott movie. *The Masks of Time* could have been on the ballot, but it isn't a scandal that it isn't. Russ's *Picnic on Paradise,* though, that's a classic. That shouldn't have been overlooked.

Other possibilities: Arthur C. Clarke's *2001: A Space Odyssey.* Paint me amazed this wasn't nominated. It should have been. *SoZ* should still have won, but . . . wow. Ursula Le Guin's *A Wizard of Earthsea.* That would be another absolutely worthy nominee.

Other things they might have looked at but it doesn't matter that they didn't: John Wyndham's *Chocky,* Robert Sheckley's *Dimension of Miracles,* Anne McCaffrey's *Dragonflight,* Peter S. Beagle's *The Last Unicorn,* John Boyd's *The Last Starship from Earth,* Lloyd Biggle Jr.'s *The Still, Small Voice of Trumpets,* Larry Niven's *A Gift from Earth.*

The other thing I'm noticing is that so much more SF is being published now than in earlier years, where I could list almost everything without my hands falling off. So this is a year where I'm happy with the winner but where the five nominees definitely don't seem to me to be the five best books published that year or the five books that showed where the field was in 1969.

Part of this multiplicity of titles is the burgeoning mass market paperback original market, and part of the excellence is because of Terry Carr's Ace Specials line, one of the most effective and brilliant sets of books ever published. Carr was an amazing editor, with an eye for both excellence and marketability. The line started in 1968. *Rite of Passage* was an Ace Special, as was Nebula nominee *Picnic on Paradise.* The line ran from 1968 to 1971, and I'll note them as they show up in our lists.

OTHER CATEGORIES

BEST NOVELLA

Winner: *Nightwings,* by Robert Silverberg (*Galaxy,* September 1968)

Nominees:

Dragonrider, by Anne McCaffrey (*Analog,* December 1967, January 1968)

Hawk Among the Sparrows, by Dean McLaughlin (*Analog,* July 1968)

Lines of Power, by Samuel R. Delany (*F&SF,* May 1968)

The Nebula went to McCaffrey. It seems to me that there's a perception that the Hugo was more "popular" and the Nebula more "literary," and it seems to me that for the years so far, this perception is what's technically known as "wrong."

Best Novelette

Winner: "The Sharing of Flesh," by Poul Anderson (*Galaxy,* December 1968)

Nominees:

"Getting Through University," by Piers Anthony (*If,* August 1968)

"Mother to the World," by Richard Wilson (*Orbit*)

"Total Environment," by Brian W. Aldiss (*Galaxy,* February 1968)

Nebula: "Mother to the World." Both good stories.

Best Short Story

Winner: "The Beast that Shouted Love at the Heart of the World," by Harlan Ellison (*Galaxy,* June 1968)

Nominees:

"All the Myriad Ways," by Larry Niven (*Galaxy,* October 1968)

"The Dance of the Changer and the Three," by Terry Carr (*The Farthest Reaches*)

"Masks," by Damon Knight (*Playboy,* July 1968)

"The Steiger Effect," by Betsy Curtis (*Analog,* October 1968)

Nebula to Kate Wilhelm's "The Planners."

BEST DRAMATIC PRESENTATION

Winner: *2001: A Space Odyssey*

Nominees:
Charly
The Prisoner: "Fall Out"
Rosemary's Baby
Yellow Submarine

So we ignored the book but honored the movie? Oh well, it's a pretty good movie.

BEST PROFESSIONAL MAGAZINE

Winner: *F&SF*, edited by Edward L. Ferman

Nominees:
Analog, edited by John W. Campbell Jr.
Galaxy, edited by Frederik Pohl
If, edited by Frederik Pohl
New Worlds, edited by Michael Moorcock

BEST PROFESSIONAL ARTIST

Winner: Jack Gaughan

Nominees:
Vaughn Bodé
Leo and Diane Dillon
Frank Kelly Freas

BEST FANZINE

Winner: *Science Fiction Review*, edited by Richard E. Geis

Nominees:
Riverside Quarterly, edited by Leland Sapiro
Shangri L'Affaires, edited by Ken Rudolph
Trumpet, edited by Tom Reamy
Warhoon, edited by Richard Bergeron

Best Fan Writer

Winner: Harry Warner Jr.

Nominees:
Richard Delap
Banks Mebane
Ted White (nomination withdrawn)
Walt Willis

White withdrew because he won the year before, as Panshin did.

Best Fan Artist

Winner: Vaughn Bodé

Nominees:
George Barr
Tim Kirk
Doug Lovenstein
Bill Rotsler

Vaughn Bodé was in both Pro and Fan categories; he must have burst upon the field and made a big impression.

COMMENTS ON 1969

10. RICH HORTON

First, novella. Back in the day, I definitely would have chosen *Night-wings* among the nominees. *Dragonrider* is okay, and *Hawk Among the Sparrows* is fine work but not overwhelming. As for *Lines of Power*, I suspect most people these days know it better by Delany's preferred title, *We, in Some Strange Power's Employ, Move on a Rigorous Line*. It was Delany doing a Zelazny pastiche (complete with a character modeled on him), and I like it fine, but it's not Delany's very best work.

The Nebula nominees are the same set, with one addition: *The Day Before Forever*, by Keith Laumer, which I don't think I've read. I have only one more potential nominee to suggest: Poul Anderson's *A Tragedy of Errors*. In what seems a thinnish year for novellas, I'd say Silverberg's novella was then and remains the worthy winner.

Incidentally, I too have long thought that the Nebula's reputation as a "more literary" award was overblown. I will say that I did a study of the Hugos and Nebulas some years ago, and one thing I did was attempt—at a very crude level—to characterize the winners as more "literary" or more "popular," and, granted that such characterizations are profoundly subjective, I did find that more Nebula winners than Hugos were to the literary end of the spectrum, but not by a wide margin. (The recent several years, before the last couple—where in my opinion the Nebulas went through a bad, bad stretch—may have changed those numbers even more.)

To novelette. As Jo says, both "The Sharing of Flesh" and "Mother to the World" are fine stories, worthy award winners. I admit I don't recall either the Aldiss or the Anthony novelette, so I can't comment on them. The Nebula nomination list includes the Wilson, Aldiss, and Anderson stories, plus some further interesting choices:

"Final War," by K. M. O'Donnell (really Barry Malzberg)
"The Guerrilla Trees," by H. H. Hollis
"The Listeners," by James Gunn
"Once There Was a Giant," by Keith Laumer

All fine stories, each quite different from the next, but none would displace the winners, in my mind.

One fine novelette from 1968 not listed is Vernor Vinge's "Grimm's Story," which of course soon became his first novel.

Katherine MacLean's "The Trouble with You Earth People" is also good work.

And there are two more Delany stories to consider. One is not all that well known, though I like it a lot: "High Weir." The other is very well known indeed—in fact, it won the Nebula. But not until the next year, because it was published in *New Worlds,* and as such not eligible for the award until after its Year's Best anthologization. This is "Time Considered as a Helix of Semi-Precious Stones," a lovely story, a worthy winner in its year, and probably would have been the worthy winner this year, had it been nominated. (It's also, according to Adam Roberts, based on Wallace Stevens's great poem "The Emperor of Ice-Cream.")

And short story. I'm not that big a fan of the Ellison story. I'm not sure to whom I'd have given the Hugo, because I think all three of the next nominees are excellent: "All the Myriad Ways," "The Dance of the Changer and the Three," and "Masks." (I don't recall Betsy Curtis's "The Steiger Effect.") Any one of those would have been a good winner, much better than "The Beast Who Shouted Love at the Heart of the World." "The Planners" is a good story, a good winner, but I'd also rank it behind the Niven, Carr, and Knight stories.

Besides "The Planners," the Nebula short list includes Carr's story; Knight's story; a Robert Taylor story that I don't know, "Idiot's Mate"; an H. H. Hollis story that I recall as decent, "Sword Game"; and an excellent Poul Anderson story, "Kyrie."

Other short stories to consider include Delany's "Cage of Brass," Zelazny's "Corrida," and the funny "The Egg of the Glak," by Harvey Jacobs. But I'd say the best five-story nomination list would consist of "Kyrie," "The Planners," "Masks," "The Dance of the Changer and the Three," and "All the Myriad Ways."

I should also mention that 1968 saw the first publication of stories by "James Tiptree Jr." (though, of course, Alice Bradley had a story in

The New Yorker in the forties). These were "Birth of a Salesman," "The Mother Ship" aka "Mamma Come Home," "Fault," and "Pupa Knows Best" aka "Help." All interesting, but it was in 1969, seems to me, that it became obvious that Tiptree was truly something special.

20. GARDNER DOZOIS

A strong year for novels.

A weaker year for short fiction. Agree that Silverberg's *Nightwings* is probably the strongest of the novellas, although I would have voted for Delany's *Time Considered* over it if it had been eligible—between this and *Nova,* this year probably represented the high point of Delany's considerable powers as a science fiction writer; after this, his focus would turn elsewhere. *Lines of Power* is a fun story, but nowhere near as strong. Don't think *Hawk Among the Sparrows* or the McCaffrey were in the same league.

Novelette is a weaker category. Guess I'd go with either "The Sharing of Flesh" or "Total Environment." "Mother of the World" is a story that hasn't held up all that well, I fear.

In short story, my vote goes to "Masks," one of Damon Knight's most icily brilliant stories. Runner-up, "The Dance of the Changer and the Three."

28. NANCYLEBOVITZ

I'm putting in a nice word for *Past Master.* It's not as impressive as *Nova* or *Stand on Zanzibar,* but it's fine giddy stuff. (I'm surprised that *SoZ*'s mosaic approach hasn't become a standard method for SF.)

If you need to treat each chapter of *Past Master* as a short story—I think some of them might stand alone, but in any case, a break for something resembling more normal fiction might be good—it's worth it.

The ansels (who walk on four legs, or two, or none, and play fan-tan) are worth it. The killing of the cyclops shines in memory like green volcanic glass, not to mention the rain forest that is too dense to get to the bottom of, nor is it possible to tell one tree from another.

And opening it at random, I just found the source of something I thought was ancient Greek:

> *Then the bolts of white and gold fire began to whip from peak to peak. A bullwhip 38 kilometers long snapped from Corona Mountain to Magnetic Mountain with a crooked light that literally blinded them all for a while. Here was the mystery of motion, the old paradox solved, a whip of light going so fast that it was in more than one place at the same time. It was on every jag and crag at once, and yet it was but a single point of light, only a streak in being of simultaneous appearance. Or was it the empyrean itself, the infinity of blinding light that is everywhere in the outside but is seen only when the false sky is ripped open for the blinding moment?*

Typing it out phrase by phrase, it isn't quite as good as I thought—too many repeated words and possibly some incoherence. . . . But still, really big lightning between the mountains and the world as shell with lightning behind it.

The book also has Programmed Mechanical Killers, and demons moving into their brains.

29. GARDNER DOZOIS

It's pretty clear that either *Stand on Zanzibar* or the original Dos Passos or both had a clear influence on much of Joe Haldeman's subsequent novel work, and in fact, I think that he's admitted as much (although I believe he credits Dos Passos rather than Brunner). Brilliant, brilliant stuff in *Past Master,* and some stunning set pieces, but it's beginning to tremble on the verge of that erudite opaqueness that made his late novels almost impossible to read (for me, anyway).

36. RICH HORTON

One novel that appeared in 1968 that I forgot is nearly as good—arguably quite as good—as the three excellent novels we've been talking about. (That is to say, *Stand on Zanzibar, Nova,* and *Camp Concentration.*)

This is *Pavane,* by Keith Roberts. It's clearly one of the great alternate history novels of all time. (I'd place three others with it off the top of my head: Dick's *The Man in the High Castle,* Amis's *The Alteration,* and Chabon's *The Yiddish Policemen's Union.*)

Some may not consider it a proper novel, as it's a fix-up of five shorter stories that all appeared in 1966. But I think it works beautifully as a unified work, and that does seem to me how it is usually thought of. At any rate, we ought to list it as one of the true best novels of 1968.

Growing Up for Real: Alexei Panshin's *Rite of Passage*

Alexei Panshin's *Rite of Passage* is one of those books that has compulsive readability. It's about Mia, a girl growing up on a spaceship. Earth has been destroyed, and the Ships—which were built to take colonies from Earth to habitable planets—now cycle between the colonies bartering information for material goods. The colonies are much more desperate and primitive than the Ships. The people on the Ships barely regard the colonists as human, and refer to them as "mudeaters." All fourteen-year-olds on the Ships have to spend a month surviving on a colony planet as a Trial, a rite of passage, before being seen as adult.

This is the story of Mia growing up and doing this; it's also the story of her questioning the things she initially considers axiomatic about the way the universe works. This is a book that ought to be old-fashioned and isn't. I know Panshin did controversial critical work on Heinlein, and I think this may have been his attempt to write a Heinlein juvenile from a different perspective. Lots of people have tried this since, with varying degrees of success. Panshin makes it work, and makes it work with a message that Heinlein wouldn't have liked, a message about what growing up means that's quite alien to the way most of the coming-of-age stories in genre work.

Rite of Passage won enormous acclaim when it was published in 1968. My edition has quotes from Zelazny, Brunner, and Blish. From what they say, they were very struck by how well Panshin got into the head of a teenage girl. I also find this impressive—there's no off note in his portrayal of Mia. But I suppose I'm jaded about this kind of thing: men writing girls well doesn't seem as notable now as it was when Panshin did it.

Reading it in 1968 must have been a very odd experience. It's clearly a juvenile, because the protagonist is twelve at the beginning and fourteen at the end, but there's a sex scene, which by 1968 standards would have made it quite unsuitable for teenagers. Then there's the gender thing—most SF readers in 1968 would have found it unusual to have a book about a girl growing up instead of a boy growing up.

But far more unusual is the way the whole book works as an implied critique of a way SF often does things. There is a lot of SF even now (and even more when Panshin was writing) that consists of setting up a universe so that the heroes will be forced by circumstances into some action that saves everything. I'm thinking of things like Pournelle's *Birth of Fire,* Piper's *Space Viking,* Heinlein's *Starship Troopers*—there are a lot of them. The characteristic is that things narrow down to alternatives where it's absolutely necessary to do a terrible thing for the overriding good of humanity, which the text and characters approve as a morally correct thing—a hard choice, but the right one.

This is such a staple of SF expectations that it's possible not to notice it until Panshin subverts it here. The people of the Ship are wrong in their behavior to the colonists, and Mia comes to see that. She spends a horrible month on the planet, but she finds kindness there as well as cruelty. She is looked after by an old man who has lost his family, and she gulls a policeman with a story about a school project. This isn't a nice world at all, but it's a real world full of people, and the Ship votes to destroy it. The people of the Ship are very harsh to their own people—they evict a woman who is having a baby against eugenic advice, and they impose the Trial on their children. Their whole way of life is set up to preserve science for humanity, and it comes to a hard choice you'd expect the text to approve and it doesn't. Neither the text nor Mia consider the genocide acceptable, and both have to live with it.

This is a way of showing growing up that isn't walking in your father's shoes. It's a way of becoming mature and self-reliant that isn't simple or self-congratulatory. Heroes in SF juveniles from *Between Planets* to *Little Brother* save the day. Mia doesn't. She survives, and she grows up, but the Ship goes ahead and kills all the people on Tintera. This must have been a mind-blowing book in 1968, and it's still powerful now. It's a little didactic, as juveniles tend to be, but it is an honest portrayal of coming-of-age and of a fascinating society.

1970

Best Novel

Winner: *The Left Hand of Darkness,* by Ursula K. Le Guin

Nominees:
Slaughterhouse-Five, by Kurt Vonnegut
Up the Line, by Robert Silverberg
Macroscope, by Piers Anthony
Bug Jack Barron, by Norman Spinrad

The 1970 Worldcon was Heicon '70, in Heidelberg, Germany, the first time it was in a non-Anglophone country. The Hugo Awards could be assumed to have more international voters than normal. The novel winner was Ursula K. Le Guin's *The Left Hand of Darkness,* an absolutely wonderful book, an undoubted classic, and one of the best books ever to have won the Hugo. This was also the first book by a woman to win, and so it's appropriate that it's this book, with its exploration of gender ambiguities. It was one of Terry Carr's Ace Specials. It's in print, it's still widely read and discussed, and it's in the library in both languages. (The French title is *La main gauche de la nuit,* which gives me quite a different image.)

There are four other nominees, of which I've read only two. Kurt Vonnegut's *Slaughterhouse-Five* is probably his best book, certainly his best-known one. It's about a time traveler and the firebombing of Dresden, and Vonnegut makes all the weird stuff point in the same direction for once so that it makes sense as SF. It's also pretty thoroughly in print and in the library in both languages.

Robert Silverberg's *Up the Line* is a funny book about time travel that hasn't lasted well. It doesn't seem to be in print. It's in the library in French only.

I haven't read Piers Anthony's *Macroscope*, because I've not enjoyed other things of Anthony's I've read. It's in print from Mundania, a small press. It's not in the library. I haven't read Norman Spinrad's *Bug Jack Barron*, because I've never gotten around to it. I sometimes enjoy Spinrad, but I think he's best at short lengths. *Bug Jack Barron* is in print and in the library in both languages.

So, four out of five in print, pretty good.

Four men, one woman, all American. Silverberg, Delany, and Anthony are previous nominees, Spinrad and Le Guin are newcomers. Two near-future SF, two time travel romps, and one anthropological SF. What did they miss?

The Nebulas have all of these except *Macroscope*, and add Zelazny's *Isle of the Dead*, which I like a lot, and Brunner's *The Jagged Orbit*, both Ace Specials. Either of these would have been a fine Hugo nominee. Oh, and they gave the Nebula to Le Guin, of course. I almost didn't say so, because it's so obvious.

Was there anything everyone missed? Not really. They could have looked at Fritz Leiber's *A Specter Is Haunting Texas*; Brian Aldiss's *Barefoot in the Head*; Philip K. Dick's *Galactic Pot-Healer*; Vernor Vinge's *Grimm's World*; Frederik Pohl's *The Age of the Pussyfoot*; Daphne Du Maurier's *The House on the Strand*—but really, there was no need.

OTHER CATEGORIES

BEST NOVELLA

Winner: *Ship of Shadows*, by Fritz Leiber (*F&SF*, July 1969)

Nominees:
A Boy and His Dog, by Harlan Ellison (*The Beast That Shouted Love at the Heart of the World*)

Dramatic Mission, by Anne McCaffrey (*Analog,* June 1969)
To Jorslem, by Robert Silverberg (*Galaxy,* February 1969)
We All Die Naked, by James Blish (*Three for Tomorrow*)

Well, first, I'd have voted for *A Boy and His Dog,* and second, what happened to the novelette category? Did they forget?

Best Short Story

Winner: "Time Considered as a Helix of Semi-Precious Stones," by Samuel R. Delany (*World's Best Science Fiction: 1969; New Worlds,* December 1968)

Nominees:
"Deeper than the Darkness," by Gregory Benford (*F&SF,* April 1969)
"Not Long Before the End," by Larry Niven (*F&SF,* April 1969)
"Passengers," by Robert Silverberg (*Orbit 4,* 1968)
"Winter's King," by Ursula K. Le Guin (*Orbit 5*)

I'd have given it to the Delany too. It seems to have had extended eligibility because of non-US first publication, despite *New Worlds'* being nominated for magazine Hugos, indicating that people were reading it, and this con's being in Europe.

Best Dramatic Presentation

Winner: "News coverage of *Apollo XI*"

Nominee:
The Bed-Sitting Room
The Illustrated Man
The Immortal
Marooned

Well, that's an interesting interpretation of a dramatic presentation, but it's hard to argue with. It would have been cool if this had started a trend, so that every year there was NASA TV and science programs up there with all the sci-fi.

BEST PROFESSIONAL MAGAZINE

Winner: *F&SF*, edited by Edward L. Ferman

Nominees:
Amazing Stories, edited by Ted White
Analog, edited by John W. Campbell Jr.
Galaxy, edited by Frederik Pohl and Ejler Jakobsson
New Worlds, edited by Michael Moorcock

BEST PROFESSIONAL ARTIST

Winner: Frank Kelly Freas

Nominees:
Vaughn Bodé
Leo and Diane Dillon
Jack Gaughan
Eddie Jones
Jeff Jones

BEST FANZINE

Winner: *Science Fiction Review*, edited by Richard E. Geis

Nominees:
Beabohema, edited by Frank Lunney
Locus, edited by Charles Brown
Riverside Quarterly, edited by Leland Sapiro
Speculation, edited by Peter R. Weston

Best Fan Writer

Winner: Wilson (Bob) Tucker

Nominees:
Piers Anthony
Charles Brown
Richard Delap
Richard E. Geis

Best Fan Artist

Winner: Tim Kirk

Nominees:
Alicia Austin
George Barr
Steve Fabian
Bill Rotsler

Comments on 1970

17. Rich Horton

There is actually quite a list of additional SF novels of note from 1969. First I'll mention John Sladek's *Mechasm*, brilliant satire, although it was actually first published in the UK in 1968, under his preferred title of *The Reproductive System*.

I'll also mention some books from the mainstream. Most notable, to me, is Vladimir Nabokov's *Ada*. I am also a fan of Kingsley Amis's *The Green Man*, something of a horror story. And according to the ISFDB, Hermann Hesse's *Magister Ludi* (*The Glass Bead Game*) was published in the United States in translation that year.

And from the genre:

Novel versions of a couple of award-winning novellas: Michael Moorcock's *Behold the Man*, and Robert Silverberg's *Nightwings*. (His novella nominee from this year, *To Jorslem*, is also part of that novel.)

Another Moorcock book, not a masterpiece but plenty of fun: *The Ice Schooner*.

A Lafferty novel that I don't much like, but others do: *Fourth Mansions*.

Every UK teenage boy's favorite Jack Vance title, *Servants of the Wankh*. (Also its sequel, *The Dirdir*.)

Two wonderful Avram Davidson fantasies: *The Island Under the Earth* and *The Phoenix and the Mirror*.

And Philip K. Dick's *Ubik*, one of his major novels. (Much more significant than *Galactic Pot-Healer*.)

I suppose my ideal five-novel short list would have been *The Left Hand of Darkness*, *A Specter Is Haunting Texas*, *Ada*, *The Green Man*, and *Ubik*. With Le Guin still winning.

21. RICH HORTON

The short fiction.

Obviously the Hugo had not yet settled on a fixed set of three short fiction categories—as I noted earlier, they moved in that direction in fits and starts, though I think it was not long until that was standardized. At any rate, this year's "Short Story" winner was a novelette by today's standards. Be that as it may . . .

In novella, I have to say that I really do enjoy Fritz Leiber's *Ship of Shadows*. It's not that well remembered these days, at least not relative to the rest of Leiber's work, but I do think it's worthwhile. That said, *A Boy and His Dog* is obviously more influential (though I think Ellison grossly overstates the case when he accuses Cormac McCarthy of "ripping off" his story in writing *The Road*) and more viscerally effective. I still think I like *Ship of Shadows* better, but I certainly do also like *A Boy and His Dog*, and can't argue with its Nebula win. The other Hugo nominees seem much lesser than those two stories to me. The Nebulas also nominated a good-but-not-great Charles Harness story, *Probable Cause*.

Of the other potential novella nominees from 1969, I can cite only three of particular interest: T. J. Bass's *Half Past Human,* which I have read only as part of the later novel; James Tiptree Jr.'s *Your Haploid Heart;* and Larry Niven's *The Organleggers,* better known by now as "Death by Ecstasy." I think the latter story good enough to have deserved a spot on the short list, but not good enough to displace either the Ellison or the Leiber story for their awards.

Novelette is a richer category. Delany's "Time Considered as a Helix of Semi-Precious Stones" won the Nebula for Novelette, to go along with its Best Short Story Hugo. Two other short story nominees were really novelettes: Gregory Benford's "Deeper Than the Darkness" (which was a Nebula nominee) and Ursula K. Le Guin's "Winter's King." The other Nebula nominees for Best Novelette were Norman Spinrad's "The Big Flash" and another Le Guin story, "Nine Lives."

Of those, it's hard to argue with Delany's story as the best—it's wonderful. But so too is "Winter's King"—which is a sequel of sorts to *The Left Hand of Darkness.* I think it's a great story, and it has one of several tremendous last lines in Le Guin's fiction. And perhaps even better is Le Guin's "Nine Lives," one of my favorite SF stories, also with a great climactic line (though it occurs a half page or so before the end of the story). I think on balance I'd vote for "Nine Lives" as the Best Novelette of 1969, though "Time Considered . . ." is certainly a fine choice too.

There were some other quite wonderful novelettes, though. One appeared in a publication few in the genre (probably few outside it, truth be told) saw—Peter Beagle's "Farrell and Lila the Werewolf," from the first issue of a little magazine called *Guabi.* I think it became better known when Terry Carr reprinted it a couple of years later in his anthology *New Worlds of Fantasy,* under the now standard shorter title "Lila the Werewolf."

A few more fine novelettes: Sonya Dorman's Roxy Rimidon story "Bye, Bye, Banana Bird," Philip José Farmer's "Down in the Black Gang," James Tiptree Jr.'s "Beam Us Home," and Kate Wilhelm's "Somerset Dreams."

Short story, now. The Nebula short list includes the two true short stories from the Hugo list, and three more strong stories, so: Silverberg's "Passengers," Niven's "Not Long Before the End," plus Tiptree's "The

Last Flight of Dr. Ain," Ellison's "Shattered Like a Glass Goblin," and Theodore Sturgeon's "The Man Who Learned Loving" (called "Brownshoe" on its first publication in the men's magazine *Adam*).

That's a good list. "Passengers" is first rate, and a worthy winner. I really, really enjoy "Not Long Before the End." The Sturgeon and Ellison stories are nice work. But for me, the clear best short story of the year was "The Last Flight of Dr. Ain," by James Tiptree Jr., just stunning and perfectly oblique in its telling.

There were several other very fine short stories that year: another Tiptree piece, "The Snows Are Melted, the Snows Are Gone"; another Niven piece, "Get a Horse!" (the first of his "time travel fantasies"); another Silverberg story, "Sundance"; and the Brian Aldiss story that became the source material for the movie *AI:* "Supertoys Last All Summer Long."

24. TNH

What an amazing time that was. I felt like I was rich.

25. NancyLebovitz

I liked *Macroscope* a lot when I was a kid—one aspect that hasn't been mentioned in the thread is that there's an interstellar information gift economy (for a while, information can be sent FTL, but matter can't be), and as I recall, it was quite well worked out.

Unfortunately, the suck fairy visited my copy and I noticed that the relationship between the brilliant male main character and the beautiful woman who just wasn't smart enough was kind of creepy. I still might reread it to see how it looks on another pass, especially since I thought the section where the action was related to astrology was the weakest thing in the book (the descriptions of the signs of the zodiac were very lively, though), and perhaps I missed something.

I've heard that Anthony compared the sales from *Macroscope* (poor) to those from *A Spell for Chameleon* (excellent) and shaped his career accordingly.

1971

Winner: *Ringworld,* by Larry Niven

Nominees:
Star Light, by Hal Clement
Tau Zero, by Poul Anderson
Tower of Glass, by Robert Silverberg
The Year of the Quiet Sun, by Wilson Tucker

The 1971 Hugo Awards were given at Noreascon I in Boston. The Best Novel award went to Larry Niven's *Ringworld,* a picaresque adventure story with aliens and interstellar engineering set in Niven's Known Space universe. It's bursting with science fiction ideas—breeding humans for luck and Kzinti for pacifism, the "cowardly" alien puppeteers, the Ringworld itself, a flat inhabitable plane circling its sun like a slice of a Dyson sphere. The human characters are there just to lead us through the universe and have adventures, but there's some lovely dialogue. ("You scream and you leap!") I loved *Ringworld* when I was fourteen, and if it blows me away rather less now, that's because the ideas and the story have become familiar—and also I can't help noticing that both sets of aliens have nonsentient females, and the human females don't do much to help with this problem. There have been multiple sequels. It's still part of the conversation of SF. It's in print and it's in the library in French only.

There were four other nominees, of which I've read only two.

Hal Clement's *Star Light* is a physics-oriented hard SF novel in which the very weird aliens from *Mission of Gravity* go with humans to an even stranger world. I haven't read it for years, and what I most remember is the atmosphere—lots of ammonia! It's in print from NESFA, in a compilation with the other connected works. It's not in the library.

Poul Anderson's *Tau Zero* is another big-concept hard SF novel, this one focused on relativity—there's an FTL spaceship that can't slow down and which keeps right on going through the whole universe and out the other end. The ship does have a crew, but I'd have to walk over to the bookshelves to tell you their names. This has never been one of my favorite Andersons. It's in print from Gollancz, but it's not in the library and I haven't heard anybody talk about it for ages.

Tower of Glass seems to be a Robert Silverberg novel that I've completely missed, because I idiotically thought that it was a variant title for *The World Inside*. Fantastic Fiction say it's about a man and some androids building a glass tower in the Arctic to communicate with aliens, and I couldn't possibly have forgotten that if I'd read it. It's not in print, and it's not in the library, so it may be a little while before I can get hold of it.

At least I knew I hadn't read Wilson Tucker's *The Year of the Quiet Sun*. I haven't read it, because it looks like a bit of a downer—somebody time travels to a radiation-scarred future. It's neither in print nor in the library.

Five nominees, all American men. Silverberg and Anderson were previous nominees, Niven had won a short-form Hugo, Tucker and Clement were newcomers. We have one mysterious world and great aliens, one relativistic spaceship novel, one novel of doubly alien exploration, a novel of architecture and alien communication, and one of time travel to the future. The thing that strikes me about these five books is how very hard SF they are when seen as a set, compared to the nominees I've been looking at for the last few years. Not just *Ringworld*, which is actually closer to space opera, but the whole lot of them. Indeed, I think this is the set of five hardest SF books nominated since we've had nominees.

What else might they have picked? The Nebula also went to *Ringworld*, again disproving the "more literary" theory of the Nebulas. Their nominees included the Silverberg and the Tucker, and added Joanna

Russ's *And Chaos Died,* R. A. Lafferty's *Fourth Mansions,* and D. G. Compton's *The Steel Crocodile.* I think the Russ at least should have been on the Hugo list, and the addition of any of these would have made it feel more representative of where SF was in 1971.

Locus began giving its awards this year. *Locus* is a news magazine for the SF field. It has appeared here before, nominated as a fanzine, and it will appear a lot more, winning as a "semiprozine" when that category gets established in the Hugos. The award was voted on by the magazine's subscribers, and thus is, like the Hugos, a popular award from a self-selected group of enthusiasts. The award is an engraved plaque.

Locus's award is a fairly prestigious thing, and the way it mirrors, or does not mirror, the Hugo and the Nebula is interesting. These days, there are an immense number of categories, but in the early years, there were fewer. The notable thing about the Locus Award for these purposes is that it has a huge list of nominees—often twenty books per category. So finding books that should have been on the Hugo list has just become immensely easier.

The first Locus Award went to *Ringworld,* which was clearly blowing everybody away. I think it is worth noting that it won everything it could possibly win and that this represents a high level of enthusiasm for the book within the community.

Other Locus nominees not previously noted: Gordon Dickson's *Tactics of Mistake;* Heinlein's *I Will Fear No Evil;* Dean Koontz's *Beastchild;* Katherine Kurtz's *Deryni Rising;* D. G. Compton's *Chronocules;* Roger Zelazny's *Nine Princes in Amber;* Ron Goulart's *After Things Fell Apart.*

The one that leaps out at me here is *I Will Fear No Evil*—the first of the late-period Heinleins, and not a good book. I'm surprised by the good sense the Hugo voters showed in neglecting a weak work by a popular writer. Then there's the Zelazny—one of his best-loved works and beginning his significant series, but it got no attention at all? Very strange.

It was nominated for the other new award in 1971, the Mythopoeic Award. This was established by the Mythopoeic Society, and is voted on by its members. It is for "fiction in the spirit of the Inklings," which I always interpreted as "fantasy the members imagine Tolkien and C. S.

Lewis would have liked" until it was won by Eleanor Arnason's *A Woman of the Iron People,* science fiction that apparently reminded the members of Lewis's Space trilogy. The award is a delightful small marble replica of one of the lions at the New York Public Library.

This first year, it was won by Mary Stewart's *The Crystal Cave,* demonstrating the members' willingness to look outside what was published within genre. Other nominees were the Kurtz, and Lloyd Alexander's *The Marvelous Misadventures of Sebastian.*

So in 1971, genre awards doubled, from two to four, and have continued to increase since.

Looking at the ISFDB for anything everybody missed, I see a number of possibilities but no real probabilities and no screaming injustices. The only thing I'd really like to note is Ira Levin's *This Perfect Day,* a dystopia written by a thriller writer who always hovered on the edges of genre, and which happened to be one of the first SF books I ever read.

OTHER CATEGORIES

BEST NOVELLA

Winner: *Ill Met in Lankhmar,* by Fritz Leiber (*F&SF,* April 1970)

Nominees:
Beastchild, by Dean R. Koontz (*Venture,* August 1970)
The Region Between, by Harlan Ellison (*Galaxy,* March 1970)
The Snow Women, by Fritz Leiber (*Fantastic,* April 1970) [nomination withdrawn]
The Thing in the Stone, by Clifford D. Simak (*If,* March 1970)
The World Outside, by Robert Silverberg (*Galaxy,* October/November 1970)

No novelette category? Good winner, and I suppose Leiber withdrew the other story because he didn't want to split the vote, not that it works that way with the Hugos. The Nebulas also gave the award to Leiber.

Best Short Story

Winner: "Slow Sculpture," by Theodore Sturgeon (*Galaxy*, February 1970)

Nominees:
"Brillo," by Ben Bova and Harlan Ellison (*Analog*, August 1970)
"Continued on Next Rock," by R. A. Lafferty (*Orbit 7*)
"In the Queue," by Keith Laumer (*Orbit 7*)
"Jean Duprès," by Gordon R. Dickson (*Nova 1*)

Definitely the right winner—but as it won the Nebulas as a novelette, it's a pity we didn't have a novelette category too.

Best Dramatic Presentation

Winner: No Award

Nominees:
Blows Against the Empire LP, The Jefferson Airplane
Colossus: The Forbin Project
Don't Crush That Dwarf, Hand Me the Pliers LP, The Firesign Theater
Hauser's Memory (TV drama)
No Blade of Grass

Best Professional Magazine

Winner: *F&SF*, edited by Edward L. Ferman

Nominees:
Amazing Stories, edited by Ted White
Analog, edited by John W. Campbell Jr.

Galaxy, edited by Ejler Jakobsson
Vision of Tomorrow, edited by Philip Harbottle

BEST PROFESSIONAL ARTIST

Winner: Leo and Diane Dillon

Nominees:
Frank Kelly Freas
Jack Gaughan
Eddie Jones
Jeff Jones

BEST FANZINE

Winner: *Locus*, edited by Charles Brown and Dena Brown

Nominees:
Energumen, edited by Michael Glicksohn and Susan Glicksohn
Outworlds, edited by Bill Bowers and Joan Bowers
Science Fiction Review, edited by Richard E. Geis
Speculation, edited by Peter R. Weston

BEST FAN WRITER

Winner: Richard E. Geis

Nominees:
Terry Carr
Tom Digby
Elizabeth Fishman
Ted Pauls

BEST FAN ARTIST

Winner: Alicia Austin

Nominees:
Steve Fabian
Mike Gilbert
Tim Kirk
Bill Rotsler

Comments on 1971

1. Alter S. Reiss

While *Ill Met in Lankhmar* is a classic that deserved the award, there's another novella from 1970 that's still a part of the conversation of SF. I speak, of course, of Jim Theis's *The Eye of Argon*. This is a story that fans get together to read aloud, as a group; there aren't many other stories that can claim that distinction.

There was a 2007 edition of *The Eye of Argon* from Wildside Press, apparently.

2. Rich Horton

Early post today—before I left for church!

Other potential novel nominees: From the genre: Robert Silverberg's *Downward to the Earth*

From the YA shelves: Sylvia Louise Engdahl's *Enchantress from the Stars*

Joy Chant's *Red Moon and Black Mountain*

John Christopher's *The Prince in Waiting*

Books of interest that don't strike me as Hugo quality but do seem worth mentioning: *The Star Virus,* by Barrington Bayley

The Communipaths, by Suzette Haden Elgin

Alien Island, by T. L. Sherred

The first two are early novels by interesting writers, and both were published as Ace Doubles. The third is the first novel by a writer who made a huge splash with the SF Hall of Fame story "E for Effort" in the late forties, published a few stories in the early fifties, then disappeared until this novel.

And from the mainstream:

The Ice People, by René Barjavel—first published in French in 1968, but 1970 saw the English translation.

Jonathan Livingston Seagull, by Richard Bach—okay, it's pretty crappy. And it's not a novel—probably no more than novelette length. But it was a huge bestseller.

Fifth Business, by Robertson Davies. This is a great, great novel, but while, as with much of Davies's work, it skirts the edge of the fantastic without, to my mind, crossing over. Still, a better novel than any of those I've mentioned.

And finally, *Time and Again,* by Jack Finney, a very well regarded novel by a writer who, of course, published some other fine SF work (*The Body Snatchers,* most notably), but who seemed regarded as a popular mainstream writer rather than an SF writer.

3. RICH HORTON

And as to the short fiction—first, Alter, *The Eye of Argon* is probably only novelette length. But by all means, let's add it to the list!

I find it interesting that both the Hugo and Nebulas gave only two short fiction awards this year, for different reasons, and they went to the same two stories in each case, which were a novella and a novelette. Both are very good: I fully endorse the awards to *Ill Met in Lankhmar,* and while I'd have given the award to another novelette, I do like "Slow Sculpture."

Of the other novella nominees in Hugo, all seem okay but not great. However, there is one Nebula nominee I like a great deal: *A Style in Treason,* by James Blish, which does not seem to be that well known.

I don't actually see any other 1970 novellas that seemed worthy of a nomination, either. One might note the presence of Ellison's *The Region Between* and Anderson's *The Fatal Fulfillment* on the Nebula (and Hugo in the case of the Ellison) ballots: those both first appeared in magazines; they were commissioned for a themed original anthology, *Five Fates.* This sort of thing hadn't happened much before (except maybe for the Twayne Triplets in the 1950s), but it was about to become very common indeed!

As to novelette, as I said, I really do like "Slow Sculpture." But there is another story on the Nebula short list that to my mind is one of the enduring classics of SF of that era, or any era, and which in retrospect should clearly have won:

Joanna Russ's "The Second Inquisition." This is truly a masterwork, a very moving story, and metafictional in the best way. Remember how it ends: "no more stories." Heartbreaking.

I also think Thomas Disch's "The Asian Shore" is wonderful. I'd have placed "Slow Sculpture" third behind "The Second Inquisition" and "The Asian Shore."

The other 1970 novelette I love is a curious beast: it's an Avram Davidson story that appeared in *Ellery Queen's Mystery Magazine* as "Manhattan Night's Entertainment." Latter-day readers (like me) will know it better as "The Lord of Central Park," the title Davidson gave it when he reprinted it in his 1978 collection *The Redward Edward Papers*. It's a lovely story.

My novelette short list of five would have been closed out with R. A. Lafferty's very fine "Continued on Next Rock."

A couple further novelettes of interest: another Roxy Rimidon story from Sonya Dorman, "Alpha Bets"; and Edgar Pangborn's "Longtooth."

The story of the Nebula short story is interesting. For the only time in Nebula history, the Best Short Story award went to "No Award." I have heard that this was possibly a result of confusing ballot instructions. At any rate, supposedly when Isaac Asimov was reading the results, he missed the "No Award" and announced the winner as the second-place piece: Gene Wolfe's "The Island of Doctor Death and Other Stories." Much embarrassment ensued. It is my assumption that Wolfe deserved the award anyway, and presumably would have won had the ballot instructions been clearer, but that's just me guessing—I don't know the details. Anyway, it's a great story, and it would have been a worthy winner. And Wolfe had a great year, publishing a ton of first-rate pieces—besides "The Island of Doctor Death and Other Stories," the best was probably "How the Whip Came Back." It was at this point, I think, that it became obvious he was a major, major writer.

The other Nebula short story nominees are quite good too. Harry Harrison's "By the Falls" is a strange story, and perhaps his best single work. Lafferty appears with "Entire and Perfect Chrysolite," which is excellent, but he also published such fine stories as "About a Secret Crocodile" and "All Pieces of a River Shore." Gardner Dozois's "A Dream at Noonday" was his first major story, but he also had the excellent "Horse of Air," which oddly enough appeared on the following year's Nebula short list.

Other strong short stories included:

"Gone Fishin'," by Robin Scott Wilson
"The Man Who Could Not See Devils," by Joanna Russ
"The Same to You Doubled," by Robert Sheckley
"Things" aka "The End," by Ursula K. Le Guin
"America the Beautiful," by Fritz Leiber

One should also note how excellent Damon Knight's *Orbit* was in this period. No fewer than three editions were published in 1970, numbers six through eight, and *Orbit 6* was particularly strong, featuring "The Second Inquisition," "The Asian Shore," "Entire and Perfect Chrysolite," and "Things." *Orbit 7* had "Continued on Next Rock," "The Island of Doctor Death and Other Stories," "A Dream at Noonday," and also Kate Wilhelm's "April Fool's Day Forever" and Keith Laumer's "In the Queue." And *Orbit 8* had "Horse of Air," "All Pieces of a River Shore," plus Ellison's "One Life, Furnished in Early Poverty." The gibes by people like Alexei Panshin (as I recall—maybe it was someone else) that *Orbit* was dominated by "nonfunctional word patterns" or some such phrasing have always struck me as simply stupid.

11. GARDNER DOZOIS

There's no "supposedly" about it, Rich. I was there, sitting at Gene Wolfe's table, in fact. He'd actually stood up, and was starting to walk toward the podium, when Isaac was told about his mistake. Gene shrugged and sat down quietly, like the gentleman he is, while Isaac stammered an explanation of what had happened. It was the one time

I ever saw Isaac totally flustered, and, in fact, he felt guilty about the incident to the end of his days.

It's bullshit that this was the result of confusing ballot instructions. This was the height of the War of the New Wave, and passions between the New Wave camp and the conservative Old Guard camp were running high. (The same year, Michael Moorcock said in a review that the only way SFWA could have found a worse thing than *Ringworld* to give the Nebula to was to give it to a comic book.) The fact that the short story ballot was almost completely made up of stuff from *Orbit* had outraged the Old Guard, particularly James Sallis's surreal "The Creation of Bennie Good," and they block-voted for No Award as a protest against "nonfunctional word patterns" making the ballot. Judy-Lynn del Rey told me as much immediately after the banquet, when she was exuberantly gloating about how they'd "put *Orbit* in its place" with the voting results, and actually said, "We won!"

All this passion and choler seems far away now, as if we were arguing over which end of the egg to break.

If we were going to give novella to one of those on the list, I think I'd go with Leiber's *The Snow Women* rather than *Ill Met in Lankhmar*. For novelette, if there had been such a category, I'd have voted for "The Second Inquisition," "The Asian Shore," or "Longtooth" before "Slow Sculpture," although I've always liked "Continued on Next Rock" and "All Pieces of a River Shore" too.

Short story should have gone to "The Island of Doctor Death and Other Stories," although Leiber's "America the Beautiful" would have been a strong choice too.

13. RICH HORTON

Gardner—I had never heard the story about block voting for "No Award" from the Old Guard keeping Wolfe's story from winning. Thanks for the correction. I think I read the "ballot instruction" story in one of Asimov's autobiographical works, but perhaps I simply mis-remembered it.

Such silliness, really. (Though with real costs to people.) Wolfe has won the Hugos and Nebulas he deserves since then, but I always count that in my head as one more for him.

I might note re: Moorcock's comic book comment that it would not be too many years before there was actual controversy about giving awards to comic books (and if anything, it was people on Moorcock's side of the divide more determined that they ought to be eligible).

Blows Against the Empire, by the way, adds to its SFnal cred (such as it is) by having the lyrics to one song ("Mau Mau (Amerikon)"), derived rather directly from the epigraph to a Mark Clifton–Alex Apostolides story ("Hide! Hide! Witch!," one of the precursor stories to "They'd Rather Be Right," as I recall). Uncredited, natch.

14. GARDNER DOZOIS

The "confused by ballot instructions" was come up with later as an explanation/justification for the whole affair, in my opinion, after passions had faded, but I never believed it, especially as I saw Old Guard members celebrating and congratulating themselves before everybody had even left the banquet room. And that was certainly the way the New Wave people there took it, as a deliberate rebuff.

I suppose *Blows Against the Empire* has points in its favor, but after having been trapped in the sixties as the only non-stoned person in a room full of stoned people who insisted on playing the same side of *Blows Against the Empire* forty times in a row, I'm afraid that it's forever lost its luster for me.

1972

Winner: *To Your Scattered Bodies Go,* by Philip José Farmer

Nominees:
Dragonquest, by Anne McCaffrey
Jack of Shadows, by Roger Zelazny
The Lathe of Heaven, by Ursula K. Le Guin
A Time of Changes, by Robert Silverberg
The World Inside, by Robert Silverberg (withdrawn)

The 1972 Hugo Awards were held at LACon I, in Los Angeles. The Best Novel Hugo was won by Philip José Farmer's *To Your Scattered Bodies Go,* the first of the Riverworld books. The premise is that everybody who was ever alive wakes up, naked, on the shore of a very long river that resembles the Mississippi. If they're killed, they wake up again naked somewhere else along the river. Strange containers they call grails provide food at regular intervals. Nobody knows why they're there or where they are or what's going on. *To Your Scattered Bodies Go* follows the adventures of Richard Francis Burton, the Victorian explorer, as he meets an interesting assortment of all the people who ever lived. It's a great book, and if the sequels are less great, it's only because no explanation can possibly live up to that premise. I loved this book with wild enthusiasm when I was a teenager, and it will always have a place in my heart. I think it's a fine Hugo winner. It's in print and in the library in English.

There were six nominees, of which one was withdrawn. I've read all of them.

Anne McCaffrey's *Dragonquest* is the second novel of the Pern series. I loved it to pieces when I was fourteen, but I can now see problematic gender issues and find the sex scenes squicky. It's not as good as the first volume, but it widens the scope of the series and stands alone well. I think this is the first time we've had a sequel nominated, and it didn't win, which is an overall trend with the Hugos; the voters tend to prefer stand-alones or first volumes. It reads like fantasy, but it's actually about a lost colony on a world where dragons have been bred to fight the destructive menace of Thread, which falls from the sky. It's in print, and it's in the library in French and English.

Roger Zelazny's *Jack of Shadows* is a fairly weak Zelazny novel about a thief in a fantasy world. It lacks his usual sparkle. It isn't in print. It's in the library in French only. I don't think it had lasted well.

The Lathe of Heaven is one of my favorite of Ursula K. Le Guin's works. It's near future, and it's about a man whose dreams can change reality. It's a classic. It's in print, and it's in the library in English.

Robert Silverberg's *A Time of Changes* is one of two Silverberg novels nominated; the other, *The World Inside*, was withdrawn. This is generally unnecessary with Hugo voting. *A Time of Changes* is set far in the future on the strange colony world of Borthan, where people keep themselves sealed off from one another. A visitor from Earth and a telepathic experience change one man into a revolutionary who wants everybody to share themselves instead of keeping apart. *The World Inside* is about overpopulation considered as a good thing, with everyone encouraged to have sex and children and live in huge towers. They are both in print and in the library in both languages.

These are all good books and, except for *Jack of Shadows*, worthy nominees.

We have four men and two women, all American. Le Guin and Zelazny were previous winners, Farmer had won a best new writer Hugo and a short fiction Hugo, McCaffrey had also won a short fiction Hugo, but they're both new to the best novel list. We have two planetary SF, one near future about overpopulation, one inexplicable weird future, one meditation on reality, and a fantasy. They are pretty much all New Wave books. I'd have voted for *The Lathe of Heaven*, but I think the Farmer is also a good winner.

What else might they have chosen? The Nebula went to *A Time of Changes*, with Le Guin also nominated. Other nominees were Poul Anderson's *The Byworlder*, one of Anderson's best—that would have been a fine addition to the Hugo ballot. There's also R. A. Lafferty's *The Devil Is Dead*, which I haven't read, T. J. Bass's *Half Past Human*, which I remember fondly but which is mostly forgotten now, and Kate Wilhelm's *Margaret and I*, which is again largely forgotten and which I found disappointing.

The Locus Award went to *The Lathe of Heaven*. I like it when the awards are spread out between the good books this way. Other nominees not previously mentioned: Philip José Farmer's *The Fabulous Riverboat* (Riverworld 2); Robert Silverberg's *Son of Man* and *The Second Trip*—he was having a really productive year!—Lloyd Biggle Jr.'s *The World Menders;* Suzette Haden Elgin's *Furthest;* R. A. Lafferty's *Arrive at Easterwine*, and Thomas Burnett Swann's *The Forest of Forever.*

The Mythopoeic Award went to Joy Chant's *Red Moon and Black Mountain.* Also nominated and not already mentioned: Evangeline Walton's (no relation) *The Children of Llyr;* Michael Moorcock's The Corum Trilogy (*The Prince in the Scarlet Robe*); John Gardner's horrible *Grendel;* Joan North's *The Light Maze;* Ursula Le Guin's *The Tombs of Atuan;* and Isidore Haiblum's *The Tsaddik of the Seven Wonders.*

Can there possibly be anything of note that all these lists missed? Well, yes. The ISFDB gives me James Blish's *And All the Stars a Stage* and *The Day After Judgment*, Doris Lessing's *Briefing for a Descent into Hell*, and Moorcock's *A Cure for Cancer.*

So our list of nominees this year looks pretty good—not "everything good" or "Jo's favorite books of the year" but a representative set of good books, almost any of which would have been a worthy winner.

OTHER CATEGORIES

....

BEST NOVELLA

Winner: *The Queen of Air and Darkness,* by Poul Anderson (*F&SF,* April 1971)

Nominees:
Dread Empire, by John Brunner (*Fantastic,* April 1971)
The Fourth Profession, by Larry Niven (*Quark 4*)
A Meeting with Medusa, by Arthur C. Clarke (*Playboy,* December 1971)
A Special Kind of Morning, by Gardner Dozois (*New Dimensions 1*)

Wow, another great year. I think the Anderson is the best, but I'd have had a very hard time voting here.

BEST SHORT STORY

Winner: "Inconstant Moon," by Larry Niven (*All the Myriad Ways*)

Nominees:
"All the Last Wars at Once," by George Alec Effinger (*Universe 1*)
"The Autumn Land," by Clifford D. Simak (*F&SF,* October 1971)
"The Bear with the Knot on His Tail," by Stephen Tall (*F&SF,* May 1971)
"Sky," by R. A. Lafferty (*New Dimensions 1*)
"Vaster Than Empires and More Slow," by Ursula K. Le Guin (*New Dimensions 1*)

Now, here the Niven definitely deserved to win, a real classic. But also some other memorable stories. The Nebulas had three short fiction categories, which were won by Katherine MacLean's "The Missing Man," the Anderson, and Robert Silverberg's "Good News from the Vatican."

Best Dramatic Presentation

Winner: *A Clockwork Orange*

Nominees:
The Andromeda Strain
I Think We're All Bozos on This Bus LP, Firesign Theater
The Name of the Game: "L.A. 2017" (screenplay by Philip Wylie;
    directed by Steven Spielberg)
THX 1138

Best Professional Magazine

Winner: *F&SF*, edited by Edward L. Ferman

Nominees:
Amazing Stories, edited by Ted White
Analog, edited by John W. Campbell Jr.
Fantastic, edited by Ted White
Galaxy, edited by Ejler Jakobsson

Best Professional Artist

Winner: Frank Kelly Freas

Nominees:
Vincent Di Fate
Jack Gaughan
Jeff Jones
John Schoenherr

Best Amateur Magazine

Winner: *Locus*, edited by Charles Brown and Dena Brown

Nominees:

Energumen, edited by Michael Glicksohn and Susan Glicksohn

Granfalloon, edited by Ron and Linda Bushyager

SF Commentary, edited by Bruce Gillespie

BEST FAN WRITER

Winner: Harry Warner Jr.

Nominees:

Terry Carr

Tom Digby

Susan Glicksohn

Rosemary Ullyot

Bob Vardeman

BEST FAN ARTIST

Winner: Tim Kirk

Nominees:

Alicia Austin

Grant Canfield

Wendy Fletcher

Bill Rotsler

COMMENTS ON 1972

5. RICH HORTON

Other potential novel nominees:

Tom Robbins's *Another Roadside Attraction*

Sylvia Louise Engdahl's *The Far Side of Evil*

K. M. O'Donnell's (Barry Malzberg's) *Universe Day*

I actually wouldn't add any of those to the short lists—just thought they deserved a mention.

I actually find the whole list, and the short fiction as well, vaguely disappointing. (In quantity more than quality—the best short fiction is very good.) I think 1971 was a sort of local minimum for SF—I blame Ejler Jakobsson. (Half-jokingly.)

6. RICH HORTON

As for the short fiction . . . this was the last year that the Hugos had only two categories. Beginning the next year, they aligned with the Nebulas. (I'm not sure when the word-count boundaries also came into alignment—very possibly the same year.)

So, Best Novella. Indeed, the Hugo short list is very, very good. I can't argue with the winner, couldn't argue with any of the choices. The Brunner is one of his *The Traveler in Black* stories, very fine stuff. The Dozois is what we might call "late high New Wave," and it blew me away on first reading. Clarke's is crackling pure hard SF, as really Clarke was the best practioner of. But my favorite is probably Niven's *The Fourth Profession,* which appeared in what might seem a very unusual place for a Niven story, a very New Wavy anthology coedited by Delany and his wife, Marilyn Hacker, herself an absolutely first-rate poet.

However the Nebula short lists put *The Queen of Air and Darkness* and *A Special Kind of Morning* in novelette. I imagine the short story–novella dividing point for the Hugo was something like ten thousand words. ("Inconstant Moon," I'm pretty sure, is novelette length by today's definitions, for example.) So, arguably, both Hugo Awards went to novelettes. I suspect "The Fourth Profession" is also novelette length, though fairly long.

The Nebula short list for novella is a bit curious: the winner is Katherine MacLean's *The Missing Man,* a very fine story. The others on the list are Jerzy Kosinski's *Being There* (which for me is insufficiently fantastical for this award, but that's just my bias), Kate Wilhelm's *The Infinity Box* and *The Plastic Abyss,* and Keith Roberts's *The God House.* I don't remember any of these stories all that well—I should seek out the Roberts, as he's a favorite of mine. I do recall enjoying *The Infinity Box,* but I couldn't tell you now what it was about.

The only other novella I can come up with that I recall with particular affection is John Brunner's *The Easy Way Out*.

To further add to the confusion, Clarke's *A Meeting with Medusa*, from the December 1971 *Playboy*, won the Nebula the following year! (When nominally stories from 1972 were eligible.)

Novelette:

As noted, the Hugos' not aligning with current (or Nebula) definitions complicates things. I'm pretty sure that from the Hugo short list three of the short stories ("Inconstant Moon," "Vaster Than Empires and More Slow," and "The Bear with a Knot in Its Tail") and three of the novellas (*The Fourth Profession, The Queen of Air and Darkness,* and *A Special Kind of Morning*) are novelettes. Of those, I would definitely choose "Inconstant Moon," a wonderful story. That said, all the others of those six are really good too.

Stephen Tall's story is perhaps the least remembered—Tall's real name was Compton Crook. (An award for Best First SF Novel is named for him.) He was born in 1908 (same year as Jack Williamson), and had stories in *Galaxy* in 1955 and *Worlds of Tomorrow* in 1966, but really started publishing regularly in 1970. His stories, many of them linked and fixed up into two novels, *The Stardust Voyages* and *The Ramsgate Paradox*, were colorful and fun. But he died in 1981, not terribly young but early in his writing career.

The Nebula novelette nominees, besides the Anderson story (which won) and the Dozois, were Kate Wilhelm's "The Encounter," Joanna Russ's "Poor Man, Beggar Man," and Edgar Pangborn's "Mount Charity." All good stories, but I'd stick with "Inconstant Moon."

Other good novelettes from 1971:

Robert Sheckley's "Pas de Trois of the Chef, the Waiter, and the Customer" (originally in *Playboy* as "Three Sinners in the Green Jade Moon")—not really SF or fantasy, but a neat, neat story, highly recommended

M. John Harrison's "The Lamia and Lord Cromis" (a Viriconium story)

James Tiptree Jr.'s "Mother in the Sky with Diamonds"

Best Short Story:

As noted, the Hugo winner and a couple of other nominees are really novelettes. The other three short fiction nominees ("All the Last Wars at Once" [the first George Alec Effinger story to really get notice], "Sky," and "The Autumn Land") are all fine. The Nebula nominees were Silverberg's "Good News from the Vatican" (the winner and a nice story, but a bit slight to my taste), George Zebrowski's "Heathen God," Gardner Dozois's "Horse of Air," and Stephen Goldin's "The Last Ghost." Of all these, I think I'd vote for "Horse of Air" for Best Short Story of 1971, except it really appeared in 1970!

Other potential nominees:

James Tiptree Jr.'s "The Peacefulness of Vivyan" (This and "Mother in the Sky with Diamonds" are fine stories, but not Tiptree at her best—but check out 1972, one of the most amazing collections of stories in a single year by a single writer in the history of the field.)
Arthur Jean Cox's "A Collector of Ambroses"
Thomas Disch's "Angoulême" (another part of *334*)
Silverberg's "In Entropy's Jaws"
Octavia Butler's first story, which appeared in the *Clarion* anthology: "Crossover." (Her first novel wouldn't appear for five more years, and no more short fiction until the eighties.)
And, finally, my actual choice for best short story published in 1971: Philip José Farmer's "The Sliced-Crosswise Only-on-Tuesday World" (I know, I said I don't get on well with Farmer, but this story is an exception. And I'm shocked it didn't appear on short lists: it made multiple Best of the Year anthologies, it appeared in a prominent place, *New Dimensions*, and Farmer was a prominent writer and a previous award winner.)

I might note also the primacy of original anthologies: the eleven short-listed Hugo stories included one from *Playboy*, one from a collection, four from the SF magazines, and five from anthologies (*New Dimensions*, *Universe*, and *Quark*). Of the fourteen Nebula nominees, one was from a collection, one was a stand-alone book, one was from an anthology that had previously been a magazine (*New Worlds Quarterly*), three were from the SF magazines, and the remaining eight were from original anthologies (*New Dimensions, Universe, Orbit,* and *Protostars*).

The key event leading to that was that this was the first year for two of the great original anthology series in the field's history, Terry Carr's *Universe* and Robert Silverberg's *New Dimensions*. (It occurs to me that Silverberg all but qualified for Grand Master status in 1971 by itself, with four major novels including a Nebula winner, some strong short fiction including a Nebula winner, and founding one of the major anthology series ever.)

21. GARDNER DOZOIS

In novella, *The Queen of Air and Darkness* is really the only one that has lasted and is still read and talked about today, so that's a good indication that the right one was picked. Next best, there is the Clarke, although it is a bit traveloguish.

The novella that I really think should have won was not on the Hugo ballot—Gene Wolfe's *The Fifth Head of Cerberus,* one of the most brilliant SF novellas ever written. Clarke beat it for the Nebula.

The God House is good Roberts, by the way, Rich, maybe not quite on the level of the best of the Pavane stories, but still a damn good read.

"Inconstant Moon" has met the test of time better than the rest of the Hugo Short Fiction category, and is about the only one still remembered, but I'd rather have seen the award go to Tom Disch's brilliant and melancholy "Angoulême." I was not as impressed with "The Sliced-Crossways Only-on-Tuesday World" as Rich was, and wouldn't have voted for it.

23. RICH HORTON

Definitely *The Fifth Head of Cerberus* is one of the greatest SF novellas of all time, and next week I'll be complaining that it didn't win! (Losing to a lesser Le Guin story and to an enjoyable but, as Gardner says, rather traveloguish Clarke story.)

I admit I haven't reread Farmer's "Sliced-Crosswise" in decades—perhaps it will have diminished. And I never read the novel it became (*Dayworld*). (Indeed, I think it became a series of novels, or at least two.) But at the time, I found the central idea irresistible.

26. GARDNER DOZOIS

Yes, I was the first person George met at his very first SF convention, as I was running the registration desk that day at that particular Dis-clave, so the first SF fan he ever met recognized him as being a writer and approved of his work—a foreshadowing of things to come!

27. TNH

Gardner @26, shouldn't there be a diorama of that scene in a museum somewhere?

29. GARDNER DOZOIS

When you paint it, remember that I was skinny in those days, not fat. (Neither was George.) I also had long hair—of an "eerie, voluminous sort," Silverberg once said—that grew down past my ass.

EFFECTIVE DREAMING: URSULA K. LE GUIN'S
THE LATHE OF HEAVEN

The Lathe of Heaven is a short novel, and one that holds a special place in my heart. It was the third grown-up science fiction novel I read. I didn't understand a word of it, but I loved it anyway.

The Lathe of Heaven is about George Orr, a man who has dreams that change reality, and he's afraid of having those dreams. He gets sent to a psychiatrist, Haber, who becomes fascinated with changing reality. He then finds a lawyer, Heather LeLache, who he hopes will rescue him from Haber as the world changes around them. It's his dreams that change reality, and dreams produce answers from the subconscious to questions rationally asked. Dreams are not daydreams. Asked to pro-duce peace on earth, George dreams of alien invasions; asked to solve overcrowding, he dreams of a plague fifteen years ago that killed off six billion people. When he wakes up, the world has always been that way, and that's how everyone remembers it except for those in the room with him.

What makes the book brilliant is that it's told from the points of view of the three central characters, and they're all real. George Orr is naturally worried about having this ability. Haber wants to use the power to do good; he's essentially benevolent but has no sense of proportion. Heather LeLache is the most interesting of them all. She's a black civil rights lawyer. When everyone becomes gray (and has always been gray—Haber told George to solve the problem of racism), she doesn't exist, because her blackness is an essential part of what has made her. Then George does manage to evoke her in that world, and she's different, as a gray person. Her point of view is the most interesting of all.

The book cycles through their points of view in order, and in the gray world, while she's missing, the point of view remains with George and that asymmetry reflects the asymmetry of a world without her. I'm sure I didn't consciously notice that the first time I read it, I'm not sure when I consciously noticed it, but I think any reader would unconsciously notice it. The changing world is evoked rather than described—you mainly see the changes to the world through the changes to the people, and you see some of the smaller changes more than some of the bigger ones.

The aliens are wonderful, but again seen very briefly—I most like the way that after they are revealed never to have been a menace, there's one running a junk shop. People have sometimes compared this book with Philip K. Dick's work with shifting realities, especially *Ubik* and *Eye in the Sky*. The real difference is that Dick liked to torture his characters, and he often didn't distinguish them enough for anyone to care about them anyway. Le Guin wrote a novel about the effect of world-changing on three-dimensional characters. Philip Dick wrote world-changing from the point of view of alienated, miserable people nobody could care about. Le Guin wrote from a position of hope and Dick from a position of existential despair. There may not be any difference, except in whether I enjoy reading the result or not.

1973

Best Novel

Winner: *The Gods Themselves*, by Isaac Asimov

Nominees:
Dying Inside, by Robert Silverberg
The Book of Skulls, by Robert Silverberg
A Choice of Gods, by Clifford Simak
There Will Be Time, by Poul Anderson
When HARLIE Was One, by David Gerrold

The 1973 Hugo Awards were held at Torcon II in Toronto. The novel winner was Isaac Asimov's *The Gods Themselves*. I find this win inexplicable. I reread it because I started to wonder if I'd just totally missed something about it when I first read it. Oh dear. It also won the Nebula and the Locus. It's in print and in the library in both languages, so it has lasted. But for me, this is one of those "Really? They gave the Hugo to that?" winners. It was Asimov's first science fiction for some time, and he was a very popular writer, and many of his books are excellent—but *The Gods Themselves* considered as a whole book seems to me to be among his weakest. But maybe everybody else thought the middle bit with the aliens was sufficiently great to carry the whole book alone?

There were five other nominees, and I've read all of them. I think Robert Silverberg's *Dying Inside* is the standout book here, and I'd definitely have voted for it. It's a close-up study of why telepathy isn't a good idea, and it's absolutely brilliant. It's in print and in the library in French only.

The other Silverberg nominated that year is *The Book of Skulls*, a comparatively weaker novel about immortality and a secret cult that broadens out to be more than that. It's also in print and also in the library in French only.

Clifford Simak's *A Choice of Gods* is a strange far-future pastoral—most of humanity has vanished, the ones who are left live very long lives quietly puttering about in a typical Simak way, and then the missing ones come back. It's extremely out of print, but it's in the library in French.

Poul Anderson's *There Will Be Time* is a Golden Age–style adventure of a man who can move through time, saving the world. I'd have thought it was a lot older than 1972, and I'd forgotten about it until I looked it up. (He wrote a lot of books with "time" in the title.) It's minor Anderson. It's not in print, and it's not in the library.

David Gerrold's *When HARLIE Was One* is about a computer becoming conscious. I suppose I technically haven't read it, as what I read was the eighties rewrite "Release 2.0" with updated (to the eighties) technology. It's a pleasant novel about AI but nothing special.

So, all American men. Anderson, Silverberg, and Simak are previous nominees. Asimov had won "Best Series Ever" and a Hugo for his science writing, but this was his first novel nomination. Gerrold had previously been nominated for a *Star Trek* episode, but not for written fiction. We have a book about aliens and parauniverses, a character study about telepathy, a novel about an immortality cult, a far-future pastoral, a time travel adventure, and a computer becoming conscious. *Dying Inside* is the standout for me; all the rest of them are fairly forgettable.

Was it really such a dull year?

Non-overlapping Nebula nominees were Spinrad's *The Iron Dream* (which is brilliant but goes on too long and shouldn't have been a novel—one idea is not enough for a whole book): John Brunner's wonderful but depressing environmental disaster, *The Sheep Look Up*, and George Alec Effinger's romp *What Entropy Means to Me*.

The John W. Campbell Memorial Award for science fiction novels started this year—it's an odd thing to choose to honor Campbell, who died in 1971. He was a magazine editor all his life. I suppose he did publish novels as serials, but it's not what he's best known for. The Campbell Memorial Award is administered by a jury, mostly consisting of the same people every year. There is a permanent award, engraved with the name of every winner, and since 2004, there have been individual lucite plaques for the winners to keep. The Campbell jury have made what seems to me some very odd choices, which we will be examining as we go on.

The judges this first year gave it to Barry Malzberg's *Beyond Apollo*. Second place was James E. Gunn's *The Listeners,* a book about SETI; and third was Christopher Priest's *A Darkening Island* aka *Fugue for a Darkening Island,* a very uncozy catastrophe novel. They also gave a special award for excellent writing to Silverberg for *Dying Inside.*

Previously unlisted Locus nominees are Zelazny's *The Guns of Avalon;* Gordon R. Dickson's *The Pritcher Mass;* Katherine Kurtz's *Deryni Checkmate;* Bob Shaw's *Other Days, Other Eyes;* Harry Harrison's *A Transatlantic Tunnel, Hurrah!;* David Gerrold's *Yesterday's Children;* Andrew J. Offutt's *The Castle Keeps;* and Gordon Eklund's *Beyond the Resurrection.*

The Mythopoeic Award went to Evangeline Walton's *The Song of Rhiannon.* Other nominees not yet mentioned were Poul Anderson's *The Dancer from Atlantis,* Ursula K. Le Guin's *The Farthest Shore,* and Thomas Burnett Swann's *Green Phoenix.*

Could there possibly be anything of note that all these lists missed?

Well, there's Sylvia Engdahl's *Heritage of the Star* aka *This Star Shall Abide,* Michael Coney's *Mirror Image,* and Richard Adams's *Watership Down.* I think the five Hugo nominees are an unadventurous lot this year, and I don't think they're the five best books of the year.

OTHER CATEGORIES

BEST NOVELLA

Winner: *The Word for World Is Forest,* by Ursula K. Le Guin (*Again, Dangerous Visions*)

Nominees:
The Fifth Head of Cerberus, by Gene Wolfe (*Orbit 10*)
The Gold at the Starbow's End, by Frederik Pohl (*Analog,* March 1972)
Hero, by Joe Haldeman (*Analog,* June 1972)
The Mercenary, by Jerry Pournelle (*Analog,* July 1972)

Wow. Another great novella year, and I wouldn't have given it to Le Guin. While I generally love her work, I think *Forest* is one of her thinnest and preachiest, and it hasn't lasted well. Either the Wolfe or the Pohl would have been a better winner—and I kind of like the Pournelle too, actually.

BEST NOVELETTE

Winner: "Goat Song," by Poul Anderson (*F&SF,* February 1972)

Nominees:
"Basilisk," by Harlan Ellison (*F&SF,* August 1972)
"A Kingdom by the Sea," by Gardner Dozois (*Orbit 10*)
"Painwise," by James Tiptree Jr. (*F&SF,* February 1972)
"Patron of the Arts," by William Rotsler (*Universe 2*)

Another really good set, and here the winner is one of my all-time-favorite short works, Anderson doing what he did best.

BEST SHORT STORY

Winner: (tie) "Eurema's Dam," by R. A. Lafferty (*New Dimensions 2*)
"The Meeting," by Frederik Pohl and C. M. Kornbluth (*F&SF*, November 1972)

Nominees:
"And I Awoke and Found Me Here on the Cold Hill's Side," by James
  Tiptree Jr. (*F&SF*, March 1972)
"When It Changed," by Joanna Russ (*Again, Dangerous Visions*)
"When We Went to See the End of the World," by Robert Silverberg
  (*Universe 2*)

Gosh. A tie, but not between the two stories everyone remembers, the
Tiptree and the Russ. Oh, and note three categories again, thank goodness.

BEST DRAMATIC PRESENTATION

Winner: *Slaughterhouse-Five*

Nominees:
Between Time and Timbuktu
The People
Silent Running

BEST PROFESSIONAL EDITOR

Winner: Ben Bova

Nominees:
Terry Carr
Edward L. Ferman
Ted White
Donald A. Wollheim

We've changed from "best magazine" to "best editor." Was this a good idea at the time? Maybe it was, because more SF was starting to be published in original anthologies.

Best Professional Artist

Winner: Frank Kelly Freas

Nominees:
Vincent Di Fate
Jack Gaughan
Mike Hinge
John Schoenherr

Best Amateur Magazine

Winner: *Energumen,* edited by Michael Glicksohn and Susan Wood Glicksohn

Nominees:
Agol, edited by Andrew Porter
Granfalloon, edited by Ron and Linda Bushyager
Locus, edited by Charles Brown and Dena Brown
SF Commentary, edited by Bruce Gillespie

Best Fan Writer

Winner: Terry Carr

Nominees:
Charles Brown
Richard E. Geis
Susan Glicksohn
Sandra Miesel
Rosemary Ullyot

Three women! That's notable.

BEST FAN ARTIST

Winner: Tim Kirk

Nominees:
Grant Canfield
Bill Rotsler
Jim Shull
Arthur Thomson

JOHN W. CAMPBELL AWARD FOR BEST NEW WRITER

Winner: Jerry Pournelle

Nominees:
Ruth Berman
George Alec Effinger
George R. R. Martin
Robert Thurston
Lisa Tuttle

The Campbell is an odd award, and it's not a Hugo, but I'm going to be considering it with them, as it's voted for with them. It recognizes writers at the beginning of their careers, and it honors Campbell very well because he did work with so many new writers. The trophy is an inscribed marble slab nicknamed the "cheeseboard."

The Campbell is supposed to be for the "best new writer." Obviously the voters were going on what was available—how else! But with the benefit of hindsight, we need to look at the nominees' subsequent careers too, to see whether they were in fact the "best new writer" or "a pretty good new writer" or "somebody who looked good but fizzled out."

Writers are eligible for the Campbell in the first two years of their careers. It therefore rewards only people who emerge fully formed—people who take time to mature, or people who sell a few stories over a long time and then have an exciting first novel are essentially never eligible when they could win. If we had a Hugo for Best First Novel instead, it would be much easier to compare like with like and to know what was eligible. But on the other hand, it might blight the prospects of astonishingly brilliant first novels that would otherwise make the main Hugo ballot like 2011's *The Hundred Thousand Kingdoms* and 2010's *The Windup Girl*, or 1993's *China Mountain Zhang* and 1985's *Neuromancer*, if people nominated them only as Best First Novel and not for the Best Novel Hugo.

Looking at this first list, four of them (including the winner) have gone on to become notable writers. Ruth Berman is primarily a poet, who has won the Rhysling and the Dwarf Stars Award in this decade. Robert Thurston has gone on to have a career writing a lot of tie-in novels. I like to think I'd have voted for Martin, but he really was at the very start of his career, and I don't know if I'd have noticed him. I might have voted for Effinger or Pournelle instead, if I'd been at Torcon II without the benefit of hindsight. (I'd also have been eight years old, but let's just forget about that.)

COMMENTS ON 1973

16. GARDNER DOZOIS

I think there's little doubt that the win for *The Gods Themselves* was a beloved-writer-is-writing-fiction-again-after-a-long-absence award, just as the Lafferty may have been a he's-old-and-sick-and-will-probably-die-soon award. Such things are common not only in the Hugos and the Nebulas also but in the Oscars and the Emmys—in fact, in just about every award.

The winner SHOULD have been *Dying Inside*, not only the best SF novel of the year but also the best from Silverberg's whole Middle Period. If it couldn't go to *Dying Inside*, for some reason, I'd rather have seen it go to *Watership Down*, actually, than most of the other finalists and potential finalists, a landmark of sorts in fantasy, and frequently read even to this day, unlike most of the others, including the nearly forgotten *The Gods Themselves*.

By this time, few people probably remember the firestorm kicked up by Malzberg's *Beyond Apollo* winning the first John W. Campbell Memorial Award. The War of the New Wave was still grumbling along at this point, and the Old Guard went ballistic at the win, some saying that it was a disgrace to Campbell's memory that such a book won (it had Lots of Sex in it, and was widely considered to be an attack on astronauts and the space program), and others saying that Campbell must be spinning in horror in his grave.

Another artifact of the War this year was the "anti-hippie" glossary in the Anderson novel.

In novella, *The Word for World Is Forest* is one of my least favorite Le Guin works, being much too diadactic and heavy-handed, even approaching shrill. (It does appear to be one of the elements that went into the mix for *Avatar*, though, so it did have a lasting effect.) I have no doubt whatever that the award should have gone to Gene Wolfe's *The Fifth Head of Cerebus*, one of the best SF novellas ever written, and a high point in Gene's career. If for some reason it couldn't go to Wolfe, then it should have gone to *The Gold at the Starbow's End*, although *Hero*, the opening section of *The Forever War*, would have been a reasonable choice too. I'd have voted for the Le Guin well toward the end of the category.

It seems to have been a weak year for novelette. "Goat Song" is a reasonable choice, although I don't think it was as strong as "The Queen of Air and Darkness" from the year before. Almost all the other novelettes are long forgotten (and, actually, "Goat Song" isn't usually counted among Poul's key works these days, either).

"The Meeting" is a good story, but I don't think either it or the Lafferty (one of Laffery's weaker stories, actually) deserved the Hugo. What should have won out of that field was Tiptree's "And I Awoke and Found Me Here on the Cold Hill's Side," although a respectable argument can be made for "When It Changed" too (although it also touched off one of the fiercest battles of the War, and the fanzines ran red with blood for months after it was published).

What I think REALLY should have won, though, was Russ's "Nobody's Home," her other story for the year, a story so amazingly ahead of its time that it reads like something Greg Egan might have written in the nineties, even though it was published in 1973.

I was told by a BNF who was involved in running the Worldcon that year that I'd actually won in the John W. Campbell Award voting, but was disqualified after the fact because I'd published a story professionally back in 1966. Whether this is actually true or not, I have no idea.

17. Rich Horton

Now to the short fiction. This was really an amazing year. And yet the Hugo voters got it mostly wrong. (The novelette award is pretty good.)

It was my "Golden Age" year, according to Peter Graham's formulation ("The Golden Age of SF is when you were twelve"), and one of the first adult SF anthologies I remember reading is *Nebula Award Stories Eight*, which collects stories from 1972.

I'd place the Hugo winner fifth of five on the Hugo short list. The winner, by a wide, wide margin, should have been *The Fifth Head of Cerberus*, one of the most amazing SF novellas ever. But Fred Pohl's *The Gold at the Starbow's End* is also exceptional. And I also quite enjoyed the two very different examples of military SF on the ballot, the Haldeman and the Pournelle. (Both stories appeared in *Analog*, by the way, as did Pohl's story, and it was immediately clear that Ben Bova was really revitalizing the magazine.)

A couple further novellas were nominated for the Nebula but not the Hugo, interesting stories, too, though they wouldn't have been my winner:

Son of the Morning, by Phyllis Gotlieb
With the Bentfin Boomer Boys on Little Old New Alabama, by Richard A. Lupoff

The Lupoff story, along with the Le Guin and a couple further stories on the ballots this year, was from Harlan Ellison's *Again, Dangerous Visions*.

One other fine novella was Frederik Pohl's *The Merchants of Venus* (his first Heechee story).

19. RICH HORTON

Novelettes:

As I said, I think "Goat Song" was a decent choice for the Best Novelette award. But there were at least two better choices, neither of which got nominated. These are Keith Roberts's chilling and powerful "Nazis win" alternate history story, "Weihnachtsabend"; and Gary Jennings's incredibly funny "Sooner or Later or Never Never."

The Hugo nomination list is pretty good, with a strong Tiptree story and a very good Gardner Dozois story. I'd also mention, from the Nebula nominations, a really nice story from another Golden Age writer making a return to the field, Alfred Bester: "The Animal Fair."

A couple other novelettes worth a mention—another Tiptree, a personal favorite of mine, though in all honesty perhaps not quite her best work, "Forever to a Hudson Bay Blanket"; and Robert Silverberg's "{Now + n, Now − n}."

Now on to Short Story. I am almost completely in agreement with Gardner in this category. Neither the Pohl/Kornbluth nor the Lafferty story was all that great a winner. (Though they are okay stories.) "When It Changed" is undoubtedly profoundly influential, but as a story, it falls well behind Gardner's choice, perhaps my favorite Joanna Russ story ever (other choice: "The Second Inquisition")—"Nobody's Home." A complete masterpiece. A great, great story. As Gardner notes, it is in some ways almost Eganesque—yet it is also astonishingly moving.

But there remains the Tiptree question. What a truly amazing year Tiptree had. The two novelettes already mentioned ("Painwise" and "Forever to a Hudson Bay Blanket"). And look at these short stories:

"And I Awoke and Found Me Here on the Cold Hill's Side"
"And I Have Come Upon This Place by Lost Ways"
"Filomena & Greg & Rikki-Tikki & Barlow & the Alien" (aka "All the Kinds of Yes")
"The Man Who Walked Home"
"On the Last Afternoon"

All of those are amazing stories. "And I Awoke" is just brilliant. But they weren't even Tiptree's best, in my opinion. I thought the best short story of 1972 was another *Again, Dangerous Visions* story—Tiptree's "The Milk of Paradise." Talk about totally blowing me away! That's my choice for the 1972 Hugo—though I will say that if you pick "Nobody's Home," I'm not really arguing.

A couple further stories worth a mention:

"Alien Stones," by Gene Wolfe
"Lamia Mutable," by M. John Harrison
"Zirn Left Unguarded, the Jenghik Palace in Flames, Jon Westerly Dead," by Robert Sheckley (best title ever!)

One might also note that 1972 saw the publication of famed film critic Roger Ebert's only two SF stories (that I know of), which appeared in *Amazing* and *Fantastic:* "After the Last Mass" and "In Dying Venice." Neither Hugo-worthy, mind you.

20. GARDNER DOZOIS

I'd forgotten about *The Merchants of Venus*. I might even have given it the Hugo over *The Gold at the Starbow's End*, although nothing beats *The Fifth Head of Cerberus* in my opinion. (I prefer the novella to the novel, which is why I usually think of it as novella instead of part of a novel.) Those two Pohl stories represent the first stirrings of the New Pohl, as he revitalized his writing career.

And, yes, Bova did a startlingly effective job of revitalizing a moribund *Analog*, bringing in new blood such as Haldeman, Pohl, Niven, and Zelazny, and that's why he won the Hugo that year, and for a couple of years thereafter, if memory serves.

21. GARDNER DOZOIS

Yes, Keith Roberts's "Weihnachtsabend" certainly deserved a place on the list, and I think I may have given it the Hugo over "Goat Song."

I've never been crazy enough about "The Milk of Paradise" to give it the award over "Nobody's Home"—the clear winner, in my opinion—but "The Man Who Walked Home" is also a classic, and has been reprinted many times since. Yes, this was in some ways the high point of Tiptree's career, and her output that year was amazing.

Thanks for the kind words about "A Kingdom by the Sea," Rich, but it's even more completely forgotten than the other novelettes in the category.

24. GARDNER DOZOIS

In some circles, Russ may well have been the most loathed figure in SF in the day, and certainly the most controversial, at the forefront of both the War of the New Wave and the Feminist Revolution, not only as writer but also as one of the field's leading critics—although she's been out of the field for so long that probably most readers don't remember that.

25. RICH HORTON

I forgot two novelettes that I really wanted to mention, both probably deserving a spot on my fictional "short list":

Thomas Disch's "Things Lost" (also from *Again, Dangerous Visions*); and Edgar Pangborn's "Tiger Boy."

And one short story, one of my favorite Harlan Ellison stories, "On the Downhill Side." (First Ellison story I read.)

26. JO

Gardner: I can't believe you think so little of "Goat Song"! It's one of my favorite Anderson shorts. Who else would write Orpheus and Eurydice science fiction? I have always—well, for the last twenty-odd years that I've been reading your "Best Of" collections—thought that you had if not impeccable taste in SF short stories, then tastes that were remarkably congruent with mine. So I really am taken aback.

48. RICH HORTON

One book from the mainstream recently popped into my mind. I believe it's from 1972. And it's a book Jo introduced to me (by mentioning it on rec.arts.sf.written many years ago). This is Sumner Locke Elliott's *The Man Who Got Away*. It's about a man who disappears one day, and ends up revisiting his entire life in reverse, until he gets to his childhood and we see why he turned out the way he did (which is to say, not so good). It's only borderline SF, in that the fantastical device, the backward time traveling, is fundamentally a device to tell the story—although it is in a sense "real" because the main character really does disappear in order to travel in time.

GREAT ALIENS, RUBBER HUMANS: ISAAC ASIMOV'S *THE GODS THEMSELVES*

I reread *The Gods Themselves* because all I could remember about it was three-gendered aliens, which didn't really seem fair. The part of the book I remembered is the middle. It does indeed have three-gendered aliens who feed on energy. Their genders are left, right, and mid—or parental, logical, and emotional. Their sex is very weird, but it's described in detail—it's as if Asimov read that Tenn story about alien amoeba porn and thought, "I could write that!"

Asimov didn't often do aliens, but he does them very well here. It's almost Tiptree-esque, and when I say that, I am thinking of "Love Is the Plan the Plan Is Death." They feel alien and they feel like people and they have odd, weird life cycles. I could have lived without the emotional one being "she" but since the parental one is "he" and making up pronouns gets clunky fast, I guess it's reasonable. This really is a good novella about three-gendered aquatic aliens.

It's a pity it's buried in the rest of the book, which turns out to be deeply disappointing. Everybody who complained about the physics in *Anathem*? I hope you complained just as loudly about the physics in *The Gods Themselves*, because it's wrong in exactly the same ways and much less entertainingly. I checked this with two actual scientist-type people, because Asimov was a chemist and a hard science fiction writer and I didn't want to trust the evidence of my own lying eyes, but here we have alternate universes with different physics in contact with each other and with different atoms and energy and messages and actual physical metals being exchanged between them, and this is really scientifically silly. Pu-187? I think not. But you know if I'm complaining about the science, that means there's something else wrong, because if I like a book, I'm prepared to overlook the most ridiculous scientific errors.

What's wrong here is that the human parts are boring. The first part is about squabbling scientists and the discovery of the pump shuffling energy between universes. This is frankly dull, and its one redeeming feature is that it's fairly short. The third part is set on the moon, and it's somewhat more interesting than the first part, but it has a kind of deus ex machina solution to the problem, which makes it all seem pointless. (I also thought it had been visited by the sexism fairy.)

I do like a lot of Asimov, but this is far from being his best work. However, an awful lot of people must have loved it in 1973. I've tried to see what's good in it—but, really, it's just the aliens. Maybe the aliens were enough to carry the whole book for some readers? They're the only memorable part. And they're still worth reading—that section grabbed me. I kept reading the rest in the hope that we might see them again before the end, and was disappointed.

DYING INSIDE, BY ROBERT SILVERBERG

I was very excited when I heard that Tor was reprinting *Dying Inside*. It's one of those classics of the genre that shows how amazing SF can be at its best, how it can do everything mainstream books do with good writing and depth of character and do something extra besides. It's been out of print for far too long. Science fiction readers have been born and grown up and become knowledgeable about the genre and never had the chance to read it. There's not much that I think ought to be canonical, that everyone ought to read, but this was one of my core introductory texts to how brilliant SF can be, and the kind of book I want to share with everyone. My old 1970s edition (with a cheesy wannabe-Magritte cover of a sunset inside a coffin) has been lent to more people than I can readily count. And now it's in print again. . . .

I was excited . . . but the cover looks kind of drab, and also kind of mainstream. Maybe it'll encourage lots of mainstream readers to read it, especially with quotes from Chabon and Lethem, but I hope it doesn't put off science fiction readers. This is not a boring book, people! It's a serious book, no argument there, and definitely a classic, but it's also the kind of book that makes your head explode because it's so amazing. It isn't in any way a YA book, but I loved it to pieces when I was fourteen.

The extra thing *Dying Inside* does is telepathy—not gosh-wow-wonderful telepathy, but telepathy as burden. It's as if Silverberg read one too many Campbellian superman stories about telepathy and asked himself what it would really be like to be able to see into other people's minds.

David Selig is a New York Jew. He's been telepathic since childhood. He's mostly hated it. He's forty-one, and the gift, or curse, is going away, and he hates that too. The book was published in 1972 and is set in 1976, and it's only now that I noticed 1976 was the book's near future not the historical year (I first read it in 1978) because of my inability to sufficiently distinguish science fiction and America. *Dying Inside* is written in a jaunty way, with lots of references and wordplay—several years after first reading it, I recognized various T. S. Eliot lines from it (talk about getting your culture in reverse). It's mostly present tense, first-person Selig as he experiences the world, which almost makes it omniscient at times, when he's experiencing the consciousness of others. Sections set in the past are third person and past tense. The style is Silverberg at the top of his form, playing with words, going from the present to the past, the scientific to the subjective on the bounce.

It has stood up to time fairly well. It's set in a very specific place and time, which makes it read more historically now, but that's not a problem. The only thing that did trouble me were the racial references. I think Silverberg was liberal and enlightened and ahead of his time on racial issues for 1972, but "liberal for 1972" reads weirdly in 2009 and had me looking sideways at the text a few times. It's been a long thirty-five years, and while things are still far from perfect on that front, reading this makes it quite clear how much progress there has been. I'd say the same on the gender front, but the gender stuff is easier to take anyway.

It's mostly a very serious book, but it has its hilarious moments, such as the young David reading the words from the psychiatrist's mind in a word association test. And the overall message is upbeat. I didn't realize when I was fourteen that there was a way of reading the book that made it be about aging and the death of youth while life goes on, but reading it now, that couldn't be clearer. I think that just goes to show what a masterpiece it is.

Of course, I don't have the faintest idea what I'd think if I read this now for the first time. I have loved it too long and read it too often to be able to detach myself from it sufficiently.

1974

BEST NOVEL

Winner: *Rendezvous with Rama*, by Arthur C. Clarke

Nominees:
The Man Who Folded Himself, by David Gerrold
The People of the Wind, by Poul Anderson
Protector, by Larry Niven
Time Enough for Love, by Robert A. Heinlein

The 1974 Hugos were awarded at Discon II in Washington, D.C.

The Best Novel award went to Arthur C. Clarke's *Rendezvous with Rama*. This is the first of the Big Dumb Object books, about a mysterious and huge alien object that comes into the solar system and is explored by some men from Earth. I have always felt that it was one of Clarke's weaker books. It has the poetry of space and of huge alien artifacts, and something of the puzzle of archaeology, when you're trying to make sense of something incomprehensible without enough clues. But I remember wishing it would get on with it when I read this when I was fourteen, and I was frankly bored when I reread it when I was twenty-five. It's slow, and I couldn't hazard a guess at the names of the characters even if you offered me large amounts of cash. I haven't read the sequels and I haven't reread it for a long time. It also won the Nebula and the Locus. It's in print and in the library in both languages. I think it's an acknowledged classic that everybody likes except me, so it was probably a good winner even though I don't care for it.

There are four other nominees, and I have read all of them. David Gerrold's *The Man Who Folded Himself* is a novel-length variation on the theme of Heinlein's "'—All You Zombies—'." It's not in print, it's not in the library, and it seems to be pretty well forgotten—I haven't heard anybody talk about it in a long while.

Poul Anderson's *The People of the Wind* is about a planet settled by both humans and wonderful flying aliens with a weird culture who live in complex coexistence until the Terran Empire wants to annex the planet, causing complications. It's great in a typical Poul Anderson kind of way. It's not in print and it's not in the library.

Larry Niven's *Protector* takes place in his Known Space setting. It's one of the best of the books set there—an alien Pak comes to the solar system looking for a lost colony of his own kind, and finds instead humanity, who are like the subsapient breeder Paks, but with our own intelligence. Contains a re-creation of a surrealist painting in space. It's in print, but it's not in the library.

And the last nominee is Robert A. Heinlein's *Time Enough for Love*, which is a long book of many parts about the very long life of Lazarus Long. It's sloppy and self-indulgent, it's full of embarrassing incest, it doesn't really have a plot so much as a set of meandering reminiscences in a frame that doesn't work, but bits of it are absolutely marvelous. I reread it more often than anything else on this list, and although parts of it make me wince, other parts of it bring tears to my eyes. It's late Heinlein at his most characteristic—you can't condemn it without throwing very valuable babies away with very dirty bathwater. It is in print. It is in the library in English.

So, five books by men, four US and one UK living in Sri Lanka, all previous nominees and Heinlein and Niven previous winners. One Big Dumb Object story, one personal time travel book, two books with aliens and spaceships, yay, and a far-future sprawling thing. Two of them have time travel, three of them have colonies on other planets, three of them have aliens, two of them have strong family connections driving the plot. They're a pretty solid lot, but not very exciting. What else might they have picked?

The Nebula nominees are identical except that in place of *Protector,* they have Pynchon's *Gravity's Rainbow*. (People are very strange, and SFWA is very strange even for people.)

Moving swiftly on, the John W. Campbell Memorial Award for hard SF was given jointly to the Clarke and to Robert Merle's *Malevil*, which I've not only not read, but never heard of either. The runners-up are Ian Watson's first novel *The Embedding*, and Peter Dickinson's *The Green Gene*, both of which I have read and neither of which I'd call hard SF.

Non-overlapping Locus nominees are *Trullion: Alastor 2262*, Jack Vance; *The Far Call*, Gordon R. Dickson; *To Die In Italbar* and *Today We Choose Faces*, both Roger Zelazny; *The Cloud Walker*, Edmund Cooper; *Relatives*, George Alec Effinger; *Herovit's World*, Barry N. Malzberg; *Hiero's Journey*, Sterling Lanier; and *The Doomsday Gene*, John Boyd.

The Mythopoeic Award went to Mary Stewart's *The Hollow Hills*, the second of her Merlin books. Other nominees were Susan Cooper's *The Dark Is Rising*, Sanders Anne Labenthal's *Excalibur*, Katherine Kurtz's *High Deryni*, and Poul Anderson's *Hrolf Kraki's Saga*. At last some women to counteract the rather male lean to this set of lists!

There's nothing in any of this that might plausibly have been nominated for a Hugo, or that seems to me clearly better than the five solid nominees we have.

Was there anything all of these missed?

Using ISFDB, there's Jerry Pournelle's *A Spaceship for the King;* Clifford Simak's *Cemetery World;* J. G. Ballard's *Crash;* Brian Aldiss's *Frankenstein Unbound;* Michael Coney's *Friends Come in Boxes* and *Syzygy;* Doris Piserchia's *Mister Justice;* John Brunner's *More Things in Heaven* and *The Stone That Never Came Down;* Hal Clement's *Ocean on Top;* Alan Garner's *Red Shift;* D. G. Compton's *The Continuous Katherine Mortenhoe;* and William Goldman's *The Princess Bride*. Wouldn't it have been lovely to have had Goldman on the ballot?

My general feeling looking at all this is that we had a solid representative ballot, and if it wasn't the five best books of the year, there weren't any egregious gaps either.

Other Categories

Best Novella

Winner: *The Girl Who Was Plugged In*, by James Tiptree Jr. (*New Dimensions 3*)

Nominees:
Chains of the Sea, by Gardner Dozois (*Chains of the Sea*)
Death and Designation Among the Asadi, by Michael Bishop (*If*, February 1973)
The Death of Doctor Island, by Gene Wolfe (*Universe 3*)
The White Otters of Childhood, by Michael Bishop (*F&SF*, July 1973)

Okay, the novella award was won by one of the best novellas of all time, so that's okay! The others were pretty strong stories, but I can't imagine anything but the Tiptree winning.

Best Novelette

Winner: "The Deathbird," by Harlan Ellison (*F&SF*, March 1973)

Nominees:
"The City on the Sand," by George Alec Effinger (*F&SF*, April 1973)
"He Fell into a Dark Hole," by Jerry Pournelle (*Analog*, March 1973)
"Love Is the Plan the Plan Is Death," by James Tiptree Jr. (*The Alien Condition*)
"Of Mist, and Grass, and Sand," by Vonda N. McIntyre (*Analog*, October 1973)

I'd have given that one to Tiptree as well. And I didn't know it was written the year after *The Gods Themselves*.

Best Short Story

Winner: "The Ones Who Walk Away from Omelas," by Ursula K. Le Guin (*New Dimensions 3*)

Nominees:
"Construction Shack," by Clifford D. Simak (*If,* February 1973)
"Wings," by Vonda N. McIntyre (*The Alien Condition*)
"With Morning Comes Mistfall," by George R. R. Martin (*Analog,* May 1973)

Another good decision, or one with which I entirely agree. I like the Martin, but "The Ones Who Walk Away from Omelas" is an enduring classic that people are still arguing over. Worth noting also what a good year *New Dimensions* was having.

Best Dramatic Presentation

Winner: *Sleeper*

Nominees:
Genesis II
The Six Million Dollar Man
Soylent Green
Westworld

Best Professional Editor

Winner: Ben Bova

Nominees:
Terry Carr
Edward L. Ferman
Robert Silverberg
Ted White
Donald A. Wollheim

Silverberg's nomination no doubt reflects the voters' appreciation of the excellence of the New Dimensions series

Best Professional Artist

Winner: Frank Kelly Freas

Nominees:
Vincent Di Fate
Frank Frazetta
Jack Gaughan
John Schoenherr

Best Amateur Magazine

Winner: (tie) *Algol,* edited by Andrew I. Porter
The Alien Critic, edited by Richard E. Geis

Nominees:
Locus, edited by Charles Brown and Dena Brown
Outworlds, edited by Bill Bowers and Joan Bowers

Best Fan Writer

Winner: Susan Wood

Nominees:
Laura Basta
Richard E. Geis
Jacqueline Lichtenberg
Sandra Miesel

Four women. Well, now, isn't that nice to see!

Best Fan Artist

Winner: Tim Kirk

Nominees:
Alicia Austin
Grant Canfield
Bill Rotsler
Arthur Thomson

John W. Campbell Award

Winner: (tie) Spider Robinson
Lisa Tuttle

Nominees:
Jesse Miller
Thomas F. Monteleone
Guy Snyder

Not such a good lineup as the year before. The two winners have gone on to become major writers, so they were definitely the right choices. Monteleone has become a major horror writer, but I'm not aware of anything significant from Snyder or Miller.

Comments on 1974

12. Bruce A.

Back when *Time Enough for Love* first came out, I made the observation that it was less than the sum of its parts. If the book had been broken up and various sections published independently, as short story, novella, novelette, Heinlein might have managed to pull off a clean sweep of the Hugos. As a novel, it didn't work well.

Hmm, several people mention the squicky incest in *TEFL*, but not the similar element in *The Man Who Folded Himself*, where the time-traveling protagonist has sex with himself at multiple points in the convoluted timeline. (Giving rise to the book's nickname as *The Man Who Fondled Himself*.)

13. RICH HORTON

The novella nomination list is quite remarkable. I have to confess that *The Girl Who Was Plugged In* impresses me, but I don't love it. (And don't get me wrong, I truly love a lot of Tiptree.) I can't argue with its award, but my vote back then would surely have gone to *Death and Designation Among the Asadi*, which was mind-blowing stuff for me back then. I'm not sure it entirely holds up, however.

Similarly to the Tiptree, the Nebula winner for novella, *The Death of Doctor Island*, is a great story by one of my most favorite writers ever that I still don't quite love. It's hard to know why. The Nebula short list, just as in novel, has four stories the same as for the Hugo, with a new one being a good Jack Dann story, *Junction*.

Oddly, the reason the Tiptree didn't make the Nebula short list is that it was listed as a novelette for those awards (and it did make that short list). A quick and dirty word count suggests that it's about sixteen thousand words, technically a novelette, but by current rules eligible for the Hugo nomination in either category depending on where the nominations fell. (As it's within 10 percent of the boundary.) For that matter, I don't know what the Hugo rules, or boundaries, were back in 1974.

Other potential novella nominees:

Two stories from a very good "three novella" anthology edited by Terry Carr, *An Exaltation of Stars:* "'Kjwalll'kje'k'koothai'lll'kje'k," by Roger Zelazny; "The Feast of St. Dionysius," by Robert Silverberg. (The third story from that book is a very good long novelette, "My Brother Leopold," by Edgar Pangborn.)

Also:

Brothers, by Gordon R. Dickson
In the Problem Pit, by Frederik Pohl

Novelettes:

I rather liked "The Deathbird" at the time, and I don't think it's a bad Hugo Award. That said, I definitely would have given the Hugo to "Love Is the Plan the Plan Is Death," a far more powerful and different story.

But speaking of Tiptree, she published a much more important story historically in 1973, that it now seems odd wasn't on award ballots— "The Women Men Don't See." I personally prefer "Love Is the Plan the Plan Is Death," but an award for either of them wouldn't have gone amiss. ("The Woman Men Don't See" appeared in the December *F&SF*, which may account for its absence from in particular the Nebula ballot.)

The novelette Nebula went to Vonda McIntyre's "Of Mist, and Grass, and Sand," a nice story (which became her novel *Dreamsnake*), but no patch on the Tiptree stories, that's for sure. The other potential novelette nominees are a couple of Edgar Pangborn pieces, "My Brother Leopold" and "The Freshman Angle."

In short story, again a Tiptree story was in a shorter category for the Nebulas, and "Love Is the Plan the Plan Is Death" won. I like it better than Le Guin's "Omelas," but both stories are excellent and it's nice they both won awards. (For what it's worth, my quick and dirty estimate of "Love Is the Plan the Plan Is Death's" word count is 7,500, exactly on the borderline between short story and novelette.)

Le Guin had two more short stories I like, "The Field of Vision" and "Imaginary Countries." The latter is a story I love, actually, though only marginally SF—it's the final story in *Orsinian Tales*. (It appeared in 1973 in *The Harvard Advocate*. I suspect most SF readers didn't see it until the book came out a few years later.)

My other favorite 1973 short story is Gene Wolfe's "La Befana." Other enjoyable stories from that year include Ed Bryant's "The Legend of Cougar Lou Landis," Damon Knight's "Down There," Terry Carr's "They Live on Levels," P. J. Plauger's "Epicycle," R. A. Lafferty's "The World as Will and Wallpaper," and Alfred Bester's "Something Up There Likes Me."

Anyway, I think the Hugo/Nebula split between the Le Guin and Tiptree stories is pretty just, though I wouldn't have complained if "La

Befana" got an award too. But Wolfe did finally get his Nebula this year. . . .

14. Rich Horton

And I forgot to mention how much fun Gene Wolfe's "How I Lost the Second World War and Helped Turn Back the German Invasion" is. I think it was Wolfe's first story in *Analog*. (Bova again!) It's not as serious as many of Wolfe's stories, but it is tremendous fun.

22. Gardner Dozois

A weak year for novels. I kind of have a sneaking fondness for *Rendezvous with Rama*, although all the flaws that have been pointed out in it are valid—still, I don't see anything else here that is obviously and unambiguously stronger, so I'd probably let the win ride. Parts of *Time Enough for Love* were good, particularly the stuff on the frontier planet, and parts of it were Really Awful; on balance, it's probably one of the most self-indulgent SF novels ever written, and badly needed an editor to cut at least a third of it away, perhaps more. David is right that the incest theme is integral to the book—EVERYONE here wants to fuck Lazurus Long and have his babies, even the computer, who has itself put into a clone body for just this purpose. It's amusing to me that here on the downslope of the War of the New Wave (which pretty much faded away over the next few years, the combatants having battered themselves into exhaustion), the icon of the Old Guard, Robert A. Heinlein himself, published a book that was MUCH DIRTIER, and much kinkier, than anything the loathed New Wavers had produced— Spinrad's *Bug Jack Barron* was held up at the time as the dirtiest and most morally objectionable SF book ever written, a book so loathsome that it had irreversibly polluted SF's precious bodily fluids all by itself, and yet, although it's got plenty of four-letter words in it, all the sex portrayed is conventional one-man-on-one-woman heterosexuality, and NOBODY SLEEPS WITH HIS MOTHER—or has her give him a lock of her pubic hair as a love token, either.

I'm in disagreement with almost all the shorter fiction winners. I liked *The Girl Who Was Plugged In*, but it wasn't the best Tiptree published that year; I would have given the award to Gene Wolfe's *The*

Death of Doctor Island—not as strong as *The Fifth Head of Cerberus*, but still stronger than most everything else published in that category that year. Never much liked "The Deathbird," and the rest of the stories in that category, including the other Tiptree, strike me as somewhat weak. The award in novelette should have gone to a story that wasn't even on the ballot, Tiptree's "The Women Men Don't See." Short story is the weakest category. Although it's now regarded as a classic, I was never all that fond of Le Guin's "Omelas." Of the stories on the ballot, I guess I'd have given it to Martin, although he would later write much stronger stories. (I was sitting next to George at the table when the award was announced, by the way, after the second most boring Toastmaster gig I've ever had to suffer through.) Guess I would have been okay with "La Befana," out of the stories mentioned, although it wasn't as strong as "The Death of Doctor Island."

Menopause, Aliens, and Fun: Larry Niven's *Protector*

Protector is like a type example of the benefits of writing a future history. It's set in Niven's Known Space universe, early in it, before humanity has FTL travel or contact with aliens. It begins with the point of view of a seeming alien, a Pak Protector in a spaceship headed for Earth and a first contact. We learn all about what it means to be a Pak and a Protector, and they really are a fascinating invention. Then the Pak get to the solar system, and it's a fully developed and complex solar system, full of intricate details that Niven thought up for other stories and can therefore just throw in here to provide texture—Belters, organlegging, and so on.

Niven later wrote about the disadvantages of having a future history when it comes to painting yourself into corners because you have too much stuff, but he wasn't at that point with *Protector*. Here it has everything going for it, he can take his new nifty science-fictional idea, the Pak, and bring them to a future solar system that has enough worked-out complexity to be interesting. This has always been one of my favorite early Nivens, and I enjoyed rereading it now almost as much as I did when I was twelve.

Is it just me, or are Niven's best characters always aliens? When I think about his characters, it's Speaker-to-Animals and Nessus I like from *Ringworld,* and it's Phssthpok I like here. All his human characters blur together—they're all competent men or perky girls, but his aliens really stand out. Maybe it's because he has to make an effort to get into their mind-set?

In any case, Phssthpok is great. He's a Protector, the supposed third stage of humanity. On the Pak planet, this happens to everyone—they get to a certain age and go through another form of puberty. Niven has taken the visible signs of aging and made them into a failed transformation—what a terrific idea. After transformation, they are entirely focused on protecting their descendants. Niven's finding an interestingly odd answer to the question of why we live on after we can no longer breed—animals pretty much don't. It's also an interesting take on the Eden myth, the tree of life is the root people need to become Protectors.

But the Pak aren't sentient before they become Protectors, and humans, of course, are, and so the other terrific character is the Brennan monster—a human transformed into a Protector, who gets the enhanced strength and intelligence and the drive to protect. In his case, what he wants to protect is humanity from the Pak, who he is sure are coming.

Of course, the biology is a little old-fashioned. In 1973, it was more reasonable to suggest that *Homo habilis* might have come from another planet. Niven first played with the idea of the Pak in a short work called "The Adults" in 1967. Since then, we have learned a lot more about how much genetic code we share with the rest of this planet, but he can't be blamed for not predicting that. Also, clearly on the Pak homeland this is a change that happens to everyone, but absolutely all the Protectors we see are male, to the point that I hadn't considered the possibility of a female Protector until I read *Ringworld Engineers,* even though the transformation really is more analogous to menopause than anything else.

Women in this book are just sexy scenery, but they are very ignorable. And Niven pays lip service at least to the idea of gender equality in the

Belt, and it was 1973, just at the beginning of second-wave feminism, so I'm giving him points for trying.

There's a bouncy enthusiasm about early Niven that's charming to read but very hard to pin down. This is a story of a first contact and Earth as a lost alien colony and an alien war, but what's great about it is how much fun it is to read, how the details dovetail just so, how the shiny ideas get thrown at you just precisely as fast as you can catch them and toss them back before you get hit with another one. It's not a very long book—I tore through it in an afternoon—but there's just precisely enough of it. It's like a well-simmered dish where the ingredients complement each other to make something delicious if not subtle, so you can't stop until you've licked the plate.

1975

Best Novel

Winner: *The Dispossessed*, by Ursula K. Le Guin

Nominees:
Fire Time, by Poul Anderson
Flow My Tears, the Policeman Said, by Philip K. Dick
Inverted World, by Christopher Priest
The Mote in God's Eye, by Larry Niven and Jerry Pournelle

The 1975 Hugo Awards were given at Aussiecon I, in Melbourne, the first time the Worldcon was in the Southern Hemisphere. The Best Novel award was won by Ursula Le Guin's *The Dispossessed*, a book that's an acknowledged and beloved classic, one of the best books science fiction has ever produced. Le Guin's subtitle is *An Ambiguous Utopia*. It's the story of Shevek, a brilliant physicist discovering a new principle of physics, which will make possible instantaneous communication, and it's the story of two worlds, each other's moon, one of them anarchist and one of them capitalist. It also won the Nebula and the Locus. It's in print and in the library in English and French.

There are four other nominees, of which I have read three. I know I've read Poul Anderson's *Fire Time*, but I can't remember it well. It's about a war on an alien planet with a weird orbit. I don't think it's in print, but it's in the library in English.

I have not read and do not intend to read Philip K. Dick's *Flow My Tears, the Policeman Said*, but I'm sure it's a worthy nominee that's not to my taste and an excellent example of Dick's work. I'm astonished to see that it won the Campbell Memorial Award for hard SF, as I'd never have guessed that Dick had written something eligible. Wow. It's in print, and it's in the library in French only.

Christopher Priest's *Inverted World* is really weird. It's about a boy growing up in a city that has to keep moving because time and space are so weird and it has to keep at one point in a curve—it's on rails. Only it turns out that they only think this, and actually they're in Africa. Or something. Great special effects, but I didn't understand the end. I'm not even sure if it's SF, so it surprises me that this was a Hugo nominee. It won the BSFA Award. It's in print. And, for a change, it's in the library in French and Italian.

Larry Niven and Jerry Pournelle's *The Mote in God's Eye* is a fun book about aliens, a first contact with a species limited to their own solar system who experience periodic collapses in civilization due to overpopulation. They're great aliens, and while the humans are very much token characters to take you through the adventure, that's a plus for a book like this. It's in print, and it's in the library in English and French, it has less-good sequels, and it's still part of the conversation of science fiction.

So, one woman and five men, four American and one English, an excellent winner, and undoubtedly an interesting set of nominees. Le Guin and Niven are previous winners, Anderson is a previous nominee, Pournelle and Priest are newcomers. We have one ambiguous utopia, one speculative fiction, two slightly surreal books, and one straight-up space opera with alien overpopulation.

What else could they have chosen?

Other Nebula nominees were Thomas M. Disch's masterpiece *334*, which should also have been on the Hugo ballot, and T. J. Bass's *The Godwhale*, which I remember as enjoyable biological SF.

Other Locus nominees were D. G. Compton's *The Unsleeping Eye* aka *The Continuous Katherine Mortenhoe*, which would have been a very good nominee; James White's *The Dream Millennium*; Richard Cowper's *The Twilight of Briareus*—I remember that, it's a cozy catastrophe with aliens! Edgar Pangborn's *The Company of Glory;* Jack Vance's *The*

Domains of Koryphon; Thomas Burnett Swann's *How Are the Mighty Fallen;* John Brunner's *Total Eclipse;* Barry Malzberg's *The Destruction of the Temple;* Doris Piserchia's *Star Rider;* Evangeline Walton's *Prince of Annwn;* Suzy McGee Charnas's *Walk to the End of the World,* which I think would have made a great addition to the Hugo ballot; and Alan Dean Foster's *Icerigger.*

The first World Fantasy Award was given in 1975 to Patricia McKillip's *The Forgotten Beasts of Eld.* This was the last of the major awards to be established. It's a partly juried award. Members of the World Fantasy Convention can nominate books, but the short list and the winner are chosen by a jury made up of SF professionals, and participants vary year by year. The trophy is a controversial and very ugly bust of H. P. Lovecraft.*

Other nominees were Poul Anderson's *A Midsummer Tempest* and H. Warner Munn's *Merlin's Ring.* The Anderson won the Mythopoeic Award; the only other nominee not previously mentioned was *Watership Down.*

With all of this, can there possibly be anything significant that none of the awards noticed?

There's Brian Aldiss's *Barefoot in the Head;* Stephen King's *Carrie;* William Sleator's *House of Stairs;* and Lloyd Biggle Jr.'s *Monument.* On the whole, I think we could have had a better five nominees from these options, but the five we have are pretty good and the winner is wonderful.

OTHER CATEGORIES

BEST NOVELLA

Winner: *A Song for Lya,* by George R. R. Martin (*Analog,* June 1974)

---

*Replaced in 2016 by a delightful tree.

Nominees:

Assault on a City, by Jack Vance (*Universe 4*)

Born with the Dead, by Robert Silverberg (*F&SF,* April 1974)

Riding the Torch, by Norman Spinrad (*Threads of Time*)

Strangers, by Gardner Dozois (*New Dimensions IV*)

I like *A Song for Lya,* but I think I'd have voted for *Strangers. Born with the Dead* is also excellent.

BEST NOVELETTE

Winner: "Adrift Just Off the Islets of Langerhans: Latitude 38° 54′ N, Longitude 77° 00′ 13″ W," by Harlan Ellison (*F&SF,* October 1974)

Nominees:

"After the Dreamtime," by Richard Lupoff (*New Dimensions IV*)

"A Brother to Dragons, a Companion of Owls," by Kate Wilhelm (*Orbit 14*)

"Extreme Prejudice," by Jerry Pournelle (*Analog,* July 1974)

"Midnight by the Morphy Watch," by Fritz Leiber (*If,* August 1974)

"Nix Olympica," by William Walling (*Analog,* December 1974)

"—That Thou Art Mindful of Him!," by Isaac Asimov (*F&SF,* May 1974)

Good winner from a good field.

BEST SHORT STORY

Winner: "The Hole Man," by Larry Niven (*Analog,* January 1974)

Nominees:

"Cathadonian Odyssey," by Michael Bishop (*F&SF,* September 1974)

"The Day Before the Revolution," by Ursula K. Le Guin (*Galaxy,* August 1974)

"The Four-Hour Fugue," by Alfred Bester (*Analog,* June 1974)

"Schwartz Between the Galaxies," by Robert Silverberg (*Stellar 1*)

I'd have definitely voted for Le Guin here; I love that story. But any of them would have been good winners—except I don't remember the Bishop.

Best Dramatic Presentation

Winner: *Young Frankenstein*

Nominees:
Flesh Gordon
Phantom of the Paradise
The Questor Tapes
Zardoz

Best Professional Editor

Winner: Ben Bova

Nominees:
Jim Baen
Terry Carr
Edward L. Ferman
Robert Silverberg
Ted White

Best Professional Artist

Winner: Frank Kelly Freas

Nominees:
Steve Fabian
Tim Kirk
John Schoenherr
Rick Sternbach

Best Amateur Magazine

Winner: *The Alien Critic*, edited by Richard E. Geis

Nominees:
Algol, edited by Andrew I. Porter
Locus, edited by Charles Brown and Dena Brown
Outworlds, edited by Bill Bowers and Joan Bowers
SF Commentary, edited by Bruce Gillespie
Starling, edited by Hank and Lesleigh Luttrell

Best Fan Writer

Winner: Richard E. Geis

Nominees:
John Bangsund
Sandra Miesel
Don C. Thompson
Susan Wood

Geis was having a good year!

Best Fan Artist

Winner: Bill Rotsler

Nominees:
George Barr
Grant Canfield
Jim Shull

John W. Campbell Award

Winner: P. J. Plauger

Nominees:
Alan Brennert
Suzy McKee Charnas
Felix C. Gotschalk
Brenda Pearce
John Varley

Oh dear. Plauger went on to write nonfiction books about computers. Suzy McKee Charnas and John Varley have gone on to be major writers. Brennert has had a respectable career, winning a Nebula for a short story. I'm not familiar with Gotschalk or Pearce. I have to say that taken as a list of writers at the beginning of careers, this doesn't hold up as well as some years.

COMMENTS ON 1975

1. RICH HORTON

A couple of quick comments on the Campbell Award for new writers. Felix C. Gotschalk had a brief but noticeable career in the seventies, mostly writing some very weird stories about a strange society in the middling near future. One novel, one of the curious second series of Ace Specials: *Growing Up in Tier 3000* (1975). Then he mostly disappeared. He died in 2002, age seventy-three, so his first story, from 1974, appeared when he was forty-five.

I don't remember Brenda Pearce well at all. Her nomination was due to one story, in the April 1974 *Analog*. She published only three stories and one 1977 novel.

One reason Alan Brennert, a first-rate writer, hasn't published more in the field is that he went on to do television work (presumably for lots of money). But I think what he has done is very fine.

Clearly Charnas is a major writer, and I think based on her work prior to the award, she was the most deserving to win. That said, Varley's career is the most significant eventually. And P. J. Plauger, the actual winner, had done some fine work, and went on to do some more nice stuff, but not a lot, because of his main career in computer science.

I personally might have nominated Cynthia Bunn, whose first two (of only five or so total) stories appeared in 1974, of which one was outstanding—more about that when I write about the short fiction. Also Arsen Darnay, who did some stuff I remember with affection in *Galaxy,* starting in 1974.

11. RICH HORTON

A few more novels worth a look:

Stanislaw Lem's *The Cyberiad* (Granted, perhaps it's better considered as a story collection.)

Jean Mark Gawron's *An Apology for Rain,* his first novel—much much better than his execrable second novel, *Algorithm*—though I still wouldn't really give it a Hugo nomination. Also the occasion for Theodore Sturgeon (in his *Galaxy* review) to do the opposite of what Silverberg famously did with Tiptree: not having seen a picture of the (dare I say?) ineluctably masculine Gawron, Sturgeon assumed he was in fact a she, and noted characteristics in the novel that, he said, could only have come from a woman writer.

Michael Shea's Vancean *A Quest for Simbilis*

From the mainstream, John Hersey's *My Petition for More Space*

Also from the mainstream, and a very highly praised novel that I have second or third on my TBR pile: Edward Whittemore's *Quin's Shanghai Circus*

Barrington Bayley's *Soul of the Robot*

And perhaps my personal choice as novel I'd most like to have seen nominated that wasn't: M. John Harrison's *The Centauri Device*

12. RICH HORTON

This is a particularly important year for me personally, as it was the first year I saw (and bought) a science fiction magazine. Indeed, that first magazine was the August 1974 *Analog,* cover by John Schoenherr for Gordon Dickson's "Enter a Pilgrim." The next day, I bought the August issues of *Galaxy* and *F&SF.* A watershed day, indeed. The novella short list is excellent, and it also really includes almost all the plausible nominees. I have no huge problem with the award going to *A Song for Lya,* though I think right now I'd choose *Strangers* (and probably would have back then). Silverberg's *Born with the Dead,* which won the Nebula, is also outstanding, and a worthy winner. (Indeed, I'd place it with *Strangers* at the top of the list, with the Martin just behind.) The Vance novella, *Assault on a City,* is one of his last short pieces, and quite enjoyable.

The Nebula short list includes the Silverberg and the Martin and one other story, Michael Bishop's *On the Street of the Serpents or, The Assassination of Chairman Mao, as Effected by the Author in Seville, Spain, in the Spring of 1992, a Year of No Certain Historicity.*

Four other novellas seem worth a mention: Norman Spinrad's *Riding the Torch,* Joan D. Vinge's *Tin Soldier,* Kate Wilhelm's *Where Late the Sweet Birds Sang,* and Charles Harness's first story in years, *The Araqnid Window.*

Finally, there is one story that I think is a novella—at about nineteen thousand words, by my estimate—but which is listed as a novelette in the ISFDB and the Locus Awards, and which is anyway one of the great, and unfairly neglected, 1974 stories: "Forlesen," by Gene Wolfe. In whichever category you put it, it should have been a major award contender and perhaps won.

There is a huge list of outstanding novelettes. The Ellison story is pretty solid, but of that list of nominees, my clear-cut choice for the best is one of my favorite Fritz Leiber stories, "Midnight by the Morphy Watch." I also remember really enjoying Pournelle's "Extreme Prejudice"—I eventually went off Pournelle, but he was a very entertaining writer early in his career.

The Nebula went to Gordon Eklund and Gregory Benford's "If the Stars Are Gods," a nice story but not one I'd give the award to in retrospect. Another nominee was Tom Reamy's exceptional horror story "Twilla," his first professional publication (though he was already a very well-known fan).

Other strong novelettes, in my mind:

"And Keep Us from Our Castles," by Cynthia Bunn
"A Full Member of the Club," by Bob Shaw

"Her Smoke Rose Up Forever," by James Tiptree Jr.

"The Night Wind," by Edgar Pangborn

"The Rubber Bend," an immensely entertaining Holmesian story by Gene Wolfe

"If This Is Winnetka, You Must be Judy," by F. M. Busby

"The Seventeen Virgins," a latish Cugel story by Jack Vance

"The Pre-Persons," by Philip K. Dick

"Picnic on Nearside," by John Varley, his first good story, in that first issue of *F&SF* I bought (August 1974) (more or less simultaneously, *Vertex* published "Scoreboard," an awful Varley story that to my knowledge has not been reprinted)

The Cynthia Bunn story, "And Keep Us from Our Castles," wowed me when I first read it, in that very same August 1974 *Analog* that I bought in wonder from the newsstand at Alton Drugs in Naperville, Illinois. I still think it's a strong story—about a harsh future method of punishment. Bunn, later known as Cynthia Morgan (I'm not sure if "Bunn" is a pseudonym or if her marital status changed) only ended up publishing about five stories, but I think she was a talent.

In retrospect, I'd suggest that Shaw and Tiptree certainly could have been on the short lists, maybe Pangborn too, and that the award should have gone to either Leiber or Tiptree, unless we call "Forlesen" a novelette—in which case, it should have won.

As for short story, my personal favorite was "Cathadonian Odyssey," by Michael Bishop, which was in the second issue of *F&SF* I bought, and which knocked me flat on reading. The Niven story is certainly enjoyable, but I prefer the Bishop, and also Silverberg's amazingly moving "Schwartz Between the Galaxies," which was in a sense his farewell to the field. I have to say I've never really liked Le Guin's "The Day Before the Revolution" all that much (even though it was in the first issue of *Galaxy* I read!)—it's beautifully written, but seems too static for me. I like another 1974 Le Guin story, "'The Author of the Acacia Seeds,' and Other Extracts from the *Journal of the Association Therolinguistics*," rather better.

But far and away, my favorite Le Guin story from 1974—and in my opinion, clearly the best short story of 1974 (though I'd have guessed it was a novelette!)—is "The Stars Below," one of my three or four favorite Le Guin stories ever. I'll be honest—I don't get why "The Day Before the Revolution" would be on short lists ahead of "The Stars Below." But it appeared on the *Locus* list of Best Short Stories, and it's listed in the ISFDB as a short story, so I'll go with that. (I checked my copy of *The Wind's Twelve Quarters*, and my best estimate of the length is 7,600 words, which is close enough to the border for me to accept the "short story" categorization.)

Other good short stories:

Larry Niven's "A Kind of Murder" and "Night on Mispec Moor"
Bob Shaw's "A Little Night Flying"
Raccoona Sheldon's "Angel Fix" (Alice Sheldon had just revealed that she was the person behind "James Tiptree Jr.," and one response to that was to initiate a new pseudonym, "Raccoona Sheldon.")
Alan Brennert's "Touchplate"
Two decent stories by Craig Strete, who became controversial later when accused of plagiarism (though as best I can determine, that accusation was perhaps overblown); that said, these stories weren't bad: "Time Deer" and "The Bleeding Man"
Roger Zelazny's "The Engine at Heartspring's Center"
Eleanor Arnason's "The Warlord of Saturn's Moons"

At any rate, in final sum, and accepting the ISFDB story categories, I come up with an "ideal" Rich Horton list of 1974 short fiction awards as follows:

Novella: *Strangers* by Gardner Dozois (*Born with the Dead* just behind)
Novelette: "Forlesen" by Gene Wolfe ("Midnight by the Morphy Watch" and "Her Smoke Rose Up Forever" just behind)
Short Story: "The Stars Below" by Ursula K. Le Guin ("Cathadonian Odyssey" and "Schwartz Between the Galaxies" just behind)

I think 1974 was an exceptional year, at longer and shorter lengths.

23. Gardner Dozois

In novella, the Martin is more entertaining and accessible, the Silverberg more artistically ambitious and intellectually serious, although a bit aloof. On balance, I give it to Silverberg by a whisker. A strong year for novellas, if I do say so myself.

I like the rest of Rich's list better than any of the actual winners, and even most of the finalists. Probably would have given it to *Her Smoke Rose Up Forever*, although *The Day Before the Revolution* was strong too, as was "Midnight by the Morphy Watch." In novelette, a hard choice between Le Guin's "The Stars Below" and one of Gene Wolfe's strangest stories (which is really saying something), "Forlesen." Since I workshopped "Forlesen" at a Milford Conference (the same one where "The Fifth Head of Cerberus" was in the workshop another day), I'll give it to it by a whisker.

"The Night Wind" and "The Seventeen Virgins" are good, but not in the same class. "The Pre-Persons" was a controversial work at the time. Never liked Craig Strete's work.

As I recall, "Raccoona Sheldon" started publishing stories BEFORE "Tiptree's" identity was revealed, because I can remember critics talking about how strongly and evidently she had been influenced by Tiptree, to the point of doing an "imitation" of "him." Raccoona was her attempt to create a female persona for herself, since everyone thought that she was a man. She later told me that she was thinking of creating another pseudonym for herself, Slyvester Mule, "Slyvester" because she loved trees and "Mule" because she too was sterile, but she never did it.

As Rich said, Alan Brennert has subsequently done a lot of television work, and a few print stories, including one "The Third Sex," that I ran in one of my Year's Bests. Felix Gotschalk was a quirky presence in the field for a number of years before fading away; I wasn't even aware that he'd died.

29. Gardner Dozois

"The Warlord of Saturn's Moons" was Eleanor Arnason's first story. "The Engine at Heartspring's Center" is good Zelazny, although not absolutely first-rate. And, yes, "Picnic on Nearside" was the first Varley story most of us noticed, at a time when what he was doing was unlike what anybody else in the field was doing.

CLEAR-SIGHTED UTOPIA: URSULA K. LE GUIN'S *THE DISPOSSESSED*

Ursula K. Le Guin's *The Dispossessed* was the first grown-up science fiction novel I ever read. I was twelve, and I had read everything in the children's section of the library. I figured I wouldn't get into too much trouble if I borrowed books from the adult section that were written by people who had also written children's books, so out I went with *The Dispossessed* and Peter Dickinson's *King and Joker*. I took them to the country park, where I sat on a stone in the middle of the river, where Ursula Le Guin proceeded to blow me away to the point where I almost missed dinner.

Rereading it now, it's not so new, but it's still that good.

The Dispossessed has the subtitle *An Ambiguous Utopia,* and I think its strength lies in Le Guin's clear-eyed acknowledgment of that ambiguity. There are twin planets that are each other's moon, as if our moon had a barely-good-enough atmosphere. A hundred and fifty years before the time of the story, the revolutionaries and malcontents of rich capitalist Urras went to the moon, Anarres, to found their own anarchist society.

Anarres could so easily be irritatingly perfect, but it isn't. There are droughts and famines, petty bureaucrats and growing centralization of power. The book follows Shevek, a brilliant physicist, as he grows up on Anarres and later travels to Urras and back. The chapters alternate between planets and time periods. This was almost too much for me at twelve; I reread it instantly in chronological order. Now I regard it as masterly—the way the tensions in the two storylines wrap and reinforce each other thematically is phenomenal. Shevek grows and changes as a character; he goes from planet to planet with his hands empty but invents the ansible that allows FTL communication. The themes reinforce each other, and Shevek's true journey is at once unique and universal.

I have met people online who thought that Anarres was a dystopia, and intended that way. At twelve, I put the book down and said to myself, "Things don't have to be this way. They could be that way." I wanted to live on Anarres. The flaws made it real. I'm not so sure I'd like to live there now, but I am sure that I still want to read books that shake the walls of the world that way.

1976

Best Novel

Winner: *The Forever War*, by Joe Haldeman

Nominees:
The Computer Connection (aka *Extro*), by Alfred Bester
Doorways in the Sand, by Roger Zelazny
Inferno, by Larry Niven and Jerry Pournelle
The Stochastic Man, by Robert Silverberg

The 1976 Hugo Awards were given at MidAmeriCon in Kansas City, Missouri.

The Best Novel award was won by Joe Haldeman's *The Forever War*. It's an impressive book and a worthy winner—it's about a young man drafted under the "Elite Conscription Act" to go and fight aliens, who goes out to fight aliens and, thanks to relativity, keeps coming back to human society grown stranger and stranger. It also won the Nebula and the Locus. It's in print, and it's in the library in English and French.

There are four other nominees, and I've read all of them, but I've reread only one of them at all recently, and they all strike me as rather weak.

Alfred Bester's *The Computer Connection* (aka *Extro*) I remember as being very disappointing, without remembering much more about it. It isn't in print, but it is in the library in English and French.

Roger Zelazny's *Doorways in the Sand* is a beautiful Zelazny novel with aliens and stereoisomers, minor work but still lovely. It's not in print, and it's not in the library. It has always been hard to find—my anecdotal evidence for this is that I have a US edition. Somebody should reprint it.

Larry Niven and Jerry Pournelle's *Inferno* is about a science fiction writer escaping from Dante's Hell with Mussolini as his guide. I mildly enjoyed it the first time I read it when I was fourteen, but I haven't felt much urge to pick it up again since, nor have I read the recent sequel. It has a science-fictional sensibility, but it's definitely about the afterlife and therefore fantasy. It also shares with Dante's original a kind of vindictive pettiness. It's in print, and it's in the library in English.

Robert Silverberg's *The Stochastic Man* is a near-future SF novel about prediction and the difference between prediction and actually seeing the future. I remember it being really powerful and a bit of a downer. It's not in print, and it's in the library in French only—this is also something somebody should reprint, and probably the best of the four.

Five books, all by American men. Bester's a previous winner; all the rest are previous nominees, except Haldeman, who is a newcomer. We have four science fiction of the traditional set-in-the-future kind, and one fantasy of hell—all except the winner, books by well-established writers.

What else might they have considered?

Non-overlapping eligible Nebula nominees were Arthur Byron Cover's *Autumn Angels;* Tanith Lee's *The Birthgrave;* Ian Watson's *The Embedding* (presumably on US publication?); Vonda McIntyre's *The Exile Waiting;* Michael Bishop's *A Funeral for the Eyes of Fire;* Barry N. Malzberg's *Guernica Night;* Marion Zimmer Bradley's *The Heritage of Hastur;* Italo Calvino's *Invisible Cities;* Katherine Maclean's *Missing Man;* and E. L. Doctorow's *Ragtime,* which I didn't even know was SF. I haven't read all of these, but I'm sure most of them would have made fine Hugo nominees.

These last two Nebula nominees are in a different category, however. SFWA nominated Joanna Russ's *The Female Man* and Samuel R. Delany's *Dhalgren,* both of which should absolutely have been on the Hugo ballot too. It's ridiculous that they were overlooked. They'd have been better nominees than anything on the list except *The Forever War.*

The World Fantasy Award went to Richard Matheson's *Bid Time Return* and also short-listed Stephen King's *Salem's Lot.*

This was the year the Campbell Memorial Award went a little crazy and gave the award to Wilson Tucker's *Year of the Quiet Sun*, a 1970 book, after saying no 1975 books were worthy of the award, and then short-listed Bob Shaw's *Orbitsville* and *The Stochastic Man*. Ouch. (*Orbitsville* did win the BSFA Award, which might have been some consolation.)

The Locus Award short-listed another book that really should have been on the Hugo ballot—John Brunner's *The Shockwave Rider*. Also short-listed and not mentioned so far, Arthur C. Clarke's *Imperial Earth*; Roger Zelazny's *Sign of the Unicorn*; Jack Vance's *Showboat World*; Ray Nelson's *Blake's Progress*; M. A. Foster's *The Warriors of Dawn*; Robert Shea and Robert Anton Wilson's *Illuminatus!*; and Cordwainer Smith's *Norstrilia*, which might not have been eligible because it had already been published in two halves in magazines in the sixties.

Is there anything of note that wasn't nominated for anything? Yes! There's one of my favorite books, Michael Coney's *Hello Summer, Goodbye*, and there's George Alec Effinger and Gardner Dozois's *Nightmare Blue*.

So, not doing so well this year really, a fairly weak short list and three absolutely vital SF novels missed. If the short list had been Russ, Delany, Brunner, Silverberg, and Haldeman, I think it would have done a much better job of showing where SF was that year. I wonder what went wrong. I wonder if a lot of the previous year's Worldcon members nominating in 1976 were Australian and had had a chance to see only books published there.

OTHER CATEGORIES

BEST NOVELLA

Winner: *Home Is the Hangman*, by Roger Zelazny (*Analog*, November 1975)

Nominees:
ARM, by Larry Niven (*Epoch*)
The Custodians, by Richard Cowper (*F&SF*, October 1975)

The Silent Eyes of Time, by Algis Budrys (*F&SF*, November 1975)
The Storms of Windhaven, by Lisa Tuttle and George R. R. Martin (*Analog*, May 1975)

I'd have voted for the Cowper, I think, but these are all good (except the Budrys, which I haven't read or don't remember).

Best Novelette

Winner: "The Borderland of Sol," by Larry Niven (*Analog*, January 1975)

Nominees:
"And Seven Times Never Kill Man," by George R. R. Martin (*Analog*, July 1975)
"The New Atlantis," by Ursula K. Le Guin (*The New Atlantis*)
"San Diego Lightfoot Sue," by Tom Reamy (*F&SF*, August 1975)
"Tinker," by Jerry Pournelle (*Galaxy*, July 1975)

Martin should have had it. I adore that story, and "The Borderland of Sol" is relatively ordinary.

Best Short Story

Winner: "Catch That Zeppelin!," by Fritz Leiber (*F&SF*, March 1975)

Nominees:
"Child of All Ages," by P. J. Plauger (*Analog*, March 1975)
"Croatoan," by Harlan Ellison (*F&SF*, May 1975)
"Doing Lennon," by Gregory Benford (*Analog*, April 1975)
"Rogue Tomato," by Michael Bishop (*New Dimensions 5*)
"Sail the Tide of Mourning," by Richard Lupoff (*New Dimensions 5*)

Best Dramatic Presentation

Winner: *A Boy and His Dog*

Nominees:
"The Capture" (Phil Foglio cartoon slide show)
Dark Star
Monty Python and the Holy Grail
Rollerball

BEST PROFESSIONAL EDITOR

Winner: Ben Bova

Nominees:
Jim Baen
Edward L. Ferman
Robert Silverberg
Ted White

BEST PROFESSIONAL ARTIST

Winner: Frank Kelly Freas

Nominees:
George Barr
Vincent Di Fate
Steve Fabian
Rick Sternbach

BEST FANZINE

Winner: *Locus*, edited by Charles Brown and Dena Brown

Nominees:
Algol, edited by Andrew I. Porter
Don-O-Saur, edited by Don C. Thompson
Outworlds, edited by Bill Bowers
Science Fiction Review, edited by Richard E. Geis

Best Fan Writer

Winner: Richard E. Geis

Nominees:
Charles Brown
Don D'Ammassa
Don C. Thompson
Susan Wood

Best Fan Artist

Winner: Tim Kirk

Nominees:
Grant Canfield
Phil Foglio
Bill Rotsler
Jim Shull

John W. Campbell Award

Winner: Tom Reamy

Nominees:
Arsen Darnay
M. A. Foster
John Varley
Joan D. Vinge

Tom Reamy died young after producing one very good novel and enough stories for one collection—including a Nebula-winning novelette and numerous other Hugo and Nebula nominations for short work. I think he was a good choice and would have become a really major writer if he'd survived.

We also have three other terrific nominees—M. A. Foster, John Varley, and Joan Vinge have all produced really great work in the time since, and if they're quite not household names, I'd expect anyone reading this to know them.

Only Arsen Darnay hasn't imprinted himself on my consciousness—no idea what happened to him.

Comments on 1976

2. Rich Horton

It's interesting (to me, if to no one else) that all the novels on the Hugo short list were serialized. Albeit *The Forever War* in pieces—a few separate novellas in *Analog* over a couple of years. The *Analog* serialization of *The Computer Connection/Extro* (which I quite enjoy, by the way, though it's clearly lesser Bester than his great fifties novels) was "The Indian Giver," hence it had three titles.

Other novels worth a mention, though not a Hugo nod:

Clara Reeve, by "Leonie Hargrave" (Thomas Disch)—this is a Gothic, so it may not be fantastical at all, and I haven't read it, but I have seen it praised
Dogsbody and *Eight Days of Luke*, by the late and very much lamented Diana Wynne Jones
Marune: Alastor 933, by Jack Vance
The Grey King, by Susan Cooper
Venus on the Half-Shell, by "Kilgore Trout" (Philip José Farmer)

And, from the mainstream, *Dead Babies*, by Martin Amis—which is actually a novel I hate. But I like a lot of Martin Amis's work (and a lot of his work is SF, and he was for some time a regular SF reviewer for one of the UK papers). *Dead Babies* is set in the near future, so it certainly qualifies as SF.

I haven't read *Ragtime*, which was a major bestseller, but I didn't think it was SF. I assume it's there as some sort of alternate history, but

I always thought (maybe I was wrong?) that it was a straight historical novel that maybe played a bit fast and loose with some real people as characters. E. L. Doctorow, by the way, is apparently a distant cousin of Cory.

I would also have called Calvino's *Invisible Cities* (which I like) a story collection, not a novel.

I'll get to the short fiction in a bit, but first a brief comment on the Campbell Award—indeed, an excellent list. About Arsen Darnay: he published a number of very engaging stories in the mid-seventies, mostly in Jim Baen's wonderfully energetic *Galaxy* (my favorite magazine at that time, partly I think because I was fifteen). Then his career more or less petered out. I suspect (purely speculating) this was a mixture of day job pressures and perhaps less-than-stellar sales. At any rate, he has a blog. There we learn that he is originally from Europe, that he is now in his seventies and a great-grandfather, and that he has published a few novels more recently, through the POD outlet Lulu.

3. RICH HORTON

In novella, while I quite enjoyed Zelazny's *Home Is the Hangman*, I think I agree with you that the Cowper would have been a better choice. For that matter, the Budrys novella, *The Silent Eyes of Time*, is first-rate. Budrys was just then returning, in a slightly limited fashion, to the field after a few years' absence. I like *ARM* a lot too, and the Tuttle-Martin story is fun. The Nebula short list adds a major Tiptree story, one of her oddly toned "postrevelation" works, *A Momentary Taste of Being*. (I suppose all of Tiptree is oddly toned in some way; that's part of her specialness.)

ARM was one of a lot of pretty good stories from the much-derided Elwood–Silverberg anthology *Epoch*. *Epoch* may have also had a lot of bad stories, but the best of its TOC was very good. There was also a slight but enjoyable Vance novella in that anthology, *The Dogtown Tourist Agency*.

Poul Anderson's story collection *Homeward and Beyond* included an excellent original novella, *The Peat Bog*.

And the best novella of the year, ignored either because it was in an Elwood anthology or because that anthology, regardless of editor, just wasn't that much seen, was another utterly amazing story by Gene Wolfe: *Tracking Song*. That would be my choice, at this remove, for the best novella of 1975. (Granted that I didn't see it until 1980, when Wolfe collected it in *The Island of Doctor Death and Other Stories and Other Stories*.)

4. RICH HORTON

Novelette:

"The Borderland of Sol" is indeed somewhat minor Niven, and the Martin story would have been a better choice, but I think Le Guin's "The New Atlantis" was better still. The Nebula winner, Reamy's "San Diego Lightfoot Sue," is also excellent. It's probably my favorite Tom Reamy story.

The Nebula short list had some interesting additions: Barry Malzberg's interesting and odd "A Galaxy Called Rome" (which, expanded, was the short-listed novel *Galaxies*), Craig Strete's "The Bleeding Man," Eleanor Arnason's 1974 story (probably first published in the United States in 1975) "The Warlord of Saturn's Moons," a John Varley story I really like, "Retrograde Summer," and perhaps best of all, "Polly Charms, the Sleeping Woman," by Avram Davidson.

I should expand on "Polly Charms, the Sleeping Woman" by noting that it first appeared in *F&SF* but later in the same year was part of Davidson's *The Enquiries of Doctor Eszterhazy*, a wonderful book of which every story could probably have been short-listed. For that matter, if *Invisible Cities* is sufficiently unified to be a novel for Nebula purposes, so is *The Enquiries of Doctor Eszterhazy*, and I say it could have been short-listed in novel too.

Three novelettes from *Epoch* seem worthy of mention (one was on the Nebula short list):

"Blooded on Arachne," by Michael Bishop

"Cambridge, 1:58 A.M.," by Gregory Benford (which became *Timescape*)

And my favorite, certainly worthy of short-listing: George R. R. Martin's ". . . For a Single Yesterday."

Other good novelettes:

George Alec Effinger's American football story (Effinger was a sports nut, and wrote a number of good SF sports stories), "25 Crunch Split Right on Two"

John Varley's "The Black Hole Passes"

Joan and Vernor Vinge's "The Peddler's Apprentice" (related to Vernor's stories about bobbles, though probably not strictly speaking in the same future)

15. RICH HORTON

And now I can comment on short story. I think "Catch That Zeppelin!" is charming but fairly minor—still, a nice work. At the time, I really, really liked "Doing Lennon," but I agree it's hard to read it the same way now. The rest of the Hugo nomination list is quite good, too. I do quite like the Ellison, a very intense story but somehow quieter than some of his work. And "Child of All Ages" is first-rate, probably Plauger's best SF.

From the Nebula additions, I particularly recommend Budrys's "A Scraping at the Bones." (Yes, I am a big fan of Budrys, if anyone hasn't noticed.) Also Benford's "White Creatures"—he was really coming into his own as a writer. Craig Strete's "Time Deer" too.

Lots of Chicagoans on the list (I'm from Chicago to begin with myself)—Budrys, Pohl, Phyllis Eisenstein (her "Attachment" was a Nebula nominee).

A couple more stories worth a mention—Poul Anderson's "Wolfram," and an odd little piece Ted White published in *Fantastic* called "Solid Geometry," by Ian MacEwan. MacEwan published his story collection *First Love, Last Rites* in 1975 as well, which also included "Solid Geometry." He has gone on to become a major novelist, best known probably for *Atonement* (which I love). His work often skirts the edges of SF/fantasy/horror.

32. GARDNER DOZOIS

In the short fiction categories, again most of the strongest stuff didn't make it onto the ballot. In novella, *Home Is the Hangman* is entertaining, but I think I would have gone for *The Silent Eyes of Time* or *A Momentary Taste of Being* (although it's extremely depressing). *The Peat Bog* is one of Anderson's best and least-known stories, although it's a historical rather than SF.

In novelette, "The Borderland of Sol" is a weak winner. The clear winner for me here is Wolfe's "The Hero as Werewolf," one of my favorite Wolfe stories; I liked it better than "Tracking Song," which I liked, but always got the uneasy feeling from that I didn't really understand it. (Michael Swanwick and I once sat down and spent about an hour trying to puzzle out what was really happening in "Tracking Song," and ultimately failed.) "Retrograde Summer" is also good, and "Polly Charms, the Sleeping Woman" may be the weakest story in *The Enquiries of Doctor Eszterhazy* (one of the most delightful collections ever published), but that still makes it strong enough to make the ballot. I wouldn't have given it to "San Diego Lightfoot Sue," but it was strong enough to legitimately make the ballot, and I suspect that Tom Reamy would have won a Hugo within a few years if he'd stayed alive. (His other story that year, "Under the Hollywood Sign," is a very grim story, by the way, almost as depressing as the Tiptree.)

"Catch That Zeppelin!" is weak late Leiber, a nostalgia award. For me, the clear winner is Budrys's "A Scraping at the Bones," a really nasty bit of future noir that's sharp as a scalpel. I wasn't as crazy about "Child of All Ages" as some others, but agree that it's strong enough to deserve a place on the ballot. Most of the other stories, frankly, are either weak or intensely dated.

Monty Python and the Holy Grail is one of the great film comedies, immensely influential, and should have won.

I was at MidAmeriCon, in some ways the first "modern" Worldcon, which introduced multitrack programming and (I think) the videotaping of panels. I have many fond memories of it.

33. GARDNER DOZOIS
Oh, and for me, the clear winner in the Campbell is John Varley. Time has blurred how important and exciting his blossoming in short fiction was in the late seventies. Suddenly, here was this guy you'd never heard of doing all these great stories that did things with SF that nobody else

was doing and that nobody had ever done before. Budrys referred to it as something like "a trumpet call, waking SF out of its doldrums." The only comparable concentrated burst of excellent stories was by Roger Zelazny in the late sixties.

35. RICH HORTON

Gardner, I think you're right that time has blurred how fresh Varley's work seemed at that time. I know he was the name I looked for most eagerly those days, in *Galaxy* and *F&SF*—I gobbled every one of his stories with delight. They really were something new and special. He's had a strong career, but I think the case can be made—I'd make it— that it hasn't quite matched the promise of those early stories, in part because that's such a high bar for anyone to clear.

In 1975 I believe Plauger won because Varley hadn't quite yet published his really striking stuff, and as M. Bernstein notes, "Child of All Ages" appeared early enough for voters to have read it prior to the voting (indeed, it was probably very fresh in the mind of voters). I would give two reasons Reamy won in 1976: (1) he really had published some fine stuff ("Twilla" the year before, as well as "San Diego Lightfoot Sue"), and (2) he was a well-known and popular fan.

This is the first year I might plausibly have voted for the Hugos, though I don't think I did.

I agree that "Polly Charms" is not the best story in *The Enquiries of Doctor Eszterhazy*—I think it got the Nebula nomination because of its *F&SF* appearance, which led more voters to see it.

47. MAGNEYJ

Re: *Dhalgren* and *The Female Man*. For some odd reason, over a stretch running almost ten years, Hugo nominators wouldn't pick an original mass market paperback unless it had been serialized in a prozine or was part of an established series. Nebulas, however, nominated at least one most years.

1977

BEST NOVEL

Winner: *Where Late the Sweet Birds Sang,* by Kate Wilhelm

Nominees:
Children of Dune, by Frank Herbert
Man Plus, by Frederik Pohl
Mindbridge, by Joe Haldeman
Shadrach in the Furnace, by Robert Silverberg

The 1977 Hugos were awarded at SunCon in Miami Beach, Florida.

The Best Novel Hugo was won by Kate Wilhelm's *Where Late the Sweet Birds Sang.* It's great to see another win for a woman, making three so far. It's an odd elegaic book about cloning and the end of humanity. I've read it, but not for a long time. I can remember the tone and the characters much better than the plot. It also won the Locus Award and took third place in the John W. Campbell Memorial Award. It's in print in the United Kingdom in the Gollancz SF Masterworks list and in the United States in the Orb line, and it's in the library in English and French. This meets my standards for having lasted, but it seems to me nevertheless that this is a little-read and little-discussed book.

There are four other nominees, and again I've read them all. Frank Herbert's *Children of Dune* is the third in the Dune series. I said in my post about *Dune* that each sequel is half as good as the one before, and I stand by that, though some people think that this is better than book two, *Dune Messiah*. It's in print and in the library in both languages. The Dune sequels and the later prequels by other hands are popular and continue to sell, but not to me.

Frederik Pohl's *Man Plus* is a classic. It won the Nebula and took second place in the John W. Campbell Award. It thoroughly deserves its place on this Hugo list. It's about changing a man to survive on Mars instead of transforming the planet. It's an up-close, personal story about becoming a cyborg, but that's just where it starts. This is one of Pohl's best books. It's in print, and it's in the library in English only.

Joe Haldeman's *Mindbridge* has colonization of other planets, aliens, and telepathy. I was disappointed in it after *The Forever War*. It's not in print, and it's in the library in French only.

Shadrach in the Furnace is another excellent science fiction vision from Robert Silverberg—he really was producing at least one amazing book every year. This one is about the overstimulated future in which the dictator of the world is seeking to extend his life in a new body, and the present owner of the new body in question has his own opinions about this. It's in print, and it's in the library in both languages.

So this is a pretty good set of books—one woman and four men, all Americans. Herbert and Haldeman are previous winners, Silverberg is a previous nominee, Pohl had won a couple of Best Professional Editor Hugos and been nominated for short work, Wilhelm had also been nominated in short form. The books are all solidly SF—postapocalyptic cloning, life extension, terraforming by changing the human, aliens and telepathy, and far-future baroque. I think the Herbert is a weak spot, but overall, these are good nominees and a good snapshot of what people were writing at the time.

What else could they have chosen?

Eligible and non-overlapping Nebula nominees were Marta Randall's *Islands* and Samuel Delany's *Triton*, one of my favorite books of all time, and which I think should definitely have been on the Hugo list.

The World Fantasy Award has no overlap with either list. It was won by William Kotzwinkle's *Doctor Rat*. Other nominees were John Steinbeck's *The Acts of King Arthur and His Noble Knights*, Karl Edward Wagner's *Dark Crusade,* Ramsey Campbell's *The Doll Who Ate His*

Mother, Gordon R. Dickson's *The Dragon and the George*, and Michael Moorcock's *The Sailor on the Seas of Fate*.

The John W. Campbell Memorial Award was won by Kingsley Amis's alternate history *The Alteration*.

Non-overlapping nominees for the Locus Award were Larry Niven's *A World Out of Time*; Arthur C. Clarke's *Imperial Earth*; Ben Bova's *Millennium*, probably Bova's best book and certainly my favorite of his; Roger Zelazny's *The Hand of Oberon*; C. J. Cherryh's *Brothers of Earth*; Marion Zimmer Bradley's *The Shattered Chain*; Jack Vance's *Maske: Thaery*; Algis Budrys's *Michaelmas*; Kate Wilhelm's *The Clewiston Test*; Anne McCaffrey's *Dragonsong*; Pamela Sargent's *Cloned Lives*; Michael Moorcock's *The End of All Songs*; Cecelia Holland's *Floating Worlds*; and Chelsea Quinn Yarbro's *Time of the Fourth Horseman*.

So, is there anything notable all of these missed? Yes, lots. M. J. Engh's *Arslan*; Dick and Zelazny's *Deus Irae*; Tanith Lee's *Don't Bite the Sun*; C. J. Cherryh's *Gate of Ivrel*, the first of the Morgaine books; Peter Dickinson's *King and Joker* and *The Blue Hawk*; Octavia Butler's *Patternmaster*; Spider Robinson's *Telempath*; and Ira Levin's *The Boys from Brazil*. Overall this year, this wouldn't have been my ideal list from what's available, but it's pretty good.

OTHER CATEGORIES

BEST NOVELLA

Winner: (tie) *By Any Other Name*, by Spider Robinson (*Analog*, November 1976)
Houston, Houston, Do You Read?, by James Tiptree Jr. (*Aurora: Beyond Equality*)

Nominees:
Piper at the Gates of Dawn, by Richard Cowper (*F&SF*, March 1976)

The Samurai and the Willows, by Michael Bishop (*F&SF*, February 1976)

I don't know the Bishop, but those are three terrific novellas. I'd have voted for the Tiptree.

Best Novelette

Winner: "The Bicentennial Man," by Isaac Asimov (*Stellar 2*)

Nominees:
"The Diary of the Rose," by Ursula K. Le Guin (*Future Power*)
"Gotta Sing, Gotta Dance," by John Varley (*Galaxy*, July 1976)
"The Phantom of Kansas," by John Varley (*Galaxy*, Febuary 1976)

Gosh, how on Earth (or any other planet) could Asimov have won? All three of the others are better stories. This is inexplicable. Had they read the Varleys? Had they read the Le Guin? I think I'd have voted for "Gotta Sing, Gotta Dance," but however, I'd have put the Asimov last. Varley was robbed.

Best Short Story

Winner: "Tricentennial," by Joe Haldeman (*Analog*, July 1976)

Nominees:
"A Crowd of Shadows," by Charles L. Grant (*F&SF*, June 1976)
"Custom Fitting," by James White (*Stellar 2*)
"I See You," by Damon Knight (*F&SF*, November 1976)

Oddly enough, in a year where I know nearly all the other short fiction, I don't remember any of these.

Best Dramatic Presentation

Winner: No Award

Nominees:
Carrie
Futureworld
Logan's Run
The Man Who Fell to Earth

BEST PROFESSIONAL EDITOR

Winner: Ben Bova

Nominees:
Jim Baen
Terry Carr
Edward L. Ferman
Ted White

BEST PROFESSIONAL ARTIST

Winner: Rick Sternbach

Nominees:
George Barr
Vincent Di Fate
Steve Fabian

BEST AMATEUR MAGAZINE

Winner: *Science Fiction Review*, edited by Richard E. Geis

Nominees:
Locus, edited by Charles Brown and Dena Brown
Mythologies, edited by Don D'Ammassa
Outworlds, edited by Bill Bowers
The Spanish Inquisition, edited by Suzanne Tompkins and Jerry Kaufman

Bites tongue on obvious joke.

BEST FAN WRITER

Winner: (tie) Richard E. Geis
Susan Wood

Nominees:
Don D'Ammassa
Mike Glicksohn
Don C. Thompson

BEST FAN ARTIST

Winner: Phil Foglio

Nominees:
Grant Canfield
Tim Kirk
Bill Rotsler
Jim Shull

JOHN W. CAMPBELL AWARD

Winner: C. J. Cherryh

Nominees:
Jack L. Chalker
M. A. Foster
Carter Scholz

Well, not much doubt that they made the right call there—Cherryh has gone on to win Hugos and to have a long distinguished career, with two whole shelves on my bookshelf and getting into a third. First female winner of the Campbell too.

Chalker was also a major writer. Foster I like a great deal; he produced seven novels and a collection and seemed to just stop writing sometime in the eighties. People are still asking about him, and his two trilogies were recently reprinted, so I think he was a good nominee.

I'm not familiar with Scholz, but he had a Hugo- and Nebula-nominated novelette in 1978 and has continued to publish short work, some of it in collaboration with Jonathan Lethem.

COMMENTS ON 1977

1. RICH HORTON

I am duty bound, given my LiveJournal (and Tor.com) handle*, to mention Michael Bishop's *And Strange at Ecbatan the Trees*. (Bishop and I are both quoting Archibald MacLeish's magnificent poem "You, Andrew Marvell.") Bishop's novel (paperbacked by DAW under the infinitely less interesting title *Beneath the Shattered Moons*) is nice stuff, but not his best.

My personal choice at the time for best novel was Cecelia Holland's *Floating Worlds*. I'm not 100 percent sure it holds up—and the science is kind of silly—but it is very good. It was short-listed for the Nebula and withdrawn by the publisher, supposedly in favor of the paperback (as allowed by Nebula rules), but I always assumed because they didn't want the stink of association with SF. I doubt that was Holland's doing—she's familiar with the genre, has written several other SF or fantasy books and stories, and writes occasional reviews for *Locus*.

Maske: Thaery is another favorite of mine, and *The Alteration* is an excellent alternate history novel.

Brian Aldiss's *The Malacia Tapestry* also dates to 1976.

4. REZENDI

I think the victories of "Bicentennial" and "Tricentennial" could be put down to a fit of American patriotism.

---

*Ecbatan

11. Rich Horton

Now the short fiction. In the novella category, I admit to not being a big fan of *Houston, Houston, Do You Read?*, largely on the grounds that I don't really approve of stories that seem to call for my extermination. (I grant that that's an unfair reading of the story, which is subtler than that, but it still bothers me.) I can't deny its power, however. I'm not a big fan of the Spider Robinson novella (though I think I enjoyed it back then): of the Hugo nominees, I'd probably go for the Cowper, though the Bishop story is also excellent.

However, the best novella of 1976 was—I'm sure this will be a shock to everybody!—by Gene Wolfe—*The Eyeflash Miracles* (which did appear on the Nebula short list). I guess I'm a broken record about Wolfe and especially his novellas, but his record at that length throughout his career is astonishing, and particularly so in the middle and late seventies.

There were a lot of really good novelettes in 1976. The award to "The Bicentennial Man" is, in my opinion, the result of a mixture of patriotic feeling, sentimentality, and love for the writer. Of the Hugo-nominated novelettes—all very good—I'd lean toward "The Phantom of Kansas" for the award.

From the Nebula short list, one can add the excellent alternate history novelette "Custer's Last Jump," by Steven Utley and Howard Waldrop.

Varley had two more very good novelettes in 1976: "Overdrawn at the Memory Bank" (which became a movie that got the *MST3K* treatment—a bit unfairly, as I thought it an okay effort), and "In the Bowl."

Larry Niven's novel *A World Out of Time* was quasi-serialized in *Galaxy,* and one part of that was a good stand-alone novelette, "Rammer."

Galaxy also published a Cordwainer Smith story, "Down to a Sunless Sea," apparently "finished" by Genevieve Linebarger. I think it pretty minor in the Smith canon.

Two good Alice Sheldon stories, one as by Tiptree: "The Psychologist Who Wouldn't Do Awful Things to Rats," and one as by Raccoona Sheldon, "Your Faces, O My Sisters! Your Faces Filled of Light!"

Two early Kim Stanley Robinson stories, both of which if I

recall correctly (which I may not) became part of his novel *The Memory of Whiteness:* "In Pierson's Orchestra" and "Coming Back to Dixieland."

But my two favorite novelettes of 1976 were first, one by Fred Saberhagen, normally not a favorite of mine: "Beneath the Hills of Azlaroc," which appeared in the first issue of Roger Elwood's short-lived SF magazine *Odyssey*. That story blew me away on first reading, though it seemed less impressive when I reread it two or three years ago.

And finally, my true favorite 1976 novelette, which I think really should have won an award, was Christopher Priest's astonishing "An Infinite Summer." It was apparently first slated for *The Last Dangerous Visions,* then withdrawn by Priest and placed in Peter Weston's UK original anthology *Andromeda 1*. (This history became controversial when Priest published *The Last Deadloss Visions,* criticizing Ellison's failure to publish *TLDV*. I have to say, that if Ellison is keeping stories as good as "An Infinite Summer" from publication, I resent that—no comment on author's rights is intended, just a reader's desire to read great stories.)

In short story, I must say that I don't think "Tricentennial" that impressive a winner, though it's okay work. Howard Waldrop's "Mary Margaret Road-Grader," a Nebula nominee, would have been a good choice, though I think any of the following three stories, not on either short list, would have been better:

"My Boat," by Joanna Russ
"The Death of Princes," by Fritz Leiber
"When I Was Ming the Merciless," by Gene Wolfe

BUT, the best short story of the year did appear on the Hugo short list. I'd have given the Hugo to "I See You," by Damon Knight, one of the great Time Viewer stories. (One of my favorite sub-subgenres actually, with such other great stories as "The Dead Past," "E for Effort," "Private Eye," and "In the Western Tradition.")

12. TANSY RAYNER ROBERTS

Talk about making the right call for longevity—it's cool to see Phil Foglio up as Best Fan Artist considering his future in the Hugo Graphic Novel category. . . .

24. GARDNER DOZOIS

In the short fiction categories, I'm prejudiced, because I was the one who bought and published both Gene Wolfe's "The Eyeflash Miracles" and Ursula K. Le Guin's "The Diary of the Rose," which appeared in my original anthology with Jack Dann, *Future Power*. They were among the first stories I ever bought to appear in public in a market with my name on it, and I'm still proud of them.

I think that *The Eyeflash Miracles* probably should have been the winner in novella, although *Piper at the Gates of Dawn* is quite good too, as is *The Samurai and the Willows*, although it might be a bit dated by now. I've always been lukewarm about *Houston, Houston, Do You Read?*, which I think is a much misunderstood story. Alice Sheldon herself once told me that she considered it to be a "cautionary tale," NOT a wish-fulfillment utopia (someday, we'll get rid of all the men!), as many people read it; you're not supposed to approve of what happens to the men in the story, the idea being that either sex having complete power over the other is not a good idea. (The inverse would be "The Screwfly Solution," I guess.)

In novelette, I think the winner should probably have been "The Phantom of Kansas," although "The Diary of the Rose" is a fine story too. In short story, my vote goes to either "Custer's Last Jump" or "Mary-Margaret Road-Grader," although Russ's "My Boat" is good too.

28. HIGGINS

1977 was my first Worldcon; it was in the extravagantly tacky Fontainebleau Hotel in Miami Beach. I commuted from my parents' home in Coral Gables every day. And hated to go home each night . . .

Just before the Hugo ceremony, I had dinner with Phil Foglio, whom I had recently gotten to know. Seeing Phil win the silver rocket filled me with (unjustified) pride, and I clapped as hard as I could clap.

1978

Best Novel

Winner: *Gateway,* by Frederik Pohl

Nominees:
Time Storm, by Gordon R. Dickson
Dying of the Light, by George R. R. Martin
The Forbidden Tower, by Marion Zimmer Bradley
Lucifer's Hammer, by Larry Niven and Jerry Pournelle

The 1978 Hugo Awards were held at the legendary Iguanacon II, in Phoenix, Arizona.

The Best Novel award was won by Frederik Pohl's *Gateway,* which is a Big Dumb Object story, a psychological mystery, and a really excellent story about people trying to get rich by getting into alien ships with uncontrollable navigation systems. It's a terrific Hugo winner, a real classic. Everyone loved it; it won the John W. Campbell Memorial Award, the Locus, and the Nebula as well as the Hugo. It's in print, and it's in the library in English only.

There are four other nominees, and I have read three of them. Let's start with the one I haven't read, Gordon Dickson's *Time Storm.* Fantastic Fiction says it's about a man who sets off accompanied by a leopard and a nearly autistic woman to find his wife, who was swept off by a time storm. If that was the blurb on the back of the book, then that explains why I haven't read it. Can it really be as awful as it sounds? If I were a huge Dickson fan, I'd have read it despite the unpromising description, but I only mildly like the books of his I have read. It's in print from Baen, but it's not in the library.

George R. R. Martin's first novel, *Dying of the Light,* is a beautifully written romantic space opera with complex culture clashes on a wandering planet at the edge of the galaxy. I love it. I am nevertheless surprised it was nominated for the Hugo—it's the kind of book I tend to see on the list of things nobody noticed and think, "But I love that!" It is in print and in the library in French and English. (But to be fair, I think that's less because it's an enduring classic than because Martin subsequently became a bestseller and brought his backlist back into print. This book was hard to find for a very long time.) I think it would have received my vote over *Gateway* in 1978 (I was thirteen), but I recognize *Gateway* as a more significant novel now.

The presence on the short list of Marion Zimmer Bradley's *The Forbidden Tower* surprised me even more. It's a book from the middle of the Darkover series, and it's not actually a good book by objective standards. It's about four telepaths, one from Earth and three from Darkover, settling into a polyamorous marriage and dealing with issues. I mean, I certainly kind of like it, but it really doesn't strike me as Hugo-worthy material. Maybe in 1978, it seemed better, more original? I didn't read it until about ten years after. It's in print from Daw, and it's in the library in both languages.

Larry Niven and Jerry Pournelle's *Lucifer's Hammer* is a survivalist story about a large meteor hitting the Earth and people coping in the aftermath. I read it in 1978 or soon after, and I didn't think much of it—I remember very simplistic characters and bestseller-style point-of-view switching, always a turnoff for me. Amazon thinks it's in print but Del Rey doesn't, so I can't tell. It's in the library in English only, so I guess I could reread it and see how well it has lasted.

So this is the weirdest nominee list for a long time. One woman and five men, all American. Niven is a previous winner. Pohl, Pournelle, Bradley, and Dickson are previous nominees. Martin had been Campbell nominated and won a short-form Hugo. We have a near-future disaster story, two planetary romances, a psychological exploration, and an alternate reality story—science fiction of very different kinds, showcasing how varied SF can be.

The winner is wonderful, but the rest of them are all surprising. And two of the ones I've read, *Lucifer's Hammer* and *The Forbidden Tower*, are comfortable books of a kind that don't really belong on this list.

What else might they have picked?

The Nebulas have four other nominees, and I haven't read any of them, thus proving that for 1978 at least, the Hugos were doing better at finding things to my tastes. They are Terry Carr's *Cirque*, Gregory Benford's *In the Ocean of Night*, David Gerrold's *Moonstar Odyssey*, and Richard A. Lupoff's *Sword of the Demon*.

The World Fantasy Awards have no overlap. It was won by Fritz Leiber's *Our Lady of Darkness*, which I think should have been a Hugo nominee. Other nominees were Stephen Donaldson's *Chronicles of Thomas Covenant* and Charles L. Grant's *The Hour of the Oxrun Dead*.

The John W. Campbell Memorial Award gave second place to Arkady and Boris Strugatsky's *Roadside Picnic*, and third to Philip K. Dick's *A Scanner Darkly*. Now, as you know, I don't like Dick at all, but I still think it's ridiculous that this wasn't on the Hugo ballot. This is a major book.

The Locus Awards separated out SF and fantasy this year for the first time. Nominees for SF not previously mentioned were: John Varley's *The Ophiuchi Hotline*, which certainly should have been a Hugo nominee; *Michaelmas*, Algis Budrys; *The Dosadi Experiment*, Frank Herbert; *Dragonsinger*, Anne McCaffrey; *Hunter of Worlds*, C. J. Cherryh; *Mirkheim*, Poul Anderson; *The Dark Design*, Philip José Farmer; *A Heritage of Stars*, Clifford D. Simak; *Midnight at the Well of Souls*, Jack L. Chalker; *Inherit the Stars*, James P. Hogan; *All My Sins Remembered*, Joe Haldeman; *The Martian Inca*, Ian Watson; *A Little Knowledge*, Michael Bishop; and *If the Stars Are Gods*, Gregory Benford and Gordon Eklund.

Nominees for fantasy not previously mentioned: *The Silmarillion*, J. R. R. Tolkien, first book I ever bought in hardcover; *The Shining*, Stephen King; *The Sword of Shannara*, Terry Brooks; *Heir of Sea and Fire*, Patricia A. McKillip; *The Book of Merlyn*, T. H. White; *A Spell for Chameleon*, Piers Anthony; *The Grey Mane of Morning*, Joy Chant; *Cry Silver Bells*, Thomas Burnett Swann; *Trey of Swords*, Andre Norton;

Queens Walk in the Dusk, Thomas Burnett Swann; and *Silver on the Tree,* Susan Cooper.

It's interesting to see *The Sword of Shannara* on this list, as Lin Carter is generally considered to have invented modern genre fantasy with the way he marketed that book, and yet both the Mythopoeic and the World Fantasy Award already existed, and Locus now considered there were sufficient excellent fantasy nominees to make it worth splitting Fantasy from SF. Maybe *Shannara* was surfing the wave rather than creating it?

Any great books overlooked by all the awards?

Diana Wynne Jones's *Charmed Life;* Octavia Butler's *Mind of My Mind;* Edward Whittemore's *The Sinai Tapestry;* M. A. Foster's *The Gameplayers of Zan;* and Barrington Bayley's *The Grand Wheel.*

I think *The Ophiuchi Hotline* and *A Scanner Darkly* are both important, boundary-defining science fiction books of the kind that the Hugo ought to be recognizing, and should definitely have been on the short list, and maybe *Our Lady of Darkness* and *Mind of My Mind* too.

OTHER CATEGORIES

BEST NOVELLA

Winner: *Stardance,* by Spider Robinson and Jeanne Robinson (*Analog,* March 1977)

Nominees:
Aztecs, by Vonda N. McIntyre (*2076: The American Tricentennial*)
In the Hall of the Martian Kings, by John Varley (*F&SF,* February 1977)
A Snark in the Night, by Gregory Benford (*F&SF,* August 1977)
The Wonderful Secret, by Keith Laumer (*Analog,* September, October 1977)

I'd have given it to Varley. It seems they were a sentimental lot at Iguanacon II, and *Stardance* does have its charms.

Best Novelette

Winner: "Eyes of Amber," by Joan D. Vinge (*Analog*, June 1977)

Nominees:
"Ender's Game," by Orson Scott Card (*Analog*, August 1977)
"The Ninth Symphony of Ludwig van Beethoven and Other Lost Songs," by Carter Scholz (*Universe 7*)
"Prismatica," by Samuel R. Delany (*F&SF*, October 1977)
"The Screwfly Solution," by Raccoona Sheldon (*Analog*, June 1977)

I'd definitely have voted for Tiptree, here calling herself Sheldon.

Best Short Story

Winner: "Jeffty Is Five," by Harlan Ellison (*F&SF*, July 1977)

Nominees:
"Air Raid," by Herb Boehm (*Asimov's*, Spring 1977)
"Dog Day Evening," by Spider Robinson (*Analog*, October 1977)
"Lauralyn," by Randall Garrett (*Analog*, April 1977)
"Time-Sharing Angel," by James Tiptree Jr. (*F&SF*, October 1977)

This is the year John Varley was robbed under the name of Boehm. Wow, "Air Raid," one of the best and most memorable short stories of all time, and it didn't win? Ellison was the GoH, so that might have had some influence? Or maybe nobody had started reading *Asimov's* yet? But I remember getting hold of that issue and wondering who this Herb Boehm was and why I hadn't seen anything of his before. (That would have been a year or so afterwards, though. SF magazines were slow crossing the Atlantic in those days.)

Dramatic Presentation

Winner: *Star Wars*

Nominees:

Blood! The Life and Future Times of Jack the Ripper (recording)

Close Encounters of the Third Kind

The Hobbit

Wizards

Best Professional Editor

Winner: George Scithers

Nominees:

Jim Baen

Ben Bova

Terry Carr

Edward L. Ferman

No, they had started reading *Asimov's;* Scithers was the editor. Inexplicable.

Best Professional Artist

Winner: Rick Sternbach

Nominees:

Vincent Di Fate

Steve Fabian

Frank Kelly Freas

Michael Whelan

Best Amateur Magazine

Winner: *Locus,* edited by Charles Brown and Dena Brown

Nominees:

Don-O-Saur, edited by Don C. Thompson

Janus, edited by Janice Bogstad and Jeanne Gomoll

Maya, edited by Rob Jackson
Science Fiction Review, edited by Richard E. Geis

Best Fan Writer

Winner: Richard E. Geis

Nominees:
Charles Brown
Don D'Ammassa
Don C. Thompson
Susan Wood

Best Fan Artist

Winner: Phil Foglio

Nominees:
Grant Canfield
Alexis Gilliland
Jeanne Gomoll
Jim Shull

John W. Campbell Award

Winner: Orson Scott Card

Nominees:
Jack L. Chalker
Stephen R. Donaldson
Elizabeth A. Lynn
Bruce Sterling

Well, no losers there, a well-selected list of early-career major writers. Card is an excellent winner, and I'd definitely have voted for him on the basis of work so far. All of the others have continued to write—

with some gaps in Lynn's case—and to produce talked-about books. Sterling is perhaps the standout, but it wasn't until the eighties that he would begin to produce his really notable work. Donaldson won in 1979.

COMMENTS ON 1978

2. RICH HORTON

In my nitpicking way, I'll note that a few may remember *Our Lady of Darkness* as "The Pale Brown Thing" in its *F&SF* serialization.

A few more novels worth a look:

Diana Wynne Jones's *Drowned Ammet*
Tanith Lee's *Drinking Sapphire Wine*
Cherry Wilder's *The Luck of Brin's Five*
Joanna Russ's *We Who Are About to . . .*

5. RICH HORTON

Short fiction . . .

A curious year for novella. I can't find any to add to the list. I don't remember Laumer's *The Wonderful Secret* at all—I thought this was already "post-stroke," when he just couldn't write anymore. (The Laumer stories I do remember from this period are dire.) *Stardance* is okay, but not special. I'd give the award to either *Aztecs* or *In the Hall of the Martian Kings*. (Which is not an Eight Worlds story, by the way.) The Nebula short list, by the way, was as short as you can get—just *Aztecs* and *Stardance*.

There isn't even a Gene Wolfe novella from 1977—but no worries, he'll be back in 1978!

A few novelettes to add to consideration. Two excellent ones appeared on the Nebula short list:

"A Rite of Spring," by Fritz Leiber
"Particle Theory," by Edward Bryant

"The Screwfly Solution" won the Nebula, and it was a very worthy winner, but I just love "A Rite of Spring," and would not have objected had it won an award. The Carter Scholz story is also very good, and also appears on the Nebula short list. (The other Nebula short-listed novelette is "The Stone House," by Martin.)

Other strong novelettes:

"Equinoctial," by John Varley

"Black as the Pit, from Pole to Pole," by Howard Waldrop and Steven Utley

"Manatee Gal Ain't You Coming Out Tonight?," one of the best Jack Limekiller stories from Avram Davidson

In short story, I had no idea the model for Jeffty was Walter Koenig's son. I did think "Jeffty Is Five" quite good. "Air Raid" is better, though. I think a lot of people had no idea that "Herb Boehm" was John Varley, but that shouldn't have mattered. After all, it got enough attention to make the short list.

There was another good Avram Davidson story: "Hark! Was That the Squeal of an Angry Thoat?" And also a magnificent Gene Wolfe story, "The Marvelous Brass Chessplaying Automaton."

As for artist, I remember Rick Sternbach's work with great affection, and I think he deserved his Hugo.

20. GARDNER DOZOIS

Novella should have been *In the Hall of the Martian Kings,* one of the first of the New Mars stories, dealing with the Mars revealed by the Mariner probes, and doing so very effectively too. Nothing else in that category really rivals it.

Novelette, I think, belongs to Tiptree/Sheldon's "The Screwfly Solution," one of her strongest stories ever, although I'm also very fond of "Manatee Gal," perhaps the best of Davidson's wonderful Jack Limekiller stories (I think "Screwfly Solution" is the more significant story, though), and Bryant's "Particle Theory" is a strong story too. A case could certainly be made for "Ender's Game," and everything that's been said here about it being a gateway drug for SF is true, although I think that really applies more to the novel version than to the novelette version; talking to Clarion students over the years about what got them started reading SF, student after student cited the novel version of *Ender's Game*—you could almost count on it turning up. I'm surprised that nobody has mentioned Bishop's "The House of Compassionate Sharers," which, as I recall, showed up in all of that year's Best of the Year anthologies. I'd also mention Jack Vance's "The Bagful of Dreams," perhaps the best of his later Cugel the Clever stories. This category is overall much stronger than novella.

Short story is very weak. Probably this should have gone to "Air Raid," which didn't even make the ballot, although, since this was a story I solicited from Varley and convinced George to buy in my position at the time as associate editor of *Asimov's*, I'm prejudiced. Wasn't that 1976, though, not 1978? If "Air Raid" is in 1976, then this was a weak year indeed in short story, although, unnoticed by just about everybody in the field except for me, it did feature the publication of William Gibson's very first story, "Fragments of a Hologram Rose," in *Unearth*.

Rick Sternbach is almost forgotten these days, but he briefly dominated the field in the couple of years he was active before moving on to work on *Star Trek*, and deserved his Hugo. (In the interests of Full Disclosure, I should say that he was a friend and once painted a painting on my kitchen table, so I may be prejudiced.)

Card certainly deserved his win at the time, based on the evidence available then, although I think that Bruce Sterling would subsequently outstrip him in sheer ability. Sterling didn't deserve it based on the work visible in 1978, though, and Card did.

21. SUSAN LOYAL

I'm caught in a moment of nostalgia. In 1977, I was an adult working a job, with discretionary income (although not a lot), out of college, not yet in graduate school. I can actually remember which of these books I read when they came out, rather than years after. What I chose to read was based on what I saw in bookstores. I knew no one else who read science fiction and fantasy, so no input from others, and that year I didn't see any issues of *F&SF*, although I'd subscribed when I was in college. So no reviews, either. Of those listed, I read:

Gateway, The Forbidden Tower, Lucifer's Hammer, The Ophiuchi Hotline, In the Ocean of Night, Dragonsinger, The Book of Merlyn, Charmed Life, The Perfect Lover. I picked up *The Silmarillion* and put it back down. I tried to read *Chronicles of Thomas Covenant* and gave up. I wanted to read *Our Lady of Darkness*, but I lived alone and was afraid that I wouldn't be able to sleep afterwards, so I didn't.

If you had asked me what I thought was the best book of the year (I'd only vaguely heard of the Hugos, so it wasn't a question I asked myself), I'd have said *The Ophiuchi Hotline* or *Charmed Life*.

However, I liked *Gateway*, although it didn't make as much impression on me as *Man Plus*. I liked *Lucifer's Hammer* quite a lot. It was the first time I'd encountered the "big space object whacks Earth and you can't rely on Stouffer's frozen meals anymore so what now?" plot. I was working as an administrative assistant, and I was charmed by the idea that organizational skills went on being useful. I read it more than once, and then never again. I liked *The Forbidden Tower*, which I also read more than once. Both its structure and its prose are awkward, but it attempts discussion of how a mature person goes about setting aside convictions that hamper effective action. Oddly, when I did find someone who also read SF&F to talk to, MZB was the only point where our tastes overlapped. (While the Comyn would certainly be first up against the wall come the revolution, their charm lies mostly in offering very clear rules of the your-grandmother-did-it-this-way-and-as-long-as-you-live-in-my-house-you-will-too variety. So the plot almost always replicates the process of individuation: (1) leave the house; (2) deconstruct grandmother's reasons to see if conditions have changed, (3) change the world. In other words, it's an effective YA plot.)

22. JohnnyMac

A minor note on *Our Lady of Darkness* (one of Leiber's best, IMHO): it is set in San Francisco and one of the key locations is a sinister hill called Corona Heights. When I read the story, I was living near San Francisco, had never heard of Corona Heights, and assumed that

Leiber had invented it. A decade or so later, I was in a service station idly studying a large map of the Bay Area mounted on the wall while I waited for my car. I was both surprised and a little chilled to discover on the map CORONA HEIGHTS clearly marked.

It was rather as if I had been driving down a freeway in New England and seen a sign reading: INNSMOUTH EXIT—3 MILES.

42. RICH HORTON

I thought it would be interesting to see how the Campbell winners break down as to what length of work led to their nomination and award. That is, were they short fiction writers or novelists?

I assumed that short fiction writers would predominate early and novelists more recently, but that's not really true. Maybe very slightly— the first five winners (over four years because of one tie) had written only short fiction, and something like four of the last five were primarily novelists, but over time it spreads out very evenly.

Indeed, by my count, nineteen Campbell winners won almost certainly because of their short fiction, and nineteen won almost certainly because of their novels. Only one seems truly ambiguous to me—Judith Moffett, who had published a novel, *Pennterra,* but also some really first-rate short fiction. Elizabeth Bear might be an arguable case—she was nominated on the basis of short fiction, as her first novels appeared only about the time of the voting, but they did appear early enough that they might have influenced the voters, if not the nominators.

1979

Winner: *Dreamsnake,* by Vonda N. McIntyre

Nominees:
Blind Voices, by Tom Reamy
The Faded Sun: Kesrith, by C. J. Cherryh
Up the Walls of the World, by James Tiptree Jr.
The White Dragon, by Anne McCaffrey

The 1979 Hugo Awards were awarded at Seacon in Brighton, England, and that was another legendary convention because I've been hearing legends about it since I got into fandom ten years later. I was fourteen in the summer of 1979, but it's technically the first Worldcon I could have gone to. I did know it was happening. I saw an article about it in the *Times* the day it started. Despite not really knowing what a science fiction convention was, I spent the whole day with a railway timetable and various adults trying to arrange it. Robert Silverberg was going to be there, I kept saying. Arthur C. Clarke was going to be there! But destiny and common sense were against me.

The Best Novel Hugo went to Vonda McIntyre's *Dreamsnake,* a book I loved when I read it a year or two later but which I haven't reread in a while. It's science fiction with a fantastic feel, a quest across a post-apocalyptic wasteland with healing snakes. It won the Nebula and *Locus* Award too. It's not in print, and in the library in French only. It's a good book, but it hasn't lasted well—I think it must have really spoken to the zeitgeist at the time.

There are four other nominees, and I've read all of them. Interestingly for a British Worldcon, no British writers, and several books not published in the United Kingdom in time for nominators to have seen them.

Tom Reamy's *Blind Voices* is a Bradbury-esque story that edges on horror, about a carnival with real magic and mysterious secrets. It's beautifully written, and was also nominated for the Nebula. I'm sorry to see that it's not in print and it's not in the library. Reamy's career was cut short by his untimely death—this was his first novel, and if he'd lived and gone on writing, he might have been better remembered. (UK edition, 1979.)

C. J. Cherryh's *The Faded Sun: Kesrith* is the first of the Faded Sun trilogy. It's about aliens and being alone among aliens and realizing you're the alien one, and it's claustrophobic and depressing even for Cherryh, and I love Cherryh. It's in print from DAW in an omnibus with the two sequels, but it's not in the library. I'd say it has lasted as a minor work from a major writer. It was also nominated for a Nebula. No UK edition until the eighties. It's the only nominee that wouldn't have been available to British voters, and I wonder if it suffered by that.

James Tiptree Jr.'s *Up the Walls of the World* is Tiptree's slightly disappointing first novel—disappointing in comparison to how wonderful her shorter work was. It's science fiction with telepaths and telepathic aliens. It's not in print, and it's in the library in French only. It's not the first thing one thinks of when talking about Tiptree; in fact, it's fairly far down the list. But like *Dreamsnake*, it was also in print in the United Kingdom before the convention.

Anne McCaffrey's *The White Dragon* is the third of her trilogy of stories about Lessa and the Dragonriders of Pern. It's in print, and it's in the library in English only. It's unusual for a book in a continuing series to be nominated, even a popular series like this one. I'd say this is the weakest of the books on the list and the first one I'd throw out of the balloon. (UK edition, 1979.)

So, four women and one man, all American. Only McCaffrey is a previous nominee, Tiptree had won at short form, McIntyre had previous short-form nominations, Reamy and Cherryh had both won the Campbell, but this is the first time for any of them on the novel ballot. So postapocalyptic SF, three planetary SF, and one dark fantasy. They're all books worth reading. This is the first time there's been more than one woman on the Best Novel ballot.

But what else might they have nominated?

The Nebulas had considerable overlap—McIntyre, Reamy, and Cherryh. Their other two nominees were Gore Vidal's *Kalki*, which I haven't read, and Gardner Dozois's excellent *Strangers*, which should definitely have been on the Hugo list.

The World Fantasy Award was won by Michael Moorcock's *Gloriana*. Other nominees were Les Daniels's *The Black Castle*; Tanith Lee's *Night's Master*; Charles L. Grant's *The Sound of Midnight*; and Stephen King's *The Stand*. I'd have been surprised if any of these had made the Hugo ballot, though *The Stand* has definitely lasted.

The John W. Campbell Memorial Award was also won by *Gloriana*, which astonishes me, as it is out-and-out fantasy—literary experimental fantasy, but not SF by any stretch of the imagination. (This is a very weird award.) I haven't heard of either of the honorable mentions, Paddy Chayefsky's *Altered States* or Donald R. Benson's *And Having Writ. . . .*

The Locus Awards have a long list. Nominees not previously mentioned are: Ben Bova's *Colony*; Marion Zimmer Bradley's *Stormqueen!*; Gordon R. Dickson's *The Far Call*; Poul Anderson's *The Avatar*; Roger Zelazny's *The Courts of Chaos*; Gregory Benford's *The Stars in Shroud*; Joan Vinge's *The Outcasts of Heaven Belt*; Charles Sheffield's *Sight of Proteus*; Marta Randall's *Journey*; Katherine Kurtz's *Saint Camber*; Chelsea Quinn Yarbro's *Hôtel Transylvania*; Marvin Kaye and Parke Godwin's *The Masters of Solitude*; and Elizabeth Lynn's *A Different Light*. A lot of good stuff here, and several books that could well have deserved a Hugo nomination, but nothing that makes me feel it was an injustice.

The Libertarian Futurist Society instituted its Prometheus Award in 1979, though it wasn't given again until 1982 and has henceforth been annual. It is given by Libertarians, but it honors genre fiction that advances the cause of liberty, rather than being explicitly Libertarian in a doctrinaire way. The award is an ounce of gold, made into a coin portraying Liberty. The first one was given to F. Paul Wilson's *Wheels Within Wheels.*

Is there anything all of these missed?

Robin McKinley's *Beauty;* Suzy McKee Charnas's *Motherlines;* Octavia Butler's *Survivor;* Richard Cowper's *The Road to Corlay;* and Hal Clement's *Through the Eye of a Needle.*

Out of all these books, I could find five I like more and are more significant and have lasted better, but I think the five we have do represent the totality pretty well.

OTHER CATEGORIES

BEST NOVELLA

Winner: *The Persistence of Vision,* by John Varley (*F&SF,* March 1978)

Nominees:
Enemies of the System, by Brian W. Aldiss (*F&SF,* June 1978)
Fireship, by Joan D. Vinge (*Analog,* December 1978)
Seven American Nights, by Gene Wolfe (*Orbit 20*)
The Watched, by Christopher Priest (*F&SF,* April 1978)

Thank goodness Varley did eventually win one! Very good set of stories here.

BEST NOVELETTE

Winner: "Hunter's Moon," by Poul Anderson (*Analog,* November 1978)

Nominees:
"The Barbie Murders," by John Varley (*Asimov's,* January/February 1978)

"Devil You Don't Know," by Dean Ing (*Analog*, January 1978)
"The Man Who Had No Idea," by Thomas M. Disch (*F&SF*, October 1978)
"Mikal's Songbird," by Orson Scott Card (*Analog*, May 1978)

I'd have definitely voted for the Card here, with the Varley a hair behind.

Best Short Story

Winner: "Cassandra," by C. J. Cherryh (*F&SF*, October 1978)

Nominees:
"Count the Clock That Tells the Time," by Harlan Ellison (*Omni*, December 1978)
"Stone," by Edward Bryant (*F&SF*, February 1978)
"The Very Slow Time Machine," by Ian Watson (*Anticipations*)
"View from a Height," by Joan D. Vinge (*Analog*, June 1978)

I don't remember the Cherryh, though I'm sure I've read it. I'd have voted for the Watson, a story that has stayed with me for a long time.

Best Dramatic Presentation

Winner: *Superman: The Movie*

Nominees:
The Hitchhiker's Guide to the Galaxy (radio series)
Invasion of the Body Snatchers
The Lord of the Rings
Watership Down

Seriously? Good grief. I would have voted for *Hitchhiker's*, and then very emphatically for No Award.

Best Professional Editor

Winner: Ben Bova

Nominees:
Jim Baen
Terry Carr
Edward L. Ferman
George Scithers

I'd definitely have voted for Baen. Words cannot express how much *Destinies* meant to me in 1979.

Best Professional Artist

Winner: Vincent Di Fate

Nominees:
Steve Fabian
David Hardy
Boris Vallejo
Michael Whelan

Best Fanzine

Winner: *Science Fiction Review*, edited by Richard E. Geis

Nominees:
Janus, edited by Janice Bogstad and Jeanne Gomoll
Maya, edited by Rob Jackson
Mota, edited by Terry Hughes
Twll-Ddu, edited by Dave Langford

Ugol's Law suggests that I am not the only person reading this who can pronounce the name of Langford's fanzine. It means "Black Hole," by the way.

Best Fan Writer

Winner: Bob Shaw

Nominees:
Richard E. Geis
Leroy Kettle
Dave Langford
D. West

Best Fan Artist

Winner: Bill Rotsler

Nominees:
Jim Barker
Harry Bell
Alexis Gilliland
Stu Shiffman

John W. Campbell Award

Winner: Stephen R. Donaldson

Nominees:
Cynthia Felice
James P. Hogan
Barry B. Longyear
Elizabeth A. Lynn
Charles Sheffield

A good year for the Campbells—all of them have gone on to have careers in the field, and I know who they are. I think Donaldson was the obvious winner, but there's not a dud there—any one of them would have made a good solid winner.

Comments on 1979

1. Rich Horton

A couple potential nominees I might add:

Space War Blues, by Richard Lupoff (the long-awaited novel version of his *Again, Dangerous Visions* story "With the Bentfin Boomer Boys on Little Old New Alabama")
The Book of the Dun Cow, by Walter Wangerin

Perhaps more interesting are a few YA novels:

A Swiftly Tilting Planet, by Madeleine L'Engle (one of the sequels to *A Wrinkle in Time*, but not as good)
Very Far Away from Anywhere Else, by Ursula K. Le Guin (I remember liking it quite a bit, but I don't remember much else about it—it's not very long, maybe novella length, and it might not really be SF or fantasy)
And finally, a very interesting novel that actually probably did deserve a place on the award short lists: *The Ennead*, by Jan Mark

As for the Campbells, it's kind of hard to argue with the award to Donaldson based on his career to that date, and even perhaps since, but I'm not a fan. I'd have given it to Lynn at the time, and probably to Sheffield for his career.

And, yes, absolutely a Hugo for Baen would have been just. I loved his *Galaxy*, and I loved *Destinies*.

2. Rich Horton

In the novella category, *The Persistence of Vision* is a famous story, a significant story, a story a lot of people love. And it's good that Varley finally got his award. But—I really dislike it.

The obvious best novella of the year was Gene Wolfe's *Seven American Nights*. (I told you Wolfe would be back!) But, really!

Other potential nominees, neither of which really thrill me: Wolfe's

The Death of Doctor Island (the gimmick of the title seems a bit forced), and Michael Bishop's *Old Folks at Home.*

There's also Larry Niven's *The Magic Goes Away,* which was a separate illustrated book from Ace (and indeed came third on the *Locus* Art Book list), but which was novella length. However, it may have been the same text as the 1976 story from *Odyssey* magazine.

In novelette, this is one of the first years I remember being disappointed by the winner as it was announced—I was thrilled to see Anderson's "Hunter's Moon" when it appeared, then quite let down by the story. Not one of his best, at all. I'd have probably given it to "The Barbie Murders," though I was impressed with "Mikal's Songbird" too. (Card again mining his favorite subject, abused brilliant children.)

C. L. Grant's "A Glow of Candles, a Unicorn's Eye" won the Nebula—but I don't remember the story. I did like Dean Ing's "Devil You Don't Know" quite a lot. Others to mention: James Tiptree's "We Who Stole the Dream," Hilbert Schenck's "The Morphology of the Kirkham Wreck" (Schenck had published a couple of stories and poems in *F&SF* in the fifties, but returned in the late seventies and into the eighties with a number of nice stories, mostly on sea-related subjects), Spider Robinson's "Antinomy."

In short story, I agree with Jo: I'd have given the award to Ian Watson's "The Very Slow Time Machine." Edward Bryant's "Stone" won the Nebula—I don't remember it well, but I think it was good.

One other short story to mention is from the wonderful John Crowley. It's an excellent story, but I really like it because it has two separate titles, each taken from the same poem, one of the greatest poems of all time, Wallace Stevens's "Sunday Morning." (And I shall soon enough be drinking coffee, in my pajamas if not a peignoir. . . .) Anyway, the story is "Her Bounty to the Dead," originally called "Where Spirits Gat Them Home."

12. CARBONEL

The audience at those Hugos, not surprisingly, were much more enthusiastic about *The Hitchhiker's Guide to the Galaxy* than the actual winner, *Superman.* Which Christopher Reeve, the star of *Superman* who was there to accept the Hugo, was entirely gracious about. He said something to the effect that he could tell he wasn't the audience's favorite, but was nevertheless very pleased.

39. Gardner Dozois

Generally, a pretty weak year. The strongest story of the entire year is Gene Wolfe's magnificent *Seven American Nights,* which definitely should have won in novella.

I'm not sure what I'd vote for in novel (my own Really Terrific novel aside, of course!). I don't think that *Dreamsnake* has aged well, and most of the other novels mentioned are weak. I'd almost go for *The Stand,* even though several hundred pages could be cut out of it without any loss (with improvement, in fact) and it features one of the worst endings in the history of world literature, causing me to throw the very heavy book across the room, killing the cat. Still, the middle sections, after everbody dies from the Snot Plague, are very fine in spots. Guess I would have to go for *Up the Walls of the World,* on the theory that middle-level Tiptree is better than no Tiptree at all.

I've already told you my pick for novella, *Seven American Nights,* although Brian Aldiss's little-known *A Chinese Perspective* is good too, as is *The Persistence of Vision* and Algis Budrys's *The Nuptial Flight of Warbirds.* Although it's a fantasy, I'd also mention Avram Davidson's *Sleep Well of Nights,* another of the strongest Jack Limekiller stories. Novella was by far the strongest category this year.

Novelette, I think should have gone to Thomas Disch's heartbreaking "Mutability," a story from an SF novel that Disch was putting together at one point, but never finished. James P. Girard's "September Song" was also pretty jazzy, and he looked like a pretty hot new writer at this point, but he subsequently disappeared without a trace. King's "The Gunslinger" also certainly deserved to be in the race.

Short story, I'd give to Jack Vance's little-known (almost unknown, in fact) story "The Secret"—a very untypical Vance story. Aldiss's "The Small Stones of Tu Fu" is also good, and again a little-known story by a major author.

Charles Sheffield, the best SF writer of the group, should have won the Campbell, in my opinion.

1980

BEST NOVEL

Winner: *The Fountains of Paradise,* by Arthur C. Clarke

Nominees:
Harpist in the Wind, by Patricia McKillip
Jem, by Frederik Pohl
On Wings of Song, by Thomas M. Disch
Titan, by John Varley

The 1980 Hugo Awards were presented at Noreascon II in Boston.

The Best Novel award was given to Arthur C. Clarke's *The Fountains of Paradise,* a hard SF novel about building a space elevator beanstalk from Sri Lanka into space. It's an old-fashioned kind of book, and it was old-fashioned even in 1979. It's the story of one engineering project and one engineer. It has thin characterization, few women, and not a lot of plot. It also won the Nebula. It's in print from Warner, and in the library in English only. I don't hear a lot of discussion about it these days, and I don't think many people would say it is their favorite Clarke. I don't think it's a good Hugo winner.

There are four other nominees, and I've read all of them. Patricia McKillip's *Harpist in the Wind* is unquestionably fantasy. It's also brilliant. But I'm very surprised to see it with a Hugo nomination, because it's the third book in the Riddlemaster trilogy, and it in no way stands alone. An unconventional choice, but a terrific book. It won the Locus Fantasy Award. It's in print as part of an omnibus in the Gollancz

Fantasy Masterworks series and also as part of an omnibus from Ace, and in the library as part of an omnibus.

Frederik Pohl's *Jem* is science fiction—humans colonize a planet that already has alien inhabitants, and everything goes wrong. The aliens are very well done, and so is the conflict. This is a good solid complex SF novel and would have been a much better winner. It's not in print, and it's in the library in French only. Somebody should reissue it.

Thomas M. Disch's *On Wings of Song* is . . . indescribable. It's a brilliant masterpiece, depressing, like all Disch, but thought provoking and amazing. It won the Campbell Memorial. It's out of print, and in the library in French only. Somebody should reprint it immediately if not sooner. This would have had my first-place vote.

John Varley's *Titan* is excellent until the very end, where it all falls apart. It's about a woman exploring an alien ecology, Big Dumb Object orbiting Saturn, in the great tradition of *Rendezvous with Rama*, only with more centaur sex. I adored everything Varley wrote up to nearly the end of this book, and have been disappointed by most of what he has written since. It won the Locus SF Award. It's not in print, and it's not in the library, though for some reason the two sequels are.

What an odd set! Four men and one woman, four Americans and one Englishman living in Sri Lanka. Clarke and Pohl were previous winners, Varley was a previous nominee, Disch had been nominated in short form but not for a novel before, McKillip was a complete newcomer to the Hugos. We have one very traditional SF novel about engineering, one epic fantasy, two complex SF novels, and one SF exploration adventure.

What else might they have chosen?

The only eligible non-overlapping Nebula nominee was Kate Wilhelm's *Juniper Time*.

The World Fantasy Award went to Elizabeth Lynn's wonderful *Watchtower*. They also short-listed the McKillip; and Lynn's *Dancers of Arun*; Patricia Wrightson's *The Dark Bright Water*; Charles L. Grant's *The Last Call of Mourning*; and Chelsea Quinn Yarbro's *The Palace*.

The John W. Campbell Memorial Award gave second place to John Crowley's *Engine Summer*, a significant book that would have been a worthy Hugo nominee, and third to J. G. Ballard's very odd *The Unlimited Dream Company.*

Locus SF nominees that haven't been mentioned so far: Spider and Jeanne Robinson's *Stardance;* C. J. Cherryh's *Kutath;* Anne McCaffrey's *Dragondrums;* Jack Vance's *The Face;* Michael Bishop's *Transfigurations;* Roger Zelazny's *Roadmarks;* Ben Bova's *Kinsman;* Len Deighton's *SS-GB;* Michael Bishop's *Catacomb Years;* Charles Sheffield's *The Web Between the Worlds;* Kevin O'Donnell's *Mayflies;* Orson Scott Card's *A Planet Called Treason;* Norman Spinrad's *A World Between;* James P. Hogan's *The Two Faces of Tomorrow;* M. A. Foster's *The Day of the Klesh;* Larry Niven's *The Ringworld Engineers;* and Jerry Pournelle's *Janissaries.* Lots there that could have been nominated.

Despite the fact that *Janissaries* is the only one I've written about, the book I've read most frequently out of that selection is undoubtedly *A Planet Called Treason,* which is flawed but fascinating.

Locus Fantasy nominees not already mentioned: Stephen King's *The Dead Zone;* Samuel R. Delany's *Tales of Nevèrÿon*—No, stop! I can't type the next nominee without cognitive dissonance upon seeing them on the same line, so I might as well say something. I don't understand. Why was this not Hugo nominated? It's fantasy, yes, but we were nominating fantasy this year. This is a really major book!

To continue: Piers Anthony's *Castle Roogna;* Poul Anderson's *The Merman's Children;* C. J. Cherryh's *The Fires of Azeroth* (SF, actually)*;* Mary Stewart's *The Last Enchantment;* Ursula Le Guin's *Malafrena;* Tanith Lee's *Death's Master;* Octavia Butler's *Kindred;* Lynn Abbey's *Daughter of the Bright Moon;* Diane Duane's *The Door into Fire;* Phyllis Eisenstein's *Sorceror's Son;* and Tim Powers's *The Drawing of the Dark.*

The Delany and the Butler should both have had Hugo nominations, but it's not really the Hugos so much as the World Fantasy Awards falling down on the job here—good winner, but their selections seem really conventional when I look at this list.

Is there anything all these awards missed?

Looking at the ISFDB, I see Brian Aldiss's *Brothers of the Head* and *Cryptozoic!;* Philip José Farmer's *Jesus on Mars;* K. W. Jeter's *Morlock Night;* Bob Shaw's *Night Walk;* and Douglas Adams's *The Hitchhiker's*

Guide to the Galaxy. I think this is another year for the negative side—these five nominees are definitely not the five best or most significant of the year.

OTHER CATEGORIES

BEST NOVELLA

Winner: *Enemy Mine*, by Barry B. Longyear (*Asimov's*, September 1979)

Nominees:
The Battle of the Abaco Reefs, by Hilbert Schenck (*F&SF*, June 1979)
Ker-Plop, by Ted Reynolds (*Asimov's*, January 1979)
The Moon Goddess and the Son, by Donald Kingsbury (*Analog*, December 1979)
Songhouse, by Orson Scott Card (*Analog*, September 1979)

Good winner. I had the Hugo winners anthology for this year and can remember actually crying at this story.

BEST NOVELETTE

Winner: "Sandkings," by George R. R. Martin (*Omni*, August 1979)

Nominees:
"Fireflood," by Vonda N. McIntyre (*F&SF*, November 1979)
"Homecoming," by Barry B. Longyear (*Asimov's*, October 1979)
"The Locusts," by Larry Niven and Steve Barnes (*Analog*, June 1979)
"Options," by John Varley (*Universe 9*)
"Palely Loitering," by Christopher Priest (*F&SF*, January 1979)

Again, good winner. I've been a fan of Martin's from this story onward.

Best Short Story

Winner: "The Way of Cross and Dragon," by George R. R. Martin (*Omni*, June 1979)

Nominees:
"Can These Bones Live?," by Ted Reynolds (*Analog*, March 1979)
"Daisy, In the Sun," by Connie Willis (*Galileo*, November 1979)
"giANTS," by Edward Bryant (*Analog*, August 1979)
"Unaccompanied Sonata," by Orson Scott Card (*Omni*, March 1979)

Good winner and an awesome list of nominees. I had no idea Willis had been writing this long.

Best Nonfiction Book

Winner: *The Science Fiction Encyclopedia*, edited by Peter Nicholls (Doubleday)

Nominees:
Barlowe's Guide to Extraterrestrials, by Wayne Douglas Barlowe and Ian Summers (Workman)
In Memory Yet Green, by Isaac Asimov (Doubleday)
The Language of the Night, by Ursula K. Le Guin, edited by Susan Wood (Putnam)
Wonderworks, by Michael Whelan (Donning)

Look, new category! And what a great set of nominees to start off— and as usual, a set of things not very like each other and hard to compare. I've read four of these (everything but the Whelan, which I assume is an art book) if you can say you've read an encyclopedia, and I have no idea which I'd vote for. Probably the Le Guin, but . . . when you have four novels, no matter how different, they are at least all novels.

Best Dramatic Presentation

Winner: *Alien*

Nominees:
The Black Hole
The Muppet Movie
Star Trek: The Motion Picture
Time After Time

Best Professional Editor

Winner: George H. Scithers

Nominees:
Jim Baen
Ben Bova
Edward L. Ferman
Stanley Schmidt

Best Professional Artist

Winner: Michael Whelan

Nominees:
Vincent Di Fate
Steve Fabian
Paul Lehr
Boris Vallejo

Best Fanzine

Winner: *Locus*, edited by Charles N. Brown

Nominees:
File 770, edited by Mike Glyer

Janus, edited by Janice Bogstad and Jeanne Gomoll
Science Fiction Review, edited by Richard E. Geis
Thrust, edited by Doug Fratz

BEST FAN WRITER

Winner: Bob Shaw

Nominees:
Richard E. Geis
Mike Glyer
Arthur D. Hlavaty
David Langford

People could still nominate Arthur Hlavaty now. He's still a terrific fan writer. He has a wonderful way of putting things.

BEST FAN ARTIST

Winner: Alexis Gilliland

Nominees:
Jeanne Gomoll
Joan Hanke-Woods
Victoria Poyser
Bill Rotsler
Stu Shiffman

JOHN W. CAMPBELL AWARD

Winner: Barry B. Longyear

Nominees:
Lynn Abbey
Diane Duane
Karen Jollie

Alan Ryan

Somtow Sucharitkul

Interesting list. Longyear produced that one wonderful novella, and I entirely see why people voted for him. He's kept writing but never been very prolific or written anything else that's had the same kind of attention since.

Lynn Abbey edited some collections with Asprin and did some writing in the Cherryh's Merovingian universe. I haven't heard anything about her in a while.

Diane Duane has gone on to have a major career, largely in YA. She'd also have been a good winner.

Karen Jollie is a complete blank to me. I don't know Alan Ryan either, but *Locus* says he won a World Fantasy Award for short story in 1984 and edited a pile of anthologies in the eighties but nothing recent.

Somtow Sucharitkul is a writer I really like. He has published a lot of books, science fiction, fantasy, horror, and historical, some under the more pronounceable name S. P. Somtow; he's wonderful but he's never really had the sales to go with his talent. He'd have been another good winner, and he won in 1981 in his second year of eligibility.

COMMENTS ON 1980

2. RICH HORTON

My choice of the Hugo nominees is *Jem*—I loved that novel, it made me furious, it made me cry (in a bitter, not tragic, sense). I actually threw the book across the room, in anger at the mess Pohl depicted so well.

But even ahead of *Jem*, there are two novels I love even more. One of these is *Malafrena*, which arguably is not eligible—it's SF only in the "Ruritanian" sense. But it's a book I passionately devoured at the time. Some of this is for personal, or temporary, reasons: it was a gift from my then girlfriend, and I read it at just the right age. (I was twenty.) But I do think it a lovely book.

The other novel, though, is my actual pick for the best novel of 1979, and that is John Crowley's *Engine Summer*, which is simply beautiful and heartbreaking.* And the last line is purely wonderful.

Other novels to mention: Barrington Bayley's *Collision with Chronos,* and the original Italian edition of Italo Calvino's *If on a Winter's Night a Traveller* (which would have had a better chance after the English translation appeared in 1981). Also, L. Neil Smith's enjoyable first novel, *The Probability Broach.* And more YA in tone: *The Spellcoats,* one of Diana Wynne Jones's excellent Dalemark Quartet, and *Which Witch?* by Eva Ibbotson, which I haven't read but which seems to get good press.

As to the Campbell, no I don't remember anything about Karen Jollie at all. It should perhaps be noted that besides his SF and horror, Somtow Sucharitkul is a major composer, and is the artistic director of the Bangkok Opera.

5. RICH HORTON

And for the short fiction . . . in novella at the time, *Enemy Mine* seemed a clear-enough winner, and it holds up fairly well. Longyear's weird career (affected in part by some personal issues he had [alcoholism] that he chronicled to some extent in a later novel) hasn't backed up that story much, and even his early work was terribly uneven, but he does still show up with a pretty strong story, as with last year's "Alten Kameraden."

As to the other novellas—generally a decent but not brilliant set. One more story from the Nebula short list was one of my favorites, Samuel R. Delany's "The Tale of Gorgik." One might also note the presence on the Nebula short list of a story by Richard Wilson, "The Story Writer," which appeared in *Destinies.* Wilson hadn't been much heard of since his Nebula-winning late sixties story, *Mother to the World.*

In novelette, no argument with "Sandkings," first-rate stuff. (Something of a revisiting of Sturgeon's SF Hall of Fame story "Microcos-

---

*"Heartbreaking" is a term that can also be applied, in slightly different ways, to *Jem, Malafrena,* and *On Wings of Song.* . . .

mic God.") But other potential nominees worthy of a mention include a really good Spider Robinson story, "God Is an Iron," and a late Alfred Bester story, "Galatea Galante." I also really like Richard Cowper's "Out There Where the Big Ships Go," and perhaps the first John M. Ford story to make a big impact, "Mandalay."

In short story, I would probably vote for "Daisy, in the Sun" as the best. This was Willis's first story to get much notice, but she had first published SF as early as 1970, with an apparently justly forgotten story called "The Secret of Santa Titicaca," in *Worlds of Fantasy*, a short-lived companion to *Galaxy*.

I also really like Ed Bryant's "giANTS," which won the Nebula.

Some more stories to mention:

"A Day in Mallworld," by Somtow Sucharitkul
"And Come from Miles Around," by Connie Willis
"In the Country of the Blind, No One Can See," by Melisa Michaels

And an interesting one: "The Colonel Came Back from Nothing-at-all," by Cordwainer Smith. This is apparently an early Instrumentality story that Smith never published, partly because it conflicts with some of the later stories. He rewrote aspects of it as "Drunkboat." This version first appeared in the Del Rey collection *The Instrumentality of Mankind*.

25. GARDNER DOZOIS

I never warmed to *Enemy Mine,* perhaps because it always struck me as a direct one-to-one translation into SF of an old Frank Sinatra war movie. The win for Longyear and the presence of him and Somtow Sucharitkul on the Campbell ballot are certainly related to the win for George Scithers in the Best Professional Editor category. Longyear was hugely prolific at short lengths during Scithers's reign at *Asimov's*—the joke at the time was that the magazine ought to be called *Barry B. Longyear and Somtow Sucharitkul's Science Fiction Magazine,* since it seemed that every issue featured a story from one or the other of them, and sometimes both—and his lapse into silence pretty much corrolated with George leaving *Asimov's*. Novella is a weak category this year, unlike the previous year, when it was the strongest. I think my vote at the time went to Hilbert Schenck's *The Battle of the Abaco Reefs*, although I suspect that it's seriously dated by now. Another good novella that was overlooked was Suzy McKee Charnas's *The Ancient Mind at Work*, one of the stories at the start of the Big Vampire Revival, the floodgates of which would really swing wide in coming decades.

Novelette clearly goes to "Sandkings," although Jack Dann's "Camps," which didn't make the ballot, is powerful stuff, and Zelazny's "The Last Defender of Camelot" is a strong fantasy. I think Martin deserved his win in short story too; in fact, in some ways, I like "The Way of Cross and Dragon" better than "Sandkings." I liked Bryant's "giANTS" too, and Zelazny's very short "Halfjack" was good as well. Connie Willis would be doing much stronger work in just a year or two, so I wouldn't have voted for "Daisy, in the Sun," although it probably deserved a place on the ballot.

Nonfiction is a tough category, but I guess I'd give it to *The Encyclopedia*, a book of significance to the genre that I still use to this day. Asimov's autobiography is probably the most fun to read, though.

Sunlit Clouds Beyond the Iron Grating: Thomas M. Disch's *On Wings of Song*

When I wrote about Samuel Delany's *Nova*, I said that if it were published today, it would still be a book we'd be excited about. I can say the same about Thomas M. Disch's *On Wings of Song*. It was published in 1979, but it doesn't at all read as if it was. It's set in a satiric, dystopic, future collapsed USA, where the country has fragmented and the economy has gone to pieces. It reads as if it could still be the future—I mean, it doesn't have cell phones and the internet, but then it makes sense that it wouldn't. It's a fascinating, complex world. There are machines that you hook up to and sing sincerely, and if you do it right, you have an out-of-body experience. They call this flying, and it's banned in the same way that drugs are banned—illegal but available.

The world is also full of phonies, white people who dye their skin black for personal reasons, fashion reasons, to please their partners, or just to get on. They always leave one part white, though, sometimes a finger, sometimes the tip of their nose. There are famines when rations get cut to starvation levels, and prisons where you have to get McDonald's takeout to survive. There are rich people and there are people who have to hustle to get by, and there's a movie called *Gold Diggers of 1984*, and Bel Canto is a popular art form.

We don't seem to have a word to describe the kind of story this is. It's the whole life story, from age five to death, of Daniel Weinreb. He lives in New York and then in Iowa, with one trip to the bright lights of Minneapolis, and then back in New York. He spends a while in prison for distributing the Minneapolis *Star Tribune* in Iowa—I was so surprised when I found out that was a real newspaper! He wants to fly, he wants it more than anything. His life is complicated and largely unheroic, the kind of life people actually have in reality and seldom have in fiction. But it's a life he could have only in that time and place, in the world he lives in. It's a book about how he grows up and what happens to him and what he wants and what he has to do to get by.

The book is depressing and hilarious in a way that's very hard to describe. Most of Disch is brilliant and depressing; this is brilliant and depressing and moving and funny. I can talk about the world, and if I wanted to do spoilers, I could talk about Daniel and the plot, but I can't possibly describe to you the experience of reading the book. The best I can do is to say that it's as if Dostoyevsky and Douglas Adams collaborated on the Great American novel.

You really want to read *On Wings of Song*. You might not like it, but it's one of the books that marks the boundaries of what it's possible to do with SF—still right out there on the edge, thirty years on. And furthermore, somebody should reprint it.

1 9 8 1

Winner: *The Snow Queen,* by Joan D. Vinge

Nominees:
Beyond the Blue Event Horizon, by Frederik Pohl
Lord Valentine's Castle, by Robert Silverberg
The Ringworld Engineers, by Larry Niven
Wizard, by John Varley

The 1981 Hugo Awards were handed out in Denvention II in Denver, and shoot me now, because this is the year when I don't like anything.

The Best Novel award went to Joan Vinge's *The Snow Queen.* It's science fiction that uses the Hans Christian Andersen story of "The Snow Queen" to shape the story and for resonance, and I really ought to love it—but in fact, I've never been able to force myself all the way through it. Maybe I am too young for it, but I tried it again last year. It's a beloved classic for many people, but it just does nothing for me. I'm sorry. I'm quite prepared to see this as a flaw in me rather than a flaw in it. It won the Locus SF award. It's in print, and it's in the library in English. I've heard people talking about it recently. It has definitely lasted. And despite not liking it, I think it was the right winner.

There are four other nominees, and I've read them all. I hate three of them, and I'm tepid on the other.

Frederik Pohl's *Beyond the Blue Event Horizon* is the sequel to his brilliant *Gateway.* It has a wonderful title. And it's in the Gateway universe. What could possibly go wrong? Well, everything. This is one of the most disappointing books I have ever read, because I had such high hopes for it. It is not as bad as the later sequels, and it is enlivened by Pohl's always delightful prose, but . . . *Gateway* did not need sequels, and this book isn't only bad but it also spoils what went before. If the Lacuna Corporation ever really advertised its memory blocking, the memory of these sequels would be one of the first things I'd erase. ("Then you'd read them again," my son said. And he's right. I wouldn't be able to stop myself.) It's in print from Tor, and it's in the library in French only.

Next, the one I'm tepid about. Robert Silverberg's *Lord Valentine's Castle* is what I'd probably have voted for if I'd had a vote in 1981. It's the first of Silverberg's Majipoor books, introducing the world, which feels like fantasy but is science fiction. It's a huge, sprawling picaresque adventure about a man who loses his memory and his body. I liked it when I was sixteen, but it hasn't worn well and I have come to feel that it's one of Silverberg's weaker books. I don't care for the sequels, and it doesn't reread well. It won the Locus Fantasy award. It doesn't seem to be in print, but it's in the library in English and French.

Larry Niven's *The Ringworld Engineers* is the first sequel to *Ringworld,* and it has some of the same flaws as *Beyond the Blue Event Horizon,* explaining things best left unexplained, revisiting characters whose stories were finished. It's in print from Orbit, and in the library in French and English. I've also heard people refer to its word for interspecies sex fairly recently, so maybe everybody else likes it.

Which brings me to John Varley's *Wizard,* which is just—spare me. I hated this so much, I didn't ever read the third one. It's the sequel to *Titan.* It has centaur sex.

So four men and one woman, all Americans. Niven and Pohl are previous winners, Silverberg and Varley are previous nominees, Vinge had won at short form but this is her first appearance on the novel ballot. They're all science fiction—one book I can't read, three feeble sequels, and one okay book by an author who has done much better. I understand why the Vinge and the Silverberg got nominated, but the rest of this is a mystery to me.

Wasn't there anything better available to represent 1980 than this collection of warmed-over stuff?

The Nebula was won by Gregory Benford's *Timescape*, a solid work of hard SF, which would have been a good nominee. They had three non-overlapping nominees—Gene Wolfe's *The Shadow of the Torturer*, a work of sufficient outstanding excellence that it should have made the Hugo ballot in any year, and two books I haven't read: Walter S. Tevis's *Mockingbird* and Robert Stallman's *The Orphan*.

The World Fantasy Award went to *The Shadow of the Torturer*. Good. (Though it's SF, you know.) Their other nominees were Chelsea Quinn Yarbro's *Aristo*, Parke Godwin's *Firelord*, Stephen King's *The Mist*, and Peter Straub's *Shadowland*.

The Campbell Memorial also went to *Timescape*, for once a book Campbell would have liked, with Damien Broderick's *The Dreaming Dragons* in second place and *The Shadow of the Torturer* third. (They knew it was SF.)

Locus SF nominees not already mentioned: C. J. Cherryh's *Serpent's Reach*; Stephen King's *Firestarter*; Robert Heinlein's *The Number of the Beast*; Philip José Farmer's *The Magic Labyrinth*; Marion Zimmer Bradley's *Two to Conquer*; Octavia Butler's *Wild Seed*; Alfred Bester's *Golem^{100}*; Robert L. Forward's *Dragon's Egg*; Marta Randall's *Dangerous Games*; Norman Spinrad's *Songs from the Stars*; Orson Scott Card's *Songmaster*; Michael Bishop's *Eyes of Fire*; Ian Watson's *The Gardens of Delight*; Keith Roberts's *Molly Zero*; James P. Hogan's *Thrice Upon a Time*; M. A. Foster's *Waves*; Jean Lorrah and Jacqueline Lichtenberg's *First Channel*; and John Shirley's *City Come A-Walkin'*.

My opinion is that you could throw a dart into that paragraph anywhere and find a better nominee than the ones we have.

I'd choose *Wild Seed, Molly Zero, Serpent's Reach*, and *Dragon's Egg*, along with the Wolfe. Oh dear, Hugos, you are letting me down badly here.

Locus Fantasy nominees not mentioned so far: Stephen R. Donaldson's *The Wounded Land*; Roger Zelazny's *Changeling*; Elizabeth Lynn's *The Northern Girl*; Piers Anthony's *Split Infinity*; Ursula Le Guin's *The Beginning Place*; Suzy McGee Charnas's *The Vampire Tapestry*; Tanith Lee's *Kill the Dead* and *Sabella*; Fred Saberhagen's *Thorn*; Manly Wade Wellman's *After Dark*; M. John Harrison's *A Storm of Wings*;

William Horwood's *Duncton Wood;* Glen Cook's *All Darkness Met;* Basil Cooper's *Necropolis;* and Lyndon Hardy's *Master of the Five Magics.*

Locus First Novel Award, new category there, went to Robert Forward's *Dragon's Egg.* Other notable nominees are John M. Ford's *Web of Angels;* David Brin's *Sundiver;* Rudy Rucker's *White Light;* Joan Sloncxewski's *Still Forms on Foxfield;* and Gillian Bradshaw's *Hawk of May.* If the Hugo list had been five of these, I'd still have been asking where the Wolfe was, but otherwise I'd have been happy.

The Mythopoeic Award went to Tolkien's *Unfinished Tales,* which seems a little recursive—it's for work "in the spirit of the Inklings." Nominees not previously mentioned were Joy Chant's *Grey Mane of Morning* and Morgan Llewellyn's *Lion of Ireland.*

So, was there anything else?

There's Anthony Burgess's *Earthly Powers* and Salman Rushdie's *Midnight's Children,* both published as mainstream but wonderful readable genre books that would have graced the Hugo ballot—and I expect they'd have had some chance of being nominated for the Nebula if they'd been American books.

So this was a great year, with lots of good books, and there's no excuse for nominating the feeble offerings that made the ballot.

OTHER CATEGORIES

BEST NOVELLA

Winner: *Lost Dorsai,* by Gordon R. Dickson (*Destinies* Vol. 2, No. 1, February–March 1980)

Nominees:
All the Lies That Are My Life, by Harlan Ellison (*F&SF,* November 1980)
The Brave Little Toaster, by Thomas M. Disch (*F&SF,* August 1980)

Nightflyers, by George R. R. Martin (*Analog,* April 1980)
One-Wing, by Lisa Tuttle and George R. R. Martin (*Analog,* January/
February 1980)

You know, whatever happens with the novels, the novella category always seems to have great stuff. It's true that this is where a lot of the
life of the genre has always been.

BEST NOVELETTE

Winner: "The Cloak and the Staff," by Gordon R. Dickson (*Analog,*
August 1980)

Nominees:
"The Autopsy," by Michael Shea (*F&SF,* December 1980)
"Beatnik Bayou," by John Varley (*New Voices III*)
"The Lordly Ones," by Keith Roberts (*F&SF,* March 1980)
"Savage Planet," by Barry B. Longyear (*Analog,* February 1980)
"The Ugly Chickens," by Howard Waldrop (*Universe 10*)

On the other hand, one of the best Varley stories ever, a great Roberts
story, and an awesome Waldrop one—and they give it to one of Dickson's more forgettable pieces? Maybe the nominators and voters at Denver were an odd lot.

BEST SHORT STORY

Winner: "Grotto of the Dancing Deer," by Clifford D. Simak (*Analog,*
April 1980)

Nominees:
"Cold Hands," by Jeff Duntemann (*Asimov's,* June 1980)
"Guardian," by Jeff Duntemann (*Asimov's,* September 1980)
"Our Lady of the Sauropods," by Robert Silverberg (*Omni,* Septem-
ber 1980)
"Spidersong," by Susan C. Petrey (*F&SF,* September 1980)

Best Nonfiction Book

Winner: *Cosmos,* by Carl Sagan (Random House)

Nominees:
Di Fate's Catalog of Science Fiction Hardware, by Vincent Di Fate and
  Ian Summers (Workman)
Dream Makers, by Charles Platt (Berkley)
In Joy Still Felt: The Autobiography of Isaac Asimov, 1954–1978, by Isaac
  Asimov (Doubleday)
Warhoon 28, by Richard Bergeron (Richard Bergeron)

I want to say I'd have voted for the Asimov, which in fact I didn't
read for another seven years, whereas I did read *Cosmos* then, and it was
good. Again, these things are not much like each other and make an
odd kind of category, hard to evaluate.

Best Dramatic Presentation

Winner: *The Empire Strikes Back*

Nominees:
Cosmos (TV series)
Flash Gordon
The Lathe of Heaven
The Martian Chronicles (TV series)

Best Professional Editor

Winner: Edward L. Ferman

Nominees:
Jim Baen
Terry Carr
Stanley Schmidt
George Scithers

Best Professional Artist

Winner: Michael Whelan

Nominees:
Vincent Di Fate
Steve Fabian
Paul Lehr
Don Maitz

Best Fanzine

Winner: *Locus,* edited by Charles N. Brown

Nominees:
File 770, edited by Mike Glyer
Science Fiction Chronicle, edited by Andrew Porter
Science Fiction Review, edited by Richard E. Geis
Starship, edited by Andrew I. Porter

File 770 is nominated this year too. Good for three decades.

Best Fan Writer

Winner: Susan Wood

Nominees:
Richard E. Geis
Mike Glyer
Arthur D. Hlavaty
Dave Langford

Sadly, this was a posthumous win for Susan Wood.

Best Fan Artist

Winner: Victoria Poyser

Nominees:
Alexis Gilliland
Joan Hanke-Woods
Bill Rotsler
Stu Shiffman

John W. Campbell Award

Winner: Somtow Sucharitkul

Nominees:
Kevin Christensen
Diane Duane
Robert L. Forward
Susan C. Petrey
Robert Stallman

I think Somtow is an excellent winner, as I said under 1979. I also talked about Duane there. Robert Forward was an aerospace engineer who wrote excellent hard SF for years—he was a mainstay of *Analog* until his death in 2002. Susan Petrey had a Hugo-nominated short story in 1981, but she was already at the end of her short career; she died in 1980. There's a scholarship fund named for her that raises money to send young writers to Clarion. Robert Stallman had a 1981 Nebula-nominated novel that I haven't read, and I'm not familiar with his work generally. I know nothing at all about Kevin Christensen. So three good nominees, one career cut sadly short, and two don't knows.

COMMENTS ON 1981

3. MORDICAI KNODE
Gene Wolfe should win the Hugo for *Book of the New Sun* every single year, again & again & again, over & over.

6. RICH HORTON
I'm at my brother's house in Indianapolis, so a more detailed response will have to wait, but I did want to say right off the bat that, obviously, *The Shadow of the Torturer* is the great novel of 1980, and should have won every award (except perhaps the one it won, since, as Jo notes, it's actually SF and not fantasy).

And one quick comment on the novelettes—"The Autopsy" should have won. It's an amazing SF horror story, and for all that it's horror it's uplifting (especially important in horror, which so often accepts a sort of po-faced "the universe is horrible and we can do nothing in the face of it" attitude that might be bracing the first time but is simply tedious on constant unexamined repetition). Anyway, as I said, "The Autopsy" is great, and even with a good Varley story and a good Waldrop story and a good Roberts story on the ballot, it should have won.

24. GARDNER DOZOIS
For me, there's no contest. The winner should have been *The Shadow of the Torturer*, my favorite of the *Book of the New Sun* volumes, and a reading experience unlike any that I'd ever had before; it's the only one of the possibilities that approaches greatness, and I think that it's still one of Wolfe's best three or four books.

I liked *Nightflyers*, but the novella Hugo should have gone to the heartbreaking *Slow Music*, in my opinion perhaps Tiptree's last really good story, and one of the saddest stories I've ever read. It certainly shouldn't have gone to a fair-to-middling Dickson novella. Other good novellas included Suzy McKee Charnas's *Unicorn Tapestry*, and M. J. Engh's troubling *The Oracle*. Davidson's *There Beneath the Silky-Trees and Whelmed in Deeper Gulphs Than Me*, another Jack Limekiller story, is worth reading, although a bit overcomplicated.

Novelette should have gone to Howard Waldrop's "The Ugly Chickens," one of the strangest and most unique stories ever written; I'll never forget Howard's reading of it at some convention. Another worthy choice would have been Michael Swanwick's "Ginnungagap," a clear cyberpunk precursor. "Strata" was also good. Again, certainly not the Dickson.

Short story is the weakest category. I guess you'd have to give it to Simak, although I'm not wildly enthusiastic. Another good, and almost unknown, story was Naomi Mitchison's "The Finger." Le Guin's "The White Donkey" is good, although not major Le Guin.

Somtow was the clear winner in the Campbell (although *The Laughing Dead* is one of the worst movies ever made), although Stallman was a significant talent who might have developed interestingly if he had survived.

Judith Moffett's first novel, *Pennterra,* which I bought and published, was a Quaker SF novel.

25. RICH HORTON

I've already noted my view that *The Shadow of the Torturer* deserved all the awards in 1981—I don't think its incompleteness is a flaw, in particular as it does bring to a close one aspect of the overall work's narrative arc.

Of the non-nominated novels Jo mentioned, I think *Wild Seed* and *Dangerous Games* of particular note. Marta Randall in particular I'd like to mention—she published some very nice stuff in the late seventies and early eighties, but seems to have disappeared since then. I think she could have had a major career.

A few more novels worth at least a mention, if probably not a Hugo nomination:

F. Paul Wilson's *An Enemy of the State*
Dean Ing's *Anasazi*
Rachel Pollack's *Golden Vanity*
Glen Cook's *October's Baby*
Sam Nicholson's *The Light-Bearer*
Diana Wynne Jones's *The Magicians of Caprona*

Lee Killough's *The Monitor, the Miners, and the Shree*
Damon Knight's *The World and Thorinn*

And a couple from the mainstream—one I wouldn't particularly recommend, but I note as it was a major bestseller: Jean Auel's *The Clan of the Cave Bear;* and a fairly minor Kingsley Amis novel, but perhaps his most overtly SFnal, *Russian Hide and Seek.* And finally, a novel I'm surprised not to see mentioned yet: John Sladek's *Roderick.*

27. RICH HORTON

In novella, then.

At the time, *Nightflyers* might have had my vote—an excellent story. I wasn't ready for *Slow Music* yet, but it might get my vote now. I agree with Bob that *Buoyant Ascent* is fine work, and that Hilbert Schenck is worth a rediscovery.

A couple that weren't mentioned: one of Somtow Sucharitkul's best stories, *Light on the Sound.* And one of Orson Scott Card's best stories, *Hart's Hope.*

In novelette, as I mentioned already, "The Autopsy" was the best story of 1980. (I see that it was a Nebula nominee in novella, in which case, it should have won there!) "The Ugly Chickens" is significant, very good, very original, but as a story qua story, it's not quite as good. (Perhaps I guessed what was going on too easily. There's an Avram Davidson story on the same subject, "Full Chicken Richness.")

The novelettes Bob mentions are all good additions to the list. But there's a really good one that I just discovered a year or two back—Damien Broderick's "The Ballad of Bowsprit Bear's Stead," from Ursula Le Guin and Viriginia Kidd's anthology *Edges.* As I wrote in my review of Broderick's collection *Uncle Bones:* "This is a bravura performance, spectacularly written and stuffed with SFnal ideas." It's also very funny. It definitely should have been nominated.

I also really liked at the time a story by Karl Hansen called "Sergeant Pepper," a cynical and action-packed milSF story. And Richard S. McEnroe's "Wolkenheim Fairday," from *Asimov's,* was enjoyable enough to stick in my memory. Also, Avram Davidson's "Peregrine: Perplexed," part of his second Peregrine novel.

Two more stories to mention from the short story category: Gene Wolfe's "Suzanne Delage" and Howard Waldrop's "All About Strange Monsters of the Recent Past." Leman's "Window" is very good too. That said, I don't have a problem with Simak's fine late story winning.

51. DAVID G. HARTWELL

I had a good year. I published the Benford, the Wolfe, the Charnas, the Stallman, the Spinrad, the Ford, Sucharitkul, and a bunch of others. Don't miss the Stallman; it's a fine book and belongs in its company.

1982

Winner: *Downbelow Station,* by C. J. Cherryh

Nominees:
The Claw of the Conciliator, by Gene Wolfe
Little, Big, by John Crowley
The Many-Colored Land, by Julian May
Project Pope, by Clifford D. Simak

The 1982 Hugo Awards were presented at Chicon IV in Chicago.

The award for Best Novel was given to C. J. Cherryh's *Downbelow Station.* It's a story of interstellar war and diplomacy set in a complex and thoroughly developed universe—it feels like history in a way that science fiction seldom manages. It's about what it means to be human, when the boundaries start to blur, what people will do to survive, and shifting definitions of home and independence and loyalty. I didn't like *Downbelow Station* in 1982—I started to like it only after I liked other books in the same universe. It's not where I suggest people start with Cherryh. But it's a major achievement and a major novel, and I'm very glad it won a Hugo and encouraged her to keep on with this kind of thing. It's in print from DAW, and it's in the library in English only.

There are four other nominees, three of which I've read.

Making up in a small way for overlooking *The Shadow of the Torturer* in 1981, we have *The Claw of the Conciliator* here. It's still brilliant, but it really doesn't stand alone, so I'm not surprised it didn't win, though it did win the Nebula and the Locus Fantasy award, although it is of course SF. *The Book of the New Sun* is so much one thing that it's a pity we don't have an award for completed things that take more than one year to publish. It's in print in a beautiful Orb edition, and in the library in French and English. It's definitely still part of the dialogue of science fiction.

John Crowley's *Little, Big* is—well. It's strange. It's definitely fantasy, and it's contemporary, and it's about a family and magic and strangeness. It's one of those books that seems to dance along the edge of dreams. I have read it once and never again because I didn't like the way it seemed to creep up on me when I wasn't looking. Many of my friends count it as a favorite book. It's undoubtedly a significant book and thoroughly deserves to be on this list. It won the World Fantasy Award and the Mythopoeic Award. It's in print from Harper, and in the library in English.

Julian May's *The Many-Colored Land* is what I'd have voted for in 1982, though now I think it's the weakest book on the list. It was so exactly to my taste then and so little to my taste now that you could use it to graph precisely how my tastes have changed. It's about people in a multi-planet future with psi powers who have a one-way gate to the Pliocene of Earth, through which people can go into Exile, and when they get there, they discover to their astonishment a society of Celtic aliens. There are sequels, which I kept reading for far longer than I should have. It won the Locus Award. It's not in print, and it's not in the library, but if anybody's interested, I remember exactly how all the magic-enhancing torcs worked and the names of the different kinds of psi.

I don't know how I missed Clifford Simak's *Project Pope*. It's not in print, and it's not in the library—and I suppose nobody ever mentioned it to me and I never happened to see a copy. I usually like Simak.

So, three men and two women, all American. Cherryh and Simak are previous nominees; Wolfe had previous short-form nominations, but this is his first novel nomination; May and Crowley are completely new to the Hugos. We have one space science fiction, one far-future science fiction, one fantasy, one science fantasy, and the one I haven't read looks like theological SF.

These are a pretty good bunch, and I'm feeling good about them, especially after 1981.

What else could they have chosen?

Non-overlapping Nebula nominees are A. A. Attanasio's *Radix;* Russell Hoban's *Riddley Walker;* and Suzy McKee Charnas's *The Vampire Tapestry.*

Non-overlapping World Fantasy nominees: Ramsey Campbell's *The Nameless;* Michael Moorcock's *The War Hound and the World's Pain;* D. M. Thomas's *The White Hotel.*

The John W. Campbell Memorial Award went to *Riddley Walker.*

Non-overlapping Locus nominees: *Windhaven,* George R. R. Martin and Lisa Tuttle; *Dream Park,* Larry Niven and Steven Barnes; *God Emperor of Dune,* Frank Herbert; *The Cool War,* Frederik Pohl; *Sharra's Exile,* Marion Zimmer Bradley; *Oath of Fealty,* Larry Niven and Jerry Pournelle; *The Divine Invasion,* Philip K. Dick; *The Book of Dreams,* Jack Vance; *The Sardonyx Net,* Elizabeth A. Lynn; *King David's Spaceship,* Jerry Pournelle; *Worlds,* Joe Haldeman; *At the Eye of the Ocean,* Hilbert Schenck; *The Unreasoning Mask,* Philip José Farmer; *Voyagers,* Ben Bova; *Dream Dancer,* Janet Morris; *The Dreamers,* James Gunn; *Twelve Fair Kingdoms,* Suzette Haden Elgin; *Giants' Star,* James Hogan; *The Affirmation,* Christopher Priest; *Deathhunter,* Ian Watson; *VALIS,* Philip K. Dick; *Lilith,* Jack L. Chalker; *Systemic Shock,* Dean Ing; *In the Hands of Glory,* Phyllis Eisenstein; *Wave Without a Shore,* C. J. Cherryh.

Non-overlapping Locus fantasy nominees: *The Changing Land,* Roger Zelazny; *The Captive,* Robert Stallman; *Camber the Heretic,* Katherine Kurtz; *The Keep,* F. Paul Wilson; *Horn Crown,* Andre Norton; *A Sense of Shadow,* Kate Wilhelm; *Lycanthia,* Tanith Lee; *Path of the Eclipse,* Chelsea Quinn Yarbro; *Delusion's Master,* Tanith Lee; *Peregrine: Secundus,* Avram Davidson; *Kingdom of Summer,* Gillian Bradshaw; *Esbae: A Winter's Tale,* Linda Haldeman; *Journey Behind the Wind,* Patricia Wrightson; *The Sable Moon,* Nancy Springer; *Madwand,* Roger Zelazny; *Gryphon in Glory,* Andre Norton; *Too Long a Sacrifice,* Mildred Downey Broxon; *Cujo,* Stephen King; *Blue Adept,* Piers Anthony.

The winner of the Prometheus Award was L. Neil Smith's *The Probability Broach.*

Was there anything everybody missed?

There's Richard Cowper's *A Dream of Kinship*, and Elisabeth Vonarburg's *The Silent City* in the original French publication, and M. A. Foster's *The Morphodite*, and Diana Wynne Jones's *The Time of the Ghost*.

A lot of good stuff, but nothing that stands out as a clear omission, or clearly better than the nominees we have. So I'd say 1982 was a year where the nominations did what they should. Good!

Other Categories

Best Novella

Winner: *The Saturn Game*, by Poul Anderson (*Analog*, February 1981)

Nominees:
Blue Champagne, by John Varley (*New Voices 4*)
Emergence, by David R. Palmer (*Analog*, January 1981)
In the Western Tradition, by Phyllis Eisenstein (*F&SF*, March 1981)
True Names, by Vernor Vinge (*Binary Star 5*)
With Thimbles, with Forks and Hope, by Kate Wilhelm (*Asimov's*, November 1981)

Really? Gosh. The Anderson is okay, but the Varley and the Vinge are classics.

Best Novelette

Winner: "Unicorn Variation," by Roger Zelazny (*Asimov's*, April 1981)

Nominees:
"The Fire When It Comes," by Parke Godwin (*F&SF*, May 1981)
"Guardians," by George R. R. Martin (*Analog*, October 1981)
"The Quickening," by Michael Bishop (*Universe 11*)
"The Thermals of August," by Edward Bryant (*F&SF*, May 1981)

BEST SHORT STORY

Winner: "The Pusher," by John Varley (*F&SF*, October 1981)

Nominees:
"Absent Thee from Felicity Awhile," by Somtow Sucharitkul (*Analog*, September 1981)
"The Quiet," by George Florance-Guthridge (*F&SF*, July 1981)
"The Woman the Unicorn Loved," by Gene Wolfe (*Asimov's*, June 1981)

BEST NONFICTION BOOK

Winner: *Danse Macabre*, by Stephen King (Everest)

Nominees:
After Man, by Dougal Dixon (Macmillan)
Anatomy of Wonder, 2nd Edition, edited by Neil Barron (R. R. Bowker)
The Art of Leo & Diane Dillon, by Leo and Diane Dillon, edited by Byron Preiss (Ballantine)
The Grand Tour, by Ron Miller and William K. Hartmann (Workman)

I love *After Man*, though I wouldn't call it nonfiction exactly. What an odd category this is!

BEST DRAMATIC PRESENTATION

Winner: *Raiders of the Lost Ark*

Nominees:
Dragonslayer
Excalibur
Outland
Time Bandits

BEST PROFESSIONAL EDITOR

Winner: Edward L. Ferman

Nominees:
Terry Carr
David G. Hartwell
Stanley Schmidt
George Scithers

David Hartwell said last week that he'd been having a good year that year, but this must have been the year people noticed!

BEST PROFESSIONAL ARTIST

Winner: Michael Whelan

Nominees:
Vincent Di Fate
Carl Lundgren
Don Maitz
Rowena Morrill

BEST FANZINE

Winner: *Locus*, edited by Charles N. Brown

Nominees:
File 770, edited by Mike Glyer
Science Fiction Chronicle, edited by Andrew I. Porter
Science Fiction Review, edited by Richard E. Geis

BEST FAN WRITER

Winner: Richard E. Geis

Nominees:
Mike Glyer
Arthur D. Hlavaty
Dave Langford

BEST FAN ARTIST

Winner: Victoria Poyser

Nominees:
Alexis Gilliland
Joan Hanke-Woods
Bill Rotsler
Stu Shiffman

JOHN W. CAMPBELL AWARD

Winner: Alexis Gilliland

Nominees:
David Brin
Robert Stallman
Michael Swanwick
Paul O. Williams

This is a year where two of the nominees went on to become major writers, writing important books and winning Hugos. Unfortunately, neither Brin nor Swanwick was the winner, though they'd both have been really excellent ones, just the kind the award was designed for, significant writers at the beginning of their careers.

Gilliland had already won a Hugo as Fan Artist in 1980. He published six books between 1981 and 1992, none of which I've read.

Robert Stallman was already dead before being nominated, but it shows how impressed people were with his work.

Paul O. Williams wrote seven postapocalyptic SF novels between

1981 and 2004, and apparently was also devoted to the haiku form and was president of the US Haiku society. He died in 2009.

So one nominee who didn't achieve any more because he was dead, two minor writers, including the winner, and two major writers.

COMMENTS ON 1982

1. RICH HORTON

One more significant mainstream novel seems worth mentioning: Alasdair Gray's *Lanark*, which I believe has been cited as a major influence by Iain Banks.

2. RICH HORTON

In novella, as you say, *The Saturn Game* is merely okay. *True Names* is a classic, though its significance was not as clear at the time. *Blue Champagne* is very good. But my favorite novella that year, in one of my personal favorite sub-subgenres (time viewers), was Phyllis Eisenstein's *In the Western Tradition*. It obviously wasn't ignored—it got the award nominations and all—but to me, it still seems a bit underappreciated.

Only a few more novellas seem worth mentioning: Michael Shea's *Polyphemus*, David Brin's *The Loom of Thessaly*, and a wacky courtroom story by Charles Harness, *The Venetian Court*.

In novelette, I might have gone for "The Quickening," or even for Brin's "The Tides of Kithrup," but I can't argue with the award to "Unicorn Variations."

In short story, I had a clear favorite, which didn't appear on the Hugo or Nebula ballots (though it was fourth on the *Locus* list!)—perhaps it was missed because it was published as part of a book marketed as a novel, C. J. Cherryh's *Sunfall*. The story is "The Only Death in the City," and I think it's wonderful.

We should also note a couple of William Gibson stories: "Johnny Mnemonic" and "The Gernsback Continuum," and John Kessel's "Not Responsible! Park and Lock It!," and also Joe Haldeman's "A !Tangled Web."

And the Nebula short story award was controversial, because Lisa Tuttle, who won for "The Bone Flute," declined the award.

8. DemetriosX

The interesting thing to me about the novellas is that so many of them deal in one way or another with artificial realities influencing and bleeding over into real life. I suppose it's part of the mix leading up to the birth of cyberpunk. *Emergence* really works better when it's integrated into the novel. My favorite was the Wilhelm, which kicked off one of her more popular mystery series.

51. Gardner Dozois

True Names is the clear winner here in retrospect, and the only one of these novellas of any historical importance or that is still read today, although I too liked *In the Western Tradition*. *The Winter Beach* was also good.

"Unicorn Variations" is cute and amusing, but I don't think I'd have given it a Hugo. Novelette seems weak this year. Might have gone for Jack Dann's "Going Under."

With the advantage of 20/20 hindsight, the short story probably should have gone to "Johnny Mnemonic," the story that heralded the birth of cyberpunk, and was certainly doing something different from what anybody else was doing at the time. The much quieter "Exposures" was also good, as was "Venice Drowned," Kim Stanley Robinson's first major story.

My opinion should probably be taken with a grain of salt, since I was Swanwick's mentor and we've remained close colleagues and collaborators ever since, but I think Swanwick deserved the Campbell even on the strength of the work he'd already done by that point, particularly the brilliant "Ginnungagap."

55. James Davis Nicoll

"Johnny Mnemonic," the story that heralded the birth of cyberpunk

Web of Angels heralded the birth of cyberpunk; it's just that sometimes people don't listen carefully enough.

56. James Davis Nicoll

Wow, that looks a lot snarkier in print than it sounded in my head. What I meant was, "It is my belief that had readers in general noted the Ford novel, they would have seen in it elements that would be now seen as Cyberpunk. The novel was tragically not as well known as it should have been. Curse you, readers of the early 1980s whose tastes diverged ever so slightly from my own!"

57. Gardner Dozois

Although the cyberpunks would always contend that the movement had sprung full-grown from the head of William Gibson, there was other work being done here and there simultaneously that had at least some of the same elements and feel to it. *True Names*, for instance, which is certainly at least "cyber" if not particularly "punk." Or the aforementioned "Ginnungagap," for that matter. That's why I've always believed that cyberpunk was an organic evolutionary movement—it was Cyberpunk Time, so several different artists were independently trying to invent it, without consulting with each other at all. It was Gibson, though, who pretty much set the tone and aesthetic feel of it with high-profile stories like "Johnny Mnenomic" and "Burning Chrome," and subsequent work was at least in dialogue with that to some extent, even if not directly influenced by it.

1983

Winner: *Foundation's Edge,* by Isaac Asimov

Nominees:
2010: Odyssey Two, by Arthur C. Clarke
Courtship Rite, by Donald Kingsbury
Friday, by Robert A. Heinlein
The Pride of Chanur, by C. J. Cherryh
The Sword of the Lictor, by Gene Wolfe

The 1983 Hugo Awards were awarded in ConStellation, in Baltimore.

The Best Novel winner was Isaac Asimov's *Foundation's Edge,* a late addition to his wonderful Foundation trilogy. I have read it, and it struck me as fairly entertaining but ill advised—it was thirty years since he'd written about this universe. I felt that going back to it, and especially connecting it up to the Robots universe, diminished the originals. But it was popular, and so were the other sequels and prequels. It seemed to me to be nailing down corners of the universe that were better left unpinned, but other people evidently liked it. It doesn't seem to be in print, but it's in the library in English and French.

There are five nominees, and I have read them all.

Arthur C. Clarke's *2010: Odyssey Two* is another disappointing sequel by a beloved veteran writer. The strange thing is that the original *2001* novel didn't get nominated. I suppose the subgenre is near-future hard SF. It's in print, and it's in the library in English and French.

I've already written about my reactions to Robert Heinlein's *Friday* under the title "The Worst Book I Love." There's a future world that anticipated some aspects of the internet. There's genetic engineering, and FTL travel and corporations that can't be trusted. There's a first person female action hero who worries about her humanity. It's a deeply flawed book with a plot that gets lost, but I love it anyway. It's in print, and it's in the library in English only. I think it's a reasonably good nominee, but I'm glad it didn't win.

Donald Kingsbury's *Courtship Rite* is wonderful but very odd. It's about a lost colony on a planet where there's very little to eat except other people, and it's a sweet love story about evolutionary fitness and cannibalism. It's quite unforgettable, and exactly the kind of thing that should be nominated, and I'd have been quite happy for it to have won. It did win the Compton Crook Award for Best First Novel.

C. J. Cherryh's *The Pride of Chanur* is what I'd have voted for then or now, an outstandingly good book in my absolute favorite subgenre—aliens and space stations. It has wonderful aliens, and wonderful space stations to come to that. It's in print, but it's not in the library.

Gene Wolfe's *The Sword of the Lictor* is part three of the *Book of the New Sun,* and it really doesn't stand alone even a bit. It's in print and in the library in English.

So, five men and one woman, one UK, one Canadian, and four Americans. Clarke, Asimov, and Cherryh were former winners. Wolfe was a former nominee. Kingsbury was a newcomer. We have one far-future SF, one far-future SF disguised as fantasy, one space opera with aliens, one SF novel about extreme colonization, and one solar system exploration with aliens.

What else might they have chosen?

Michael Bishop's *No Enemy but Time* won the Nebula. Other non-overlapping nominees were Philip K. Dick's *The Transmigration of Timothy Archer* and Brian Aldiss's *Helliconia Spring.* The only one I've read is the Aldiss. It's probably his best work and should have made the Hugo list. It won the John W. Campbell Memorial Award and the BSFA Award—good!

The World Fantasy Award was won by Michael Shea's *Nifft the Lean.* Non-overlapping nominees were *Fevre Dream,* by George R. R. Martin; *The Nestling,* by Charles L. Grant; and *Phantom,* by Thomas Tessier.

The Philip K. Dick Award began this year. It honors paperback original SF, and it is one of my favorite awards, consistently finding good books nobody is paying attention to. The award consists of a cash prize and a framed certificate.

The first one was won by Rudy Rucker's *Software*, another book from the incipient cyberpunk movement as noted in comments to 1982, and one that would have been a great Hugo nominee. They gave a special citation to *The Prometheus Man*, by Ray Faraday Nelson. Other nominees were *Aurelia*, by R. A. Lafferty; *Roderick*, by John Sladek; *The Umbral Anthology of Science Fiction Poetry*, edited by Steve Rasnic Tem; and *Waiting for the Barbarians*, by J. M. Coetzee.

The Locus Award went to the Asimov. Non-overlapping nominees were: *The Crystal Singer*, by Anne McCaffrey; *Starburst*, by Frederik Pohl; *Merchanter's Luck*, by C. J. Cherryh; *Life, the Universe and Everything*, by Douglas Adams; *The Golden Torc*, by Julian May; *Hawkmistress!*, by Marion Zimmer Bradley; *Eye of Cat*, by Roger Zelazny; *The Descent of Anansi*, by Larry Niven and Steven Barnes; *Mindkiller*, by Spider Robinson; *A Rose for Armageddon*, by Hilbert Schenck; *The White Plague*, by Frank Herbert; *Coils*, by Fred Saberhagen and Roger Zelazny; *Wintermind*, by Marvin Kaye and Parke Godwin; *Birthright: The Book of Man*, by Mike Resnick; *Light on the Sound*, by Somtow Sucharitkul; *Nor Crystal Tears*, by Alan Dean Foster; *The Fall of the Shell*, by Paul O. Williams.

The Mythopoeic Award went to Carol Kendall's *The Firelings*. Nominees not so far mentioned were *The Blue Sword*, by Robin McKinley; *The Darkangel*, by Meredith Ann Pierce; *God Stalk*, by P. C. Hodgell; *Lady of Light*, by Diana L. Paxson; *The Mists of Avalon*, by Marion Zimmer Bradley; *The One Tree*, by Stephen R. Donaldson; *Queen of Sorcery*, by David Eddings.

The Prometheus Award went to James P. Hogan's *Voyage from Yesteryear*.

Is there anything all these awards missed?

There's John M. Ford's *The Princes of the Air*, but I think most of the things worth noting did get on one of these lists.

So, is the Hugo list doing its job this year? Nearly. I think the winner is weak, and I'd have liked to see the Aldiss and the Rucker on it in place of any of the Asimov/Clarke/Heinlein, but . . . it's okay. Not perfect, but okay. These are representative books of 1982, and there aren't many of the lasting significant books of 1982 that got missed.

OTHER CATEGORIES

BEST NOVELLA

Winner: *Souls*, by Joanna Russ (*F&SF*, January 1982)

Nominees:
Another Orphan, by John Kessel (*F&SF*, September 1982)
Brainchild, by Joseph H. Delaney (*Analog*, June 1982)
The Postman, by David Brin (*Asimov's*, November 1982)
To Leave a Mark, by Kim Stanley Robinson (*F&SF*, November 1982)
Unsound Variations, by George R. R. Martin (*Amazing Stories*, January 1982)

Unsound Variations is one of Martin's most chilling stories, and one that I remember better than I want to. The rest of these are also excellent—it seems to me that we keep having a set of brilliant novellas year after year, that it's consistently a really strong category.

BEST NOVELETTE

Winner: "Fire Watch," by Connie Willis (*Asimov's*, February 1982)

Nominees:
"Aquila," by Somtow Sucharitkul (*Asimov's*, January 1982)
"Nightlife," by Phyllis Eisenstein (*F&SF*, February 1982)
"Pawn's Gambit," by Timothy Zahn (*Analog*, March 1982)
"Swarm," by Bruce Sterling (*F&SF*, April 1982)

Best Short Story

Winner: "Melancholy Elephants," by Spider Robinson (*Analog*, June 1982)

Nominees:
"The Boy Who Waterskied to Forever," by James Tiptree Jr. (*F&SF*, October 1982)
"Ike at the Mike," by Howard Waldrop (*Omni*, June 1982)
"Spider Rose," by Bruce Sterling (*F&SF*, August 1982)
"Sur," by Ursula K. Le Guin (*The New Yorker*, February 1, 1982; *The Compass Rose* [revised])

Best Nonfiction Book

Winner: *Isaac Asimov: The Foundations of Science Fiction*, by James Gunn

Nominees:
The Engines of the Night, by Barry N. Malzberg
Fear Itself: The Horror Fiction of Stephen King, edited by Tim Underwood and Chuck Miller
A Reader's Guide to Fantasy, by Baird Searles, Beth Meacham, and Michael Franklin
The World of the Dark Crystal, by J. J. Llewellyn, text; Brian Froud, illustrator

Dramatic Presentation

Winner: *Blade Runner*

Nominees:
The Dark Crystal
E. T. The Extraterrestrial
The Road Warrior
Star Trek II: The Wrath of Khan

Best Professional Editor

Winner: Edward L. Ferman

Nominees:
Terry Carr
David G. Hartwell
Stanley Schmidt
George Scithers

Best Professional Artist

Winner: Michael Whelan

Nominees:
Frank Kelly Freas
Don Maitz
Rowena Morrill
Barclay Shaw
Darrell Sweet

Best Fanzine

Winner: *Locus*, edited by Charles N. Brown

Nominees:
Fantasy Newsletter, edited by Robert A. Collins
File 770, edited by Mike Glyer
Science Fiction Chronicle, edited by Andrew I. Porter
Science Fiction Review, edited by Richard E. Geis

Best Fan Writer

Winner: Richard E. Geis

Nominees:
Mike Glyer
Arthur Hlavaty
Dave Langford

BEST FAN ARTIST

Winner: Alexis Gilliland

Nominees:
Joan Hanke-Woods
Bill Rotsler
Stu Shiffman
Dan Steffan

JOHN W. CAMPBELL AWARD

Winner: Paul O. Williams

Nominees:
Joseph H. Delaney
Lisa Goldstein
Sandra Miesel
Warren G. Norwood
David R. Palmer

Paul O. Williams seems to have won on the strength of his first novel, *The Breaking of Northwall*. He published half a dozen more novels, but he was a minor writer.

Joseph H. Delaney had a novella on the Hugo ballot, and he went on to write other award-nominated short work through the eighties.

Lisa Goldstein is the standout on this list—she has continued to produce excellent fantasy right up to the present day. She has been nominated for Nebulas, Mythopoeics, and World Fantasy Awards. I think hindsight would make her the best winner from this list—and not just because she's one of my favorite writers.

I don't know much about Sandra Miesel or Warren G. Norwood—anyone?

David R. Palmer had published a handful of notable short work over the couple of years prior to this nomination, and then the much-praised novel *Emergence* in 1984 and a sequel, *Threshold*, in 1985, and since then nothing but rumors of a third in the sequence.

So not a great year for the Campbells overall.

COMMENTS ON 1983

5. RICH HORTON

I should mention Damien Broderick's *The Judas Mandala* and a couple from the YA field:

Diana Wynne Jones's *Witch Week*.

Lloyd Alexander's *The Kestrel*, which is not really SF or fantasy but "other world historical" sort of like *Malafrena* (which it reminds me of) or *Swordspoint* without the sequels (which reveal the presence of magic). *The Kestrel* is the second book of Alexander's Westmark trilogy.

6. RICH HORTON

Indeed, quite a remarkable list of novellas. *Souls* is brilliant and a very worthy winner, but at the time, I probably voted for *To Leave a Mark*, which I totally loved and which was my introduction to KSR. I also think *Another Orphan* (which won the Nebula) is a great, great story. Any of those three do the award proud. For that matter, *The Postman* is first-rate too—as DemetriosX notes, it is perhaps diminished in our memory by the rest of the novel and by the movie.

The only other novella I'd mention, though not really as a potential nominee, is Pauline Ashwell's return to her Lizzie Lee series, *Rats in the Moon*, which is fun but minor.

"Fire Watch" is one of my favorite Connie Willis stories, and certainly is a strong winner. But I think my vote might have gone to Sterling's "Swarm," which is really scary in its way, as well as great SFnal speculation.

I'd have voted for Sterling again in short story—I think "Spider Rose" is a masterpiece. I really felt blessed at the time—the field was blessed—with the emergence of Sterling, KSR, Kessel, Goldstein, and Gibson. There's a strong Le Guin story too, in "Sur." Gibson's "Burning Chrome" is also good, as is Willis's Nebula winner, "A Letter from the Clearys," and Barry Malzberg's "Corridors," and Greg Bear's "Petra."

I should also mention three strong stories from Howard Waldrop, who was at his most productive: ". . . The World as We Know't," "Ike at the Mike," and "God's Hooks!" Also, J. G. Ballard published a significant short story that got onto the Nebula short list, "Myths of the Near Future," which is interesting in that it recapitulates the themes (and style) of his early- to mid-sixties stories like "The Terminal Beach" long after Ballard had pretty much moved on.

12. TexAnne

Warren Norwood was a frequent guest at AggieCon. He wrote a series called The Windhover Tapes, which I don't think I ever got around to reading. I'm sure they're long out of print. He taught me to play mountain dulcimer, and he was a ruthless yet encouraging workshop teacher.

31. Gardner Dozois

Souls, Joanna Russ's last major SF story, is the clear winner for me in novella, although the Kessel and the Robinson are good stories too.

In novelette, at the time I might have given it to Sterling's "Swarm," and still might, in fact, but it's hard to ignore Gibson's other seminal story at short lengths, "Burning Chrome"; it and "Johnny Mnenomic" carried most of the weight of Gibson's influence at the time—and influence other young writers, he did indeed do—although *Neuromancer* largely supplanted them once it came out. "Firewatch" and "Understanding Human Behavior" were also very fine; in fact, I think that overall, counting nominees and stuff that didn't get nominated, novelette was stronger than novella this year.

Never liked "Sur" or "Melancholy Elephants." "A Letter from the Clearys" was good, but "Firewatch" was stronger, and "The Boy Who Waterskied to Forever" is weak Tiptree. At the time, I'd probably have voted for "Spider Rose," although I like it less overall than "Swarm." Now I'd be tempted by "God's Hooks!," to my mind a much stronger Waldrop story than "Ike at the Mike," although "The Pope of the Chimps" is a very underrated story, one of Silverberg's best.

32. RICH HORTON

Gardner—"Burning Chrome" and "Johnny Mnemonic" are fine works, and very influential, but I think "Swarm" (and "Spider Rose") are better stories, if indeed perhaps less obviously influential. The greatest Gibson short story came a couple of years later—"New Rose Hotel." (Ignore the movie, please!) That was just before *Neuromancer,* and of course after "Burning Chrome" and "Johnny Mnemonic," so it didn't have the same "shock of the new" influence. But, man, is it a great story. The other best single piece of writing Gibson has done (in my opinion) is the "artist of the boxes" chapter from *Count Zero.*

1984

Winner: *Startide Rising,* by David Brin

Nominees:
Millennium, by John Varley
Moreta: Dragonlady of Pern, by Anne McCaffrey
The Robots of Dawn, by Isaac Asimov
Tea with the Black Dragon, by R. A. MacAvoy

The 1984 Hugo Awards were given at LACon II in Anaheim, California.

David Brin's *Startide Rising,* the second of his Uplift series, is an excellent winner, exactly the kind of book that ought to win—imaginative, innovative, full of new ideas. The concept of "uplift" is wonderful, where each species raises others to sentience and there's a galaxy full of alien species who have done this for each other and are freaked out by the mystery of humans, who managed it for themselves. *Startide Rising* is in print, and it's in the library in French and English. It's a classic, and it's definitely still part of the conversation of SF. It also won the Nebula and the Locus—it really was the standout book of the year.

There are four other nominees, and I've read all of them.

John Varley's *Millennium* is an expansion of his wonderful novella *Air Raid,* about a world where people with time travel but a ruined future Earth are trying to rescue people from plane crashes. I really looked forward to the book and then found it disappointing. I much prefer *Air Raid* as a stand-alone. It's in print, and it's in the library in French only.

Anne McCaffrey's *Moreta: Dragonlady of Pern* is the last of the Pern books that I read. I don't remember it all that well, but I do remember finding it repetitive. It's in print, and it's in the library in French and English, so I suppose it has lasted.

I loved Isaac Asimov's *The Robots of Dawn,* which was great especially after having not enjoyed *Foundation's Edge* the year before. I haven't reread it for a long time, but I thought at the time that it was a fresh, thoughtful addition to the Robots series. It's in print and in the library in French only.

R. A. MacAvoy's *Tea with the Black Dragon* is delightful. It's an unusual Hugo nominee for several reasons—it's fantasy, it was a paperback original, and it's a first novel, but a terrific thing to see on the ballot. It's in print, but it's not in the library. It was also nominated for the Nebula, the World Fantasy Award, and the Philip K. Dick Award.

So, three men and two women, all American. MacAvoy's a newcomer, Asimov is a previous winner, McCaffrey and Varley are previous nominees, Brin was a Campbell nominee and a short fiction nominee but a newcomer to the novel ballot. We have three additions to existing series, one fantasy, one science fantasy, two space operas, and one uncategorizable. *Moreta* seems weak, but this seems like a reasonable-to-good set of five.

What else might they have chosen?

Non-overlapping Nebula nominees are Gregory Benford's *Against Infinity,* Gene Wolfe's *The Citadel of the Autarch,* Jack Vance's *Lyonesse,* and Norman Spinrad's *The Void Captain's Tale.* Any of the ones I've read would have been perfectly good Hugo nominees too, but not notably better than the ones we have.

The World Fantasy Award went to John M. Ford's astonishing *The Dragon Waiting.* Other non-overlapping nominees are George R. R. Martin's *The Armageddon Rag,* Stephen King's *Pet Sematary,* and Manuel Mujica Láinez's *The Wandering Unicorn.*

The John W. Campbell Memorial Award went to *The Citadel of the Autarch,* as somebody belatedly realized that those books are SF, or maybe it was an award for the whole series. I do think *The Book of the New Sun* as a whole thing should have won a Hugo, but I'm not sure any of the parts after *The Shadow of the Torturer* actually stand alone sufficiently to be considered. Second place is John Calvin Batchelor's *The Birth of the People's Republic of Antarctica*, which I loathed, and third John Sladek's *Tik-Tok*.

The Philip K. Dick Award went to Tim Powers's *The Anubis Gates*. Finalists not mentioned yet are Zoe Fairbairns's *Benefits*, M. John Harrison's *The Floating Gods*, and Barrington J. Bayley's *The Zen Gun*.

Other Locus nominees not previously mentioned: *Helliconia Summer*, Brian W. Aldiss; *Thendara House*, Marion Zimmer Bradley; *Orion Shall Rise*, Poul Anderson; *The Nonborn King*, Julian May; *Superluminal*, Vonda N. McIntyre; *Welcome, Chaos*, Kate Wilhelm; *The Crucible of Time*, John Brunner; *Worlds Apart*, Joe Haldeman; *Valentine Pontifex*, Robert Silverberg; *Gods of Riverworld*, Philip José Farmer; *Forty Thousand in Gehenna*, C. J. Cherryh; *A Matter for Men*, David Gerrold; *Wall Around a Star*, Jack Williamson and Frederik Pohl; *Golden Witchbreed*, Mary Gentle; *Broken Symmetries*, Paul Preuss; *Roderick at Random*, John Sladek; *There Is No Darkness*, Joe Haldeman and Jack C. Haldeman II; *Code of the Lifemaker*, James P. Hogan; *Transformer*, M. A. Foster.

The Locus Fantasy Award, in a year with so much excellent fantasy, went to one of my least favorite books, Marion Zimmer Bradley's *The Mists of Avalon*. Nominees not previously mentioned: *White Gold Wielder*, Stephen R. Donaldson; *Christine*, Stephen King; *The Dreamstone*, C. J. Cherryh; *Damiano*, R. A. MacAvoy; *Neveryóna*, Samuel R. Delany; *Dragon on a Pedestal*, Piers Anthony; *Hart's Hope*, Orson Scott Card; *Cugel's Saga*, Jack Vance; *The Sword of Winter*, Marta Randall; *Magician's Gambit*, David Eddings; *The Tree of Swords and Jewels*, C. J. Cherryh; *On a Pale Horse*, Piers Anthony; *Floating Dragon*, Peter Straub; *The Neverending Story*, Michael Ende; *Anackire*, Tanith Lee; *Sung in Shadow*, Tanith Lee; *'Ware Hawk*, Andre Norton; *The Silent Gondoliers*, S. Morgenstern; *The Sword Is Forged*, Evangeline Walton.

The Mythopoeic Award went to Joy Chant's *When Voiha Wakes*, another book I really like.

The Prometheus Award went to J. Neil Schulman's *The Rainbow Cadenza*.

And looking to see if there's anything they all overlooked, I find Steven Brust's *Jhereg*, which really should have been on the World Fantasy list, and also had a Campbell nomination!

So out of all this, there are *The Dragon Waiting* and *The Anubis Gates*, both of which I think the Hugo voters overlooked unfairly in favor of weak books by better-known writers. And I'd have liked to see *The Crucible of Time* get more visibility too. But a good winner and a reasonable field—I think this is another year where I'm coming down on "meh, sort of" doing their job.

OTHER CATEGORIES

BEST NOVELLA

Winner: *Cascade Point,* by Timothy Zahn (*Analog,* December 1983)

Nominees:
Hardfought, by Greg Bear (*Asimov's,* February 1983)
Hurricane Claude, by Hilbert Schenck (*F&SF,* April 1983)
In the Face of My Enemy, by Joseph H. Delaney (*Analog,* April 1983)
Seeking, by David R. Palmer (*Analog,* February 1983)

So did I suddenly stop reading novellas in 1983? Why are none of these familiar? Weird.

BEST NOVELETTE

Winner: "Blood Music," by Greg Bear (*Analog,* June 1983)

Nominees:
"Black Air," by Kim Stanley Robinson (*F&SF,* March 1983)
"The Monkey Treatment," by George R. R. Martin (*F&SF,* July 1983)
"The Sidon in the Mirror," by Connie Willis (*Asimov's,* April 1983)
"Slow Birds," by Ian Watson (*F&SF,* June 1983)

These, on the other hand, are great. I think the best one won, but what a terrific set.

"Black Air" was one of the first Robinsons I noticed.

Best Short Story

Winner: "Speech Sounds," by Octavia E. Butler (*Asimov's*, mid-December 1983)

Nominees:
"The Geometry of Narrative," by Hilbert Schenck (*Analog*, August 1983)
"The Peacemaker," by Gardner Dozois (*Asimov's*, August 1983)
"Servant of the People," by Frederik Pohl (*Analog*, February 1983)
"Wong's Lost and Found Emporium," by William F. Wu (*Amazing Stories*, May 1983)

Yay, another great winner. And I think this might be the first time we've had two writers of color on the same list.

Best Nonfiction Book

Winner: *The Encyclopedia of Science Fiction and Fantasy, Vol. 3*, by Donald H. Tuck

Nominees:
Dream Makers, Volume II, by Charles Platt
The Fantastic Art of Rowena, by Rowena Morrill
The High Kings, by Joy Chant
Staying Alive: A Writer's Guide, by Norman Spinrad

It makes absolutely no sense to call *The High Kings* nonfiction—it's a retelling of Celtic legends as if they were being told at the court of King Arthur. I like it, but it's definitely fiction.

Best Dramatic Presentation

Winner: *Return of the Jedi*

Nominees:
Brainstorm
The Right Stuff
Something Wicked This Way Comes
WarGames

Best Professional Editor

Winner: Shawna McCarthy

Nominees:
Terry Carr
Edward L. Ferman
David G. Hartwell
Stanley Schmidt

Best Professional Artist

Winner: Michael Whelan

Nominees:
Val Lakey Lindahn
Don Maitz
Rowena Morrill
Barclay Shaw

Best Semiprozine

Winner: *Locus*, edited by Charles N. Brown

Nominees:
Fantasy Newsletter/Fantasy Review, edited by Robert A. Collins
Science Fiction Chronicle, edited by Andrew I. Porter
Science Fiction Review, edited by Richard E. Geis
Whispers, edited by Stuart David Schiff

Ah, the introduction of the "best *Locus*" category.

BEST FANZINE

Winner: *File 770*, edited by Mike Glyer

Nominees:
Ansible, edited by Dave Langford
Holier Than Thou, edited by Marty and Robbie Cantor
Izzard, edited by Patrick Nielsen Hayden and Teresa Nielsen Hayden
The Philk Fee-Nom-Ee-Non, edited by Paul J. Willett

Yay, PNH and TNH first Hugo nomination!

BEST FAN WRITER

Winner: Mike Glyer

Nominees:
Richard E. Geis
Arthur Hlavaty
Dave Langford
Teresa Nielsen Hayden

BEST FAN ARTIST

Winner: Alexis Gilliland

Nominees:
Brad W. Foster

Joan Hanke-Woods
William Rotsler
Stu Shiffman

JOHN W. CAMPBELL AWARD

Winner: R. A. MacAvoy

Nominees:
Joseph H. Delaney
Lisa Goldstein
Warren Norwood
Joel Rosenberg
Sheri S. Tepper

R. A. MacAvoy won the Campbell, unsurprisingly, with her first novel having Hugo, Nebula, and World Fantasy nominations. She has gone on to have a quiet career writing fantasy novels at intervals. I like her work, but she hasn't had any more success to match her first book.

Joseph H. Delaney was nominated on the strength of some short stories. He continued to produce excellent short work through the eighties, and one novel.

Lisa Goldstein was nominated again; as noted before, she'd have been a fine winner.

Warren Norwood never impinged on my consciousness, but he seems to have had a first novel out in 1983 and followed it up with lots of other novels through the eighties. A reasonable nominee even if he didn't become a major writer.

Joel Rosenberg is a major writer; he's been producing well-thought-of fantasy solidly from 1983 to now. An excellent nominee.

Sheri Tepper is another excellent nominee. She's probably the standout from this group as far as later career goes—she hadn't produced much before her nomination, but since then, she has gone on to be a major serious writer.

COMMENTS ON 1984

2. RICH HORTON

One major mainstream novel needs to be mentioned—Mark Helprin's breathless *Winter's Tale*. I definitely recommend that one!

Quite an impressive list of Campbell nominees. I like a lot of MacAvoy's work—she was a good winner. Tepper does seem to have the "biggest" career of the others—though to my mind, Goldstein is a significantly better writer—but really, the whole list is beyond reproach. Steven Brust, however, would have been a very good addition, as you note.

3. RICH HORTON

As to novellas, *Hardfought* is excellent and would probably have had my vote. Otherwise, not really a great year for novellas. But it was (as so often) a magnificent year for novelettes.

Here's my list of the best:

"Black Air," by Kim Stanley Robinson
"Blood Music," by Greg Bear
"Cicada Queen," by Bruce Sterling
"Slow Birds," by Ian Watson
"The Monkey Treatment," by George R. R. Martin
"Hearts Do Not in Eyes Shine" (John Kessel, and as he recently remarked, quite similar in general theme and shape to the movie *Eternal Sunshine of the Spotless Mind*)
"The Curse of the Smalls and the Stars" (Leiber, a good Fafhrd–Grey Mouser story)
"Remembering Siri" (Dan Simmons, became part of *Hyperion*)
"Red Star, Winter Orbit" (Gibson and Sterling)

At the time, I think I voted for "Black Air," but I could just as well have voted for "Blood Music," which is brilliant. "Cicada Queen" and "Slow Birds" are nearly as good.

In short story, "Speech Sounds" is wonderful, and so is the Nebula winner (Gardner Dozois's "The Peacemaker"), and so too is Leigh Kennedy's "Her Furry Face." On balance, I think I'd stick with "Speech Sounds" for the award.

Nineteen eighty-three is also the year that Robertson Davies, a favorite writer of mine, published *High Spirits*, a collection of pretty good ghost stories.

And it's the first year of Gardner Dozois's long-running Year's Best Science Fiction series, which began with Bluejay Books. (Dozois had earlier done several slimmer volumes for Dutton, continuing a book that Lester del Rey had started.) His TOC is a pretty remarkable reflection of the best stories of the year.

26. LISA GOLDSTEIN

Im on vacation and missed all the terrific comments about the 1983 Campbell Award. Im still on vacation (in a land with no apostrophes, apparently) but had to take the time to say that I didnt mind (much) losing the Campbell to R. A. MacAvoy, who is a wonderful writer. Looking forward to her new book!

32. GARDNER DOZOIS

In retrospect, Bear's *Hardfought* is clearly the most significant of the novellas, by a good margin.

In novelette, I would go for either Bear's "Blood Music" or Sterling's "Cicada Queen," although "Black Air" is a classic too, and "Hearts Do Not in Eyes Shine" is also a good story. "Blood Music" probably had the most impact on subsequent SF, as did *Hardfought*.

"Speech Sounds" is a good story, but I'd probably have gone for "Her Furry Face" or Jack McDevitt's "Cryptic."

I too liked *The Right Stuff*, but no way that it's SF, no matter how much we liked it. Not sure there's anything else there, though, that would get my vote.

Notice Shawna McCarthy's well-deserved win for editor. I always thought that if she'd stayed on as editor of *Asimov's*, it would have been the first of many.

The Tea, the Statue, the Dragon, and You:
R. A. MacAvoy's *Tea with the Black Dragon*

When I first read *Tea with the Black Dragon*, I had never tasted oolong tea. Now I have a special pot for it.

Tea with the Black Dragon is an odd but charming book. It's the kind of book that when someone mentions it, you smile. It's unusual in a number of ways. It's set at a very precise moment of the early eighties, which can be deduced from the very specific technology—but it's a fantasy. It has an action-adventure plot with kidnapping, embezzlement, and early-eighties computer fraud—but that's secondary to what it's about. (If ever a book had plot to stop everything happening at once, this would be it.)

One of the major characters is a fifty-year-old divorced single mother who may be a boddhisattva. Another is a Chinese dragon. The whole book is infused with Chinese mythology and CPM-era computers. It's very short, barely a couple of hours' read, which was unusual even when books used to be shorter.

This was MacAvoy's first novel, and it received a lot of attention. She won the Campbell Award for Best New Writer in 1984. The book won a Locus Award for best first novel, and was nominated for the World Fantasy Award, the Hugo, and Nebula. It had a special citation for the Philip K. Dick Award, essentially coming second to *The Anubis Gates*. So a great many people liked this book, and I expect they're all smiling to think of it.

I think a great deal of the popularity and acclaim came from how lovely it is, and the rest of it came from how amazingly unusual it was in 1983 to have a fantasy novel using Chinese mythology and with a Chinese protagonist. We were parched for it and delighted with it when we got it. I can remember being excited by what seems to me today to be charming, but quite slight. We've come a long way.

MacAvoy is a hit-and-miss writer for me—when I love her books, I really love them; and when I don't, I get bored. I think I've read at least the first volume of everything she's written. She's notable for using unusual cultures and mythologies, and also for doing her homework. The direct sequel to *Tea with the Black Dragon, Twisting the Rope,* is one of the ones I don't care for.

Rene pointed out a very interesting thing about this book. Science fiction went straight from multivac to cyberpunk, without really pausing at the stage of breadboards and CPM handwritten word processors. Fantasy, however, did—we have in *Tea with the Black Dragon* a precise snapshot of an era of computing history. (I could also add Hambly's *The Silent Tower* to this, with the evil wizard's brain coded in CPM on computers that ran on despair, an idea later fully implemented by Microsoft as Windows 95.)

As in 1983 I was struck by the fascinating use of Chinese mythology. It's worth mentioning that on this read, I was a little surprised that everyone apart from Mr. Long was white—surely there were Asian geeks in California in the eighties? The Stanford students are described as all bicycling, but also all blond. Very odd.

The central questions of the book are "What does it mean to be human?" and "What is truth?"—not small things to tackle in a first novel, and MacAvoy deals with them well, and in a manner that suits the central Zen theme.

What it means to a dragon to be human is a question people don't ask often enough.

1985

Winner: *Neuromancer*, by William Gibson

Nominees:
Emergence, by David R. Palmer
The Integral Trees, by Larry Niven
Job: A Comedy of Justice, by Robert A. Heinlein
The Peace War, by Vernor Vinge

The 1985 Hugo Awards were presented at Aussiecon II in Melbourne, Australia.

The Best Novel award was given to William Gibson's *Neuromancer*. It was the book that made cyberpunk explode into everyone's consciousness. It's a huge, important book and I hated it. I haven't reread it since 1985, so I'm probably not being fair to blame it for everything I hated about cyberpunk as a movement. But even though I don't like it at all and would never read it again, I think it absolutely deserved to win the Hugo—it was a major genre-changing work that everybody was talking about and everybody is still mentioning in relevant contexts. It's in print, it's in the library in English, and unique among everything mentioned since I started doing this, the library also has two critical works about it. It also won the Nebula, the PKD Award, and came in third for the Campbell Memorial. Huge, significant book, okay? (Thank goodness cyberpunk is over.)

There were four other nominees, and I've read three of them. I haven't read David Palmer's *Emergence*—no reason why not. I think there wasn't a British edition and nobody talked to me about it much, either then or later. It seems to be postapocalyptic SF. It's not in print, and it's not in the library.

Larry Niven's *The Integral Trees* is good old-fashioned science fiction about people living somewhere with weird physics—in a cluster of floating trees and things. I remember enjoying it on a long train journey. It won the Locus Award. It's in print, and it's in the library, but I think most people would agree that while it's fun, it's minor Niven.

Robert A. Heinlein's *Job: A Comedy of Justice* is a strange Caballesque book about religion and moving between worlds. I have read it more than once and will probably read it again one day. It contains moments I will always remember. But if *The Integral Trees* is minor Niven, this is minor late Heinlein, minor among his late work. If this was one of the five best books of the year, we were having a bad year. It won the Locus Fantasy Award. It is in print, but not in the library.

Vernor Vinge's *The Peace War* is excellent. It's about the scientific invention of bobbles, which create a mirror sphere around the target, and which don't work the way the people who invent them think they do. It's also a deeply political story about control of technology, and it has great characters. I'd have voted for it, and it absolutely deserves its place on the ballot. It's in print as an ebook and as an omnibus with the sequel *Marooned in Realtime*, which is even better. And it's in the library in English only.

So, five American men. Niven and Heinlein are previous winners, Vinge had been nominated at short form, Gibson and Palmer are complete newcomers. We have a postapocalyptic diary, a Golden Age writer with a minor weird book, a Hugo favorite with solid space SF, a fascinating near-future technological speculation by an early career writer who would go on to be really major, and a first novel introducing a new subgenre.

What else might they have chosen?

Non-overlapping Nebula nominees are Lewis Shiner's *Frontera; The Man Who Melted*, Jack Dann; and Kim Stanley Robinson's *The Wild Shore*. The Robinson would surely have been an ornament to the Hugo ballot, but I don't feel it's hugely unjust to leave it off.

The World Fantasy Award was a tie between Barry Hughart's *Bridge of Birds* and Robert Holdstock's *Mythago Wood*, both classics. Other nominees were Diana Wynne Jones's *Archer's Goon*, T. E. D. Klein's *The Ceremonies*, and Stephen King and Peter Straub's *The Talisman*.

The John W. Campbell Memorial Award went to Frederik Pohl's *The Years of the City*, with Lewis Shiner's *Green Eyes* second and *Neuromancer* third. Okay, then. *The Years of the City* would have made a fine Hugo nominee.

The Philip K. Dick Award went to *Neuromancer*, with *The Wild Shore* getting a special citation. (Wow, publishing has changed. You'd never see a major book like *Neuromancer* as a paperback original now.)* Other nominees not previously mentioned: *The Alchemists*, Geary Gravel; *Them Bones*, Howard Waldrop; *Voyager in Night*, C. J. Cherryh.

Other Locus nominees not mentioned so far: *Demon*, John Varley; *Heechee Rendezvous*, Frederik Pohl; *Stars in My Pocket Like Grains of Sand*, Samuel R. Delany; *Chanur's Venture*, C. J. Cherryh; *Across the Sea of Suns*, Gregory Benford; *West of Eden*, Harry Harrison; *The Final Encyclopedia*, Gordon R. Dickson; *City of Sorcery*, Marion Zimmer Bradley; *Icehenge*, Kim Stanley Robinson; *World's End*, Joan D. Vinge; *Clay's Ark*, Octavia E. Butler; *The Adversary*, Julian May; *Heretics of Dune*, Frank Herbert; *A Day for Damnation*, David Gerrold; *Native Tongue*, Suzette Haden Elgin; *Free Live Free*, Gene Wolfe; *Star Rebel*, F. M. Busby; *Dr. Adder*, K. W. Jeter; *The Glamour*, Christopher Priest; *The Practice Effect*, David Brin; *Steam Bird*, Hilbert Schenck; *Circumpolar!*, Richard A. Lupoff.

Okay, so it wasn't a boring year, and all the major awards missed all the best books. Wow. *Chanur's Venture* is the first third of a novel, and a sequel, so maybe not. But *Stars in My Pocket Like Grains of Sand*, probably Delany's masterpiece. *Clay's Ark*, one of Butler's best. *Icehenge*! What could they be thinking, to nominate *Job* and *The Integral Trees* instead? It's ridiculous.

Other Locus Fantasy nominees not previously mentioned: *Damiano's Lute*, R. A. MacAvoy; *Raphael*, R. A. MacAvoy; *The Infinity Concerto*, Greg Bear; *Gilgamesh the King*, Robert Silverberg; *The Ladies of Mand-*

*Except that it has changed again. Now trade paperback originals are a thing, as 2014's Hugo, Nebula, and PKD Award–winning *Ancilliary Justice* shows.

rigyn, Barbara Hambly; *Enchanter's End Game*, David Eddings; *The Businessman*, Thomas M. Disch; *Bearing an Hourglass*, Piers Anthony; *Crewel Lye: A Caustic Yarn*, Piers Anthony; *Castle of Wizardry*, David Eddings; *Who Made Stevie Crye?*, Michael Bishop; *Vampire Junction*, S. P. Somtow; *Cards of Grief*, Jane Yolen; *The Hero and the Crown*, Robin McKinley; *Maia*, Richard Adams; *Nights at the Circus*, Angela Carter; *Brisingamen*, Diana L. Paxson; *Moonheart*, Charles de Lint; *The Third Book of Swords*, Fred Saberhagen; *Fire and Hemlock*, Diana Wynne Jones; *Half a Sky*, R. A. Lafferty; *The Bishop's Heir*, Katherine Kurtz; *The Beggar Queen*, Lloyd Alexander.

The Mythopoeic Award went to Jane Yolen's *Cards of Grief*, which would be great, since I love that book, except that it's SF. What were they thinking? It has spaceships and everything. The only nominee not already mentioned is Tolkien's *The Book of Lost Tales*, which makes it even odder.

Looking at the ISFDB, I see some good books, but nothing that seriously deserves Hugo consideration. Though if *Job* is on there, Brust's *To Reign in Hell* is just as deserving.

To sum up: I think through the eighties so far, there has been a pattern emerging of nominating "old masters" with weak new works in place of the best books. This is a tendency we should watch out for in ourselves as nominators. Nominating Heinlein because he's Heinlein and ignoring *Clay's Ark* and *Stars in My Pocket* is nonsensical. *Neuromancer* would have won against almost any competition. But every one of those top five slots should be something that's potentially a worthy winner, so that future generations can look at them and say, "Yes, that was where the genre was that year." Not "What were they thinking?"

OTHER CATEGORIES

BEST NOVELLA

Winner: *Press Enter*, by John Varley (*Asimov's*, May 1984)

Nominees:

Cyclops, by David Brin (*Asimov's,* March 1984)

Elemental, by Geoffrey A. Landis (*Analog,* December 1984)

Summer Solstice, by Charles L. Harness (*Analog,* June 1984)

Valentina, by Joseph H. Delaney and Marc Stiegler (*Analog,* May 1984)

Oh, I know! They'd just invented home computers, and everybody was trying to find a way to think about them!

Best Novelette

Winner: "Bloodchild," by Octavia E. Butler (*Asimov's,* June 1984)

Nominees:

"Blued Moon," by Connie Willis (*Asimov's,* January 1984)

"The Lucky Strike," by Kim Stanley Robinson (*Universe 14*)

"The Man Who Painted the Dragon Griaule," by Lucius Shepard (*F&SF,* December 1984)

"Return to the Fold," by Timothy Zahn (*Analog,* September 1984)

"Silicon Muse," by Hilbert Schenck (*Analog,* September 1984)

"The Weigher," by Eric Vinicoff and Marcia Martin (*Analog,* October 1984)

Brilliant winner. Some very good nominees.

Best Short Story

Winner: "The Crystal Spheres," by David Brin (*Analog,* January 1984)

Nominees:

"The Aliens Who Knew, I Mean, Everything," by George Alec Effinger (*F&SF,* October 1984)

"Ridge Running," by Kim Stanley Robinson (*F&SF,* January 1984)

"Rory," by Steven Gould (*Analog,* April 1984)

"Salvador," by Lucius Shepard (*F&SF,* April 1984)

"Symphony for a Lost Traveler," by Lee Killough (*Analog,* March 1984)

Good winner, but I think I'd have voted for the Effinger. Look how many of these short fiction nominees are from the new generation. Also, all Big Three magazines except for one from an anthology.

BEST NONFICTION BOOK

Winner: *Wonder's Child: My Life in Science Fiction,* by Jack Williamson

Nominees:
The Dune Encyclopedia, edited by Dr. Willis E. McNelly
The Faces of Science Fiction, by Patti Perret
In the Heart or in the Head: An Essay in Time Travel, by George Turner
Sleepless Nights in the Procrustean Bed, by Harlan Ellison

BEST DRAMATIC PRESENTATION

Winner: *2010*

Nominees:
Dune
Ghostbusters
The Last Starfighter
Star Trek III: The Search for Spock

BEST PROFESSIONAL EDITOR

Winner: Terry Carr

Nominees:
Edward L. Ferman
Shawna McCarthy
Stanley Schmidt
George Scithers

Carr, a book editor rather than a magazine editor, had Hugo recognition only after his death.*

BEST PROFESSIONAL ARTIST

Winner: Michael Whelan

Nominees:
Vincent Di Fate
Tom Kidd
Val Lakey Lindahn
Barclay Shaw

BEST SEMIPROZINE

Winner: *Locus,* edited by Charles N. Brown

Nominees:
Fantasy Review, edited by Robert A. Collins
Science Fiction Chronicle, edited by Andrew I. Porter
Science Fiction Review, edited by Richard E. Geis
Whispers, edited by Stuart David Schiff

BEST FANZINE

Winner: *File 770,* edited by Mike Glyer

Nominees:
Ansible, edited by Dave Langford
Holier Than Thou, edited by Marty and Robbie Cantor
Mythologies, edited by Don D'Ammassa
Rataplan, edited by Leigh Edmonds

---

*I was mistaken about this. See comments.

Best Fan Writer

Winner: Dave Langford

Nominees:
Leigh Edmonds
Richard E. Geis
Mike Glyer
Arthur Hlavaty

First win for Dave, who really is an excellent fan writer.

Best Fan Artist

Winner: Alexis Gilliland

Nominees:
Brad W. Foster
Steven Fox
Joan Hanke-Woods
William Rotsler
Stu Shiffman

John W. Campbell Award

Winner: Lucius Shepard

Nominees:
Bradley Denton
Geoffrey A. Landis
Elissa Malcohn
Ian McDonald
Melissa Scott

Well, a much better year than the previous year. All these nominees have gone on to have significant careers in SF writing. I've heard of all of them!

Lucius Shepard had published some award-nominated short work and one novel, and won on that basis. Since then, he has gone on to produce more work of the same quality, regularly being nominated for awards for long and short work, right up to the present day. I don't think he has ever been a bestselling writer, but he is a respected literary writer within SF, and a very good winner.

Of the others, Bradley Denton has kept writing and producing well-thought-of, slightly off-the-wall work; "Sergeant Chip" won the Sturgeon a few years ago. I'd say he's not quite a major writer, but he's a significant minor one.

Geoffrey Landis has been a major SF poet and a major writer at short lengths—though it took him until 2000 to produce a novel. He's also a NASA scientist, so maybe he was busy living SF. Great nominee.

Elissa Malcohn has continued to produce poems, short stories, and novels without ever having a breakout hit to bring her visibility.

Ian McDonald is unquestionably a major writer—his last three novels have been nominated for Hugos, including *The Dervish House* in 2010. I don't know what he had published before the nomination—I didn't become aware of him until *Desolation Road* in 1988. I think judging on subsequent careers, he was the new writer of 1985 who has gone furthest, but I think the voters made the right decision on the available evidence.

Melissa Scott won in 1986, so we can leave talking about her until next week.

COMMENTS ON 1985

2. JAMES DAVIS NICOLL

Carr, a book editor rather than a magazine editor, had Hugo recognition only after his death.

Not true! This is the grand exception to the general rule (prior to the split in Best Editor Hugo to long and short form) that book editors have to die to win a Best Editor Hugo. At this time, Carr was editing his second Ace Science Fiction Specials series (the third Ace Science Fiction Specials series overall). In 1984, the books released in that series were Kim Stanley Robinson's *The Wild Shore;* Carter Scholz and Glenn Harcourt's *Palimpsests;* Lucius Shepard's *Green Eyes;* Howard Waldrop's *Them Bones;* and William Gibson's *Neuromancer.*

Carr died in 1987 and won the Best Dead Book Editor Hugo that year.

4. CSTROSS

Palmer's *Emergence* was indeed published in the United Kingdom. Warning for Jo: I don't recommend reading it. Not only have its core premises not aged well but it also has some monumentally icky sexual issues, race politics straight out of the 1930s (and not in a good way), an overdose of "fans are slans" exceptionalism, and a degree of foaming-at-the-mouth anti-Communism that makes me fear for the purity of my bodily fluids. The one thing it *does* have going for it is a really strong narrative voice and some Heinleinian resonances; I'd peg it as the zenith (or, perhaps more accurately, the nadir) of a particular kind of John W. Campbell–influenced SF. A hideous example of a particularly reprehensible ideological subtext within American SF, in other words.

23. CSTROSS

To say I *really liked Neuromancer* would be an understatement; it warped my literary development! Took me a few years to shake the influence off and start trying to innovate rather than imitate.

26. RUSS ALLBERY

Count me as another who disliked *Neuromancer.* I think there are a lot of problems with that book, but the one that stands out in my memory is how completely egregiously wrong it got computers. And not only did it blow computer technology completely, but it did so in such an influential way that the same egregious errors continue and multiply in other influenced works to this day. (See, for example, Robert Sawyer, particularly *The Terminal Experiment*.) I blame *Neuromancer*, at least in part, for the fictional conception of computers that lead to programs that run on any computer they find, running programs "moving" through a network, ridiculous visual representations of computer security, and the general tendency to portray computer security as an analogue to medieval fortresses, leading to innumerable major errors about how computer security actually functions.

Note: I do not blame Gibson for this. Computers and networks were very new to the general population, and extrapolation is very hard. *Neuromancer* wasn't any more wrong than many, many other "predictions" in SF. It just had the misfortune (from my perspective) to be wrong in ways that for me make it very difficult to read, and it was wrong in such a persistent and influential way that it turned cyberpunk and cyberpunk-derived writing into a sort of magical alternative technology subgenre that has nothing to do with how computers actually work, but which is persistently used by others as a model for computers.

46. GARDNER DOZOIS

Novella is a bit weak this year. *Press Enter* was a product of its time, and inevitably has dated quite a bit by now. In retrospect, the best novella of the year was Geoff Ryman's *The Unconquered Country*, but as it appeared in *Interzone*, which wasn't being seen much on this side of the Atlantic at the time, very few people actually read it. (A few more might have seen it if Ryman's then-agent had let me use it in my Best of the Year that year, but he would not.) Nancy Kress's *Trinity* was also first-rate, one of her first major stories. Lucius Shepard's *A Traveller's Tale* was also vivid and good, and, in retrospect, any of these novellas would have made a better choice than the Varley.

Novelette and short story are both very strong this year, with lots of good stuff both on the ballot and left off the ballot.

In novelette, it's hard to argue with the emotionally grueling "Blood-child" as the winner, although "The Man Who Painted the Dragon Griaule" is acknowledged as a fantasy classic by now, and "Blued Moon" is still funny, one of Connie Willis's first major stories. There was lots of good stuff that didn't make the ballot. I've always had a sneaking fondness for Frederik Pohl's "The Kindly Isle," and Swanwick's "Trojan

Horse" (also edging toward post-cyberpunk before cyberpunk had even fully developed) and Shepard's "Black Coral" are also good, as is Robinson's "The Lucky Strike," although it's heavy political content makes it controversial, and I know some (usually those who don't agree with its politics) who loathe it. Joanna Russ's little-known "Bodies" is also good.

In short story, leaving my own two stories out of consideration, Shepard's "Salvador" is my clear choice among the stories that made the ballot. There was lots of good stuff that didn't make it, though, including Gibson's "New Rose Hotel" (which I think is the only story on this entire ballot that was later made into a movie, for what that's worth), Richard Cowper's chilling "A Message to the King of Brobdingnag," Bruce Sterling's "Sunken Gardens," Molly Gloss's early story "Interlocking Pieces," Tanith Lee's "Draco, Draco," O. Niemand's "Two Bits," and Gene Wolfe's classic fantasy short, "A Cabin on the Coast."

Based on the work that was available to be read at the time, there's absolutely no doubt that Lucius Shepard deserved the Campbell. He had one of the biggest explosions of high-quality stories in one year the field had seen since Varley, with "Salvador," "The Man Who Painted the Dragon Griaule," "A Traveller's Tale," and at least a half dozen other stories coming out that year, plus a novel. It was overwhelming, and it seemed like a good new Shepard story was coming along every five minutes. In retrospect, most of Shepard's subsequent impact would be on horror/fantasy, while Ian McDonald, whom you really couldn't have picked on the basis of the work he'd produced to that point, would turn out to be far more influential on science fiction—in fact, I think McDonald may be one of the best SF writers working in the field today, if not THE best. It was a strong ballot, though, and all the other candidates have subsequently produced good work, especially Geoff Landis, who's on the Hugo ballot again here in 2011.

48. RICH HORTON

I'm late to the party—and what a party! Forty-seven comments so far—because I was off at ConQuesT.

Other novels of at least some note that I haven't seen mentioned (though I may have missed them):

A Quiet of Stone, by Stephen Leigh (not a masterpiece but a nice book)

Divine Endurance, Gwyneth Jones's first novel (I actually hated this novel, and it started an odd pattern—I think Jones's short fiction is excellent to brilliant, but I have never gotten on with her novels. But I do think the first novel of such a major writer deserves note.)

Planet of Whispers, by James Patrick Kelly (Not a great book, but a good one—and Kelly's first novel, so important from that point of view)

Moon-Flash, by Patricia McKillip (if I'm not mistaken, McKillip's only SF)

The Digging Leviathan, by James P. Blaylock

The Final Reflection, by John M. Ford (a Star Trek novel, of course)

The Man in the Tree, by Damon Knight

Interstellar Pig, by William Sleator

The Black Company, by Glen Cook

As to the Campbell, it's very hard to argue with Shepard's win, based on his body of work to that date. That said, I'd rank him no better than fourth among these writers.

Ian McDonald (who had already published a first-rate story, "The Catharine Wheel," sort of a beta version of the Mars of his wonderful novels *Desolation Road* and *Ares Express*) is clearly, far and away, the best in terms of having published the best novels and also having a long and varied career.

Geoffrey A. Landis has published only one novel, and it's a minor work, but he's had lots of excellent short fiction.

And Brad Denton (besides being a really fine guitar player, as I can attest from hearing him play just two nights ago), has done plenty of outstanding work, and his serial killer novel *Blackburn* is not to be missed.

1986

Best Novel

Winner: *Ender's Game*, by Orson Scott Card

Nominees:
Blood Music, by Greg Bear
Cuckoo's Egg, by C. J. Cherryh
Footfall, by Larry Niven and Jerry Pournelle
The Postman, by David Brin

The 1986 Hugo Awards were presented at ConFederation in Atlanta, Georgia.

The Best Novel award was given to Orson Scott Card's *Ender's Game*, a book about which I am deeply conflicted. I read it in 1985 when it was new, and absolutely loved it. I'd already been a fan of Card's for some time, and this is the pure essence of Card—a conflicted genius child forced into the act of atrocity. It has wonderful characters and a wonderful story and alien dreams . . . and a very troubling set of axioms that it took me a long time to recognize. Every novel has the author palming cards in the world-building to get things to come out the way they want so that it looks like cold equations but it's actually a cold deck. Sometimes when you stop and think, it's worrying that that is what they wanted. I loved *Ender's Game* in 1985; I read it straight through twice. I know the names of all the characters and can quote large chunks of the text. And yet I can't help seeing that there's this pure tormented innocent forced, forced, into killing *all* the aliens while having perfect compassion for them, and it makes me feel slightly ill.

It's a great book and a worthy Hugo winner. It won the Nebula too. I'd have absolutely voted for it in 1986. It's in print and in the library in English and French. It's still being talked about and stirring up controversy. But I find its view of necessity disturbing, and I doubt I will read it again.

There are four other nominees, and I've read all of them.

Greg Bear's *Blood Music* is a short fascinating novel of genetic engineering, nanotech, and artificial intelligence. This is probably Bear's best work. It's in print and in the library in French and English. The novelette form won the Hugo and the Nebula, and this may have made people reluctant to vote for it, feeling it had already won.

C. J. Cherryh's *Cuckoo's Egg* is a space opera about aliens, communication, and responsibility. It's infuriating that it didn't get a British edition until years later. It's in print in an omnibus, but it's not in the library. My entirely unscientific perception is that this is not one of Cherryh's better-known books and it hasn't lasted well.

Footfall, by Larry Niven and Jerry Pournelle is a big blockbuster about a near-future alien invasion. I liked the aliens, but this is a style of book I tend to read fast and forget—multiple POVs, not much depth, fun, but only fun. I don't think it's the kind of thing that really belongs on the Hugo ballot. It's in print and in the library in English only.

David Brin's *The Postman* is an intelligent, tightly focused, near-future disaster novel that asks interesting questions about the nature of civilization. I think the original novella-length version was the best. It didn't lose by being expanded, but it didn't gain much either. I believe it was later made into a movie. It's good, but it isn't as original or innovative as Brin's Uplift books. It won the Locus SF Award and the Campbell Memorial. It's in print, and it's in the library in English and French.

So, five men and one woman, all American. Cherryh, Niven, and Brin are previous winners. Pournelle and Bear are previous nominees. Card had won the Campbell and been nominated for short-form Hugos, but this was his first novel nomination.

Interestingly, we have three novels expanded from previously nominated short work—the Card, the Bear, and the Brin. All these books are science fiction, but they are very different. We have two disaster novels (one with aliens), two space operas (with aliens), and one pretty much pure-science near future, also with aliens arising. So 1986 was a year where everyone wanted aliens. Lovely.

What else might the voters have chosen?

Other non-overlapping Nebula nominees were Tim Powers's *Dinner at Deviant's Palace;* Brian W. Aldiss's *Helliconia Winter;* Barry N. Maltzberg's *The Remaking of Sigmund Freud;* and Bruce Sterling's *Schismatrix.* I don't like *Schismatrix,* but I recognize it as an excellent example of emergent cyberpunk and would have preferred to see it on the Hugo ballot in place of *Footfall.*

The World Fantasy Award was won by *Song of Kali* by Dan Simmons, which is too much horror for it to be seriously considered for the Hugo. Other nominees were *The Damnation Game,* Clive Barker; *The Dream Years,* Lisa Goldstein; *Illywhacker,* Peter Carey; *The Vampire Lestat,* Anne Rice; and *Winterking,* Paul Hazel.

The John W. Campbell Memorial Award gave second place to Vonnegut's *Galápagos,* with *Blood Music* and Keith Roberts's *Kiteworld* joint third.

The Philip K. Dick Award was won by *Dinner at Deviant's Palace,* with a special citation of Richard Grant's *Saraband of Lost Time.* Other finalists not already mentioned were *Emprise,* Michael P. Kube-McDowell; *Knight Moves,* Walter Jon Williams; *Terrarium,* Scott Russell Sanders; and *The Timeservers,* Russell Griffin.

Other *Locus* nominees not mentioned so far: *Robots and Empire,* Isaac Asimov; *The Cat Who Walks Through Walls,* Robert A. Heinlein; *Brightness Falls from the Air,* James Tiptree Jr.; *Always Coming Home,* Ursula K. Le Guin; *Eon,* Greg Bear; *The Proteus Operation,* James P. Hogan; *The Kif Strike Back,* C. J. Cherryh; *Contact,* Carl Sagan; *Artifact,* Gregory Benford; *The Memory of Whiteness,* Kim Stanley Robinson; *Between the Strokes of Night,* Charles Sheffield; *Chapterhouse: Dune,* Frank Herbert; *Ancient of Days,* Michael Bishop; *Dayworld,* Philip José Farmer; *Child of Fortune,* Norman Spinrad; *Tom O'Bedlam,* Robert Silverberg; *Starquake,* Robert L. Forward; *Five-Twelfths of Heaven,* Melissa Scott; *The Darkling Wind,* Somtow Sucharitkul.

I can't tell you how happy it makes me to see the Heinlein, the Asimov, and the Herbert down here instead of up among the Hugo nominees. Of the rest, the Tiptree and the Le Guin are great but flawed; they'd have been good nominees but not outstanding ones. The Cherryh is wonderful but doesn't stand alone any more than one organ ripped out of a body would.

The Locus Fantasy Award went to Roger Zelazny's *The Trumps of Doom,* an Amber book. Other nominees not previously mentioned: *The Book of Kells,* R. A. MacAvoy; *Dragonsbane,* Barbara Hambly; *Lyonesse II: The Green Pearl,* Jack Vance; *The King's Justice,* Katherine Kurtz; *The Summer Tree,* Guy Gavriel Kay; *With a Tangled Skein,* Piers Anthony; *Dark of the Moon,* P. C. Hodgell; *Silverthorn,* Raymond E. Feist; *Mulengro,* Charles de Lint; *Lovecraft's Book,* Richard A. Lupoff; *Brokedown Palace,* Steven Brust; *The Damnation Game,* Clive Barker; *The Wishsong of Shannara,* Terry Brooks; *Wizard of the Pigeons,* Megan Lindholm; *In Yana, the Touch of Undying,* Michael Shea; *The Last Rainbow,* Parke Godwin; *Things Invisible to See,* Nancy Willard; *The Song of Mavin Manyshaped,* Sheri S. Tepper; *Wings of Flame,* Nancy Springer; *The Bronze King,* Suzy McKee Charnas; *Marianne, the Magus, and the Manticore,* Sheri S. Tepper.

The Mythopoeic Award was won by Barry Hughart's *Bridge of Birds,* which wasn't Hugo eligible, as it was published in 1984. Other nominees not already mentioned: Diana Wynne Jones's *Fire and Hemlock* and Manuel Mujica Láinez's *The Wandering Unicorn.*

The Prometheus Award was won by Victor Milán's *The Cybernetic Samurai.* Other nominees were: *Elegy for a Soprano,* Kay Nolte Smith; *The Gallatin Divergence,* L. Neil Smith; *A Matter of Time,* Glen Cook; and *Radio Free Albemuth,* Philip K. Dick.

Looking for things they all missed, I see Pamela Dean's *The Secret Country;* Geoff Ryman's *The Warrior Who Carried Life;* Michael Swanwick's *In the Drift;* and John Kessel and James Patrick Kelly's *Freedom Beach.*

So . . . on the whole, this was a pretty good year, where the Hugo nominations were doing what they're supposed to. There are a number of things I'd rather have seen on the list than *Footfall,* but nothing that it seems really unjust to leave out. And there were three weak "old master" books that the 1986 nominators decided not to nominate, and good for them. So, well done, voters of 1986.

OTHER CATEGORIES

BEST NOVELLA

Winner: "24 Views of Mt. Fuji, by Hokusai," by Roger Zelazny (*Asimov's*, July 1985)

Nominees:
Green Mars, by Kim Stanley Robinson (*Asimov's*, September 1985)
The Only Neat Thing to Do, by James Tiptree Jr. (*F&SF*, October 1985)
Sailing to Byzantium, by Robert Silverberg (*Asimov's*, February 1985)
The Scapegoat, by C. J. Cherryh (*Alien Stars*)

Okay, that's another great set of novellas, and I'd have had a hard time voting. I think I'd have put the Silverberg first . . . no, the Tiptree, no . . . I don't know. The Cherryh is good, and all the others are outstanding. This is the kind of nomination list that makes me happy.

BEST NOVELETTE

Winner: "Paladin of the Lost Hour," by Harlan Ellison (*Universe 15; Twilight Zone*, December 1985)

Nominees:
"Dogfight," by Michael Swanwick and William Gibson (*Omni*, July 1985)
"The Fringe," by Orson Scott Card (*F&SF*, October 1985)
"A Gift from the GrayLanders," by Michael Bishop (*Asimov's*, September 1985)
"Portraits of His Children," by George R. R. Martin (*Asimov's*, November 1985)

I'd have voted for the Martin, but I can't argue too much here.

Best Short Story

Winner: "Fermi and Frost," by Frederik Pohl (*Asimov's*, January 1985)

Nominees:
"Dinner in Audoghast," by Bruce Sterling (*Asimov's*, May 1985)
"Flying Saucer Rock & Roll," by Howard Waldrop (*Omni*, January 1985)
"Hong's Bluff," by William F. Wu (*Omni*, March 1985)
"Snow," by John Crowley (*Omni*, November 1985)

Oooh, "Fermi and Frost"!

Best Nonfiction Book

Winner: *Science Made Stupid*, by Tom Weller

Nominees:
Benchmarks: Galaxy Bookshelf, by Algis Budrys
An Edge in My Voice, by Harlan Ellison
Faces of Fear: Encounters with the Creators of Modern Horror, edited by Douglas E. Winter
The John W. Campbell Letters, Vol. 1, edited by Perry A. Chapdelaine Sr., Tony Chapdelaine, and George Hay
The Pale Shadow of Science, by Brian W. Aldiss

Best Dramatic Presentation

Winner: *Back to the Future*

Nominees:
Brazil
Cocoon
Enemy Mine
Ladyhawke

BEST PROFESSIONAL EDITOR

Winner: Judy-Lynn del Rey (refused)

Nominees:
Terry Carr
Edward L. Ferman
Shawna McCarthy
Stanley Schmidt

The note at *Locus* says that Lester del Rey refused the Hugo because of Judy-Lynn's opposition to posthumous awards. This led to the present system, where you have to accept or decline nominations.

BEST PROFESSIONAL ARTIST

Winner: Michael Whelan

Nominees:
Frank Kelly Freas
Don Maitz
Rowena Morrill
Barclay Shaw

Whelan deserved it just for the *Cuckoo's Egg* cover.

BEST SEMIPROZINE

Winner: *Locus,* edited by Charles N. Brown

Nominees:
Fantasy Review, edited by Robert A. Collins
Interzone, edited by Simon Ounsley and David Pringle
Science Fiction Chronicle, edited by Andrew Porter
Science Fiction Review, edited by Richard E. Geis

Best Fanzine

Winner: *Lan's Lantern*, edited by George "Lan" Laskowski

Nominees:
Anvil, edited by Charlotte Proctor
Greater Columbia Fantasy Costumers Guild Newsletter, edited by Bobby
  Gear
Holier Than Thou, edited by Marty and Robbie Cantor
Universal Translator, edited by Susan Bridges

Best Fan Writer

Winner: Mike Glyer

Nominees:
Don D'Ammassa
Richard E. Geis
Arthur Hlavaty
David Langford
Patrick Nielsen Hayden

Best Fan Artist

Winner: Joan Hanke-Woods

Nominees:
Brad W. Foster
Steven Fox
William Rotsler
Stu Shiffman

John W. Campbell Award

Winner: Melissa Scott

Nominees:
Karen Joy Fowler
Guy Gavriel Kay
Carl Sagan
Tad Williams
David Zindell

Okay, a pretty good year. I've not only heard of all of them, but I've read things by them too.

Melissa Scott was nominated on the strength of two novels, *The Game Beyond* and *Five-Twelfths of Heaven*, which is the first of the only trilogy of alchemical polyamorous space opera I know of. Since then, she has gone on to write lots of acclaimed SF, including *The Kindly Ones* and *Point of Hopes*. I really like her work. I think she's a great winner. She's still writing.

Karen Joy Fowler won in 1987, so let's leave her until next time.

In retrospect, Guy Gavriel Kay should perhaps have won—he's one of the greatest living fantasy writers. He had only published *The Summer Tree*, which isn't representative of what he would go on to achieve. But the people who nominated and voted for him at the very start of his career were getting it right.

Carl Sagan was really a science writer whose only SF novel was *Contact*. He died in 1996.

Tad Williams has gone on to be a major fantasy writer. He's still writing.

David Zindell must have been nominated for his only publication, the novella *Shanidar*, which was the basis for his 1988 post-scientific wide-screen baroque space opera, *Neverness*. He wrote four ambitious books in that universe, and has since been publishing his Ea Cycle.

All good Campbell nominees, winding up a pretty good slate altogether.

COMMENTS ON 1986

16. RICH HORTON

Some not-yet-mentioned novels:

CV, by Damon Knight–very readable, very enjoyable, kind of went
  weird at the end (though there are two sequels, which presumably
  take off from that point and might justify the weirdness)
The Nick of Time, by George Alec Effinger
Alien Main, by Lloyd Biggle and T. L. Sherred

And from the "mainstream":

A Maggot, by John Fowles
Last Letters from Hav, by Jan Morris
The Handmaid's Tale, by Margaret Atwood

That is a pretty significant set of three books, really!

19. RICH HORTON

Okay, short fiction.

Nineteen eighty-five was one of the great years for short fiction in
SF history, in my view. I think that's reflected in the winners being all
fine stories that didn't deserve to win.

For example, in novella. Yes, Zelazny's *24 Views of Mount Fuji, by
Hokusai,* is a fine story. But it's not the best of the year. Tiptree's *The
Only Neat Thing to Do* is her best late story, and it's arguably the best
"Cold Equations" reexamination ever—well, or second best, Kelly's
"Think Like a Dinosaur" is probably the best. But it's not the best. Nei-
ther is the very good Silverberg story, nor the okay Cherryh story.

For me, and by a wide margin, Kim Stanley Robinson's *Green
Mars* was the best novella of 1985. I admit some personal investment
there—it's one of the stories I credit with bringing me back to the field
after a few years drifting away a bit. But it's also a great, great story. With
a great last line—"A new creature steps on the peak of green Mars."

And it's not correct to say it has nothing to do with the RGB Mars novels. It's true that it's not in the strict continuity of the novels, but it's clearly a beta version of that Mars, with some shared characters (or at least versions of characters), and with similar ideas (terraforming Mars, and longevity). It was eventually collected in *The Martians*, Robinson's short story collection that was a pendant to the trilogy.

There were quite a few more very fine novellas in 1985. Bruce Sterling's *Green Days in Brunei* is excellent—it surely should have made the short list. Vernor Vinge's *The Ungoverned* is a good story, if not quite Hugo-worthy. Kate Wilhelm's *The Gorgon Field* is also good.

Now to novelette. I'd have voted for "Dogfight" among the nominees. But there were some outstanding ones that didn't even make the short list.

My favorite novelette of 1985 was Avram Davidson's "The Slovo Stove," which doesn't seem that well known these days, but which is thoroughly marvelous.

In addition, one of William Gibson's best stories was first published in 1985, though few people in the field saw it. This was "The Winter Market," which first appeared in *Vancouver Magazine* in November 1985. It got more notice after it appeared in *Interzone* and *Burning Chrome* in 1986, and the following year's Dozois "Best Of."

There's also:

"Solstice," by James Patrick Kelly
"The Warm Space," by David Brin
"The Road Not Taken," by Harry Turtledove
"Lord Kelvin's Machine," by James P. Blaylock
"Mercurial," by Kim Stanley Robinson
"Tunicate, Tunicate, Wilt Thou Be Mine?," by Charles Sheffield
"Empire Dreams," by Ian McDonald
"Shanidar," by David Zindell (the first significant story, I think, from
    the Writers of the Future anthologies—of course, this was the first
    year of the anthologies!)

The short story field was particularly brilliant. Again, the best story did not appear on the Hugo short list, though it did win the Nebula. This is Nancy Kress's "Out of All Them Bright Stars," in my opinion, one of the very best SF short stories of all time.

Of the Hugo short list, to my mind, the best story is "Snow," by John Crowley. Sterling's "Dinner in Audoghast" is also very good. I'd rank the Zelazny story behind those two. Perhaps, as Jo suggests, a reread of the whole short list would be productive. The Crowley story is pure SF, by the way (and very moving)—we think of him as primarily a fantastist, because of *Little, Big* and the Ægypt sequence, but some of his very best work ("Snow," *Engine Summer,* and *Great Work of Time*) is SF.

Other good short stories (some very good indeed):

Connie Willis's famously controversial "All My Darling Daughters"
James P. Blaylock's "Paper Dragons"
John Kessel's "A Clean Escape"
Andrew Weiner's "Klein's Machine"
My favorite Lucius Shepard story, "A Spanish Lesson"
Karen Joy Fowler's "The Lake Was Full of Artificial Things" (one of a
     few great SF stories with titles from Wallace Stevens)
John M. Ford's "Scrabble with God"
Greg Bear's "Through Road No Wither"
Lisa Goldstein's "Tourists"

Taken all in all, I think the list of short stories, including the Hugo short list, is about as good a list at that length as ever.

25. GARDNER DOZOIS

Another strong year for novella. The voters went for the most flamboyant story—the Zelazny, which is one of the best of the late Zelazny stories, but not up to the best of his earlier work—but my vote would have gone to *Sailing to Byzantium,* with *Green Mars* as second choice. *The Only Neat Thing to Do* is not my favorite late Tiptree—it seems too sentimental to me, in a manner that's calculated to work the audience: a tearjerker. My favorite late Tiptree is *Slow Music,* from a couple of years before.

In novelette, I'd go for "The Winter Market," perhaps Gibson's single best story, with "Dogfight" as a follow-up, although the Martin, the Bishop, and even the Card are also strong. As someone mentioned, Lucius Shepard published two of his best stories that year, "The Jaguar Hunter" and "A Spanish Lesson."

In short story, I'd go for "Snow," one of my favorite stories of the whole period. "Flying Saucer Rock and Roll" is a hoot—no other term really describes it, one of Waldrop's best. The Sterling and the Pohl are also very strong, as is the Blaylock.

I was in the audience when Lester del Rey refused Judy-Lynn's Hugo, saying bitterly, "If you wouldn't give it to her while she was alive, she wouldn't want it after she was dead."

53. GARDNER DOZOIS

Oddly, for the chief drum-beater and propagandist for cyberpunk, especially through his fanzine *Cheap Truth*, Sterling himself never wrote much cyberpunk. Most of his work is early posthuman stuff, although he also wrote a lot of historical fantasy that is rather reminiscent of a somewhat less gonzo Howard Waldrop.

WHO IS ALIEN? C. J. CHERRYH'S *CUCKOO'S EGG*

Cuckoo's Egg is in many ways the quintessential Cherryh novel. There are terrific aliens and an alien society. There's one human. It starts off slowly and gets faster and faster. And nobody tells you what's going on until the very end, when you find out at whiplash speed. *Cuckoo's Egg* starts off with Duun, whose race is shonun and whose rank is hatani. Duun is given what is clearly a human baby, amid alien complications. We don't know why, or what's going on. For the rest of the book, the viewpoint alternates between Duun and his fosterling, Haras Thorn, as he grows up entirely baffled about who and what he is.

It's a good book because the alien society is interesting and well done, and so is the part about growing up surrounded by aliens and wanting to belong and knowing you never really can. Cherryh is excellent at aliens, as always. If you don't like it, it will be because you don't enjoy being bewildered. I like it a lot more, rereading it, than I did the first time.

Duun gives Thorn a childhood as best he can contrive—his own childhood, in the countryside. He teaches him to be hatani, and we slowly learn what it means to be hatani, not just to fight but also to judge. I think Cherryh was somewhat influenced in making this society by reading about medieval Asia—the ghota are ninjalike, and there's something of that feel to the castes, and the tiny details like raked sand on the floors and low-tech bathing. The speeded-up industrialization in response to the initial human probe also has something about it of Meiji Japan. The shonun are themselves, but it's interesting to see how she has used Earth history to make them, especially in reference to the whole colonial thing, considering the presence of more technologically advanced humans out there somewhere.

Thorn spends most of the book bewildered and trying to fit in. He wants there to be other people who look like him, somewhere in the world. He wants to be what Duun wants him to be—he loves Duun, who is all he has. Yet he knows hatani aren't supposed to need anybody or anything, and Duun wants him to be hatani. He can never entirely trust Duun. It's difficult for him. He's between worlds—culturally hatani, physically human, and it gets more difficult when they start playing him tapes of humans and he starts to understand. And it's difficult for Duun too, who sees wider complications than Thorn can.

This isn't a favorite Cherryh for me—it's on the cusp between the ones I like and the ones I find go too far into misery and incomprehensibility. There's just enough safety here, just enough of a potential for things being all right that I can bear it—at least on rereading. It also has a notably good cover—Michael Whelan is actually illustrating a scene from the book and getting everything right.

She has written books I like better, and books that are easier to read, but if you want one book that is pure essence of Cherryh, no explanations, no excuses, just aliens and difficult motivations, then this is it.

1987

Winner: *Speaker for the Dead*, by Orson Scott Card

Nominees:
Black Genesis, by L. Ron Hubbard
Count Zero, by William Gibson
Marooned in Realtime, by Vernor Vinge
The Ragged Astronauts, by Bob Shaw

The 1987 Hugo Awards were awarded at Conspiracy, in Brighton, England.

The Best Novel award went to Orson Scott Card for *Speaker for the Dead*, the sequel to the 1986 winner, *Ender's Game*. It's unusual for a sequel to win, and this is the first time it happened two years in a row like this. And it's another good winner, and another book about which I am conflicted.

I remember buying *Speaker for the Dead*. I can often remember reading a book for the first time, but it's not often I remember buying one. It was in Forbidden Planet in London, and I didn't know it existed, but of course, the title told me it was connected to *Ender's Game*, and I can still remember that shock of joy when I found it. And I did love it—even more than *Ender's Game*. It has aliens and spaceships and an intelligent computer. It has distance between the stars measured not in kilometers but in years. It had the fascinating comparison of human, ramen, and varelse. I wish I still loved it; I really do. But you can't unsee the man behind the curtain. It's so very manipulative. It pushed my buttons then, and now it doesn't.

It also won the Nebula and Locus Awards. It's in print; it's in the library in French only. It's definitely still being read and talked about. I would absolutely have voted for it in 1987.

There are four other nominees, of which I have read two—the lowest for some time.

Let's start with the ones I haven't read. I haven't read L. Ron Hubbard's *Black Genesis*, because it didn't look like my kind of thing. It's not in print, and it's in the library in English only. There was some controversy about the nomination and the role of the publishers at the con, and it came last in the voting below No Award.

I haven't read William Gibson's *Count Zero*, because I hated *Neuromancer*. It's in print, and it's in the library in English. It came third in the voting.

I have read, and written about, Vernor Vinge's *Marooned in Realtime*. I loved it in 1987; I continue to love it. It's a post-singularity story about a murder investigation in geological time. It's in print, but it's not in the library. It's a sequel to *The Peace War*, but it stands alone. This is what I'd vote for if I had to vote on this list now. It came fourth in the voting, perhaps because this was a British Worldcon and there was not yet a UK edition, so many of the voters wouldn't have had the chance to read it.

Bob Shaw's *The Ragged Astronauts* is a romp about two planets close enough to share an atmosphere and travel between them in a balloon. It was a lot of fun, but not really Hugo-worthy. It's not in print, and it's not in the library, and I don't think it has lasted. However, it won the BSFA Award and came second in the Hugo voting, so clearly other people liked it more than I did.

All men, four American and one Northern Irish. Hubbard is a Hugo newcomer. Cherryh and Card are former winners; Vinge is a former nominee. Shaw had a prior short-form nomination, and two prior fan writer wins. The books are all SF: one with aliens and spaceships, one cyberpunk, one novel of ideas, one romp, and I have no idea how to categorize the Hubbard.

An odd year. What else might they have chosen?

Eligible non-overlapping Nebula nominees were Leigh Kennedy's *The Journal of Nicholas the American* and James Morrow's brilliant and chilling *This Is the Way the World Ends*, which I think would have made a good addition to the Hugo ballot.

Patrick Suskind's *Perfume* won the World Fantasy Award. Other nominees were Stephen King's *It;* Charles L. Grant's *The Pet;* Gene Wolfe's *Soldier of the Mist;* Dean R. Koontz's *Strangers;* Terry Bisson's phenomenal *Talking Man;* and Margaret Mahy's *The Tricksters.*

The John W. Campbell Memorial Award went to Joan Slonczewski's *A Door into Ocean*, a book that really should have been a Hugo nominee. Second place went to Morrow, and third to Card.

The Philip K. Dick Award went to James Blaylock's *Homunculus*, with a special citation to Jack McDevitt's *The Hercules Text*. Other nominees were *Artificial Things*, Karen Joy Fowler; and *A Hidden Place*, Robert Charles Wilson.

Other Locus SF nominees not already mentioned: *Heart of the Comet*, Gregory Benford and David Brin; *The Handmaid's Tale*, Margaret Atwood; *Foundation and Earth*, Isaac Asimov; *Chanur's Homecoming*, C. J. Cherryh; *The Songs of Distant Earth*, Arthur C. Clarke; *The Coming of the Quantum Cats*, Frederik Pohl; *Santiago*, Mike Resnick; *Enigma*, Michael P. Kube-McDowell; *Lear's Daughters*, M. Bradley Kellogg with William Rossow; *Star of Gypsies*, Robert Silverberg; *Nerilka's Story*, Anne McCaffrey; *The Warrior's Apprentice*, Lois McMaster Bujold; *The Moon Goddess and the Son*, Donald Kingsbury; *Hardwired*, Walter Jon Williams; *The Architect of Sleep*, Steven R. Boyett; *Venus of Dreams*, Pamela Sargent; *The Nimrod Hunt*, Charles Sheffield; *The Forever Man*, Gordon R. Dickson; *Rebels' Seed*, F. M. Busby.

The Locus Fantasy Award went to *Soldier of the Mist*. Other nominees not yet mentioned: *Blood of Amber*, Roger Zelazny; *Godbody*, Theodore Sturgeon; *Twisting the Rope*, R. A. MacAvoy; *The Folk of the Air*, Peter S. Beagle; *The Serpent Mage*, Greg Bear; *Wizard of the Pigeons*, Megan Lindholm; *The Quest for Saint Camber*, Katherine Kurtz; *A Darkness at Sethanon*, Raymond E. Feist; *The Mirror of Her Dreams*, Stephen R. Donaldson; *The Darkest Road*, Guy Gavriel Kay; *Magic Kingdom for Sale—Sold!*, Terry Brooks; *Wielding a Red Sword*, Piers Anthony; *The Falling Woman*, Pat Murphy; *The Dragon in the Sword*, Michael Moorcock;

Jinian Star-Eye, Sheri S. Tepper; *New York by Knight*, Esther M. Friesner; *The King of Ys: Roma Mater*, Poul Anderson and Karen Anderson; *The Hounds of God*, Judith Tarr; *The Unconquered Country*, Geoff Ryman; *Yarrow*, Charles de Lint; *The Hungry Moon*, Ramsey Campbell; *Dragonsbane*, Barbara Hambly; *A Voice for Princess*, John Morressey.

Peter Beagle's *The Folk of the Air* won the Mythopoeic Award.

Marooned in Realtime won the Prometheus Award.

So the Hugo list missed *The Warrior's Apprentice* and *The Door into Ocean* and *This Is the Way the World Ends* and *Talking Man*—a lot of really excellent stuff wasn't on the ballot. So I'd say this wasn't a good year.

OTHER CATEGORIES

BEST NOVELLA

Winner: *Gilgamesh in the Outback*, by Robert Silverberg (*Asimov's*, July 1986; *Rebels in Hell*, 1986)

Nominees:

Escape from Kathmandu, by Kim Stanley Robinson (*Asimov's*, September 1986)

R & R, by Lucius Shepard (*Asimov's*, April 1986)

Spice Pogrom, by Connie Willis (*Asimov's*, October 1986)

Eifelheim, by Michael F. Flynn (*Analog*, November 1986)

For the first time, these are in order of how they ranked in the voting.

BEST NOVELETTE

Winner: "Permafrost," by Roger Zelazny (*Omni*, April 1986)

Nominees:

"Thor Meets Captain America," by David Brin (*F&SF*, July 1986)

"The Winter Market," by William Gibson (*Stardate*, March/April 1986;
Interzone, April 1986)

"Hatrack River," by Orson Scott Card (*Asimov's*, August 1986)

"The Barbarian Princess," by Vernor Vinge (*Analog*, September 1986)

I'd have voted for the Card, for sure. British voters would not have seen it. I remember when I got hold of the *Asimov's* with that in it, which was June of 1987—I was reading it when I moved into my house in Lancaster. I sat down on the kitchen counter to finish it because the furniture hadn't been delivered yet. And I'd have bought the magazine as soon as I saw it. *Omni*, on the other hand, was easily available, and *Interzone*, of course.

Best Short Story

Winner: "Tangents," by Greg Bear (*Omni*, January 1986)

Nominees:

"Robot Dreams," by Isaac Asimov (*Robot Dreams; Asimov's*, mid-December 1986)

"The Boy Who Plaited Manes," by Nancy Springer (*F&SF*, October 1986)

"Still Life," by David S. Garnett (*F&SF*, March 1986)

"Rat," by James Patrick Kelly (*F&SF*, June 1986)

Best Related Nonfiction

Winner: *Trillion Year Spree*, by Brian W. Aldiss and David Wingrove (Gollancz, 1986; Atheneum, 1986)

Nominees:

The Dark Knight Returns, by Frank Miller, Klaus Jenson, and Lynn Varley (DC/Warner, 1986)

Industrial Light and Magic: The Art of Special Effects, by Thomas G. Smith (Ballantine Del Rey, 1986)

Science Fiction in Print: 1985, by Charles N. Brown and William G. Contento (*Locus* Press, 1986)

Only Apparently Real: The World of Philip K. Dick, by Paul Williams (Arbor House, 1986)

BEST DRAMATIC PRESENTATION

Winner: *Aliens*

Nominees:
Star Trek IV: The Voyage Home
The Fly
Little Shop of Horrors
Labyrinth

BEST PROFESSIONAL EDITOR

Winner: Terry Carr

Nominees:
Gardner Dozois
David G. Hartwell
Edward L. Ferman
Stanley Schmidt

This was Terry's posthumous win.

BEST PROFESSIONAL ARTIST

Winner: Jim Burns

Nominees:
Frank Kelly Freas
Don Maitz

Barclay Shaw
Tom Kidd
J. K. Potter

BEST SEMIPROZINE

Winner: *Locus*, edited by Charles N. Brown

Nominees:
Interzone, edited by Simon Ounsley and David Pringle
Science Fiction Chronicle, edited by Andrew I. Porter
Science Fiction Review, edited by Richard E. Geis
Fantasy Review, edited by Robert A. Collins

BEST FANZINE

Winner: *Ansible*, edited by Dave Langford

Nominees:
File 770, edited by Mike Glyer
Lan's Lantern, edited by George "Lan" Laskowski
Texas SF Inquirer, edited by Pat Mueller
Trap Door, edited by Robert Lichtman

Ansible 1987 is so good, I'm still linking to it.

BEST FAN WRITER

Winner: Dave Langford

Nominees:
Patrick Nielsen Hayden*
Simon Ounsley
Mike Glyer

---

*Six Lousy Votes-Ed

No Award
D. West
Arthur D. Hlavaty
Owen Whiteoak (Nomination Declined)

Best Fan Artist

Winner: Brad W. Foster

Nominees:
Arthur "ATom" Thomson
Stu Shiffman
Taral Wayne
Steve Fox

John W. Campbell Award

Winner: Karen Joy Fowler

Nominees:
Lois McMaster Bujold
Katharine Eliska Kimbriel
Rebecca Ore
Leo Frankowski
Robert Reed

Wow. Well, Fowler was a very good winner on past productions, and a perfectly good winner on what she has done since—she's a major writer, but most of her work is interstitial, on the borders of genre.

But really, Bujold is the standout major writer on this list—and she had three novels out in 1986. I wonder if she was hurt by the vote's being in Britain, where she didn't have anything out until 1988. She is, of course, one of the most significant writers working today, the winner of five Hugos and three Nebulas, and on this year's Hugo ballot again.

I'm not familiar with Kimbriel. *Locus* tells me she had a first novel out in 1986, which must have impressed some nominators.

Rebecca Ore has gone on to write a pile of award-nominated SF novels over the next couple of decades.

Robert Reed has written a number of novels and an incredible number of wonderful short things. He's one of my favorite writers at short length—I'll buy a magazine if he's in it, and this keeps me buying magazines because he's prolific. He won a Hugo in 2006 with *A Billion Eves*. He was right at the beginning of his career, but I see this as just the kind of Campbell nomination one would wish to see.

COMMENTS ON 1987

48. RICH HORTON

I'll discuss the short fiction awards this year, because 1986 was a pretty strong year for short fiction, but the awards kind of let me down.

In novella, a fine Robert Silverberg story won, but to be honest, it was probably last of the Hugo nominees for me. *R & R* is early intense Shepard, a very strong story, if just a bit cliché by now. *Spice Pogrom* and *Escape from Kathmandu* are both comedies, as noted, but wonderful comedies. And *Eifelheim* is a really neat mysterious story— as someone said, the novel wasn't as good, but it's not bad either! (A bit too long, too dry, probably.) Of those nominees, I think KSR's *Escape from Kathmandu* gets my vote.

I also really liked Greg Benford's *As Big as the Ritz*, F. Paul Wilson's *Dydeetown Girl*, and the late Ronald Anthony Cross's *Hotel Mind Slaves*. Plus another excellent John Varley story, *Tango Charlie and Foxtrot Romeo*. Add another Benford story, *Newton Sleep*, and you've got a second short list pretty much the equal of the Hugo list.

I'd say that's a ten-deep short list you could throw a blanket over and pick any one as a pretty worthy winner. (The Nebula short list, by the way, included *Dydeetown Girl* and Benford's *Newton Sleep* in addition to *R & R* [which won], *Escape from Kathmandu,* and *Gilgamesh in the Outback.*)

As for novelette, both short lists are disappointing to me. "Permafrost" is, as someone said, a case of revered writer winning with a just decent story. Card's "Hatrack River" is very good (though it spawned a series that started strong and went downhill . . . sigh, like so many). Gibson's "The Winter Market" is brilliant, but technically not eligible, having first been published (outside the field) in 1985. It'd have been a worthy winner, though. The Nebula winner is very fine, Kate Wilhelm's "The Girl Who Fell into the Sky."

But my personal favorite 1986 novelette seemed all but ignored. Maybe it just spoke to me—but I loved John M. Ford's "Walkaway Clause." And there were two more quite brilliant 1986 novelettes—John Kessel's searing "The Pure Product" (which reminded me to an extent of "Vintage Season") and Bruce Sterling's "The Beautiful and the Sublime," which is, well, beautiful and sublime. Any of those three are better than any story on either the Hugo or Nebula short list, in my opinion (except maybe the 1985 story, "The Winter Market"). A bad miss by the nominators to include NONE of those.

There was great stuff in short story as well. To begin with, "Tangents" is great, and I have no real problem with it winning. But my favorite 1986 short story is James Patrick Kelly's "Rat," that famous "humanist" SF writer doing cyberpunk, and doing it very well. I also love Pat Cadigan's "Pretty Boy Crossover." So—"Tangents" is a good choice, but either the Kelly or Cadigan would have been just as good.

Other good short stories: "A Cup of Worrynot Tea," by Ford; "A Transect," by KSR; "Freezeframe," by Benford; "Down and Out in the Year 2000," by KSR; "Senses Three and Six," by David Brin; and perhaps most overlooked, Michael Blumlein's "The Brains of Rats."

49. GARDNER DOZOIS

It probably is a bit dated now, but Shepard's *R & R* remains a powerful story, and probably was the best choice at the time. Robinson's *Escape from Kathmandu* is also good, although much more lighthearted. Flynn's *Eifelheim* is good too, better than the later novel version.

Agree that Zelazny's "Permafrost," although solid, is relatively minor Zelazny. We discussed "The Winter Market" last time; it may be Gibson's best story, and would be a worthy winner. Also playing in the same class is Kessel's "The Pure Product," one of Kessel's best stories, and the choice between them would be a hard one. Sterling's little-known "The Beautiful and the Sublime" is also good, as is Connie Willis's "Chance" and Tanith Lee's "Into Gold." The appearance of Judith Moffett's first story, "Surviving," should probably be noted.

(For the sake of Full Disclosure, it should probably be mentioned that a lot of the stories from here on out will have been bought and published by me—including "The Pure Product," "The Beautiful and the Sublime," *R & R, Escape from Kathmandu,* "Chance," "Into Gold," and several of the short stories, so I may be prejudiced in their favor.)

Never warmed to "Rat." I'm okay with "Tangents" winning in short story, although Cadigan's "Pretty Boy Crossover" and a late Damon Knight story, "Strangers on Paradise," are also good.

1988

BEST NOVEL

Winner: *The Uplift War*, by David Brin

Nominees:
When Gravity Fails, by George Alec Effinger
Seventh Son, by Orson Scott Card
The Forge of God, by Greg Bear
The Urth of the New Sun, by Gene Wolfe

The 1988 Hugo Awards were presented in Nolacon II in New Orleans.

The Best Novel award was won by David Brin's *The Uplift War*, third of the Uplift trilogy. The second book, *Startide Rising*, also won the Hugo, in 1984. This was another ambitious volume, expanding the scope of the previous books in the series and opening up questions about the nature of humanity. An excellent Hugo winner. It also won the Locus Award. It's in print and in the library in English only. It's still part of the conversation of SF, and these books are widely regarded as Brin's best work.

There are four other nominees, and I've read three of them. I'm listing them in order of votes received.

George Alec Effinger's *When Gravity Fails* is a splendid book and a terrific nominee. It's the story of a noir detective in an Islamic future; it's about people changing their minds and their bodies. It's a really good book, definitely Effinger's masterpiece, and I think I'd have voted for it. It's in print, and it's in the library in French only.

Orson Scott Card's *Seventh Son* is the first volume of the Chronicles of Alvin Maker. It's a fantasy alternate early United States and a fantasy retelling of the life of Joseph Smith, founder of Mormonism. The folk magic is really well done. This is another good nominee, Card was doing something here that hadn't really been done before, a fantasy America. It won the Locus Fantasy award. It's in print, and it's in the library in French and English.

I haven't read Greg Bear's *The Forge of God*, though I have read the sequel, *Anvil of Stars*, so I know what it's about. Aliens attack the Earth, and unlike all the other books like this, they destroy it all but a handful of children who escape in a spaceship. I haven't read it, because I accidentally read the sequel first and thus got comprehensively spoiled. It's in print, and it's in the library in English.

Gene Wolfe's *The Urth of the New Sun* is a sequel to the four-volume *The Book of the New Sun*, and I didn't like it as much. It seemed like an unnecessary addition to a series that already had a good ending. Having said that, it was beautifully written and full of clever ideas, as with all Wolfe, so it's a perfectly reasonable nominee. It's in print, and in the library in both languages.

So five American men. Card and Brin were previous winners. Bear and Wolfe were previous nominees. Effinger was a previous Campbell and short-form nominee, but this is his first appearance on the novel ballot. The books are four science fiction and one fantasy, one space opera, one future of the third world, one far future, one near-future alien invasion, and one alternate history fantasy.

What else might they have chosen?

The Nebula went to Pat Murphy's *The Falling Woman*, an astonishingly brilliant but weird book that I'd have loved to see on the Hugo ballot. The only non-overlapping eligible nominee is Avram Davidson's *Vergil in Averno*.

Ken Grimwood's *Replay* won the World Fantasy Award, despite being SF, and would have been a splendid Hugo nominee. Nominees not previously mentioned: *Ægypt*, John Crowley; *Misery*, Stephen King; *On Stranger Tides*, Tim Powers; *Swan Song*, Robert R. McCammon; *Weaveworld*, Clive Barker.

The Campbell Memorial Award has no overlap at all, which is unusual. The winner was Connie Willis's strange but wonderful first novel,

Lincoln's Dreams. (So this is the year the World Fantasy was won by SF and the Campbell was won by a fantasy . . . okay!) Second place was George Turner's *The Sea and the Summer*, and third was Geoff Ryman's *The Unconquered Country*.

The Philip K. Dick Award, as always, turns up some interesting and unusual things. The winner was *Strange Toys*, Patricia Geary, and the special citation was *Memories*, Mike McQuay. The finalists were *Dark Seeker*, K. W. Jeter; *Dover Beach*, Richard Bowker; *Life During Wartime*, Lucius Shepard; *Mindplayers*, Pat Cadigan—which struck me as one of the better things to come out of cyberpunk.

Other Locus nominees not previously mentioned were: *The Annals of the Heechee*, Frederik Pohl; *Vacuum Flowers*, Michael Swanwick; *The Smoke Ring*, Larry Niven; *Great Sky River*, Gregory Benford; *2061: Odyssey Three*, Arthur C. Clarke; *The Legacy of Heorot*, Larry Niven, Jerry Pournelle, and Steven Barnes; *To Sail Beyond the Sunset*, Robert A. Heinlein; *Fool's Run*, Patricia A. McKillip; *The Secret Ascension*, Michael Bishop; *The Tommyknockers*, Stephen King; *Dawn*, Octavia E. Butler; *Intervention*, Julian May; *After Long Silence*, Sheri S. Tepper; *Code Blue—Emergency*, James White; *Way of the Pilgrim*, Gordon R. Dickson; *Araminta Station*, Jack Vance; *Voice of the Whirlwind*, Walter Jon Williams; *The Awakeners*, Sheri S. Tepper; *Still River*, Hal Clement; *Rumors of Spring*, Richard Grant; *Liege-Killer*, Christopher Hinz; *In Conquest Born*, C. S. Friedman; *Little Heroes*, Norman Spinrad; *Watchmen*, Alan Moore and Dave Gibbons; *A Mask for the General*, Lisa Goldstein.

Looking at this list, I'm cheered to see the Clarke, the Pohl, and the Heinlein in it—thank goodness people had stopped nominating weak works by beloved masters. However, I am disappointed that Butler's *Dawn* didn't get a Hugo nomination—it's the first of the Xenogenesis books, one of Butler's best, and the first thing of hers I read. And *Code Blue—Emergency* is White's masterpiece and could have done with more recognition. Oh well.

Previously unmentioned Locus Fantasy nominees: *Sign of Chaos*, Roger Zelazny; *The Witches of Wenshar*, Barbara Hambly; *The Grey Horse*, R. A. MacAvoy; *Guardians of the West*, David Eddings; *A Man Rides*

Through, Stephen R. Donaldson; *Being a Green Mother*, Piers Anthony; *War for the Oaks*, Emma Bull; *Bones of the Moon*, Jonathan Carroll; *Swan Song*, Robert R. McCammon; *The Dark Tower II: The Drawing of the Three*, Stephen King; *Land of Dreams*, James P. Blaylock; *Daughter of the Empire*, Raymond E. Feist and Janny Wurts; *The Firebrand*, Marion Zimmer Bradley; *Never the Twain*, Kirk Mitchell; *Darkspell*, Katharine Kerr; *Equal Rites*, Terry Pratchett.

On the Best First Novel list, I see Ellen Kushner's *Swordspoint*. I'm surprised it didn't get more attention, as it has deservedly become a classic.

The Mythopoeic Award went to *Seventh Son*.

So, there are some books I'd really have liked to see on the Hugo ballot, especially the Butler, but this was a pretty good year, with the five nominees doing a fairly good job of demonstrating where the field was.

OTHER CATEGORIES

BEST NOVELLA

Winner: *Eye for Eye*, by Orson Scott Card (*Asimov's*, March 1987)

Nominees:
The Blind Geometer, by Kim Stanley Robinson (*Asimov's*, August 1987)
The Forest of Time, by Michael F. Flynn (*Analog*, June 1987)
Mother Goddess of the World, by Kim Stanley Robinson (*Asimov's*, October 1987)
The Secret Sharer, by Robert Silverberg (*Asimov's*, September 1987)

Gardner Dozois Year's Best anthologies started to be published in Britain this year, so I actually have most of the nominees in one useful place from now on, so I can check if I can't remember something. I'd have voted for the Robinson, with the Silverberg a close second.

Best Novelette

Winner: "Buffalo Gals, Won't You Come Out Tonight," by Ursula K. Le Guin (*Buffalo Gals and Other Animal Presences; F&SF*, November 1987)

Nominees:
"Dinosaurs," by Walter Jon Williams (*Asimov's*, June 1987)
"Dream Baby," by Bruce McAllister (*In the Field of Fire; Asimov's*, October 1987)
"Flowers of Edo," by Bruce Sterling (*Asimov's*, May 1987)
"Rachel in Love," by Pat Murphy (*Asimov's*, April 1987)

Amazingly excellent novelettes this year. I'd have had a very hard time deciding.

Best Short Story

Winner: "Why I Left Harry's All-Night Hamburgers," by Lawrence Watt-Evans (*Asimov's*, July 1987)

Nominees:
"Angel," by Pat Cadigan (*Asimov's*, May 1987)
"Cassandra's Photographs," by Lisa Goldstein (*Asimov's*, August 1987)
"The Faithful Companion at Forty," by Karen Joy Fowler (*Asimov's*, July 1987)
"Forever Yours, Anna," by Kate Wilhelm (*Omni*, July 1987)
"Night of the Cooters," by Howard Waldrop (*Omni*, April 1987)

Best Nonfiction Book

Winner: *Michael Whelan's Works of Wonder*, by Michael Whelan

Nominees:
Anatomy of Wonder, 3rd Edition, edited by Neil Barron

The Battle of Brazil, by Jack Matthews

Imagination: The Art & Technique of David A. Cherry, by David A. Cherry

Science Fiction, Fantasy, & Horror: 1986, by Charles N. Brown and William G. Contento

BEST OTHER FORMS

Winner: *Watchmen,* by Alan Moore and Dave Gibbons

Nominees:

Cvltvre Made Stvpid, by Tom Weller

The Essential Ellison, by Harlan Ellison

I, Robot: The Movie, by Harlan Ellison (*Asimov's,* November, December, mid-December 1987)

Wild Cards series, edited by George R. R. Martin

So, a new category, the first for some time, and one that wouldn't last—though comparing apples to oranges didn't seem to bother people in nonfiction. But I don't know what Wild Cards is doing here; it's words-in-a-row fiction.

BEST DRAMATIC PRESENTATION

Winner: *The Princess Bride*

Nominees:

Predator

Robocop

Star Trek: The Next Generation: "Encounter at Farpoint"

The Witches of Eastwick

BEST PROFESSIONAL EDITOR

Winner: Gardner Dozois

Nominees:
Edward L. Ferman
David G. Hartwell
Stanley Schmidt
Brian Thomsen

Gardner mentioned in last week's comments that he'd bought a lot of the stories and wasn't unbiased talking about them. And it's true, he bought a lot of the best stories of the year, and look, the voters recognized that.

Best Professional Artist

Winner: Michael Whelan

Nominees:
David A. Cherry
Bob Eggleton
Tom Kidd
Don Maitz
J. K. Potter

Best Semiprozine

Winner: *Locus,* edited by Charles N. Brown

Nominees:
Aboriginal SF, edited by Charles C. Ryan
Interzone, edited by Simon Ounsley and David Pringle
Science Fiction Chronicle, edited by Andrew Porter
Thrust, edited by D. Douglas Fratz

Best Fanzine

Winner: *Texas SF Inquirer,* edited by Pat Mueller

Nominees:
File 770, edited by Mike Glyer
FOSFAX, edited by Timothy Lane
Lan's Lantern, edited by George "Lan" Laskowski
The Mad 3 Party, edited by Leslie Turek

BEST FAN WRITER

Winner: Mike Glyer

Nominees:
Arthur Hlavaty
Dave Langford
Guy H. Lillian III
Leslie Turek

BEST FAN ARTIST

Winner: Brad W. Foster

Nominees:
Steve Fox
Teddy Harvia
Merle Insinga
Taral Wayne
Diana Gallagher Wu

JOHN W. CAMPBELL AWARD

Winner: Judith Moffett

Nominees:
Rebecca Ore
Martha Soukup
C. S. Friedman
Loren J. MacGregor

Interesting to note that with all five novel nominees by men, four of the Campbell nominees are women.

Judith Moffett had written the brilliant short story "Surviving" and the Quakers in Space novel *Pennterra*. She shone like a supernova in 1988. I've read all her books, and I would happily read more if she'd write more, but I haven't seen anything by her in the last decade. It's hard to say if she was a good Campbell winner—she's a good *writer,* and I'd absolutely have voted for her, but she hasn't gone on to be a major writer.

I talked about Ore last week.

Martha Soukup had written some excellent short work, and she has continued to do so steadily, though I haven't seen anything from her in a while. Wikipedia suggests that she has been writing plays.

C. S. Friedman had just published her first novel, *In Conquest Born,* a wide-screen baroque space opera. She went on to write the True Night trilogy, and a number of other books on odd edges of SF and fantasy, all from DAW. She's a significant minor writer and one of my husband's favorites.

Loren MacGregor had published his excellent first novel, *The Net,* and never wrote anything else. I used to hang out with him on Usenet, and he was a really nice guy, but some people just have one book and that's that.

There are a lot of people who could have been nominated who in hindsight might have looked better—Emma Bull, Pat Cadigan, Mercedes Lackey, Ellen Kushner, Geoff Ryman . . . and Lois McMaster Bujold, who was nominated the year before and was still eligible.

COMMENTS ON 1988

6. SUPERGEE

Wild Cards was an Other Form because it was a novel-like thing written by numerous people. That made sense to me at the time.

14. Kevin Standlee

"Other Forms" was the 1988 committee using its authority to create a one-shot category, and as far as I can tell, there was no momentum generated to make this a permanent category. Subsequent Worldcons have also used their one-shot authority to create special categories, with mixed success. Sometimes (1993 Best Translator, 1995 Best Music, 2006 Best Interactive Video Game), there were so few nominations that the category never reached the final ballot. Sometimes (2002 and 2005 Best Web Site) the category was fairly successful, but the Business Meeting rejected attempts to add a permanent category. In that last case, it's rather likely that incremental changes in Best Related Work (formerly Best Related Book) have broadened the category sufficiently that websites might be eligible in the category, but we won't know until a website gets enough nominations to make the ballot and an administrator rules on the subject.

The WSFS Business Meeting has become so skeptical of new Hugo Award categories that there is strong pressure for any proposed new category to "prove itself" by having a Worldcon trial it, at least where it's possible to do so. (You can't do it when the proposal is to split another category into pieces, on the principle that no work should be eligible simultaneously in two categories.)

28. Gardner Dozois

I bought a lot of the short work for *Asimov's* this year, so take the disclaimer as still in effect.

Novella's a tight category; think I might go with *The Blind Geometer,* by a slight margin, although the Flynn is good too.

In novelette, the winner isn't one of my top favorite Le Guins, although still pretty good. Think I'd go with "Rachel in Love" or "Flowers of Edo," one of the historical fantasies that Sterling actually wrote more of than cyberpunk, although Neal Barrett Jr.'s "Perpetuity Blues" is one of the funniest gonzo stories ever written. Octavia Butler's "The Evening and the Morning and the Night" and Charles Sheffield's "Trapalanda" are also strong. Worth noting are early stories by Alexander Jablokov and Paul McAuley, "At the Cross-Time Jaunters' Ball" and "The Temporary King," respectively, and what I think may be R. Garcia y Robertson's first story, "The Moon of Popping Trees."

In short story, I think I'd go for Waldrop's delightful "Night of the Cooters," by a small margin.

At the time, I certainly would have voted for Judith Moffett for the Campbell, and although she never quite became the powerhouse she seemed to have the potential to become, as was pointed out, she hasn't stopped writing entirely either, with new stuff out every few years. Judging from the work they'd published to date, I don't think either Greg Egan or Stephen Baxter would have been likely Campbell candidates at the time. (Interestingly, Egan's first few genre stories were horror, not SF.)

34. RICH HORTON

Short fiction.

Novellas first—the Hugo short list is very good, but my clear-cut choice for winner is *The Forest of Time*, by Michael F. Flynn. It's interesting in that its theme is pretty much the same as that of Watt-Evans's Hugo-winning short story, which is also very good, two exceedingly differing ways of getting at the same point.

As I said, all the rest are good—my second-place vote probably goes to KSR's *The Blind Geometer*.

But there were some other fine novellas: Geoff Ryman's *Love Sickness*, James Patrick Kelly's *Glass Cloud*, and perhaps above all, John M. Ford's difficult but fascinating *Fugue State*.

In novelette, I'm with Gardner—my choice for the best of the short list lies between "Rachel in Love" and "Flowers of Edo." I also really liked Octavia Butler's "The Evening and the Morning and the Night," and Barrett's "Perpetuity Blues," and Jablokov's "At the Cross-Time Jaunters' Ball." Others worth a mention: one of Connie Willis's best stories, "Schwarzschild Radius"; Howard Waldrop's "He-We-Await"; a rare true SF story from Lucius Shepard, "The Sun Spider"; and Susan Palwick's "Ever After."

I'd also like to mention a story I saw in the ISFDB listing of 1987 genre novelettes that's not really genre, though from a mainstream writer who has written a lot of very nice fantasy. This is A. S. Byatt's

"Sugar," an utterly amazing, gorgeously written story. It's perhaps her most autobiographical fiction, and it's just stunning. It's not fantasy or SF, but it's great, and you should all read it.

As for short story, I certainly have no argument with the winner, a lovely story. (Watt-Evans has long been self-deprecating about its win, suggesting that it won only because voters who had read any of the stories thought its title was cool, or something like that—I doubt that, it's an excellent story, and a worthy winner.) Wilhelm's Nebula winner is good too, and I also quite like the Waldrop and Fowler stories. (And the Cadigan and Goldstein stories are nice enough too.)

Other strong short stories:

Gene Wolfe's "All the Hues of Hell"
Jonathan Carroll's "Friend's Best Man"
Neal Barrett's "Highbrow"
Paul Di Filippo's "Kid Charlemagne"
Lucius Shepard's "The Glassblower's Dragon" (practically a drabble relative to his usual length!)

60. GARDNER DOZOIS

Before this thread moves off into history, I should probably mention that this year's Hugo must surely be the HEAVIEST Hugo of all time. It has a solid stone base, stands about three feet high, and must weigh about twenty pounds. You could easily kill somebody with it.

61. JO

Gardner: And what a wonderful mystery somebody could write that had it as a murder weapon! There are a very limited number of suspects. Murder in New Orleans—somebody whom everyone has a motive to kill is struck down, which of the Hugo winners dunnit?

66. GARDNER DOZOIS

That was the first Hugo I won, and I had to deal with getting it all the way back from New Orleans to Philadelphia on the train. It was very awkward and tricky to handle, took up a lot of floor space, and even in those more innocent pre-9/11 days, the conductors looked at it with suspicion. As well as being probably the heaviest Hugo, it may be in competition for the ugliest Hugo, although there it has a couple of rivals. Having the Hugo rocket balanced on top of what looks like an outpouring of boiling black diarrhea has always seemed like odd symbolism to me.

Jo, you should go ahead and write it! This time next year, you could be picking up an Edgar.

There was also the one on the Alfred Hitchcock show about the woman who killed her husband with the frozen leg of lamb, and then thawed it and cooked it and served it to the police.

69. RICH HORTON

I missed one really major novelette, indeed probably the best novelette of 1987, in my earlier summary.

This is "Empires of Foliage and Flower," by Gene Wolfe. It's a New Sun story, though not obviously so, a really remarkable piece. Apparently, it first appeared as a chapbook from Cheap Street, an odd little publishing company run by Jan and George O'Nale. I saw it first in an issue of Bryan Cholfin's excellent magazine, *Crank*, several years later.

At any rate, a great story, the best of 1987, I think.

1989

Best Novel

Winner: *Cyteen*, by C. J. Cherryh

Nominees:
Red Prophet, by Orson Scott Card
Falling Free, by Lois McMaster Bujold
Islands in the Net, by Bruce Sterling
Mona Lisa Overdrive, by William Gibson
The Guardsman, by P. J. Beese and Todd Cameron Hamilton (withdrawn)

The 1989 Hugo Awards were presented at Noreascon III in Boston.

The Best Novel award was won by C. J. Cherryh's *Cyteen*, one of my favorite books of all time. It's about cloning and personality—physical cloning is taken for granted, building artificial personalities is all in a day's work, replicating a famous dead scientist and politician. Making the cloned "son" of another scientist a "custom job" and different from his progenitor is slightly harder, and when it comes to replicating a whole society from the genes on up to the memes, nobody knows if it will work a few generations down the line. It's a huge, brilliant, ambitious book with a wide vision; it blew me away when I first read it and would be in my personal top five books of all time. It also won the Locus Award. It's in print and in the library in English and French. I think this is exactly the kind of book that should be winning the Hugo.

There were four other nominees, and I've read three of them.

Orson Scott Card's *Red Prophet* was the sequel to 1988's nominee *Seventh Son*, another fantasy of the American frontier with folk magic.

I liked it a lot less—in fact, I liked every book in this series less than the one before. It won the Locus fantasy award. It's in print, and it's in the library in English and French. I don't think it's a terrible Hugo nominee, but I think it's an unimaginative one.

Lois McMaster Bujold got her first Hugo nomination this year with the Nebula-winning *Falling Free*. I think of this as minor Bujold, but minor Bujold would be a major book from most writers. This is another book about using cloning to solve problems—in this case, solving engineering problems by genetically engineering Quaddies, people with four arms and no legs, who can work well in zero gravity, until they're suddenly made technologically obsolete when gravity control is invented. It's in print and in the library in English and French. I think it has been eclipsed somewhat by Bujold's later work.

Bruce Sterling's *Islands in the Net* was one of those books everybody was talking about at the time. I didn't read it for ages, because I felt generally negative about cyberpunk. By the time Sterling had won me over by writing great short stories and I gave in and read this in the mid-nineties, it was already laughably technologically obsolete. It's a problem when writing about the near future, and especially writing about the near future of computers in 1988. *Cyteen* and *Falling Free* could still be in the future. *Islands in the Net,* not so much. However, it's a well-written book in a popular subgenre, and one of the best cyberpunk books out there. I think it was a good nominee. It won the Campbell Memorial. It's not in print, but it's in the library in English and French.

I haven't read William Gibson's *Mona Lisa Overdrive,* because I hated *Neuromancer.* It's in print, and it's in the library in English and French.

So, two women and three men, all American. Cherryh, Card, and Gibson were previous winners, Bujold and Sterling had been nominated for the Campbell, and Sterling had several short-form nominations, but this was the first appearance for either of them on the novel slate. We have two books set in multi-planet futures with cloning, two near-future cyberpunk Earths, and one historical fantasy. What else might they have chosen?

There's a curious withdrawal—apparently P. J. Beese and Todd Cameron Hamilton's novel *The Guardian,* which I have neither read nor previously heard of, had enough votes for a nomination, but the administrators concluded that the votes were bloc votes and disqualified them. *Locus* says, "A group of enthusiastic New York area fans was later discovered to be responsible for the votes, exonerating Beese and Hamilton." Whatever was going on, it's not in print and not in the library, and I'd say it has sunk pretty much without a trace.

Non-overlapping eligible Nebula nominees: Lewis Shiner's *Deserted Cities of the Heart* and George Turner's *Drowning Towers*.

The World Fantasy Award went to *Koko*, by Peter Straub. Other nominees: *The Drive-In*, by Joe R. Lansdale; *Fade*, by Robert Cormier; *The Last Coin*, by James P. Blaylock; *The Silence of the Lambs*, by Thomas Harris; *Sleeping in Flame*, by Jonathan Carroll.

The John W. Campbell Memorial Award gave second place to Kim Stanley Robinson's *The Gold Coast*, which would have been a fine Hugo nominee, with Anne McCaffrey's *Dragonsdawn* third. (I really do find the jury's decision-making completely bizarre. There's hardly a year I don't type their stuff without a side order of "Huh?" Ignore *Falling Free* and *Cyteen* and commend *Dragonsdawn*? Oooookay.)

The Philip K. Dick Award had a tie. The two winners were Paul McAuley's *Four Hundred Billion Stars* and Rudy Rucker's *Wetware*. Other nominees: *Becoming Alien*, Rebecca Ore; *Neon Lotus*, Marc Laidlaw; *Orphan of Creation*, Roger MacBride Allen; *Rendezvous*, D. Alexander Smith.

Other Locus nominees not already mentioned: *Prelude to Foundation*, Isaac Asimov; *Eternity*, Greg Bear; *Araminta Station*, Jack Vance; *Alternities*, Michael P. Kube-McDowell; *Adulthood Rites*, Octavia E. Butler; *Catspaw*, Joan D. Vinge; *At Winter's End*, Robert Silverberg; *Brothers in Arms*, Lois McMaster Bujold; *Ivory*, Mike Resnick; *Crazy Time*, Kate Wilhelm; *Venus of Shadows*, Pamela Sargent; *The Gate to Women's Country*, Sheri S. Tepper; *The Player of Games*, Iain M. Banks; *Hellspark*, Janet Kagan; *Chronosequence*, Hilbert Schenck; *Children of the Thunder*, John Brunner; *Fire on the Mountain*, Terry Bisson; *Terraplane*, Jack Womack; *Starfire*, Paul Preuss; *An Alien Light*, Nancy Kress; *The Company Man*, Joe Clifford Faust.

Of the ones I've read, I'd love to have seen *Hellspark* or *Fire on the Mountain* get more recognition, and either of them would have made a really good Hugo nominee. *Adulthood Rites* is excellent, but doesn't stand alone.

Locus fantasy award nominees not previously mentioned: *The Paladin*, C. J. Cherryh (and wasn't she having a good year!); *There Are Doors*, Gene Wolfe; *Unicorn Mountain*, Michael Bishop; *King of the Murgos*, David Eddings; *The Story of the Stone*, Barry Hughart; *Greenmantle*, Charles de Lint; *Lavondyss*, Robert Holdstock; *The Dragonbone Chair*, Tad Williams; *Wyvern*, A. A. Attanasio; *The Healer's War*, Elizabeth Ann Scarborough; *Druid's Blood*, Esther M. Friesner; *The White Serpent*, Tanith Lee; *Sister Light, Sister Dark*, Jane Yolen; *Wyrd Sisters*, Terry Pratchett; *Who's Afraid of Beowulf?*, Tom Holt; *The Changeling Sea*, Patricia A. McKillip; *The Reindeer People*, Megan Lindholm; *The White Raven*, Diana L. Paxson; *Walkabout Woman*, Michaela Roessner; *Silk Roads and Shadows*, Susan Shwartz; *The Nightingale*, Kara Dalkey; *Death in the Spirit House*, Craig Strete.

You can practically see modern fantasy becoming a commercial genre before your very eyes!

Locus Best First Novel was won by Ian McDonald's *Desolation Road*, which I think would have been a splendid Hugo nominee. I also notice David Zindell's *Neverness* on the list.

The Mythopoeic Award went to Michael Bishop's *Unicorn Mountain*.

And anything all the awards missed? Helen Wright's *A Matter of Oaths;* Steve Miller and Sharon Lee's *Agent of Change,* first of the Liaden series; Peter Dickinson's wonderful YA *Eva;* S. M. Stirling's controversial *Marching Through Georgia,* first of the Draka books; Patricia Wrede and Caroline Stevermer's *Sorcery & Cecelia;* Salman Rushdie's *The Satanic Verses;* Elisabeth Vonarburg's *The Silent City;* Rachel Pollack's *Unquenchable Fire;* Parke Godwin's *Waiting for the Galactic Bus;* and Neal Stephenson's *Zodiac.*

So, while this was a good year overall, with a lot of great books I'd have liked to see recognized, I don't see any howling omissions from the Hugo ballot, and I think the five we have are pretty representative. So, thumbs-up for 1989's list.

Other Categories

....

Best Novella

Winner: *The Last of the Winnebagos*, by Connie Willis (*Asimov's*, July 1988)

Nominees:
The Scalehunter's Beautiful Daughter, by Lucius Shepard (*Ziesing*, 1988; *Asimov's*, September 1988)
Journals of the Plague Years, by Norman Spinrad (*Full Spectrum*, 1988)
The Calvin Coolidge Home for Dead Comedians, by Bradley Denton (*F&SF*, June 1988)
Surfacing, by Walter Jon Williams (*Asimov's*, April 1988)

Again, terrific novellas. All five of them are memorable and excellent. I think this is consistently the category with the highest quality nominees.

Best Novelette

Winner: "Schrödinger's Kitten," by George Alec Effinger (*Omni*, September 1988)

Nominees:
"Peaches for Mad Molly," by Steven Gould (*Analog*, February 1988)
"Do Ya, Do Ya, Wanna Dance?" by Howard Waldrop (*Asimov's*, August 1988)
"The Function of Dream Sleep," by Harlan Ellison (*Midnight Graffiti*, June 1988; *Asimov's*, mid-December 1988)
"Ginny Sweethips' Flying Circus," by Neal Barrett Jr. (*Asimov's*, February 1988)

I'd have voted for the Waldrop. No, the Gould.

Best Short Story

Winner: "Kirinyaga," by Mike Resnick (*F&SF*, November 1988)

Nominees:
"The Giving Plague," by David Brin (*Interzone 23*, Spring 1988; *Full Spectrum 2*, 1988)
"Ripples in the Dirac Sea," by Geoffrey A. Landis (*Asimov's*, October 1988)
"Our Neural Chernobyl," by Bruce Sterling (*F&SF*, June 1988)
"Stable Strategies for Middle Management," by Eileen Gunn (*Asimov's*, June 1988)
"The Fort Moxie Branch," by Jack McDevitt (*Full Spectrum*, 1988)

Best Related Nonfiction Book

Winner: *The Motion of Light in Water: Sex and Science Fiction Writing in the East Village 1957–1965*, by Samuel R. Delany

Nominees:
First Maitz, by Don Maitz
The New Encyclopedia of Science Fiction, by James E. Gunn
A Biographical Dictionary of Science Fiction and Fantasy Artists, by Robert Weinberg
Science Fiction, Fantasy, and Horror: 1987, by Charles N. Brown and William G. Contento

Best Dramatic Presentation

Winner: *Who Framed Roger Rabbit*

Nominees:
Beetlejuice
Big
Willow
Alien Nation

BEST PROFESSIONAL EDITOR

Winner: Gardner Dozois

Nominees:
David G. Hartwell
Edward L. Ferman
Stanley Schmidt
Charles C. Ryan

BEST PROFESSIONAL ARTIST

Winner: Michael Whelan

Nominees:
Don Maitz
David A. Cherry
Bob Eggleton
Thomas Canty

BEST SEMIPROZINE

Winner: *Locus*, edited by Charles N. Brown

Nominees:
Science Fiction Chronicle, edited by Andrew I. Porter
The New York Review of Science Fiction, edited by David G. Hartwell, Patrick Nielsen Hayden, Teresa Nielsen Hayden, Susan Palwick, and Kathryn Cramer
Interzone, edited by David Pringle and Simon Ounsley
Thrust, edited by D. Douglas Fratz

I remember buying the first issue of *The New York Review of Science Fiction* in Forbidden Planet. It was so exciting! It had an article by Delany. The whole thing was marvelous. It was twenty years before I saw another copy.

Best Fanzine

Winner: *File 770*, edited by Mike Glyer

Nominees:
Lan's Lantern, edited by George "Lan" Laskowski
Niekas, edited by Edmund R. Meskys, Mike Bastraw, and Anne Brande
FOSFAX, edited by Timothy Lane
Other Realms, edited by Chuq Von Rospach

Best Fan Writer

Winner: Dave Langford

Nominees:
Mike Glyer
Arthur D. Hlavaty
Avedon Carol
Chuq Von Rospach
Guy H. Lillian III

Best Fan Artist

Winner: (tie) Brad W. Foster
Diana Gallagher Wu

Nominees:
Stu Shiffman
Teddy Harvia
Taral Wayne
Merle Insinga

Special Awards
Saul Jaffe—SF-Lovers Digest
Alex Schomburg—Noreascon III Special Art Award

SF-Lovers Digest was the first online anything to get an award. It was a mailing list that later evolved into the newsgroup rec.arts.sf.written. I'm here today only because of that newsgroup, for whatever values of "here" you like. Without it, I'd never have met Emmet, I'd never have moved to Montreal, I wouldn't be writing for Tor.com, and I might never have taken my writing seriously. So go Saul Jaffe and the Noreascon III administrators.

John W. Campbell Award

Winner: Michaela Roessner

Nominees:
Delia Sherman
Christopher Hinz
Kristine Kathryn Rusch
Melanie Rawn
P. J. Beese and Todd Cameron Hamilton
William Sanders

Interestingly long list.

Michaela Roessner's first novel, *Walkabout Woman*, had been nominated for the Mythopoeic Award and won the Crawford Award for best first novel. It was followed by three more novels in the nineties, but I haven't seen anything from her in the last decade. I don't think she's one of the more spectacular successes of the Campbells.

Delia Sherman had also just published a well-received first novel, *Through a Brazen Mirror*. Sherman has gone on to have a solid career, writing with her wife, Ellen Kushner, and alone, and is publishing these days mostly YA fantasy. Her work has been nominated for the Nebula, the World Fantasy, the Mythopoeic, and the Tiptree.*

---

*Since then, she has become even more successful, winning a Norton Award in 2012.

Christopher Hinz's first novel, *Liege-Killer*, won the Compton Crook Award for best first novel. He has since written a couple of sequels and some comic books.

Kristine Kathryn Rusch won in 1990, so let's leave her for next year.

Melanie Rawn had also just published her first novel. She went on to have a strong career writing fat fantasies; she has published ten and has a couple more forthcoming.

I know nothing about Beese and Hamilton beyond what I've quoted above. Unlike all the other nominees, William Sanders had published only short work. He went on to have a career writing mostly short work and editing.

Writers who published first novels in 1988 and who did not get a Campbell nomination but may have been eligible include Ian McDonald, Elizabeth Moon, Daniel Keyes Moran, Matt Ruff, Paul McAuley, and Storm Constantine.

COMMENTS ON 1989

9. RICH HORTON

The great 1988 novella not nominated is *The Blabber*, by Vernor Vinge, beta version of his Zones of Thought universe, and a wonderful story on its own.

I'll have more about short fiction later. . . .

14. RENE WALLING

So, two women and three men, all American . . .

By then Gibson was living in Canada and *Mona Lisa Overdrive* won the Aurora for Best Long Form in English. It was up against *Machine Sex and Other Stories*, Candas Jane Dorsey; *Memory Wire*, Robert Charles Wilson; *The Silent City*, Elisabeth Vonarburg; and *Time Pressure*, Spider Robinson. My vote would probably have gone to *Machine Sex* or *The Silent City*. I'll also note this last book also won the Prix

Rosny-Aîné in 1982, to my knowledge, the only book by a Canadian to do so. I haven't read the Wilson—something I will have to correct, for I always enjoy his books.

So after a bit of a detour: ". . . two women and three men, four Americans and one Canadian . . ." ☺

17. James Davis Nicoll

By then Gibson was living in Canada

Having moved to Canada in 1967 as a sort of draft dodger; that is, avoiding the draft was one reason he came here, along with IIRC the promise of sexually open-minded hippie chicks and affordably priced hash, but it turned out no attempt to draft him was ever made.

Obviously anyone who is notable, not totally despicable, and who has ever seen a bottle of maple syrup will eventually be claimed as Canadian, but I am not sure when exactly Gibson became a citizen.

28. Rich Horton

As noted, the novella list is marvelous. I love *The Last of the Winnebagos,* and it's certainly the story I'd have chosen from the short list, though I also think very highly of *The Scalehunter's Beautiful Daughter.* Brad Denton is a wonderful writer, and *The Calvin Coolidge Home for Dead Comedians* is first-rate too.

But, as I said, possibly the best story of the year wasn't nominated. (Perhaps because it appeared in a story collection, not a magazine or original anthology, and thus was not thought of as "new" by some people.) This is Vernor Vinge's *The Blabber,* which shares some characters and a similar universe with *A Fire Upon the Deep,* but which (much like KSR's *Green Mars* versus the Mars trilogy) is clearly not quite in the same future as the novel. But it's a great story and, above all, just filled with true "sense of wonder."

On balance, I'd still give the award to Willis, but both stories are great.

One other novella seems worth a mention: James Tiptree Jr.'s rather creepy *Backward, Turn Backward.* I don't think the story works, but it is intriguing. Much better than the other big Tiptree story of 1988, "The Earth Doth Like a Snake Renew," which I quite frankly hate. Interestingly (to me, at any rate), both stories seem rehashes, thematically, of earlier Tiptree stories: *Backward* revisits the central idea of "Forever to a Hudson Bay Blanket," and "Earth" craps on the subtlety and elegance of "The Last Flight of Doctor Ain." ("The Earth Doth Like a Snake Renew" was apparently originally written as a Raccoona Sheldon story, but never sold. It only appeared posthumously, and I have wondered if she realized how bad it was during her life, which is why it didn't sell. Maybe not, mind you, but I'd like to think that.)

There is also a long list of excellent novelettes. The Hugo short list is okay to pretty good. I really like Gould's "Peaches for Mad Molly," and I like "Ginny Sweethips' Flying Circus" a lot as well. Either one would have been a good winner, but the Effinger is good too. I'm not a big fan of "Do Ya, Do Ya, Wanna Dance?," partly because it trips one of my hot buttons (I don't like the meme "the sixties were the best ever, man, and rock and roll could have saved the world," which is just childish), and partly because it just doesn't take off for me. The Ellison seems minor.

But there were quite a few more fine novelettes:

"The Hob," by Judith Moffett
"Mannequins," by Charles Oberndorf
"Deathbinder" and "Many Mansions," by Alexander Jablokov
"El Vilvoy de las Islas," by Avram Davidson
"King of Morning, Queen of Day," by Ian McDonald
"French Scenes," by Howard Waldrop

And an odd one: "John Ford's 'Tis Pity She's a Whore,'" by Angela Carter, which reimagines the tragedy by the Jacobean playwright John Ford as a Western by the twentieth-century film director John Ford. What we need now, I think, is a third level, a story reimagining Carter's reimagination as a science fiction story by the late John M. Ford.

There were also a lot of very good short stories. I don't think the right story won the Hugo, at all. But the remainder of the nominees are very strong. I love Gunn's dark comedy, "Stable Strategies for Middle Management," and the Sterling and Brin are exceptional, and Landis's Nebula winner (for 1990!—I think perhaps "rolling eligibility" had come in by now), "Ripples in the Dirac Sea," is also excellent.

For all that, I'd have given the Hugo to a completely different story, Neal Barrett Jr.'s lovely "Stairs."

And other good shorts include:

"The Odd Old Bird," by Avram Davidson (best of the later Eszterhazy stories, I think)

"The Other Dead Man," by Gene Wolfe (one of his best shorts)

"At the Double Solstice," by Gregory Benford (files the serial numbers off a scene from one of the Galactic Center novels to make it a stand-alone short—something Benford has done a few times)

"Bible Stories for Adults, No. 17: The Deluge," by James Morrow (the 1989 Nebula winner)

"Blit," by David Langford

"Lily Red," by Karen Joy Fowler

"Mrs. Shummel Exits a Winner," by John Kessel (probably my second favorite story, behind "Stairs"—became part of his excellent novel *Good News from Outer Space*)

"An Infinity of Karen," by Lawrence Watt-Evans

"Ado," by Connie Willis

"Remaking History," by Kim Stanley Robinson (This appeared first in 1988 in the UK anthology *Other Edens II,* and was reprinted in *Asimov's* in 1989. It got a Hugo nomination in 1990, which had to be withdrawn because the story was ineligible that year.)

"(Learning About) Machine Sex," by Candas Jane Dorsey

Glad to see Tom Canty showing up in the artist category—he's one of my favorites to this day.

DESIGNING PEOPLE AND SOCIETIES:
C. J. CHERRYH'S *CYTEEN*

....

When I was reading the Foundation books, it occurred to me how seldom one sees a designed society written about with approval in SF. I think this is a lingering legacy of the Cold War—Soviet design bad, American competition good. If we see designed societies, they're rarely like Seldon's Foundation and much more often dystopic and there to be overthrown by our heroes in the course of the plot.

C. J. Cherryh's *Cyteen* is an interesting example, because it's directly about designing people and designing societies. And it's set among the designers, who are themselves designed. It doesn't view these designs with either approval or disapproval, but as if they are historical fact. It's a book about cloning and individuality, about slavery and freedom, about historical destiny and growing up under pressure and learning to handle real power over societies. It's about mind-building and society-building, and it works in a way very like Asimov's psychohistory, by manipulating people and trends. It's a book I keep coming back to because it has so much in it; it remains rich and thought provoking even after I've read it countless times. At heart, it is a character story; it's an investigation of what it's like to be, and to become, and to create, someone with the fate of worlds in their hands.

Union is a designed society in the future, an interstellar society with one planet and a lot of space stations. It's a democratic society that has a different model of the way voting works, a society that has the rule of law, and where elections do matter, but when you see it close up, all these legal protections don't count for much when powerful people don't want them to. And it's a society that has, in addition to citizens, inhabitants who are not citizens, *azi*—who are clones with designed personalities, and something quite similar to manumittable slaves.

Cherryh chose to show us Union society first from outside in *Downbelow Station* (1982), where they are the implacable enemy. I didn't want to read *Cyteen* when it was first published, because I didn't want to spend that much time in Union. It becomes clear that Alliance doesn't understand Union. Close up, it's . . . differently claustrophobic.

Paradoxically, it's both better and worse than it seemed from outside. It has democratic institutions and safeguards—elections matter desperately, though electorates are by occupation and people have different numbers of votes, as in Shute's *In the Wet*.

This is a society only 250 years old, and that 250 years represents only two generations, because they have rejuv, a drug that keeps people biologically forty for about a hundred years. If you were an ordinary CIT in Union, your life would be much nicer and more free than I would have imagined. But for an azi or somebody who isn't ordinary, it's much worse.

Ariane Emory is one of the architects of Union, one of the designers of personality and society, and we see her from inside and out, as manipulator and as manipulated. The bulk of the book is about getting her back, producing a child who is not just a genetic replica but a psychogenetic replica too. Ariane Emory was a genius who worked at designing people and societies and who served as Councillor for Science, politically the most powerful of the nine most powerful people in Union. She's so intelligent and so powerful, she forgets that she has limits. But she knows she's dying, and she sets things up for her replica. She arranges for them to do to her replica the things that shaped her—the neglectful carping mother who dies when she is seven, the guardianship of an uncle who is very strange. They don't go so far as to replicate the abuse, for which the second Ari is grateful. Ari II is tested and manipulated and shaped into being what they want her to be, until by the end of the book, she is so much her predecessor that she would do the same.

The replication of Ari II is explicitly compared to what has been done to society. On the one hand, there's the overt setting up of Union and the different electorates and all of that. On the other, there's the covert work. Azi are an economic requirement—they needed people fast, they cloned them and gave them their personalities via "tape from the cradle"—azi are trustworthy and competent and have skills deep down, but they are permanent minors (until and unless emancipated), and they (or rather their contracts, which amounts to the same thing) are sold entirely without any input from them. Tape has given them their skills, but also their morality and their priorities. And Ari I has set up worms—self-programming replications that they will teach to their children—in the programming of the azi, which will shape society in the directions she thinks important. Ari I says in the notes she leaves for her successor that Ari II's experience of discovering what has been done to her will help her realize how Union would react if it discovers too soon what she has done.

Cyteen is a book that covers a great deal of time and space. It also leaves you to make up your own mind about Ariane Emory's manipulation of society. Ari I is plainly shown as a predator, and as somebody who believes that she is doing terrible things for what she sees as valuable ends. It says on the cover that she is murdered and replicated, and many readers spend the early part of the book hating her and longing for somebody to murder her already. It's a tribute to Cherryh's writing that many of those same readers go down the same path as her replicate and would agree at the end that getting her back is a priority.

As for society, if you accept her reasoning—that humanity will become small bands spread out across an endless plain of space mired in endless war or predation unless society finds a better way to replicate itself, then it's possible to admire what she has done. If you think that a society that needs to do this isn't worth saving, then you can keep hating her.

This manipulation of society by affecting the personalities of segments of the population so that the whole population will react the way you want it to is very like psychohistory. It's also explicitly undermined—we learn not only from Gehenna but also from the azi points of view that the designers (even Ari) aren't as good as they think they are at designing personalities. We learn from Grant that the azi whisper about ways to be free, and we keep seeing Justin fixing design problems.

We also know, because Cherryh had written books set later in the history of this universe, that it doesn't ultimately work. Ari I talks about azi as ideally a one-generation proposition for opening up frontiers, but we see future societies where azi are institutions. In *Cyteen*, azi do not always get rejuv, and in later books, we see them killed off at forty. Union does last, but not in the way she would have wanted. Cherryh believes in history and unintended consequences.

I've probably read *Cyteen* forty times, but it always grabs me and won't let go, and I always see more in it.

THE MOST EXPENSIVE PLUMBERS IN THE GALAXY: LOIS MCMASTER BUJOLD'S *FALLING FREE*

Falling Free is about as hard science as it's possible to get—it's a novel where all the good guys are engineers, with engineering mind-sets, and the solutions to social and economic problems are engineering ones. It's explicitly about how changing technology affects people's lives. But to start talking about it, you have to begin with biology.

The Quaddies have four arms and no legs. They've been developed (genetically engineered) by GalacTech for use as a zero-gravity work-force. (Thus *Falling Free,* they're designed for free fall.) They've been trained as engineers. And they're not considered as people; the company owns them and can terminate them at any time—for instance, when artificial gravity is invented, that makes their whole species technologically obsolete.

Falling Free is one of Bujold's early books, and it isn't as technically accomplished as her later work. This is the same universe as the Vorkosigan books, but set several hundred years earlier. It's both an interesting background—the company, Earth beginning to be eclipsed by its colonies, the beginnings of Quaddie culture—and an exciting story of escape and engineering. It's also a character study of how people go along with things until they realize they can't do that anymore—it's an examination of what it means to be free. And that's the other thing the title means.

Leo Graf is an engineer who is passionate about engineering. He's prepared to accept the Quaddies situation being really fairly bad, but it's only when events press it on to absolutely appalling that he decides to take action. He's an odd hero. He consoles himself by thinking how he saved three thousand people's lives inspecting welds—he really is exactly like an engineer. I find him hard to get a grip on. The Quaddies—all of them—are much more sympathetic. I especially like Silver, with her taste for illicit romance novels and men with legs. But I don't find the Silver-Graf romance very convincing even so.

This is a very traditional science fiction book in many ways—the best bit is the science. When I think about this story, I remember the bit where they remake a plasma mirror, and when I get to that bit, I can't put the book down. The whole changing-technology bit feels real. Bujold does brilliantly at getting you to accept four-armed human beings as sympathetic people.

Bujold originally planned this book as the first of a trilogy, but the other two proposed books never got written and now never will. We know what happened to the Quaddies from "Labyrinth" and *Diplomatic Immunity:* they successfully escape and set up their own gravity-free culture far away. Nevertheless, the end of *Falling Free* always leaves me wanting to know what happened to these people immediately next, not their remote descendants.

1990

Winner: *Hyperion*, by Dan Simmons

Nominees:
A Fire in the Sun, by George Alec Effinger
Prentice Alvin, by Orson Scott Card
The Boat of a Million Years, by Poul Anderson
Grass, by Sheri S. Tepper

The 1990 Hugo Awards were presented in ConFiction in The Hague, Netherlands, and I would have been there—I had a supporting membership—but I was extremely pregnant at the time and couldn't make it. However, I did vote for the first time. And in the novel category, I voted for the winner, which was Dan Simmons's *Hyperion*.

Hyperion is the kind of book the Hugos were made for, the kind of book that needs to be celebrated. It's a mosaic novel, some pilgrims traveling to the planet Hyperion tell their stories, and in the process of telling, the universe is revealed. The stories are in different SFnal styles, and although the book has no resolution, it's all the better for that. There are sequels, which do explain things, and which I don't like. *Hyperion*, considered alone, is a whole thing and a masterpiece. It also won the Locus Award. It's in print and in the library in English and French.

There were four other nominees, and I've read them all.

George Alec Effinger's *A Fire in the Sun* is the first sequel to 1989's nominee *When Gravity Fails*. It's another terrific book, but it's definitely a sequel, and I'm not sure how well it would stand alone. It's in print and in the library in English and French.

Orson Scott Card's *Prentice Alvin* is the third of his Alvin Maker books, and the third of them to be nominated for a Hugo, giving Card five successive years on the ballot. I liked it less than the first two. It's in print, and in the library in English and French.

Poul Anderson's *The Boat of a Million Years* is about immortals living through all of history in the hope of eventually voyaging to the stars. There's a lot of cool history in the book, and interesting speculation about what it would be like to keep on living while everyone around you ages and dies. I really liked it, and voted it second after *Hyperion*. In retrospect and on rereading, I like it less—the historical parts are great, but the present and future bits aren't. It's in print and in the library in English only.

Sheri Tepper's *Grass* is a book I wanted to like, but couldn't. I had generally enjoyed Tepper up to this point, and I enjoyed several of her later books, but I found *Grass* impossible to engage with, and now I'm finding it hard to remember. There was an unusual planet and aliens who were right and a "Dark They Were, and Golden-Eyed" vibe, or was that the sequel, *Raising the Stones*? And a plague, I think, spreading between the stars? I'd read it again, but I do remember having trouble getting into it, and that's the kiss of death for me. It's in print, and it's in the library in English only.

So, four men and one woman, all American although the con was in Europe. Card is a previous winner, Anderson and Effinger are previous nominees, Tepper was a Campbell nominee but new to the Hugo ballot, Simmons was a Hugo newcomer. We have two novels of multiplanet civilizations, one noir Islamic future Earth, one historical science fiction and one historical fantasy.

All right, then—what else might they have chosen?

The Nebula Award went to Elizabeth Ann Scarborough's *The Healer's War*, which as a 1988 book wouldn't have been eligible for the Hugo. SFWA's rules on this were completely incomprehensible to ordinary mortals until they were rationalized a couple of years ago. The only other non-overlapping eligible nominee is John Kessel's *Good News from Outer Space*.

The World Fantasy Award was won by *Lyonesse: Madouc,* by Jack Vance. Other nominees were *Carrion Comfort,* Dan Simmons (wasn't he having a good year!); *A Child Across the Sky,* Jonathan Carroll; *In a Dark Dream,* Charles L. Grant; *Soldier of Arete,* Gene Wolfe; *The Stress of Her Regard,* Tim Powers.

The John W. Campbell Memorial Award went to Geoff Ryman's *The Child Garden,* a totally wonderful book that expands the boundaries of SF. It should have been a Hugo nominee. I don't understand why Ryman is so underrated when he's so brilliant. Second place is K. W. Jeter's *Farewell Horizontal,* and third is the Kessel.

The Philip K. Dick Award was given to Richard Paul Russo's *Subterranean Gallery.* Special commendation was Dave Wolverton's *On My Way to Paradise.* Other nominees: *Being Alien,* Rebecca Ore; *A Fearful Symmetry,* James Luceno; *Heritage of Flight,* Susan M. Shwartz; *Infinity Hold,* Barry B. Longyear.

Locus Award nominees not yet mentioned: *Rimrunners,* C. J. Cherryh; *Tides of Light,* Gregory Benford; *Rama II,* Arthur C. Clarke and Gentry Lee; *Falcon,* Emma Bull; *Phases of Gravity,* Dan Simmons; *The City, Not Long After,* Pat Murphy; *Imago,* Octavia E. Butler; *A Talent for War,* Jack McDevitt; *The Third Eagle,* R. A. MacAvoy; *Buying Time* (UK title: *The Long Habit of Living*), Joe Haldeman; *Homegoing,* Frederik Pohl; *Out on Blue Six,* Ian McDonald; *Orbital Decay,* Allen Steele; *Sugar Rain,* Paul Park; *Eden,* Stanislaw Lem; *Dawn's Uncertain Light,* Neal Barrett Jr.; *Black Milk,* Robert Reed; *On My Way to Paradise,* Dave Wolverton; *The Renegades of Pern,* Anne McCaffrey; *The Queen of Springtime* (US title: *The New Springtime*), Robert Silverberg.

I like *Rimrunners,* and I like *Falcon* and *Imago* and *A Talent for War,* but it's not a howling injustice that they're not Hugo nominees.

The Locus fantasy award went to *Prentice Alvin.* Other nominees not already mentioned: *Rusalka,* C. J. Cherryh (look, I love Cherryh, but this is a very depressing book); *Dream Baby,* Bruce McAllister; *White Jenna,* Jane Yolen; *Sorceress of Darshiva,* David Eddings; *Tourists,* Lisa Goldstein; *The Fortress of the Pearl,* Michael Moorcock; *The Stone Giant,* James P. Blaylock; *Guards! Guards!,* Terry Pratchett; *Snow White and Rose Red,* Patricia C. Wrede; *A Heroine of the World,* Tanith Lee; *Marianne, the Matchbox, and the Malachite Mouse,* Sheri S. Tepper;

Ars Magica, Judith Tarr; *Gate of Darkness, Circle of Light*, Tanya Huff; *Apocalypse*, Nancy Springer; *Queen's Gambit Declined*, Melinda Snodgrass; *Arthur*, Stephen R. Lawhead; *The Coachman Rat*, David Henry Wilson; *Tours of the Black Clock*, Steve Erickson; *The Cockroaches of Stay More*, Donald Harington.

Looking at their first novel listing, I see Rosemary Kirstein's *The Steerswoman* and Doris Egan's *The Gate of Ivory*.

The Mythopoeic Award was given to Tim Powers's *The Stress of Her Regard*. Other nominees not yet mentioned were Patricia McKillip's *The Changeling Sea* and Matt Ruff's *Fool on the Hill*.

Anything they all missed? Walter Jon Williams's *Angel Station* and Daniel Keys Moran's *The Long Run*.

So I think this is another year where the Hugo nominees are looking pretty good for the best five books of the year.

OTHER CATEGORIES

BEST NOVELLA

Winner: *The Mountains of Mourning*, by Lois McMaster Bujold (*Analog*, May 1989)

Nominees:
The Father of Stones, by Lucius Shepard (WSFA Press; *Asimov's*, September 1989)
Time-Out, by Connie Willis (*Asimov's*, July 1989)
Tiny Tango, by Judith Moffett (*Asimov's*, February 1989)
A Touch of Lavender, by Megan Lindholm (*Asimov's*, November 1989)

Again, a terrific bunch of novellas. I voted for the Lindholm, the Willis, and the Moffett in that order. I hadn't seen the Shepard or the Bujold yet. Novellas, where SF really shines.

Best Novelette

Winner: "Enter a Soldier. Later: Enter Another," by Robert Silverberg (*Asimov's*, June 1989; *Time Gate*)

Nominees:

"At the Rialto," by Connie Willis (*The Microverse; Omni*, October 1989)

"Dogwalker," by Orson Scott Card (*Asimov's*, November 1989)

"Everything but Honor," by George Alec Effinger (*Asimov's*, February 1989; *What Might Have Been? Vol. 1: Alternate Empires*)

"For I Have Touched the Sky," by Mike Resnick (*F&SF*, December 1989)

"The Price of Oranges," by Nancy Kress (*Asimov's*, April 1989)

My votes were Silverberg, Kress, Willis, and I remember agonizing over that order.

Best Short Story

Winner: "Boobs," by Suzy McKee Charnas (*Asimov's*, July 1989)

Nominees:

"Computer Friendly," by Eileen Gunn (*Asimov's*, June 1989)

"Dori Bangs," by Bruce Sterling (*Asimov's*, September 1989)

"The Edge of the World," by Michael Swanwick (*Full Spectrum 2*)

"Lost Boys," by Orson Scott Card (*F&SF*, October 1989)

"The Return of William Proxmire," by Larry Niven (*What Might Have Been? Vol. 1: Alternate Empires*)

Best Nonfiction Book

Winner: *The World Beyond the Hill: Science Fiction and the Quest for Transcendence*, by Alexei Panshin and Cory Panshin (Jeremy P. Tarcher)

Nominees:
Astounding Days, by Arthur C. Clarke (Gollancz; Bantam Spectra)
Dancing at the Edge of the World, by Ursula K. Le Guin (Grove)
Grumbles from the Grave, by Robert A. Heinlein (Ballantine Del Rey)
Harlan Ellison's Watching, by Harlan Ellison (Underwood-Miller)
Noreascon Three Souvenir Book, edited by Greg Thokar (MCFI Press)

I voted for the Le Guin only, as I hadn't read any of the others.

Best Dramatic Presentation

Winner: *Indiana Jones and the Last Crusade*

Nominees:
The Abyss
The Adventures of Baron Munchhausen
Batman
Field of Dreams

Best Professional Editor

Winner: Gardner Dozois

Nominees:
Ellen Datlow
Edward L. Ferman
David G. Hartwell
Beth Meacham
Charles C. Ryan
Stanley Schmidt

I'm sure I voted for Gardner, because not only did I love *Asimov's* and buy every issue I could find, but I also adored his Year's Best books. But Beth Meacham is a terrific editor, and she's never had a Hugo in all this time.

BEST PROFESSIONAL ARTIST

Winner: Don Maitz

Nominees:
Jim Burns
Thomas Canty
David A. Cherry
James Gurney
Tom Kidd
Michael Whelan

BEST SEMIPROZINE

Winner: *Locus*, edited by Charles N. Brown

Nominees:
Interzone, edited by David Pringle
The New York Review of Science Fiction, edited by Kathryn Cramer,
    David G. Hartwell, and Gordon Van Gelder
Science Fiction Chronicle, edited by Andrew I. Porter
Thrust, edited by D. Douglas Fratz

I voted *NYRoSF* first, trusting that the subsequent issues were all as good as the first one, and *Interzone* last because it was so irritating living in a country where that one very narrow vision was the only SF magazine.

BEST FANZINE

Winner: *The Mad 3 Party*, edited by Leslie Turek

Nominees:
File 770, edited by Mike Glyer
FOSFAX, edited by Timothy Lane

Lan's Lantern, edited by George "Lan" Laskowski
Pirate Jenny, edited by Pat Mueller

BEST FAN WRITER

Winner: Dave Langford

Nominees:
Mike Glyer
Arthur D. Hlavaty
Evelyn C. Leeper
Leslie Turek

It *just* occurred to me for the first time that Dave Langford must have been paid for his reviews in *White Dwarf,* and they weren't fan writing at all. Oh well. I voted for him on the grounds of them, but it's not like he wasn't doing lots of fan writing anyway.

BEST FAN ARTIST

Winner: Stu Shiffman

Nominees:
Steve Fox
Teddy Harvia
Merle Insinga
Joe Mayhew
Taral Wayne

WORLDCON SPECIAL AWARD, ORIGINAL ARTWORK [NOT A HUGO]

Winner: Don Maitz, cover of *Rimrunners* (by C. J. Cherryh)

Nominees:
Gary Ruddell, Cover of *Hyperion* (by Dan Simmons)

Michael Whelan, cover of *Paradise* (by Mike Resnick)

James Gurney, cover of *Quozl* (by Alan Dean Foster)

Michael Whelan, cover of *The Renegades of Pern* (by Anne Mc-Caffrey)

James Gurney, cover of *The Stress of Her Regard* (by Tim Powers)

JOHN W. CAMPBELL AWARD

Winner: Kristine Kathryn Rusch

Nominees:
Nancy A. Collins
John Cramer
Katherine Neville
Allen Steele

Rusch is an obviously terrific winner, she has been significant in the field as a writer and an editor, she's still writing and still being nominated for awards. Definitely a good choice.

Allen Steele was also a great nominee and would have been a very good winner. His first novel, *Orbital Decay*, had just come out, but I'd read only some short things in *Asimov's*. He has gone on to have a solid career as a hard SF writer, and he's still writing and being nominated for awards.

Nancy A. Collins is a horror writer, I don't know much about her, but she has had a successful career and is still around, so probably a good nominee even if not my thing.

John Cramer and Katherine Neville are completely unknown to me. *Locus* suggests that Cramer had a couple of novels in 1990 and 1991. Wikipedia tells me that Neville is a mainstream writer of adventure thrillers.

In a year where Rosemary Kirstein, Tanya Huff, Doris Egan, Teresa Edgerton, Josepha Sherman, and Matt Ruff all had first novels and were likely eligible, it seems like the Campbell was nodding.

COMMENTS ON 1990

3.JAMES DAVIS NICOLL

John Cramer

Nuclear physicist of somewhat nonconsensus views, probably best known within SF for two things: he's SF editor Kathryn Cramer's father and the author of an astounding number of Alternate View columns for *Analog*.

27.GARDNER DOZOIS

In novella, Moffett or Lindholm for me, out of stuff nominated, although I think John Crowley's *Great Work of Time,* which didn't even get on the ballot, might actually have deserved it the most. Walter Jon Williams's *No Spot of Ground* is a very good alternate history, perhaps one of the best ever written at short lengths. Steven Popkes's *The Egg* is also first-rate. Card's *Pageant Wagon* is pretty good too, although not in the same class. A good year for novellas overall, especially when you count in both the stuff that made the ballot and the stuff that didn't.

In novelette, I'd go for the Kress, although Silverberg makes a worthy winner. An almost unknown story here that ought to have made the ballot is "The Third Sex," by Alan Brennert. My own "Solace" also went completely unnoticed, sigh.

In short story, my heart belongs to "Dori Bangs," although it's alternate history rather than SF per se. A more SFnal story that would also have made a great winner is Charles Sheffield's "Out of Copyright," one of his best stories. (His *Destroyer of Worlds* was also a pretty good novella that year.) Avram Davidson's "The Odd Old Bird" is also good, although probably not major enough to win the Hugo. Of historical interest are first stories by Maureen McHugh and Janet Kagan, "Baffin Island and "The Loch Moose Monster" (considered a minor classic in some circles) respectively, and Steven Utley's first story after a silence of nearly a decade, "My Wife." The Niven may have been the worst story of the year, and I'm glad it didn't win.

This year also saw the publication of one of the first of the tribute anthologies, allowing various writers to play with the worlds and characters of Isaac Asimov, *Foundation's Friends*, the best of which were by Frederik Pohl and by Connie Willis.

Obviously, either Kristine Kathryn Rusch or Allen Steele should have won the Campbell, and a case could be made for either. The other three candidates don't really belong there, and there were other writers who could have taken their places who would have been a better fit.

38. RICH HORTON

One novel I haven't seen mentioned is Richard Grant's *Views from the Oldest House*, which I haven't read but have heard good things about—and I've seen it compared to Nabokov, a good thing I think.

Also a mainstream novel with fantastic elements, pretty good despite the author's later joining the "I don't write SF, because I don't write about squids in space" crowd (after writing a really obviously SF novel): *Sexing the Cherry*, by Jeannette Winterson.

As to the Campbell, I have no objection to KKR winning, nor would I have objected to Steele. The thing I object to is the Neville nomination. It was based on *The Eight*, a bestselling historical novel with aspects of the fantastical, or alt-historical, more or less in the Dan Brown sort of genre (except Brown's not historical). The problem with *The Eight*—a problem shared by Brown's novels, mind you—is that it is jaw-droppingly awful. Appalling writing, appalling history, stupid plotting. One of the worst books I've read in the past few decades.

39. RICH HORTON

Short fiction.

First, as noted, despite a pretty strong novella short list, the clear best novella of the year—by a very wide margin—wasn't nominated: John Crowley's *Great Work of Time*. This is one of the masterworks of the past quarter century, in my view.

Crowley published another good novella in 1989, *In Blue*.

Of the Hugo nominees, my choice at the time went to *Tiny Tango*. There was also an excellent story not yet mentioned on the Nebula ballot, *A Dozen Tough Jobs*, by Howard Waldrop. I also liked Michael

Bishop's *Apartheid, Superstrings, and Mordecai Thubana,* and Iain M. Banks's *The State of the Art* (which probably wasn't seen by enough readers to get nominated).

In novelette, "At the Rialto," by Willis, probably got my vote for the Hugo among the short-listed stories. I also liked "The Price of Oranges," but as Doug notes, it is rather "obvious and shameless." The Nebula short list included another good choice, Greg Bear's "Sisters."

Other strong novelettes:

"Cast on a Distant Shore," by R. Garcia y Robertson
"Matter's End," by Gregory Benford
"Tales from the Venia Woods," by Robert Silverberg
"The Sin-Eater of the Kaw," by Bradley Denton
"Alphas," by Gregory Benford (another example of him filing off the
    serial numbers of an episode from his novels to make an independent
    story)

In short story, well, "Boobs" is a pretty good revenge fantasy, and not an unworthy winner but not a lasting masterwork either. "Dori Bangs" is neat in its way, but has no real SFnal zing. It did prompt me to read some of Lester Bangs's writing, including a masterful analysis of the greatest rock album of all time (though, of course, it's not "rock"): Van Morrison's *Astral Weeks.*

But my actual choice for best short story of 1989 didn't get a sniff on either the Nebula or Hugo ballot: Karen Joy Fowler's "Game Night at the Fox and Goose."

Other good short stories:

Tanith Lee's "Zelle's Thursday"
Adam-Troy Castro's "Clearance to Land"
David Brin's "Dr. Pak's Preschool"
Greg Egan's "The Cutie"

And from outside the genre, Stephen Millhauser's "Eisenheim the Illusionist," a very good story that is the source material for the movie *The Illusionist.*

64. Gardner Dozois

"The Caress" is the first Egan story I bought for *Asimov's,* and may be his first publication in the United States, although he'd had several stories, mostly technohorror, published in England previously. It's also the first time he stops writing horror and steps into his more familiar identity as a hard SF writer.

It was in a 1990-dated issue, though, so for me it's a 1990 story.

1991

Winner: *The Vor Game,* by Lois McMaster Bujold

Nominees:
Earth, by David Brin
The Fall of Hyperion, by Dan Simmons
Queen of Angels, by Greg Bear
The Quiet Pools, by Michael P. Kube-McDowell

The 1991 Hugo Awards were presented at Chicon V in Chicago.

The Best Novel winner was Lois McMaster Bujold's *The Vor Game,* a book that's probably best described as military science fiction with depth and consequences. It's the sixth volume in Bujold's Vorkosigan saga, but a great place to start the series, which I think a lot of people may have done with this Hugo nomination. It's a really good book in a solidly realized universe. It's about identity and duty and the way history informs present decisions. It's a very good book, and the first of Bujold's Hugo nominations for this series. It's in print in several editions—NESFA brought out a hardcover edition in 2010—and in the library in English only. An excellent Hugo winner.

There are four other nominees, of which I have read three. David Brin's *Earth* is an ambitious failure. It's that hardest of all forms, the fifty-years-ahead novel. The near future can be assumed not to be all that different from the present, the far future can be whatever you like, but that fifty-year distance is tricky. John Brunner did it with *Stand on Zanzibar,* and *Stand on Zanzibar* is clearly what *Earth* is trying to do.

It's a big multiple-viewpoint predictive novel that was overtaken by events and technology almost the moment it hit the shelves. It's in print and in the library in English.

Dan Simmons's *The Fall of Hyperion* is a book that didn't disappoint me at the time, but which didn't stand up to rereading. The universe is still marvelous, but the answers are not as satisfying as the questions. I think I'd describe it as far-future meta-SF. It won the Locus Award. It's in print, and it's in the library in English and French. I don't think it really belongs on this list, and I'm glad it didn't win.

Greg Bear's *Queen of Angels* is a murder mystery in a fast-moving near-future world where the question isn't *who* did it, but *why* they did it, with forensic psychology and an emergent AI. This is the kind of book I'm delighted to see on the list—not entirely successful, but pushing the boundaries of genre. It's in print, and it's in the library in French.

And I haven't read Michael P. Kube-McDowell's *The Quiet Pools*— no excuse, I've just never picked it up or really looked at it. Did it have a UK edition? It seems to be about people sending out generation starships and other people trying to stop them, which sounds like something I might like. It's not in print, and it's not in the library, which reduces my chances of reading it anytime soon. Nor has anyone urged me to read it.

So, four men and one woman, all American. Brin and Simmons are previous winners, Bear and Bujold are previous nominees, Kube-McDowell is a newcomer. The books are all solidly science fiction, no fantasy at all. We have two star-spanning adventures, very different from each other, two near futures with computers but neither of them really cyberpunk, and one generation starship. I think the best book won, but I wouldn't have been sorry if any of them had won except for *Fall of Hyperion*.

What else might they have chosen?

The Nebula was won by Ursula Le Guin's *Tehanu,* a book about which I am deeply conflicted. Other non-overlapping eligible nominees are James Morrow's brilliant *Only Begotten Daughter,* which was well worthy of Hugo nomination; Jane Yolen's *White Jenna;* and two books I've never heard of: Valerie Martin's *Mary Reilly* and John E. Stith's

Redshift Rendezvous. It's not all that unusual for me not to have read something, but I'm surprised to see two books on the Nebula ballot that I haven't even heard of.

The World Fantasy Award was shared between James Morrow's *Only Begotten Daughter* and Ellen Kushner's *Thomas the Rhymer.* Other nominees not previously mentioned: Neil Gaiman and Terry Pratchett's *Good Omens* and Guy Gavriel Kay's *Tigana.*

The John W. Campbell Memorial Award went to *Pacific Edge,* which would have been a great Hugo nominee.

The Philip K. Dick Award, for paperback original science fiction, went to Pat Murphy's *Points of Departure,* with a special citation for Raymond Harris's *The Schizogenic Man.* Other nominees were Allen Steele's *Clarke County, Space;* Gregory Feeley's *The Oxygen Barons;* and Elizabeth Hand's *Winterlong.*

Locus nominees not previously mentioned were: *Voyage to the Red Planet,* Terry Bisson; *The Difference Engine,* William Gibson and Bruce Sterling; *Jurassic Park,* Michael Crichton; *The Ring of Charon,* Roger MacBride Allen; *Pegasus in Flight,* Anne McCaffrey; *Raising the Stones,* Sheri S. Tepper; *The Hemingway Hoax,* Joe Haldeman; *Summertide,* Charles Sheffield; *Polar City Blues,* Katharine Kerr; *The World at the End of Time,* Frederik Pohl; *The Hollow Earth,* Rudy Rucker; *The Rowan,* Anne McCaffrey; *In the Country of the Blind,* Michael F. Flynn (which won the Prometheus Award); *The Ghost from the Grand Banks,* Arthur C. Clarke; *The Divide,* Robert Charles Wilson; *Agviq,* Michael Armstrong; *Heathern,* Jack Womack.

The Locus fantasy award went to *Tehanu.* Nominees not yet mentioned were: *The Eye of the World,* Robert Jordan; *The Blood of Roses,* Tanith Lee; *Servant of the Empire,* Raymond E. Feist and Janny Wurts; *Drink Down the Moon,* Charles de Lint; *Rats and Gargoyles,* Mary Gentle; *Ghostwood,* Charles de Lint; *Moving Pictures,* Terry Pratchett; *Dealing with Dragons,* Patricia C. Wrede; *Time and Chance,* Alan Brennert; *In Between Dragons,* Michael Kandel; *Gossamer Axe,* Gael Baudino; *Chase the Morning,* Michael Scott Rohan; *Castleview,* Gene Wolfe.

Some good stuff, but nothing that strikes me as notably better than the Hugo list we have.

Thomas the Rhymer won the Mythopoeic Award.

And was there anything all these missed?

Nancy Kress's *Brainrose;* Salman Rushdie's *Haroun and the Sea of Stories;* Diane Duane's *High Wizardry;* Colin Greenland's *Take Back Plenty;* Dorothy Heydt (Katherine Blake)'s *The Interior Life.* I don't think any of those are likely Hugo nominees, really, but they're all good books.

I think the Hugos really did miss out on *Pacific Edge* and *Only Begotten Daughter,* but not much else, and four out of the five books we have on the list of nominees are just the kind of book I think we should be nominating. So on the whole, a pretty good year.

OTHER CATEGORIES

BEST NOVELLA

Winner: *The Hemingway Hoax,* by Joe Haldeman (*Asimov's,* April 1990)

Nominees:
Bones, by Pat Murphy (*Asimov's,* May 1990)
Bully!, by Mike Resnick (*Axolotl*)
Fool to Believe, by Pat Cadigan (*Asimov's,* February 1990)
A Short, Sharp Shock, by Kim Stanley Robinson (Mark V. Ziesing; *Asimov's,* November 1990)

The novella version of *The Hemingway Hoax* is brilliant, and I'd have voted for it by a hair from the Robinson and the Cadigan. Another great novella year.

BEST NOVELETTE

Winner: "The Manamouki," by Mike Resnick (*Asimov's,* July 1990)

Nominees:
"A Braver Thing," by Charles Sheffield (*Asimov's,* February 1990)

"The Coon Rolled Down and Ruptured His Larinks, A Squeezed
   Novel by Mr. Skunk," by Dafydd ab Hugh (*Asimov's*, August 1990)
"Over the Long Haul," by Martha Soukup (*Amazing Stories*, March
   1990)
"Tower of Babylon," by Ted Chiang (*Omni*, November 1990)

The only one of these I remember is the Chiang. His first publication,
I believe.

BEST SHORT STORY

Winner: "Bears Discover Fire," by Terry Bisson (*Asimov's*, August 1990)

Nominees:
"Cibola," by Connie Willis (*Asimov's*, December 1990)
"Godspeed," by Charles Sheffield (*Analog*, July 1990)
"The Utility Man," by Robert Reed (*Asimov's*, November 1990)
"VRM-547," by W. R. Thompson (*Analog*, February 1990)

Robert Reed's first Hugo nomination, with an excellent story. The
Willis and the Bisson are memorable too.

BEST NONFICTION BOOK

Winner: *How to Write Science Fiction and Fantasy*, by Orson Scott Card

Nominees:
Bury My Heart at W.H. Smith's, by Brian W. Aldiss
Hollywood Gothic, by David J. Skal
Science Fiction in the Real World, by Norman Spinrad
Science Fiction Writers of America Handbook, edited by Kristine Kathryn
   Rusch and Dean Wesley Smith

Bury My Heart at W.H. Smith's is my favorite book by Aldiss, a really
funny touching memoir.

Best Dramatic Presentation

Winner: *Edward Scissorhands*

Nominees:
Back to the Future III
Ghost
Total Recall
The Witches

Best Professional Editor

Winner: Gardner Dozois

Nominees:
Ellen Datlow
Edward L. Ferman
Kristine Kathryn Rusch
Stanley Schmidt

Best Professional Artist

Winner: Michael Whelan

Nominees:
Thomas Canty
David A. Cherry
Bob Eggleton
Don Maitz

Best Semiprozine

Winner: *Locus,* edited by Charles N. Brown

Nominees:
Interzone, edited by David Pringle

The New York Review of Science Fiction, edited by David G. Hartwell,
    Kathryn Cramer, and Gordon Van Gelder
Quantum (formerly *Thrust*), edited by D. Douglas Fratz
Science Fiction Chronicle, edited by Andrew I. Porter

BEST FANZINE

Winner: *Lan's Lantern*, edited by George "Lan" Laskowski

Nominees:
File 770, edited by Mike Glyer
FOSFAX, edited by Janice Moore and Timothy Lane
Mainstream, edited by Jerry Kaufman and Suzanne Tompkins
Mimosa, edited by Dick and Nicki Lynch

BEST FAN WRITER

Winner: Dave Langford

Nominees:
Avedon Carol
Mike Glyer
Arthur Hlavaty
Evelyn C. Leeper
Teresa Nielsen Hayden

BEST FAN ARTIST

Winner: Teddy Harvia

Nominees:
Merle Insinga
Peggy Ranson
Stu Shiffman
Diana Stein

John W. Campbell Award

Winner: Julia Ecklar

Nominees:
Nancy A. Collins
John Cramer
Scott Cupp
Michael Kandel

I hadn't heard of Julia Ecklar, but it seems she's a filker and short story writer who wrote a Star Trek novel under her own name and also wrote in collaboration as L. A. Graf. It's hard to feel she was the best choice for Campbell winner. But it wasn't a strong field of nominees.

Nancy A. Collins is a very successful and well-known horror writer who had a very successful first novel out that year, and with hindsight I think she'd have been the best winner.

Michael Kandel is best known as the translator of Lem, but he has also published original fiction. He's not prolific, and although well thought of, he is not well known.

We talked about John Cramer last time. I'm not familiar with Scott Cupp—anyone?

Neither of them have had the kinds of careers that one might wish from Campbell nominees.

Nominators could also have considered Tom Holt and Michael F. Flynn, who both had notable first novels out in 1990, but I don't know whether previous publications might have made them ineligible. This wasn't one of its more shining moments.

Comments on 1991

2. Rich Horton

There is one major, major novel that in retrospect, to me, is clearly the most deserving SF novel of 1990. This is *Use of Weapons,* by Iain M.

Banks. It's my favorite Banks novel, using Banks's preferred twisty structure to perfect effect, with lots of SFnal neatness and a powerful emotional story. It wasn't published in the United States until a bit later, as I recall, which probably accounts for it not getting any notice.

As to the Campbell, yes, a dispiriting group of nominees. Julia Ecklar has been mostly an *Analog* writer, and she's done some nice work, but in reality, she's had a rather insubstantial career. Perhaps Nancy Collins is indeed the right choice based on her career to that date, or even since, but I'll show my prejudices and say that I wouldn't have been happy to have a pure horror writer win.

Tom Holt's actual first novel appeared in 1985—it was a continuation of E. F. Benson's Lucia series, and as such not genre. So if he was still eligible (which I believe he was) he would have been eligible in 1988 and 1989, after the publication of *Expecting Someone Taller* in 1987.

However, he did publish a major, major novel in 1989–1990—in my opinion, his best work. This is *The Walled Orchard*. It was originally published in two parts: *Goat Song* in 1989, *The Walled Orchard* in 1990. (It has since been reissued in one volume.) If you consider it fantasy (and it's not really—it's historical fiction with a tinge of fantasy because the characters really believe in things we consider fantastical now), and if you consider the two novels as one, I retract my vote for *Use of Weapons* and put forward *The Walled Orchard* as by far the best novel of 1990. (That said, I don't consider it fantasy. But I do most strongly recommend you read *The Walled Orchard!*)

There is, though, one very intriguing potential Campbell nominee: Ian R. MacLeod. His first story appeared in *Interzone* in 1989, and it didn't make much of a splash: "Through." But four major stories appeared in 1990, in *Interzone* and *Weird Tales:* "Green," "1/72 Scale," "Well-Loved," and "Past Magic."

The curious thing is, arguably none of these stories made him Campbell-eligible, due to the technicalities of the Campbell rules, by which *Interzone* and *Weird Tales* were deemed not pro publications. By this argument, he was Campbell-eligible in 1992 and 1993, based on the appearance of "1/72 Scale" in *Best New Horror* in 1991 (and in the Nebula anthology in 1992) and "The Giving Mouth" (another major story) in *Asimov's* in 1991.

Still, he'd have been a great nominee, and clearly a better choice for a winner than anyone on the actual short list.

6.RICH HORTON

In novella, three stories were pretty much neck and neck for me: Haldeman's *The Hemingway Hoax,* which is just wonderful in its novella form; KSR's *A Short, Sharp Shock;* and also a very good Greg Bear story, in his *Queen of Angels* future: *Heads,* which probably didn't get nominated, because in 1990 it appeared only as an *Interzone* serial and a slim UK book. (It was published in book form in the United States in 1991.)

A couple more worthy novellas, besides the very good set of nominees: *Mammy Morgan Played the Organ; her Daddy Beat the Drum,* by Michael F. Flynn; and *Elegy for Angels and Dogs,* by Walter Jon Williams (channeling Zelazny).

In novelette, there are as usual a ton of worthy stories. Among the nominees, my vote would probably have gone to Ted Chiang's "Tower of Babylon," which did win the Nebula. But I would also strongly recommend Dafydd ab Hugh's "The Coon Rolled Down and Ruptured His Larinks, a Squeezed Novel by Mr. Skunk," which is exceptional, a strange postapocalyptic thing about intelligent mutated animals. Ab Hugh never did anything else remotely as good; that's quite a story.

But probably my favorite two novelettes of 1990 appeared in the same issue of *Asimov's,* the March issue. These are "Simulation Six," by Steven Gould; and "Buddha Nostril Bird," by John Kessel. Either would have been a worthy winner.

Other strong novelettes:

"Green" and "1/72 Scale," by Ian R. MacLeod
"Four Kings and an Ace" and "The Spiral Dance," by R. Garcia y Robertson
"Fin de Cyclé," by Howard Waldrop
"Final Tomte," by Judith Moffett
"Sea Change," by Alan Brennert
"The Death Artist," by Alexander Jablokov
"The Caress," by Greg Egan

"The Shores of Bohemia," by Bruce Sterling (which I think would have made the fifth of my ideal short list, along with the ab Hugh, Chiang, Kessel, and Gould stories)

Also, Ursula Le Guin returned to her Hainish universe with "The Shobies' Story," which got a lot of praise but which I don't like all that much. Later "new" Hainish stories were much better, though.

In short story, I'm a big fan of Bisson's "Bears Discover Fire," and I consider it a very worthy winnner. The Reed and Willis stories are, as you say, quite fine. W. R. Thompson did some pretty good stuff for *Analog* in that period as well, and I think "VRM-547" was solid stuff, though I confess I don't remember it well.

But there were also four major Egan short stories: "Axiomatic," "The Extra," "The Moral Virologist," and "Learning to Be Me," any one of which surely would have graced the short list.

17.Gardner Dozois

Sadly, "the answers are not as satisfying as the questions" is something that applies to many books, especially multivolume series.

In novella, my vote goes to *The Hemingway Hoax* (which, yes, I liked better than the novel version, which didn't really add anything essential). Second place probably goes to *Elegy for Angels and Dogs*, which I believe still may hold the title for longest single novella ever published in *Asimov's*. In addition to those novellas already mentioned by Rich, there was *Mr. Boy*, by James Patrick Kelly; *The Cairene Purse*, by Michael Moorcock; *Not Fade Away*, by R. Garcia y Robertson; and *The First Since Ancient Persia*, by John Brunner.

In novelette, my vote probably would have gone to Egan's "The Caress," which we discussed last week, although Jablokov's "The Death Artist" was strong too. "The Coon Rolled Down" seemed at the time to indicate that ab Hugh was going to have a much more significant career than he actually subsequently had. Ian MacLeod's "Green," which, by the way, appeared in the mid-December 1990 *Asimov's*, not in *Interzone*, was a significant step toward the type of fantasy that MacLeod would later develop; he also had a novelette, "Marnie," in the May 1991 *Asimov's*. Ian McDonald's "Toward Kilimanjaro" is also strong. And yes, agree that "The Shobies' Story" would be easily out-classed by subsequent new Hainish stories. The rest of the stories Rich lists are worth mentioning too.

In short story, "Bears Discover Fire" is really the only one still read and discussed (even argued about, since some love it and some loath it), so it's the most historically significant in retrospect. My vote might have gone to Egan's "Learning to Be Me," a very important story in shaping the SF of the nineties that was just taking form. A now-forgotten fantasy story by Keith Roberts, "Mrs. Byres and the Dragon," is also worth reading.

I'm proud to point out that the winning stories in all three short fic-tion categories came from *Asimov's*—a rare sweep for one market.

27. RICH HORTON
I should certainly have mentioned Kelly's *Mr. Boy* as one of the best novellas of the year. . . .

56. RICH HORTON
Oh—and yes, of course, the windmill scheme in *Red Mars* is dumb, dumb, dumb. But it's not that critical to the novel.

59. JAMES DAVIS NICOLL
Except to undermine any faith the reader might have that the author ac-tually gets the stuff he's writing about so authoritatively. It's like reading a book about WWII, where the author goes on about civilian massacres at Iwo Jima; you know immediately they didn't do their homework.

60. WOMZILLA
James @59—No, it just means you know they didn't do *all* their home-work.

64. JAMES DAVIS NICOLL
This is basic thermo! VERY BASIC THERMO! NO GROUP OF HIGHLY EDU-CATED PEOPLE SHOULD HAVE MADE THAT MISTAKE. INCOHERENT LOUD RANTING WITH FACIAL AND HAND GESTURES!
1: Okay, possibly Thomas Gold might.

65.WOMZILLA

Not everyone knows basic thermo, James. Nor is everyone immune to making mistakes. No author knows everything.* And no author knows as much about everything as his entire potential audience does.[†]

---

*Well, Gene Wolfe might.
[†]Not even Gene Wolfe.*

   *Now you've got me doing it.

1992

Best Novel

Winner: *Barrayar*, by Lois McMaster Bujold

Nominees:
All the Weyrs of Pern, by Anne McCaffrey
The Summer Queen, by Joan D. Vinge
Bone Dance, by Emma Bull
Stations of the Tide, by Michael Swanwick
Xenocide, by Orson Scott Card

The 1992 Hugo Awards were presented at Magicon in Orlando, Florida.

The Best Novel award went to Lois McMaster Bujold's *Barrayar*. *Barrayar* is about motherhood and reproduction as mediated by technology, society, war, and the tensions between the expectations of a galactic society and a backwater planet. It's very definitely part of the Vorkosigan saga, and a direct sequel to the first novel, *Shards of Honor*, but it also stands alone, which seems to be a requirement for a Hugo winner in a series. I think it's an excellent book and well-deserving winner. It won the Locus SF award. It's in print and in the library.

There are five other nominees, and I've read three of them. Let's start with the ones I haven't read.

Anne McCaffrey's *All the Weyrs of Pern* is book eleven of the Pern series, and I stopped reading somewhere around book seven or so because it didn't seem to be doing anything new. I am therefore not really qualified to say whether this is a worthy nominee, but I'm inclined to think not so much. It's in print, but it's not in the library.

I haven't read Joan Vinge's *The Summer Queen* for the same reason—I didn't like the previous volume, 1980's Hugo winner *The Snow Queen*. Again, I can't say if it's a good nominee, but as this is a case of my not being able to read it, in this case, it might well be. It's also in print, but it's not in the library.

Emma Bull's *Bone Dance* is a postapocalyptic fantasy about gender. It's excellent, thought provoking, and unusual, exactly the sort of book that should be on this list. It's in print but not in the library—and it never had a UK edition.

Michael Swanwick's *Stations of the Tide* is another wonderful book that's hard to describe succinctly. I think "surreal hard SF" is about as close as I can get—it's kind of cyberpunk and kind of space opera, and it's really all about the people. It begins "The bureaucrat fell from the sky." I've never written about it, because it's one of those books that makes me incoherent. It won the Nebula, and very well deserved. It's in print, but it's not in the library.

Orson Scott Card's *Xenocide* is one of my least favorite books. It's the third in the Ender series, and if there's one thing I really hate, it's a sequel that tramples all over the previous books. It's future planetary SF with AI and aliens and idiotic suspension-of-disbelief-destroying invention of FTL. I grind my teeth in its general direction. I'm sorry it was nominated for a Hugo and glad it didn't win. It's in print and in the library.

So, two men and four women, all American (one living in Ireland). Three previous winners: Card, Bujold, and Vinge. Swanwick had short-form nominations only, and Bull is a complete newcomer. We have four science fiction novels set on other planets, very different from each other, and one postapocalyptic fantasy.

What else might they have chosen?

Eligible Nebula nominees were Gibson and Sterling's *The Difference Engine*, Pat Cadigan's *Synners*, and John Barnes's *Orbital Resonance*, any of which would have been excellent Hugo nominees.

The World Fantasy Award was won by *Boy's Life*, by Robert R.

McCammon. Other nominees not previously mentioned were *Hunting the Ghost Dancer*, A. A. Attanasio; *The Little Country*, Charles de Lint; *Outside the Dog Museum*, Jonathan Carroll; and *The Paper Grail*, James P. Blaylock.

The John W. Campbell Memorial Award went to Bradley Denton's very odd *Buddy Holly Is Alive and Well on Ganymede*. Other nominees not already mentioned: *The Silicon Man*, Charles Platt; and *A Woman of the Iron People*, by Eleanor Arnason. I like the Arnason a great deal—I like everything she has written. As well as this Campbell nod, it won the Mythopoeic Award and the Tiptree. I think it was one of the most significant and talked-about books of the year, and it should have been a Hugo nominee.

The Philip K. Dick Award was given to Ian McDonald's brilliant metafantasy *King of Morning, Queen of Day*, which I wouldn't exactly call science fiction, but never mind. Other non-overlapping nominees: *A Bridge of Years*, Robert Charles Wilson; *The Cipher*, Kathe Koja; *Mojo and the Pickle Jar*, Douglas Bell.

The James Tiptree, Jr. Literary Award for genre fiction that does interesting things with gender began this year. It's a juried award, with a changing jury. The award is different every year, but includes a thousand-dollar check and a trip to WisCon. The first winners were Gwyneth Jones's *White Queen* and Arnason's *A Woman of the Iron People*. Books not previously mentioned and on the short list were: *The Architecture of Desire*, Mary Gentle; *He, She and It* (aka *Body of Glass*), Marge Piercy; *Moonwise*, Greer Ilene Gilman; *Sarah Canary*, Karen Joy Fowler.

Locus SF nominees not previously mentioned were: *Heavy Time*, C. J. Cherryh; *The Dark Beyond the Stars*, Frank M. Robinson; *Brain Child*, George Turner; *The Garden of Rama*, Arthur C. Clarke and Gentry Lee; *Ecce and Old Earth*, Jack Vance; *Russian Spring*, Norman Spinrad; *The Trinity Paradox*, Kevin J. Anderson and Doug Beason; *Death Qualified: A Mystery of Chaos*, Kate Wilhelm; *The Illegal Rebirth of Billy the Kid*, Rebecca Ore; *The Ragged World*, Judith Moffett; *Carve the Sky*, Alexander Jablokov; *Eternal Light*, Paul J. McAuley.

Some nice things, but nothing that strikes me as better than the nominees we have.

The Locus fantasy award went to Sheri Tepper's *Beauty*, a book I disliked when I first read it almost as much as *Xenocide*, but which has weathered in the memory much better. It's an odd mix of fantasy and SF.

Other nominees not previously mentioned: *Eight Skilled Gentlemen*, Barry Hughart; *The Rainbow Abyss*, Barbara Hambly; *The Hereafter Gang*, Neal Barrett Jr.; *Witches Abroad*, Terry Pratchett; *Riverrun*, S. P. Somtow; *Outside the Dog Museum*, Jonathan Carroll; *King of the Dead*, R. A. MacAvoy; *Nothing Sacred*, Elizabeth Ann Scarborough; *The Sorceress and the Cygnet*, Patricia A. McKillip; *The Revenge of the Rose*, Michael Moorcock; *Cloven Hooves*, Megan Lindholm; *The Magic Spectacles*, James P. Blaylock; *The End-of-Everything Man*, Tom De Haven; *Flying Dutch*, Tom Holt; *Elsewhere*, Will Shetterly; *The White Mists of Power*, Kristine Kathryn Rusch; *The Architecture of Desire*, Mary Gentle; *Illusion*, Paula Volsky.

The only Mythopoeic nominee not previously mentioned was Pamela Dean's *Tam Lin*, one of my favorite books.

The Prometheus Award went to Niven, Pournelle, and Flynn's *Fallen Angels*.

So, was there anything they all missed?

There was Robert Reed's very strange *Down the Bright Way*, George Alec Effinger's *The Exile Kiss*, and Steven Brust's *The Phoenix Guards*.

So looking at the year as a whole, the nominees are pretty good, but I think the absence of *A Woman of the Iron People* is regrettable. I'd also have liked to see *Orbital Resonance* and *Synners* on the ballot in place of the McCaffrey and the Card. But I do think *Barrayar* is the kind of book that should be honored by the Hugo, and the presence of *Stations of the Tide* and *Bone Dance* on the ballot is heartening. And looking at these nominees as a whole, they really do give a pretty good picture of where the field was. So a pretty good set of choices overall.

Other Categories

Best Novella

Winner: *Beggars in Spain*, by Nancy Kress (*Asimov's*, April 1991; Axolotl)

Nominees:
And Wild for to Hold, by Nancy Kress (*Asimov's*, July 1991; *What Might Have Been? Vol. 3: Alternate Wars*)
The Gallery of His Dreams, by Kristine Kathryn Rusch (Pulphouse/ Axolotl; *Asimov's*, September 1991)
Griffin's Egg, by Michael Swanwick (Legend; St. Martin's)
Jack, Connie Willis (*Asimov's*, October 1991)

If anybody had asked me before I started this series, I'd have had no idea that the novella was the Hugo category that I consistently remembered best and which had the best nominees, but year after year, there it is. Nancy Kress was having a good year, and that's a tremendous winner. But the Swanwick and the Willis are also classics. Somebody should do a collection of all the novella nominees ever, or ebooks of all of them or something. They'd make a great book club. (Novella club?)

Best Novelette

Winner: "Gold," by Isaac Asimov (*Analog*, September 1991)

Nominees:
"Dispatches from the Revolution," by Pat Cadigan (*Asimov's*, July 1991)
"Fin de Cyclé," by Howard Waldrop (*Night of the Cooters: More Neat Stories 1990; Asimov's*, mid-December 1991)
"Miracle," by Connie Willis (*Asimov's*, December 1991)
"Understand," by Ted Chiang (*Asimov's*, August 1991)

Time is a strange thing. It's so odd to see "Understand" and "Gold" on the same ballot when they feel as if they come from different eras.

BEST SHORT STORY

Winner: "A Walk in the Sun," by Geoffrey A. Landis (*Asimov's*, October 1991)

Nominees:

"Buffalo," by John Kessel (*Fires of the Past: Thirteen Contemporary Fantasies About Hometowns*, *F&SF*, January 1991)

"Dog's Life," by Martha Soukup (*Amazing Stories*, March 1991)

"In the Late Cretaceous," by Connie Willis (*Asimov's*, mid-December 1991)

"One Perfect Morning, with Jackals," by Mike Resnick (*Asimov's*, March 1991)

"Press Ann," by Terry Bisson (*Asimov's*, August 1991)

"Winter Solstice," by Mike Resnick (*F&SF*, October/November 1991)

Pretty good lineup here too. A good year for short fiction.

BEST NONFICTION BOOK

Winner: *The World of Charles Addams*, by Charles Addams

Nominees:

The Bakery Men Don't See Cookbook, edited by Diane Martin and Jeanne Gomoll

Clive Barker's Shadows in Eden, edited by Stephen Jones

The Science Fantasy Publishers: A Critical and Bibliographic History: Third Edition, by Jack L. Chalker and Mark Owings

Science-Fiction: The Early Years, by Everett F. Bleiler

Best Dramatic Presentation

Winner: *Terminator 2: Judgment Day*

Nominees:
The Addams Family
Beauty and the Beast (Disney movie)
The Rocketeer
Star Trek VI: The Undiscovered Country

Best Professional Editor

Winner: Gardner Dozois

Nominees:
Ellen Datlow
Edward L. Ferman
Kristine Kathryn Rusch
Stanley Schmidt

Rusch was editing for Pulphouse and Axolotl, which were publishing some great things and getting a lot of attention for a small press.

Best Professional Artist

Winner: Michael Whelan

Nominees:
Thomas Canty
David A. Cherry
Bob Eggleton
Don Maitz

Best Original Artwork

Winner: Michael Whelan, cover of *The Summer Queen* (by Joan D. Vinge)

Nominees:

Don Maitz, cover of *Heavy Time* (by C. J. Cherryh)

Bob Eggleton, cover of *Lunar Descent* (by Allen Steele)

Bob Eggleton, cover of *Asimov's*, January 1991 (illustrating "Stations of the Tide" by Michael Swanwick)

Thomas Canty, cover of *The White Mists of Power* (by Kristine Kathryn Rusch)

A short-lived category, and one completely oriented to US voters—I just realized I've never seen most of those covers, even though I have read the books, because the UK editions had different covers.

Best Semiprozine

Winner: *Locus,* edited by Charles N. Brown

Nominees:

Interzone, edited by David Pringle

The New York Review of Science Fiction, edited by David G. Hartwell, Kathryn Cramer, Robert K. J. Killheffer, and Gordon Van Gelder

Pulphouse, edited by Dean Wesley Smith

Science Fiction Chronicle, edited by Andrew I. Porter

Best Fanzine

Winner: *Mimosa,* edited by Dick and Nicki Lynch

Nominees:

File 770, edited by Mike Glyer

FOSFAX, edited by Timothy Lane and Janice Moore

Lan's Lantern, edited by George "Lan" Laskowski

Trapdoor, edited by Robert Lichtman

Best Fan Writer

Winner: Dave Langford

Nominees:
Avedon Carol
Mike Glyer
Andrew Hooper
Evelyn C. Leeper
Harry Warner Jr.

Best Fan Artist

Winner: Brad W. Foster

Nominees:
Teddy Harvia
Peggy Ranson
Stu Shiffman
Diana Harlan Stein

John W. Campbell Award

Winner: Ted Chiang

Nominees:
Barbara Delaplace
Greer Ilene Gilman
Laura Resnick
Michelle Sagara

Well, this is much better than 1991!

Ted Chiang is a brilliant winner, just the kind of person who ought to win. He had published two astonishing novellas, both nominated for awards, and he has gone on to have a strong career publishing some of the best short stories ever written in the genre—including a nominee for this year's Hugos.*

Greer Gilman's *Moonwise* was a first novel that had made a big impression. She has since won the World Fantasy Award with a short story and the Tiptree with her second novel, *Cloud and Ashes*. Gilman is one of the genre's great stylists, and it's great to see her nominated.†

Michella Sagara had also just published a first novel. She was to go on to have a terrific career writing fantasy as Michelle Sagara, Michelle West (her married name), and Michelle Sagara West. She also reviews for *F&SF*. Great nominee.

Barbara Delaplace had published only short work, and she went on to publish occasional short stories throughout the nineties and in the last decade. I'm not familiar with her work.

Laura Resnick won in 1993, so let's leave her for next year.

I'd say these are a good selection of the best new writers of the year, based on subsequent performance.

COMMENTS ON 1992

5.RICH HORTON

The best novel of the year, in my opinion, was Karen Joy Fowler's *Sarah Canary*. It's genre is ambiguous—I read it with Clute, as SF, but one could read it as historical fiction. Themes include gender, race, class, and the American West. It's exceptional work. I'd have given it all the awards (Tiptree included, much as I like Eleanor Arnason) (though possibly KJF, a founder of the Tiptree Awards, if memory serves, disqualified herself) . . . but . . .

Other novels worth mentioning: Paul Park's *The Cult of Loving*

---

*It won too!

†And since then, she has won a Shirley Jackson Award.

Kindness (the rather different conclusion to his trilogy that began with *Sugar Rain*); and William Sanders's *The Wild Blue and the Gray*.

And from outside the genre, two first-rate books that are arguably SFnal. Richard Powers's *The Gold Bug Variations* probably isn't really SF, but it is fiction about science, and it's very, very good. And Martin Amis's *Time's Arrow* is a holocaust novel, but with a fantastical premise (an entity that perceives that it is living backwards in the consciousness of a German doctor guilty of crimes at Auschwitz).

7.RICH HORTON

The Mill, by Paul Di Filippo—the first story I really noticed by him, and excellent, excellent work.

Candle, by Tony Daniel.

Canso de Fis de Jovent, the first segment of John Barnes's novel *A Million Open Doors,* published separately in *Analog*—it stands alone very well, and it's wonderful.

And finally, the good parts of *Xenocide,* published separately in *Analog: Gloriously Bright.* Had Card published this separately (with the ending of the novel left off this portion for spoiler avoidance), and had he replaced the odious AI Jane with another character (easily done if you don't need the story to link with the Ender stuff), this would have been a classic. (Though people would have complained, with some justice, that the portrait of the central character as from a Chinese colony trades somewhat on stereotypes about Asians.)

In novelette, Asimov's win is clearly a sentimental award. Chiang probably should have won from this list, though I don't like "Understand" as much as a lot of Chiang.

My preferred alternative is "The Perfect Stranger," a lovely story from Ian R. MacLeod.

Other strong novelettes:

"Mairzy Doats," by Paul Di Filippo
"Guide Dog," by Mike Conner
"The Happy Man," by Jonathan Lethem
"Black Glass," by Karen Joy Fowler
"Snow on Sugar Mountain," by Elizabeth Hand

"What Continues, What Fails . . . ," by David Brin

In short story, again an excellent list. A good winner. "Buffalo" is brilliant work. "In the Late Cretaceous" is excellent. Also good:

"Division by Zero," by Chiang
"They're Made Out of Meat," by Terry Bisson
"Fidelity" and "The Infinite Assassin," by Greg Egan
"The Swordsman Whose Name Was Not Death," by Ellen Kushner

22. RICH HORTON

Oh, and as to the Campbell. I have little to say except that Chiang is an obviously good choice as the winner, and Gilman and Sagara have both (in very different ways) lived up to the promise of their nominations. Resnick's work has mostly been in other genres, which is nothing to be ashamed of—she's had a solid career too. I've never heard of Delaplace. Likely she did some nice work, but still, how she could have made the ballot ahead of Ian MacLeod (eligible for a second year) is hard to understand.

56. GARDNER DOZOIS

In novella, *Beggars in Spain* is probably the best remembered of the lot, although *Griffin's Egg* is also excellent, and the choice between them is a hard one. The other Kress is also first-rate. Greg Benford's *Matter's End* is also interesting. Phil Jennings's *Blossoms* is a peculiar story, but one with some intriguing ideas in it.

There were also a number of strong novelettes this year. I probably would have gone for "Understand" (one of the few stories about supergeniuses where the supergenius is actually CONVINCING as one) over "Gold," but Ian R. MacLeod's "Marnie," Kim Stanley Robinson's "A History of the Twentieth Century, with Illustrations," Alexander Jablokov's "Living Will," and Walter Jon Williams's "Prayers on the Wind" are also very strong, as are "Dispatches from the Revolution," Waldrop's "Fin de Cyclé," and Brian Aldiss's "FOAM." Lethem's "The Happy Man" is one of the most harrowing stories ever published in *Asimov's*. "Division by Zero" is at least as strong as "Understand."

The Landis is a pretty strong winner for short story, but I think I might have voted for Paul McAuley's sly little story "Gene Wars." Greg Egan's "The Moat" and "Fidelity," as well as his "Blood Sisters."

Of historical interest is Chris Beckett's first story, "La Macchina."

Chiang was certainly a worthy winner, and has proved himself so time and again since, but if he'd been on the final ballot, I'd have given the Campbell to Ian R. MacLeod.

1993

Best Novel

Winner: (tie)
A Fire Upon the Deep, by Vernor Vinge
Doomsday Book, by Connie Willis

Nominees:
China Mountain Zhang, by Maureen F. McHugh
Red Mars, by Kim Stanley Robinson
Steel Beach, by John Varley

The 1993 Hugo Awards were given in ConFrancisco in San Francisco.

The novel award was a tie, Vernor Vinge's *A Fire Upon the Deep,* and Connie Willis's *Doomsday Book. A Fire Upon the Deep* is galactic science fiction, a book sizzling with ideas and alien names and characters and adventures. *Doomsday Book* is about time travel and disease—a quieter book altogether, and one focused on character and history. I really like both of them.

These are two genuinely great books, and they have remained poised neck and neck through time in their very different excellences. I'm sure there are people who don't like one or the other of them, and even people who don't like either of them, but I feel that the two of them between them display the best the genre has to offer in its depth and diversity. People are always saying to me, "What one book should I read?" and I am always growling ungraciously that no one book can do it; you need a cross section. Two isn't enough either. But if you read both *A Fire Upon the Deep* and *Doomsday Book* and consider that science fiction readers gave them both our highest accolade in the same year, you might get the idea.

They're both in print. The Vinge is in the library in English only, and the Willis, which also won the Nebula and the Locus, is in the library in French and English.

And it was a brilliant year even apart from them.

There were three other nominees, and I've read all of them.

Maureen McHugh's *China Mountain Zhang* was a first novel. It's a mosaic novel set in a Chinese-dominated near-future communist USA. It's exactly the kind of thing I'm delighted to see nominated. I picked it up because of the nomination. I wasn't voting that year, but I saw the nominees in Locus and wondered about this and picked it up to see, liked the beginning, and bought it. And it's wonderful. It won the Tiptree Award. It's in print, and it's in the library in English.

Kim Stanley Robinson's *Red Mars* is a huge book about people who live for a very long time terraforming Mars. I didn't like it, but I recently realized that the reason I didn't like it was because I liked *Icehenge* so much that I preferred that vision and couldn't really focus on this story. I need to read it again and be fair to it. But even not liking it, it's a good nominee—it's an ambitious SF book that's using up-to-date science and telling a story that couldn't be told any other way. It's in print and in the library in French and English.

John Varley's *Steel Beach* is perhaps the weakest of the nominees. It's set in a retconned version of his Eight Worlds stories, and it's about a journalist on the moon. It has an excellent and much-quoted first line. I wanted to like it, but I found it unsatisfying and overlong. It's not in print, and it's in the library in French only.

So, three men and two women, all Americans. Vinge and Varley had been nominated before, but this was Vinge's first win. Willis had won at short form, and Robinson had multiple short-form nominations, but this was the first time for either of them on the novel slate. McHugh was a complete newcomer. We have one far-future space opera, one time travel, one near-future Earth, two middle-distance solar systems. What else might they have picked?

Non-overlapping Nebula nominees were Jane Yolen's chilling *Briar Rose,* John Barnes's masterpiece *A Million Open Doors,* and Karen Joy

Fowler's *Sarah Canary*. Any of these would have been a good Hugo addition, and I really think the Barnes should have made it.

The World Fantasy Award was given to Tim Powers for *Last Call*. Other nominees not previously mentioned were *Anno Dracula*, Kim Newman; *Photographing Fairies*, Steve Szilagyi; *Was*, Geoff Ryman.

The John W. Campbell Memorial Award was awarded to Charles Sheffield's *Brother to Dragons*. Second place was Sheri Tepper's *Sideshow*, with Vinge third.

The Philip K. Dick Award was given to *Through the Heart*, Richard Grant; with a special citation for *In the Mothers' Land*, Elisabeth Vonarburg. Other nominees were *Æstival Tide*, Elizabeth Hand; *Iron Tears*, R. A. Lafferty; and *Take Back Plenty*, Colin Greenland. This is a consistently interesting award that often turns up things where nobody else is looking.

Tiptree nominees not mentioned so far were *Correspondence*, Sue Thomas; *Lost Futures*, Lisa Tuttle; *Time, Like an Ever-Rolling Stream*, Judith Moffett; *Venus Rising*, Carol Emshwiller.

Other Locus nominees not mentioned yet were: *The Hollow Man*, Dan Simmons; *Anvil of Stars*, Greg Bear; *Chanur's Legacy*, C. J. Cherryh; *Mars*, Ben Bova; *The Memory of Earth*, Orson Scott Card; *Snow Crash*, Neal Stephenson; *Worlds Enough and Time*, Joe Haldeman; *Crystal Line*, Anne McCaffrey; *Count Geiger's Blues*, Michael Bishop; *Hellburner*, C. J. Cherryh; *Aristoi*, Walter Jon Williams; *Labyrinth of Night*, Allen Steele; *Mining the Oort*, Frederik Pohl; *Lord Kelvin's Machine*, James P. Blaylock; *Hearts, Hands and Voices* (*The Broken Land*), Ian McDonald; *Jaran*, Kate Elliott; *Glass Houses*, Laura J. Mixon; *A Deeper Sea*, Alexander Jablokov; *Alien Earth*, Megan Lindholm.

And here we see the difference between "books I really like" and "books I think are good." I adore *Jaran* and *Hellburner*, and I don't really like *Snow Crash*, but I actually gasped when I saw that it was here and hadn't been nominated for a Hugo or a Nebula, because like it or not, I do think it was one of the most significant books of the year.

The Locus fantasy award was won by *Last Call*. Other nominees not previously mentioned were *The Spirit Ring*, Lois McMaster Bujold; *A Song for Arbonne*, Guy Gavriel Kay; *Winds of Change*, Mercedes Lackey; *The Magicians of Night* (UK title *Magicians of the Night*), Barbara

Hambly; *The Shadow Rising*, Robert Jordan; *Domes of Fire*, David Eddings; *Small Gods*, Terry Pratchett; *Last Refuge*, Elizabeth Ann Scarborough; *The Cutting Edge*, Dave Duncan; *A Sudden Wild Magic*, Diana Wynne Jones; *The Gypsy*, Steven Brust and Megan Lindholm; *Forest of the Night*, S. P. Somtow; *Flying in Place*, Susan Palwick.

The Mythopoeic Award was won by *Briar Rose*. Nominees not yet mentioned were Susan Shwartz's *Grail of Hearts* and James Blaylock's *The Paper Grail*.

So with all these awards, was there anything that was overlooked? Nicola Griffith's *Ammonite;* Greg Egan's *Quarantine;* Terry Pratchett's *Only You Can Save Mankind;* Harry Turtledove's *Guns of the South;* and Debra Doyle and James Macdonald's *The Price of the Stars*.

This is a year where I remember thinking at the time how exciting the nominees were, and yet now I can't understand how *Snow Crash* isn't on the ballot. I'm sure I read *Snow Crash* because everybody was talking about it. But maybe it was one of those books where word of mouth took time to build, because I read *Snow Crash* because everybody was talking about it in 1994. I'm also sorry *A Million Open Doors* didn't make it, not just because it's a terrific book but also because I'd then have discovered Barnes with a good book instead of *Mother of Storms*. I think it's also possible to argue that *Briar Rose* and *Last Call* could well have made the list. So on the whole, I am slightly less happy with this list than I was in 1993, but I still think it's pretty good—a good view of where the field was, with some omissions. Great winners. And *China Mountain Zhang*.

OTHER CATEGORIES

BEST NOVELLA

Winner: *Barnacle Bill the Spacer,* by Lucius Shepard (*Asimov's,* July 1992)

Nominees:
Protection, by Maureen F. McHugh (*Asimov's,* April 1992)

Stopping at Slowyear, by Frederik Pohl (Pulphouse/Axolotl; Bantam Spectra)

The Territory, by Bradley Denton (*F&SF,* July 1992)

Uh-Oh City, by Jonathan Carroll (*F&SF,* June 1992)

I'd have voted for the McHugh, which still gives me chills thinking about it. But the Shepard is also very good.

Best Novelette

Winner: "The Nutcracker Coup," by Janet Kagan (*Asimov's,* December 1992)

Nominees:

"Danny Goes to Mars," by Pamela Sargent (*Asimov's,* October 1992)

"In the Stone House," by Barry N. Malzberg (*Alternate Kennedys*)

"Suppose They Gave a Peace . . . ," by Susan Shwartz (*Alternate Presidents*)

"True Faces," by Pat Cadigan (*F&SF,* April 1992)

Best Short Story

Winner: "Even the Queen," by Connie Willis (*Asimov's,* April 1992)

Nominees:

"The Arbitrary Placement of Walls," by Martha Soukup (*Asimov's,* April 1992)

"The Lotus and the Spear," by Mike Resnick (*Asimov's,* August 1992)

"The Mountain to Mohammed," by Nancy Kress (*Asimov's,* April 1992)

"The Winterberry," by Nicholas A. DiChario (*Alternate Kennedys*)

I've never been all that excited by "Even the Queen."

Best Nonfiction Book

Winner: *A Wealth of Fable: An Informal History of Science Fiction Fandom in the 1950s*, by Harry Warner Jr.

Nominees:
The Costumemaker's Art, edited by Thom Boswell
Enterprising Women: Television Fandom and the Creation of Popular Myth, by Camille Bacon-Smith
Let's Hear It for the Deaf Man, by Dave Langford
Monad: Essays on Science Fiction 2, edited by Damon Knight
Virgil Finlay's Women of the Ages, by Virgil Finlay

Best Dramatic Presentation

Winner: *Star Trek: The Next Generation:* "The Inner Light"

Nominees:
Aladdin
Alien 3
Batman Returns
Bram Stoker's Dracula

Best Professional Editor

Winner: Gardner Dozois

Nominees:
Ellen Datlow
Beth Meacham
Kristine Kathryn Rusch
Stanley Schmidt

Best Professional Artist

Winner: Don Maitz

Nominees:
Thomas Canty
David A. Cherry
Bob Eggleton
James Gurney

BEST ORIGINAL ARTWORK

Winner: *Dinotopia*, James Gurney (Turner)

Nominees:
Ron Walotsky, cover of *F&SF*, October/November 1992
Michael Whelan, cover of *Asimov's*, November 1992
Jim Burns, cover of *Aristoi* (by Walter Jon Williams; Tor)
Michael Whelan, cover of *Illusion* (by Paula Volsky; Bantam Spectra)

BEST SEMIPROZINE

Winner: *Science Fiction Chronicle*, edited by Andrew I. Porter

Nominees:
Interzone, edited by David Pringle
Locus, edited by Charles N. Brown
The New York Review of Science Fiction, edited by David G. Hartwell, Donald G. Keller, Robert K. J. Killheffer, and Gordon Van Gelder
Pulphouse, edited by Dean Wesley Smith

Not *Locus*. Odd.

BEST FANZINE

Winner: *Mimosa*, edited by Dick and Nicki Lynch

Nominees:
File 770, edited by Mike Glyer
FOSFAX, edited by Timothy Lane and Janice Moore

Lan's Lantern, edited by George "Lan" Laskowski
STET, edited by Leah Zeldes Smith and Dick Smith

BEST FAN WRITER

Winner: Dave Langford

Nominees:
Mike Glyer
Andy Hooper
Evelyn C. Leeper
Harry Warner Jr.

BEST FAN ARTIST

Winner: Peggy Ranson

Nominees:
Teddy Harvia
Merle Insinga
Linda Michaels
Stu Shiffman
Diana Harlan Stein

JOHN W. CAMPBELL AWARD

Winner: Laura Resnick

Nominees:
Barbara Delaplace
Nicholas A. DiChario
Holly Lisle
Carrie Richerson
Michelle Sagara

Laura Resnick was nominated on the basis of some excellent short work. She has since gone on to write a large number of well-received fantasy and paranormal romance novels, with more books due out this year.

Barbara Delaplace and Michelle Sagara were discussed in their first year of eligibility.

Nicholas DiChario had also published short work only at the time of his nomination. He has gone on to have a quiet career publishing SF novels and short stories; he has been a finalist for the Campbell Memorial Award twice.

Holly Lisle's first novel, *Fire in the Mist*, had just come out at the time of her nomination. She has gone on to have a successful career publishing fantasy and paranormal romance novels, alone and with co-authors ranging from Marion Zimmer Bradley to S. M. Stirling.

Carrie Richerson had published some well-received short stories, and has gone on publishing short work, but has not had a very visible career.

Other people who might have been eligible for the Campbell this year include Susan Palwick, Stephen Gould, Maureen McHugh, Poppy Z. Brite, and Maya Kaathryn Bohnhoff.

COMMENTS ON 1993

4.RICH HORTON

In first novel, besides *China Mountain Zhang*, there was Steven Gould's *Jumper*, which is really good (much better than the movie!). And not precisely a first novel, but the first novel most people saw by him, and the first to be characteristic of him: Greg Egan's *Quarantine*. And Susan Palwick's *Flying in Place* is heartbreaking—I was in tears for the last fifty pages or so of the book, which I read in a rush at an unplanned long lunch at my desk at work.

I also really loved Michael Bishop's superhero novel *Count Geiger's Blues*, which I don't think has got as much notice as it should have.

Two more very good novels came from true SF legends, and neither got the attention it deserved either. One is Algis Budrys's *Hard Landing*, which is very short (maybe 45K?), and which was published in one issue of *F&SF*. It is really first-rate, and very underrated (as with almost all of Budrys). And Damon Knight's quite strange *Why Do Birds* was not much noticed in the field, but it too is excellent.

Other novels worth a look:

Jonathan Carroll's *After Silence*
Donald Westlake's *Humans*
James P. Blaylock's *Lord Kelvin's Machine*

Really a wonderful year in novel.

9.RICH HORTON

So, oddly perhaps for me, the short fiction was less compelling.

I think Shepard's *Barnacle Bill the Spacer* is okay, but not close to his best work, and surely not the best work on the ballot, which is probably *Protection*, though I also really like *Uh-Oh City*.

No other novellas leap out at me as criminally neglected, but there are some good ones:

Gypsy Trade and *The Virgin and the Dinosaur*, by R. Garcia y Robertson
Grownups, by Ian R. MacLeod (probably should have made the ballot,
    wouldn't have been a bad winner)
Naming the Flowers, by Kate Wilhelm
The Final Folly of Captain Dancy, by Lawrence Watt-Evans
And the two halves of A. S. Byatt's *Angels and Insects: Morpho Eugenia*
    and *The Conjugal Angel*

In novelette, "The Nutcracker Coup" is really fun. Sargent's story seems very, very dated, and indeed seemed so to me within about a year—Dan Quayle was really not important enough to expend all that much energy on, seems to me. The other novelettes are fine work—does any of them much stick with me? Not really.

Maybe Greg Egan's "Dust" would have been a better choice? Or Jonathan Lethem's "Vanilla Dunk"? Actually, I really liked Thomas Disch's rather savage (as usual for him) "The Abduction of Bunny

Steiner, or a Shameless Lie." I also like R. Garcia y Robertson's "Breakfast Cereal Killers" and Alex Jeffers's novel excerpt "From The Bridge." (I don't think *The Bridge* has ever been published. Maybe it was planned as "just an excerpt" from the beginning?)

In short story, I do like "Even the Queen," though it's a "cause célèbre" for Willis-haters. "The Arbitrary Placement of Walls" is excellent—Soukup is a good writer, shame she hasn't written much lately (that I've noticed, anyway!). A short story I really liked that year that didn't get much notice was "Steelcollar Worker," by Vonda N. McIntyre.

Also worth notice:

"The Last Robot," by Adam-Troy Castro
"Are You for 86?," by Bruce Sterling
"The Lost Sepulcher of Huascar Capec," by Paul Park
"The Cool Equations," by Deborah Wessell (one of the better reex-
    aminations of the notorious Tom Godwin classic)
"Yellow Rome," by Avram Davidson

16.CARBONEL

It's probably worth mentioning that this was the first year that a concerted effort was made to get as many as possible of the nominees together in one place. ClariNet (Brad Templeton in a corporate disguise, IIRC) published the Hugo and Nebula Anthology CD for $27 or so, which was a great bargain at the time. (These days, the Hugo Voters' Packet is even better, but I see this as a precursor.)

It was the first time I really felt like an informed voter, because I'd read everything on the fiction list, and taken a good whack at the other categories.

21.GARDNER DOZOIS

In novella, McHugh's *Protection* is a very strong story, one of her best, although it's been curiously overlooked, in spite of the Hugo nomination. (It's also one of the few stories that ever drew a six-page revision request from me, and the exchange of a half dozen subsequent letters between us, back when letters were actually written on paper and sent through the mail.) MacLeod's *Grownups* is also very strong, and very strange. I think either of those might have the edge on *Barnacle Bill,* actually, although *Barnacle Bill* is entertaining. Also completely overlooked, oddly, is one of Fred Pohl's strongest novellas ever, *Outnumbering the Dead,* which might well have gotten my vote. Wilhelm's *Naming the Flowers* is also good, and the two Robertson stories are great fun. Also of at least historic interest is the last story Isaac Asimov submitted to me while he was still alive, *Cleon the Emperor,* which, to me, demonstrates the failure of the whole idea of "predicting" the future scientifically through social calculations, since in spite of all Seldon's intricate calculations, the Emperor is unexpectedly killed by a disgruntled gardener who's pissed off over some minor offense.

Swanwick's *Griffin's Egg,* discussed last time, became eligible for the Nebula this year with its American reprint, and I think I would have given the award to it if it had been on the ballot. It would have been between it and *Outnumbering the Dead* for me, probably. (Both printed first as novella chapbooks in England.)

In novelette, I lean toward something that didn't even make the ballot, Greg Egan's "Dust," another curiously overlooked story, although I think it contains some of Egan's most profound thinking about the nature of reality. "Vanilla Dunk" is one of the field's best sports stories, written before Jonathan Lethem ascended into the Godhood of mainstream acceptance. Yes, as Rich pointed out, political satire dates fast, and the Sargent was dated within months of it coming out; I thought she was rather kinder in her portrayal of Quayle than he deserved, actually. There was also a powerful alternate history story by Ian R. MacLeod (who was having a very strong year), "Snodgrass," where the change in history is that John Lennon had left the Beatles very early on, before they became famous, and it follows, movingly, what the rest of Lennon's life might have been like. Another good overlooked story is Maureen McHugh's "The Missionary's Child."

When she won the Hugo for "The Nutcracker Coup," Janet went up to the podium and blurted out, "This was supposed to be Cadigan's!" That was very Janet.

I remain fond of "Even the Queen," although it's no longer really SF, since products to keep you from having your period are actually out on the market now. It did provide me with my moment of fannish immortality, when, accepting her Nebula for the story, Connie said at the podium that she didn't know how to describe it to friends, and I shouted out from the audience, "Call it a period piece!" Kress's "The Mountain to Mohammed" is also good, as is a little story by Robert Reed called "Birth Day."

I'm pleased to be able to point out that once again all the short fiction winners were from *Asimov's*.

The Campbell ballot is also weak. In retrospect, it clearly should have been won by Maureen McHugh.

29.JAMES DAVIS NICOLL

Flying in Place, Susan Palwick

Depending on how one sees a particular element of the story, this is either fantasy or purely mainstream. This won the Crawford Award for best first novel. And is highly recommended.

Her second novel, *The Necessary Beggar,* did not come out until 2005. In the interval, there was rueing and lamenting.

31.RICH HORTON

Flying in Place is wonderful, indeed. And the "particular element" of the story is sufficiently ambiguous that I was able to give it to my wife (not SF/fantasy reader) and she loved it too.

McHugh wasn't eligible for the Campbell—indeed, she was last eligible in 1990, as she had a pseudonymous piece in *Twilight Zone* magazine in 1988. And "Baffin Island" and "Kites" both appeared in *Asimov's* in 1989. She would have been a good nominee and worthy winner then, though KKR wasn't a bad winner herself.

45.LAKESIDEY

I remember a time in 2005 when my work required me to spend three months in a remote corner of the world. On the advice of people who'd been through that stint before ("there's nothing to do out there!!"), I took a backpack full of novels along, mostly stuff I'd heard the names of but never found the time to read until then.

And thus it was that in one magical week, I read both Brin's *Startide Rising* and Vinge's *A Fire Upon the Deep.* I knew little about either author (or either book) except that they were well spoken of. I cautiously kept my expectations low. And yet . . . and yet!

The sheer sense of wonder. How does one describe it? There were moments in both books where I had to stop, put down the book, and catch my breath, thinking to myself, this, *this*, is why I starting reading science fiction.

(I was lucky enough to also have *The Uplift War* in that backpack, so the next week was pretty awesome too. ;o) Alas, it was three years before I managed to lay hands on *A Deepness in the Sky*. Worth the wait, though.)

I don't judge whether these books are realistic, or possible, or even probable. I don't know whether they will go down in history as memorable works of literary art. I don't really care; to me, what matters is that those books made me think. And, maybe more important, made me happy.

The Net of a Million Lies: Vernor Vinge's *A Fire Upon the Deep*

It's not that I think *A Fire Upon the Deep* is perfect; it's just that it's got so much in it. There are lots of books that have fascinating universes, and there are lots of first-contact novels, and there are lots of stories with alien civilizations and human civilizations and masses of history. The thing that makes *A Fire Upon the Deep* so great is that it has all these things and more, and it's integrated into one thrilling story. It has the playful excitement and scope of pulp adventure together with the level of characterization of a really good literary work, and lots of the best characters are aliens. It really is the book that has everything. Galaxy-spanning civilizations! Thousands of kinds of aliens! Low-bandwidth speculation across light-years! Low-tech development of a medieval planet! Female point-of-view characters! A universe where computation and FTL travel are physically different in different places! An ancient evil from before the dawn of time and a quest to defeat it! A librarian, a hero, two intelligent pot plants, a brother and sister lost among aliens, and a curious mind split between four bodies. And the stakes keep going up and up.

This is a universe where not only technology but also the very ability to think increases with distance from the galactic core, and the universe is divided into "zones of thought." In the "Slow Zone" you can't have true AI or FTL. In the "Beyond" you can have those things, but nothing that takes more than human-level intelligence. In the Transcend you have singularities and godlike beings, and above that, who knows? There's an ancient godlike evil known as the Blight lurking at the edge of the Transcend, the level where it's possible to become a Power. Humans poking around wake it up and trigger a catastrophe. Their escaping ship, which might contain the seeds of the Blight's destruction, rushes to the bottom of the Beyond, where it lands on a planet where the inhabitants, the Tines, are pack minds, at a medieval tech level. Meanwhile, Ravna, a human librarian at Relay, and Pham, a human rescued from the Slowness and patched together by a Power, start a rescue mission. What Vinge gives us of his universe is like what Tolkien says of Middle Earth, "an account . . . of its end and passing away before its beginning and middle had been told." *A Fire Upon the Deep* is the story of an absolutely fascinating universe and of how it came to an end.

Vinge makes this complicated novel work by starting with the Blight, the threat at first to a lab full of human scientists at the edge of the Transcend, and then to the whole galaxy. We start close up and small with a freighter full of children escaping, and the threat of the Blight is always relentlessly there, throughout the rest of the book. Whenever a lesser writer would have a man come through the door with a gun, Vinge has the Blight destroy something big—or in one case, some aliens reacting to the Blight destroy something big. The universe is very complicated, and there are braided stories ratcheting along, but the shape of the story is very simple—the swelling threat of the Blight, the treasure at the bottom of the Beyond, the chase and pursuit.

He also keeps it focused down on the characters—Johanna and Jeffri Olnsdot on the planet of the Tines; the Tine Pilgrim with his four bodies; Ravna, the librarian who is the only human working at Relay; and Pham Nuwen, the trader from the Slow Zone with shattered pieces of a god in his head. And because there are two strands of story, they drive each other forward—you never leave one strand without wanting more of it, and Vinge keeps up this balance all the way to the climax. Vinge sets us close in, and everything is so fascinating right from the start that it's easy to really care.

This particular kind of fascination is almost unique to science fiction. There's a universe and the way it works is really weird, and he keeps handing out pieces of it and you keep fitting it together. There are two real stories here, the children on the Tines World, and Ravna and Pham's rescue attempt. The first has the Tines themselves, with their minds and personalities spread across bodies. It also has the development of technology from "dataset"—a child's computer with a portable web full of information. And there's the way Samnorsk is this wonderful language of science and opportunity for the Tines, and you can get whiplash seeing how it's a backwater dead-end language in the wider universe. In the second story, you have the wider universe with the zones. And there's the low-bandwidth usenet-like net where civilizations trade information that is sometimes incomprehensible.

Vinge does really well at making this wider universe seem real, even though we don't see all that much of it. We have what Ravna takes for granted, and what she has to explain to Pham. We see the net and get to know some of the posters—like the Aphranti Hegemony ("Death to Vermin") and Sandor at the Zoo. We see a little of Relay and a little of Harmonious Repose, but it's surprising how much detail is evoked with so little. The Beyond feels solid, with its layers of translation and weird aliens ones that walk on tusks, and ones like potted plants, and Twirlip of the Mists, who sounds demented but is always right.

This seeming solidity is conjured with evocative names and casually mentioned references that get nailed down by being referenced from different directions—for example the planet from which humanity emerged from the Slowness, Njora, is mentioned in the context of the fairy tale "Age of Princesses" several times by the kids on Tines World comparing the Tines tech; and there's a reference to the fountain flowing on Straum to say humanity would never forget its origins, not to mention the Straumli forests with mechanical copies of Njoran wildlife; and then on the ship (the *Out of Band II*, great name), when Pham makes the illusion of a castle, Ravna thinks that in the Age of Princesses, the castles were in tropical swamps so they didn't have fireplaces. That's just one tiny thing, but everything is as well sourced as this, and all the information is delicately incleud, dropped in smoothly. The details build up a picture that's consistent and interesting, and some of the delightful details are major clues you can't recognize the first time through.

All these details build up and draw you in, so that by the end of the book when you come out gasping for breath, it's almost as if you have really been there.

But yet, this is a fight of good against evil, gods and lurking evil; it begins with the metaphor of the mummy's tomb and ends with a transcendent victory. There's something of the joy of fantasy in it too, despite the spaceships and the aliens. Pham and the skroderiders are canny traders; Vrimini.org wants to make a profit; only Ravna wants an adventure, a daring rescue, to save the universe. One quest, Blueshell agrees to, but never another! But this is an epic, after all, with the scale and scope and moral compass of an epic.

Any one of the ideas in *A Fire Upon the Deep* would have kept an ordinary writer going for years. For me, it's the book that does everything right, the example of what science fiction does when it works.

Time Travel and the Black Death: Connie Willis's *Doomsday Book*

Doomsday Book is Connie Willis's second novel. I read it when it was first published, and I bought a UK paperback as soon as one was available, and I've been rereading it frequently ever since, often at Christmas, as it's set at Christmas.

This is a story about infectious diseases, history, and caritas. It is set in two epidemics in two time periods, an influenza epidemic in 2054 and the Black Death in 1348, and the two stories alternate: the future time worrying about Kivrin, the student trapped in the wrong part of the past, while Kivrin back in 1348 is trying to cope and learn and help.

The plot ratchets, going forward in both time periods in turn, until they come together again at the end. The characters all work, what happens to them hurts, and the whole thing is utterly unputdownable even after multiple rereads. I expect to be coming back to this book and enjoying it for my whole life. If you haven't read it, I highly recommend it, and I am now going to discuss it in detail, with spoilers.

I have heard *Doomsday Book* called a tragedy, especially in opposition to *To Say Nothing of the Dog,* which really is a comedy. Shakespeare's plays get divided into comedies, tragedies, histories, and "problems," and *Doomsday Book* is a history, or possibly a problem. It has sad moments and funny moments, and certainly a lot of people die, but our protagonists survive and are successful. It has a eucatastrophic ending that is perfectly satisfying. You would think that a book with two epidemics would be a "man against nature" story, but while the influenza and the Black Death can be seen as antagonists in a plot sense, the actual story here is "man learns lesson."

One of the ways Willis makes the whole book work is the way that the influenza epidemic in the future section starts immediately while the revelation of the mistake and the horrors of the Black Death come after Kivrin, and the reader has had time to understand and care about the people in the past. Along with Kivrin, we learn them as real and with their own concerns—Rosemond's worrying engagement to a much older man, Gawyn's fatal love for Eliwys, Imeyne's petty snobbery and constant carping. We see their kindness to Kivrin and we see the details of their lives before they start to die. And then we endure their deaths with Kivrin. One of the most effective parts of the book is where Kivrin starts to count deaths—she knows the Black Death killed "a third to a half" of Europe, and she thinks it will kill a third, or at most half, of the village. That kind of statistical thinking has no place in reality, and Willis wants us to be sure that this is reality. Statistics and probabilities are relentlessly mocked throughout the book. The lesson Kivrin learns is that history is real, what a third to a half of Europe really means, and that everyone through all of time is a person.

I used the Latin word "caritas" above when I was saying what the book was about. I used it instead of either of its usual translations, "charity" and "love," because both of them have specific meanings in English that aren't what Willis is interested in here. "Charity" in English has come to mean "giving money to organizations that do good" so exclusively that any other meanings are hard to reach. As for "love," while we do talk about kinds of love other than romance, we mean romance so often that we need to distinguish them as "mother love" or whatever. It's interesting that Willis here avoids romance completely and shows mother love in a very negative light, while showing us pretty much every other form of loving human relationship.

Kivrin is everyman, er, everygirl. She's a very typical Willis character: she's geeky and plucky and hardworking and unromantic. She's determined to get to the past, and she's delighted with it once she recovers from her influenza. Kivrin thinks about the people around her in the past, and when she thinks of the future she has left, she thinks of her teachers. She also thinks about God. She doesn't think about a romantic partner, and she doesn't think about her parents, though she must have some, or have had some. She never thinks of her childhood, even when dealing with children. She exists as Medieval Student only. But she's very easy to identify with; we see her in first person in her reports as well as in third person.

Through Kivrin we are shown loving friendship and that most unusual love, the love of an adult for somebody else's children. This is all through *Doomsday Book*, and yet how rare it is in the whole of the rest of literature! Kivrin loves Rosemond and Agnes, Mr. Dunworthy loves Kivrin and Colin. There's no hint of romance, or even the usual kind of parental substitution, nor are the children little angels—they are deftly characterized and real. Agnes whines and Rosemond puts on airs and Colin sucks gobstoppers and evades authority. Yet unlovable as they are, the older characters love them, and the reader also comes to care for them.

Mary Ahrens, one of the best characters in the novel, loves Colin, who is her great-nephew. How often do we see aunts, let alone great-aunts, and how often do we see them when they're not being played for laughs? She's exactly the kind of character we so rarely see in fiction—an older woman, unmarried, professional, with connections to her family, with close friends. She dies, of course. Mary Ahrens is a doctor, and as well as loving her great-nephew and her friends, she also loves humanity and lays down her life caring for them in the epidemic. In this, she's contrasted directly with Kivrin, who survives with everyone dying around her—Mary dies, while saving almost everyone.

They are both, in their own ways, shown to be saintly. Father Roche, who saw Kivrin arrive from the future, specifically believes she is a saint sent by God to help them—and he gets what he thinks is confirmation when he asks for her confession when she is feverish and she tells him she has not sinned. From the text's point of view, it's by no means sure that he's wrong. Kivrin is very human and fallible, and yet she is saint-like and what she does is more than many people would do, or did do. Yet if God has sent her, through the mistake of feverish Badri and the folds of time, he has sent her to do no more than help people die with dignity and learn a lesson. Through Mary's work in the future and Kivrin's in the past we may see the operation of Grace and of God's love—and for those who believe in Christianity, this may work better. It leaves me with teeth-gritting questions about theodicy.

It's probably worth noting in this context that everyone in this book in both time periods attends church. I didn't notice this as unusual at first, because it is Christmas, which is one of the few times British people might go to church, but it's quite clear if you pay attention that Dunworthy, Kivrin, Mary, and the other modern characters are regular churchgoers. Badri Chaudhuri, the time travel technician who is the first to fall sick with influenza, is explicitly identified as "Church of England." There has obviously been a religious revival, and people have started going to church in the United Kingdom as they do in the United States. It would be plausible for any one of them to be a churchgoer, very strange for them all to be. But social change happens; a hundred years ago, they'd have all gone to church, who can say about sixty years from when the book was written?

Our other central character, the protagonist of the future strand, is Mr. Dunworthy. He never gets a first name. He's a don, a history professor, unmarried and not in any romantic relationships. He has close friends, he has students, he has colleagues, and he cares for history and time travel more than anything. He doesn't want Kivrin to go into the fourteenth century, because it's too dangerous, and he worries about her constantly—with good cause, as it turns out. We see his love for his friends and for his students, and his relationship with Kivrin is specifically compared on several occasions to God and Jesus—clearly she is an alter ego. And Kivrin prays to him when feverish. He's an older man who takes in a waif—Colin—who is harassed by bureaucracy, though he has an able secretary who takes care of everything—Finch—and who sets everything right in the end, at least for the characters who are still alive. He appears in a number of other Willis novels in the Oxford Time Travel universe.

If Kivrin's an everyman with whom the reader is intended to identify, Dunworthy is very much a specific himself, paternal, worried, impatient with incompetence, as kind as he can be in the circumstances, which are perpetually too much for him. Everything in the book is seen through either Kivrin or Dunworthy.

We have parental figures, in Dunworthy and Mary, but real parents are represented by Colin's neglectful mother and William Gaddson's overprotective one. Colin's mother, Mary's niece Deirdre, has sent him away at Christmas, which is the one time in Britain when everyone is with their family—there's no Thanksgiving to dilute that the way there is in the United States. Deirdre has sent him away so she can be with her "new live-in," a romantic partner. Colin waits for the gifts she is sending, he clearly wants them as proof of her love, but Mary casually mentions that last time (this is not the first time he has been sent to Mary for Christmas) the gifts didn't arrive until Epiphany, twelve days late. She doesn't come for Mary's funeral, which Colin has to cope with alone, because Dunworthy is sick. She doesn't retrieve Colin afterwards even when quarantine is lifted. She's a horrible mother.

Mrs. Gaddson is at the other extreme, an almost Dickensian caricature, absolutely appalling and larger than life, the overprotective mother from hell who reads gloomy bits of the Bible to patients in the hospital. She has come to Oxford not to help but to make everything worse—though that's unfair. It isn't malice (you rarely meet real malice in Willis); it's her own nature. Her son only wants to get away from her. She's an even worse mother than the neglectful Deirdre.

In 1348, Imeyne cares so little for her daughter-in-law and grandchildren that she summons not only Sir Blouet and his family but also a plague-stricken priest, who infects them all. Even without that, she's constantly carping at them. Eliwys loves her children, but she's helpless to help them even from everyday hurts—and she has the palest characterization of all the family.

While mother love fares badly, romance fares even worse. William Gaddson is our only example of romantic love. Half the girls in Oxford are in love with him and planning to marry him, and this is a kind of running joke. William is always turning up with useful girls—girl technicians and nurses, whatever Dunworthy requires. They don't know about each other, and never find out, he's clearly so used to deceiving his mother that deceiving half the girls in Oxford is child's play. Apart from William and his changing parade of women, all we have for romantic love is Gawyn, pining for Eliwys, and her using that love to send him to fetch her husband. He never returns. Sir Blouet's engagement to Rosemond—who is thirteen to his forty—is horrible, and both Rosemond and Kivrin see it as horrible.

We have here a community of celibate academics. This isn't a requirement—Oxford dons have been allowed to marry for quite some time. Even female dons could marry well before 1992—and in any case, we don't see any female dons except the visiting American archaeologist, Lupe Montoya. We just have a group of people who happen to be academics and happen to be celibate.

In 1348, the priest, Father Roche, does need to be celibate, and is, and is shown as ideal—talking to God the way Kivrin talks into her *corder*, dealing well with everyone, although he has no education, thinking well of everyone. He's the saintliest character in the book, and he dies, and perhaps God did send Kivrin to him to help him in his last days.

What we're shown positively and from many directions all through the book is caritas, disinterested love, love of humanity, of friends and other people's children. Roche shows caritas, Mary does, Kivrin learns it.

The two themes that run through all Willis's work are the weight of history, and communication difficulties. Both of them are apparent here. History, obviously, lots here, and the reality of people in history is foregrounded. As for communication, telephones are very important, and missed messages and messages gone astray. Colin waiting for the post to bring presents, Dunworthy trying to call Basingame, trying to call Andrews, Montoya trying to call Basingame and Dunworthy, the bell ringers, the nurse writing down what Badri says in his delirium, the message Imeyne sends, and poor Gawyn, as well as Father Roche knowing where the drop is. As so often with Willis, there are no real antagonists in this book. Gilchrist and Latimer, who have opened up the medieval period while the head of department is away, and who rush Kivrin through, are wrong, but not malicious. Imeyne with her suspicion of Kivrin is definitely a force for tension. But there's no violence here and no villains; the antagonists are nature (the plagues), ignorance, and miscommunication. Even Gilchrist's shutting down the net isn't the disaster it seems at first—Badri has made a backup.

Bells are a motif, from the mechanical carrillon playing to shoppers in the streets to the visiting bell ringers and the peal they want to ring, and then the bells tolling for the dead.

It's easy to point out things that are wrong with *Doomsday Book*, from the lack of call waiting (or even answering machines) in 2054 to the snow-plowed road in 1348. Indeed, it's like shooting fish in a barrel. The thing is that these things don't matter, because the book has, as even Adam Roberts acknowledges, real emotional heft, and they're just nitpicking. It's just as easy to point to details she gets right—the language being completely incomprehensible at first, despite having studied it; Colin taking aspirin into the past because he knows it's been around forever.

Her themes and her plot come together here to make a vastly readable and most unusual book.

1994

Best Novel

Winner: *Green Mars,* by Kim Stanley Robinson

Nominees:
Beggars in Spain, by Nancy Kress
Glory Season, by David Brin
Moving Mars, by Greg Bear
Virtual Light, by William Gibson

The 1994 Hugo Awards were presented at ConAdian in Winnipeg, Manitoba.

The award for Best Novel was given to Kim Stanley Robinson's *Green Mars,* a book I have not read, because as I mentioned in last week's post, I couldn't get on with the first book in the trilogy, *Red Mars.* This is a very unusual winner: I can't think of another case where the middle book of a trilogy has won the Hugo without the first book's also winning. As I haven't read it, I can't say how well it stands alone, but Hugo voters aren't generally very tolerant of books that don't. *Green Mars* is, of course, about terraforming Mars. It also won the Locus Award. It's in print and in the library in French and English.

There are four other nominees, and I've read three of them.

Nancy Kress's *Beggars in Spain* is an expansion of the novella *Beggars in Spain.* It's near-future SF about people who do not sleep—a girl who doesn't sleep and her twin sister who does. It turns out that not sleeping has all kinds of advantages nobody would have imagined, as well as giving people twice as much time in the day. It's excellent, with well-drawn characters and thought-provoking ideas. Terrific nominee. It's in print and in the library in English only.

David Brin's *Glory Season* is set on a planet where men and women come into sexual heat in different seasons and most people are clones living in large groups of clone-sisters of different ages. It's like Sargent's *Shore of Women* and Tepper's *The Gate to Women's Country* in having women living in civilization and men outside, but quite original in having the perspective of somebody who is a rare unique individual in a society of identicals. It's in print and in the library in French and English.

Greg Bear's *Moving Mars* is also a novel of terraforming Mars, and also a sequel to an earlier Hugo nominee, in this case, *Queen of Angels*. The part of this book I remember best is the marvelous end, which overshadows all the earlier, more ordinary setup to the bit where they do, as it says on the cover, move Mars. This is another excellent nominee. It's in print and in the library in English and French.

I have not read William Gibson's *Virtual Light*, because of truly disliking *Neuromancer*. It's cyberpunk with the tag line "a mind can be a terrible thing to crash." It's in print and in the library in English only.

So, four men and one woman—four American, one Canadian. Gibson and Brin are past winners. Bear and Robinson were past nominees. Kress had short-form Hugo wins, but this is her first novel nomination. And they're all SF: one cyberpunk, two terraforming Mars, one traditional near-future one-invention SF, and one far-future planetary. What else might they have chosen?

The Nebula, being on a different schedule, went to *Red Mars*. Other eligible non-overlapping nominees were Kevin J. Anderson and Doug Beason's *Assemblers of Infinity* and Gene Wolfe's *Nightside the Long Sun*.

The World Fantasy Award was won by Lewis Shiner's *Glimpses*. Other nominees were *Drawing Blood*, Poppy Z. Brite; *The Innkeeper's Song*, Peter S. Beagle; *The Iron Dragon's Daughter*, Michael Swanwick; *Lord of the Two Lands*, Judith Tarr; *Skin*, Kathe Koja; *The Throat*, Peter Straub.

It seems to me that *The Iron Dragon's Daughter* is a major significant work that should not have been overlooked by the Hugo nominators.

The John W. Campbell Memorial Award, in another "huh" moment after seeming relatively sane for the previous few years, was won by "No Award" with *Beggars in Spain* second and *Moving Mars* third. I'd love to know what they were thinking, and also how delighted Kress and Bear were to come second to "No Award."

The Philip K. Dick Award was a tie between two excellent books, Jack Womack's *Elvissey* and John M. Ford's *Growing Up Weightless*. I think either or both of these would have been excellent Hugo nominees. Other nominees were: *Bunch!*, David R. Bunch; *CrashCourse*, Wilhelmina Baird; *Icarus Descending*, Elizabeth Hand.

The Tiptree was won by Nicola Griffith's *Ammonite*. Honor books were: *Coelestis*, Paul Park; *Dancing Jack*, Laurie J. Marks; *Illicit Passage*, Alice Nunn; *In the Garden of Dead Cars*, Sybil Claiborne; *Ring of Swords*, Eleanor Arnason; *The Robber Bride*, Margaret Atwood.

It's interesting that the top five Locus nominees are the five Hugo nominees—that doesn't often happen. Other nominees not yet mentioned: *Hard Landing*, Algis Budrys; *The Call of Earth*, Orson Scott Card; *A Plague of Angels*, Sheri S. Tepper; *Harvest of Stars*, Poul Anderson; *Against a Dark Background*, Iain M. Banks; *The Hammer of God*, Arthur C. Clarke; *Powers That Be*, Anne McCaffrey and Elizabeth Ann Scarborough; *The Broken God*, David Zindell; *Brother Termite*, Patricia Anthony; *Godspeed*, Charles Sheffield; *Vanishing Point*, Michaela Roessner; *Chimera*, Mary Rosenblum; *Red Dust*, Paul J. McAuley; *The Gripping Hand*, Larry Niven and Jerry Pournelle; *Nightside the Long Sun*, Gene Wolfe; *Timelike Infinity*, Stephen Baxter.

Against a Dark Background is the standout book here, probably Iain M. Banks's best book, and definitely the kind of groundbreaking book you'd expect to get some Hugo attention. It probably suffered from timing of UK and US publication, and that sucks.

The Beagle won the Locus Award for Best Fantasy Novel. Other nominees not yet mentioned: *To Green Angel Tower*, Tad Williams; *The Thread That Binds the Bones*, Nina Kiriki Hoffman; *Strange Devices of the Sun and Moon*, Lisa Goldstein; *The Fires of Heaven*, Robert Jordan; *Deerskin*, Robin McKinley; *Dog Wizard*, Barbara Hambly; *The Hollowing*, Robert Holdstock; *Faery in Shadow*, C. J. Cherryh; *The Porcelain Dove*, Delia Sherman; *Winter of the Wolf*, R. A. MacAvoy; *The Far Kingdoms*, Allan Cole and Chris Bunch; *The Cygnet and the Firebird*,

Patricia A. McKillip; *The Wizard's Apprentice*, S. P. Somtow; *Bones of the Past*, Holly Lisle; *Skybowl* (Dragon Star Book III), Melanie Rawn; *The Robin & the Kestrel*, Mercedes Lackey.

The Mythopoeic Award was won by Delia Sherman's *The Porcelain Dove*.

So, was there anything they all missed? Loads of things this year. Steven Brust's *Agyar*; Amy Thompson's *Virtual Girl*; M. J. Engh's *Rainbow Man*; Isaac Asimov's *Forward the Foundation*; Colin Greenland's *Harm's Way*; Diana Wynne Jones's *Hexwood*; Octavia Butler's *The Parable of the Sower*.

This was a year where there were a lot of notable novels, and where my personal choice of five would be quite different from the Hugo list. On the other hand, the books on the Hugo list have lasted and are mostly still being discussed—and they do give a good snapshot of where the field was in 1994. And it would be easy to make a list of twenty things that were theoretically all good enough for a place on the Hugo ballot.

OTHER CATEGORIES

BEST NOVELLA

Winner: *Down in the Bottomlands*, by Harry Turtledove (*Analog*, January 1993)

Nominees:
An American Childhood, by Pat Murphy (*Asimov's*, April 1993)
Into the Miranda Rift, by G. David Nordley (*Analog*, July 1993)
Mefisto in Onyx, by Harlan Ellison (*Omni*, October 1993; Mark V. Ziesing)
The Night We Buried Road Dog, by Jack Cady (*F&SF*, January 1993)
Wall, Stone, Craft, by Walter Jon Williams (*F&SF*, October/November 1993; Axolotl)

Again, terrific novellas. I think I'd have voted for the Turtledove by a hair over the Williams.

Best Novelette

Winner: "Georgia on My Mind," by Charles Sheffield (*Analog*, January 1993)

Nominees:
"Dancing on Air," by Nancy Kress (*Asimov's*, July 1993)
"Deep Eddy," by Bruce Sterling (*Asimov's*, August 1993)
"The Franchise," by John Kessel (*Asimov's*, August 1993)
"The Shadow Knows," by Terry Bisson (*Asimov's*, September 1993)

And a great set of novelettes as well.

Best Short Story

Winner: "Death on the Nile," by Connie Willis (*Asimov's*, March 1993)

Nominees:
"England Underway," by Terry Bisson (*Omni*, July 1993)
"The Good Pup," by Bridget McKenna (*F&SF*, March 1993)
"Mwalimu in the Squared Circle," by Mike Resnick (*Asimov's*, March 1993)
"The Story So Far," by Martha Soukup (*Full Spectrum 4*)

Best Nonfiction Book

Winner: *The Encyclopedia of Science Fiction*, edited by John Clute and Peter Nicholls

Nominees:
The Art of Michael Whelan: Scenes/Visions, by Michael Whelan
Once Around the Bloch: An Unauthorized Autobiography, by Robert Bloch

PITFCS: Proceedings of the Institute for Twenty-First Century Studies,
    edited by Theodore R. Cogswell
Understanding Comics: The Invisible Art, by Scott McCloud

A good set of books, but how can you compare them rationally when
they're not working in the same space?

Best Dramatic Presentation

Winner: *Jurassic Park*

Nominees:
Addams Family Values
Babylon 5: "The Gathering"
Groundhog Day
The Nightmare Before Christmas

Best Professional Editor

Winner: Kristine Kathryn Rusch

Nominees:
Ellen Datlow
Gardner Dozois
Mike Resnick
Stanley Schmidt

Best Professional Artist

Winner: Bob Eggleton

Nominees:
Thomas Canty
David A. Cherry
Don Maitz
Michael Whelan

BEST ORIGINAL ARTWORK

Winner: *Space Fantasy Commemorative Stamp Booklet*, by Stephen Hickman (US Postal Service)

Nominees:

Keith Parkinson, cover of *Asimov's*, November 1993 (illustrating *Cold Iron* by Michael Swanwick)

Thomas Canty, cover of *F&SF*, October/November 1993 (illustrating "The Little Things" by Bridget McKenna)

BEST SEMIPROZINE

Winner: *Science Fiction Chronicle*, edited by Andrew I. Porter

Nominees:

Interzone, edited by David Pringle

Locus, edited by Charles N. Brown

The New York Review of Science Fiction, edited by David G. Hartwell, Donald G. Keller, Robert K. J. Killheffer, and Gordon Van Gelder

Pulphouse, edited by Dean Wesley Smith and Jonathan E. Bond

Tomorrow Speculative Fiction, edited by Algis Budrys

BEST FANZINE

Winner: *Mimosa*, edited by Dick and Nicki Lynch

Nominees:

Ansible, edited by Dave Langford

File 770, edited by Mike Glyer

Lan's Lantern, edited by George "Lan" Laskowski

STET, edited by Leah Zeldes Smith and Dick Smith

BEST FAN WRITER

Winner: Dave Langford

Nominees:
Sharon Farber
Mike Glyer
Andy Hooper
Evelyn C. Leeper

Best Fan Artist

Winner: Brad W. Foster

Nominees:
Teddy Harvia
Linda Michaels
Peggy Ranson
William Rotsler
Stu Shiffman

John W. Campbell Award

Winner: Amy Thomson

Nominees:
Holly Lisle
Jack Nimersheim
Carrie Richerson
Elizabeth Willey

A pretty good list. Thomson is a good winner—*Virtual Girl* is a terrific first novel, and she has gone on to write other excellent books. I just wish she'd write more.

We talked about Richerson and Lisle last week.

I'm not familiar with Nimersheim, but it seems he was nominated on the basis of half a dozen short stories in anthologies. He has gone on to write more short stories, but he's not had all that much visibility.

Elizabeth Willey had just published her first fantasy novel, *A Well-*

Favored Man, which was a lot of fun. She went on to write two sequels and then nothing else that I've seen, which is a pity.

Other potential nominees might have been Poppy Z. Brite, Patricia Anthony, Mary Rosenblum, Nicola Griffith, Charles Pellegrino, and Sean Stewart.

Comments on 1994

3. Rich Horton

A few significant novels not mentioned: Bradley Denton's *Blackburn,* which is not really SF/fantasy to my mind (though parts appeared in *F&SF*), but it's very good, very involving, very dark.

Diana Wynne Jones's *Hexwood* and *The Crown of Dalemark.*

Matt Ruff's *Sewer, Gas & Electric* (which probably would have made my ideal nominee list).

Samuel R. Delany's *They Fly at Çiron* (which to be honest, I haven't read, but which I mention because it fits an interesting (to me) short list: novels expanded from collaborative short stories that were published as by only one of the original authors. Others are Poul Anderson's *Twilight World* (expanded from his first story "Tomorrow's Children," with F. N. Waldrop) and James Blish's *VOR* (expanded from "The Weakness of RVOG" with Damon Knight).

Finally, from the "mainstream":

Jeff Noon's *Vurt*

Margaret Atwood's *The Robber Bride* (perhaps not strictly speaking genre, but incorporating some genre elements)

Alan Lightman's *Einstein's Dreams*

4. Rich Horton

And the short fiction.

Again, the Hugo nominees are good to excellent, but somehow don't inspire me. Others worth mentioning:

Sister Alice, by Robert Reed
The Beauty Addict, by Ray Aldridge
The Last Castle of Christmas, by Alexander Jablokov
Walt and Emily, by Paul Di Filippo

In novelette, Sheffield's winner is a good story, but I think I'd have voted for (perhaps DID vote for) Sterling's "Deep Eddy." Also worth a look:

"Cush," by Neal Barrett Jr.
"Chaff," by Greg Egan
"The Other Magpie," by R. Garcia y Robertson
"A History of the Antipodes," by Philip C. Jennings (I quite liked Jennings's work, but he never quite seemed to gain traction, and he's published very little in the past decade or so—this story appeared in the very attractive large slick version of *Amazing* that appeared for a while in the nineties—it looked nice, but I think it got less notice than other magazines.)

In short story, I might have given Soukup the award. But other nominees might have come from this list:

"The Extra," by Greg Egan
"From the Corner of My Eye," by Michael F. Flynn
"From Our Point of View, We Had Moved to the Left," by William Shunn
"Exogamy," by John Crowley

And finally, the incomparable Avram Davidson died in 1993. He published three very fine stories this year, one in each length category, all worth mentioning:

Novella: *A Far Countrie*
Novelette: "The Spook-Box of Theobald Delafont de Brooks"
Short Story: "Sea-Scene; or, Vergil and the Ox-Thrall"

9. Rich Horton

What I remember from *Green Mars* is the constitutional convention. But little else. It's the drabbest of the RGB Mars books, a classic "middle book." (*Red Mars* is the best of that series [or, well, the novella *Green Mars*, set in a beta version of that Mars, is KSR's best Mars story], and *Blue Mars* is a bit of a mess but more interesting.)

I think SF was moving into a period of a lot of looking backwards at the genre. A lot of regret for the lost future promised in fifties SF. Some of these stories end up being brilliant, mind you (MacLeod's *New Light on the Drake Equation*), but they are still informed by that regret. (In a way, *Against a Dark Background* plays with that feeling.)

I think *The Iron Dragon's Daughter* was too dark for much of the SF community at that time (same with Swanwick's later *Jack Faust*).

So, yes, much of 1993's SF seems to me dispiriting. And it may well be because of a flagging of energy related to a feeling that the old SF "project" was permanently a dead letter.

16. Gardner Dozois

The Iron Dragon's Daughter should have been on the Hugo ballot, and certainly should have won the World Fantasy Award, being a game-changer for a great deal of the fantasy that followed it, and highly influential. *The Innkeeper's Song* is also a good fantasy. *Beggars in Spain* would have made a good Hugo winner, and I can't help but wonder if it didn't win because the original novella, *Beggars in Spain*, already had. *Ring of Swords*, *Hard Landing*, and the Banks probably should have been on the ballot.

In novella, I might have gone for *Wall, Stone, Craft*, although it's alternate history rather than SF per se; Williams has written several extremely good novellas in his career, and this is one of them. *Sister Alice* also should have been on the ballot, and is SF, one of the best far-future stories of its decade, and is the other story I'd have been tempted to vote for. *A Far Countrie* is late Davidson, and not as strong as earlier Jack Limekiller stories, but, hey, in my opinion, even weak Davidson is better than no Davidson at all. R. Garcia y Robertson's *Down the River* is a lot of fun.

Novelette is the strongest category this year, although not all the strong stories reached the ballot. I'd have preferred "Dancing on Air" or "Deep Eddy," both very strong stories, as the winner (think I would slightly favor "Dancing on Air"), and my actual favorite, Ian R. MacLeod's "Papa," didn't make the ballot at all. Greg Egan's "Chaff" is another excellent story. Steven Utley's "There and Then" is one of the best of his Silurian Tales, and Neal Barrett Jr.'s "Cush" is one of the weirder stories ever to appear in an SF magazine. Brian Aldiss's "Friendship Bridge" is also good.

The short story ballot is weak; there was better stuff elsewhere that didn't make it on. I'd have given it to Robert Reed's "Guest of Honor," one of the first, along with *Sister Alice,* of the really good Robert Reed stories. Greg Egan's "The Extra" is also strong, as is Stephen Baxter's "Lieserl" and Geoffrey A. Landis's "Beneath the Stars of Winter."

It's interesting to notice three writers this year producing good stuff by working against the sort of thing they're known for. Ian Mc-Donald's "Brody Loved the Masai Woman" is a vampire story, Steven Utley's "The Country Doctor" is one of his rare horror stories, and Eleanor Arnason's "The Hound of Merlin" is an Arthurian fantasy. Also interesting to notice that Jonathan Lethem was writing a lot of SF for *Asimov's* and elsewhere in those days.

Not germane to anything, I'll mention that the cover of my Best of the Year that year, the Eleventh Annual Collection, *Pistachio Crater,* by Kim Poor (who alas isn't painting anymore) was one of my favorite covers for the entire run of the Year's Best to date.

1995

BEST NOVEL

Winner: *Mirror Dance,* by Lois McMaster Bujold

Nominees:
Beggars and Choosers, by Nancy Kress
Brittle Innings, by Michael Bishop
Mother of Storms, by John Barnes
Towing Jehovah, by James Morrow

The 1995 Hugo Awards were presented at Intersection in Glasgow, Scotland, the first Worldcon I attended.

The Best Novel winner was Lois McMaster Bujold's *Mirror Dance,* one of the best of the Vorkosigan saga. It's a book about a clone finding family and identity, and a man who knows he cannot fail failing, it's utterly dependent on the social and technological matrix of the characters and the planets that shaped them, but it's a novel of character. It's also the kind of book that makes you think. I think it's an excellent Hugo winner. It won the Locus SF award. It's in print and in the library in English.

There were four other nominees, and although I was voting in the Hugos that year, I have read only three of them.

Nancy Kress's *Beggars and Choosers* is the sequel to *Beggars in Spain,* and I was disappointed with it. It seemed like just more story, rather than exploration of anything new. It's in print as an audiobook but not as a book, and it's not in the library.

Michael Bishop's *Brittle Innings* is a fantasy about baseball. It had no UK publication, and I couldn't get hold of it in time to read it. I can't imagine I was the only British voter with this problem, and I expect it suffered accordingly in the voting. I still haven't read it— Bishop's a really excellent writer who often gets too close to horror for my comfort, and it's about baseball. It won the Locus fantasy award. It's not in print, and it's not in the library.

John Barnes's *Mother of Storms* was a terrible introduction to John Barnes for me, although he went on to become one of my favorite writers despite it. It's a near-future disaster novel about global warming and a hurricane, written in bestseller omniscient, with really nasty sex scenes. It is, unfortunately, deeply memorable. It's in print as an ebook, and it's in the library in French and English.

James Morrow's *Towing Jehovah* is brilliant but weird. The enormous body of God is floating in the Atlantic, and a tanker has to tow it away. It's not at all the book you'd expect from that description either. Terrific nominee. I put it in second place after the Bujold and would have been happy to see it win. It won the World Fantasy Award. It's in print, and it's in the library in French and English.

So, three men and two women, all Americans despite the Worldcon's being in Scotland. Bujold's a previous winner, Kress was nominated the year before, Bishop had multiple prior short-form nominations, Barnes and Morrow are Hugo newcomers. We have one near-future disaster novel, one baseball fantasy, one theological SF, one near-future innovation novel, and one planetary SF.

What else might the nominators have considered?

The Nebula was awarded to last year's *Moving Mars*. Non-overlapping eligible nominees were Jonathan Lethem's *Gun, with Occasional Music;* Roger Zelazny's *A Night in the Lonesome October;* and Rachel Pollack's *Temporary Agency.*

Non-overlapping World Fantasy nominees were *The Circus of the Earth and the Air,* Brooke Stevens; *From the Teeth of Angels,* Jonathan Carroll; *Love & Sleep,* John Crowley; *Waking the Moon,* Elizabeth Hand.

The John W. Campbell Memorial Award went to what I thought at the time and still believe to be the best book of 1994, Greg Egan's *Permutation City.* The runner-up was *Brittle Innings. Permutation City* hadn't yet had a US release, and wasn't eligible the next year when it did have one. It does seem like a real injustice that it didn't make the Hugo ballot.

The Philip K. Dick Award was won by Robert Charles Wilson's excellently strange *Mysterium*. There was a special citation for *Inagehi*, by Jack Cady. Other nominees were: *Rim: A Novel of Virtual Reality*, Alexander Besher; *Scissors Cut Paper Wrap Stone*, Ian McDonald; *Summer of Love*, Lisa Mason; *Tonguing the Zeitgeist*, Lance Olsen.

The Tiptree Award was won by Nancy Springer's *Larque on the Wing*. They don't separate long and short form; the other winner was Le Guin's short "The Matter of Seggri." Other short-listed works not previously mentioned were *Amazon Story Bones*, Ellen Frye; *Cannon's Orb*, L. Warren Douglas; *The Furies*, Suzy McKee Charnas; *Genetic Soldier*, George Turner; *North Wind*, Gwyneth Jones; *Trouble and Her Friends*, Melissa Scott.

Locus SF non-overlapping nominees: *Parable of the Sower*, Octavia E. Butler; *Foreigner*, C. J. Cherryh; *Heavy Weather*, Bruce Sterling; *Worldwar: In the Balance*, Harry Turtledove; *Rama Revealed*, Arthur C. Clarke and Gentry Lee; *Caldé of the Long Sun*, Gene Wolfe; *The Dolphins of Pern*, Anne McCaffrey; *The Engines of God*, Jack McDevitt; *Furious Gulf*, Gregory Benford; *The Stars Are Also Fire*, Poul Anderson; *Shadow's End*, Sheri S. Tepper; *Necroville* (US title: *Terminal Café*), Ian McDonald; *Tripoint*, C. J. Cherryh; *The Voices of Heaven*, Frederik Pohl; *Feersum Endjinn*, Iain M. Banks; *Half the Day Is Night*, Maureen F. McHugh; *Ring*, Stephen Baxter; *Climbing Olympus*, Kevin J. Anderson; *Random Acts of Senseless Violence*, Jack Womack; *Wildlife*, James Patrick Kelly; *End of an Era*, Robert J. Sawyer; *Solis*, A. A. Attanasio; *Pasquale's Angel*, Paul J. McAuley; *The Jericho Iteration*, Allen Steele.

Of these, *Parable of the Sower*, *Foreigner*, and *Random Acts* would have been excellent nominees, and there are some other really good books there as well.

Locus fantasy nominees: *Lord of Chaos*, Robert Jordan; *Finder*, Emma Bull; *Memory & Dream*, Charles de Lint; *Love & Sleep*, John Crowley; *Five Hundred Years After*, Steven Brust; *Storm Warning*, Mercedes Lackey; *Summer King, Winter Fool*, Lisa Goldstein; *Merlin's Wood*, Robert Holdstock; *A College of Magics*, Caroline Stevermer; *The Warrior's Tale*, Allan Cole and Chris Bunch; *The Forest House*, Marion Zimmer

Bradley; *Slow Funeral*, Rebecca Ore; *Shadow of a Dark Queen*, Raymond E. Feist; *Rhinegold*, Stephan Grundy; *The Dubious Hills*, Pamela Dean; *Exiles 1: The Ruins of Ambrai*, Melanie Rawn.

The Mythopoeic Award was won by Patricia McKillip's *Something Rich and Strange*. The only nominee not previously mentioned was Robert Holdstock's *The Hollowing*.

Was there anything all these awards missed?

All I can see is Robert Reed's *Beyond the Veil of Stars* and S. P. Somtow's *Jasmine Nights*.

So this strikes me as a disappointing year—a couple of very good nominees, and an excellent winner, but also some disappointing nominees and a large number of really good lasting books left out—*Permutation City*, definitely, but also *Foreigner* and *Parable of the Sower*.

OTHER CATEGORIES

BEST NOVELLA

Winner: *Seven Views of Olduvai Gorge*, by Mike Resnick (*F&SF*, October/November 1994)

Nominees:
Cri de Coeur, by Michael Bishop (*Asimov's*, September 1994)
Les Fleurs du Mal, by Brian Stableford (*Asimov's*, October 1994)
Forgiveness Day, by Ursula K. Le Guin (*Asimov's*, November 1994)
Melodies of the Heart, by Michael F. Flynn (*Analog*, January 1994)

I remember I put the Le Guin first and the Flynn second, and I remember having a terrible time trying to find the *F&SF* and not actually finding it in time to vote. It was awful before the stories went up online!

Best Novelette

Winner: "The Martian Child," by David Gerrold (*F&SF*, September 1994)

Nominees:
"Cocoon," by Greg Egan (*Asimov's*, May 1994)
"A Little Knowledge," by Mike Resnick (*Asimov's*, April 1994)
"The Matter of Seggri," by Ursula K. Le Guin (*Crank! 3*, Spring 1994)
"The Singular Habits of Wasps," by Geoffrey A. Landis (*Analog*, April 1994)
"Solitude," by Ursula K. Le Guin (*F&SF*, December 1994)

For this year only, Best Novelette is my favorite category. "Solitude"! And "Cocoon"!

Best Short Story

Winner: "None So Blind," by Joe Haldeman (*Asimov's*, November 1994)

Nominees:
"Barnaby in Exile," by Mike Resnick (*Asimov's*, February 1994)
"Dead Man's Curve," by Terry Bisson (*Asimov's*, June 1994)
"I Know What You're Thinking," by Kate Wilhelm (*Asimov's*, November 1994)
"Mrs. Lincoln's China," by M. Shayne Bell (*Asimov's*, July 1994)
"Understanding Entropy," by Barry N. Malzberg (*Science Fiction Age*, July 1994)

Best Nonfiction Book

Winner: *I. Asimov: A Memoir*, by Isaac Asimov

Nominees:
The Book on the Edge of Forever, by Christopher Priest
Making Book, by Teresa Nielsen Hayden

Silent Interviews: On Language, Race, Sex, Science Fiction, and Some Comics, by Samuel R. Delany

Spectrum: The Best in Contemporary Fantastic Art, edited by Cathy Burnett and Arnie Fenner

I've read all of them except the art book, and any of them would have been a splendid winner. *I. Asimov* isn't as exciting as the Nielsen Hayden or the Delany, but it's an excellent autobiography. But I didn't vote in this category, because I hadn't been able to get hold of any of them beforehand.

BEST DRAMATIC PRESENTATION

Winner: *Star Trek: The Next Generation:* "All Good Things . . ."

Nominees:
Interview with the Vampire
The Mask
Star Trek: Generations
Stargate

BEST PROFESSIONAL EDITOR

Winner: Gardner Dozois

Nominees:
Ellen Datlow
Mike Resnick
Kristine Kathryn Rusch
Stanley Schmidt

I voted for Gardner, as *Asimov's* was my favorite magazine by miles at this time, and his Year's Best was (and remains) one of the most exciting books of any year.

Best Professional Artist

Winner: Jim Burns

Nominees:
Thomas Canty
Bob Eggleton
Don Maitz
Michael Whelan

Best Original Artwork

Winner: *Lady Cottington's Pressed Fairy Book,* by Brian Froud

Nominees:
Michael Whelan, cover of *Foreigner* (by C. J. Cherryh)
Michael Koelsch, cover of *Gun, with Occasional Music* (by Jonathan Lethem)

I voted for the *Foreigner* cover, which I still really like.

Best Semiprozine

Winner: *Interzone,* edited by David Pringle

Nominees:
Locus, edited by Charles N. Brown
The New York Review of Science Fiction, edited by David G. Hartwell, Donald G. Keller, Robert K. J. Killheffer, and Gordon Van Gelder
Science Fiction Chronicle, edited by Andrew I. Porter
Tomorrow Speculative Fiction, edited by Algis Budrys

That was the year *Interzone* had two stories I liked, one by Egan and one by Ryman. No wonder I emigrated. I voted for the *NYRoSF,* still on the strength of the first issue, which was still all I'd ever seen.

Best Fanzine

Winner: *Ansible,* edited by Dave Langford

Nominees:
File 770, edited by Mike Glyer
Habakkuk, edited by Bill Donaho
Lan's Lantern, edited by George "Lan" Laskowski
Mimosa, edited by Dick and Nicki Lynch

Best Fan Writer

Winner: Dave Langford

Nominees:
Sharon Farber
Mike Glyer
Andy Hooper
Evelyn C. Leeper

Best Fan Artist

Winner: Teddy Harvia

Nominees:
Brad W. Foster
Linda Michaels
Peggy Ranson
Bill Rotsler

John W. Campbell Award

Winner: Jeff Noon

Nominees:
Linda J. Dunn

David Feintuch
Daniel Marcus
Felicity Savage

Noon's first novel, *Vurt,* had just come out to great acclaim. Noon has gone on to write more books that are published as mainstream, but which have SFnal or fantastic elements. I disliked *Vurt,* so I haven't kept up with his career, especially as it has been mostly outside genre, but I understand that he looked like a nova at the time.

Dunn and Marcus seem to have written short work before and after nominations, without ever having a breakout or much consideration—I hadn't really been aware of them.

Feintuch won in 1996, so let's leave him for then.

Savage had just published a well-received first novel, *Humility Garden,* but nothing since.

Other people who may have been eligible: Jonathan Lethem, Kathleen Ann Goonan, Maggie Furey, Jane Lindskold, and J. R. Dunn. Not a very good year for the Campbell.

COMMENTS ON 1995

32. GARDNER DOZOIS

Brittle Innings isn't really about baseball, baseball is just a framework to hang the plot on, and almost any other sport would have served the purpose as well. It's an early precursor of what we'd now call a "mash-up," and my only problem with it is that I think it would have worked as well or better as a novelette than a novel, being the kind of idea that it's hard to get to stretch well that far.

Of course, there's a cultural bias involved (although I didn't grow up paying any attention whatsoever to baseball either, not getting interested in it until a few decades back), but I do think the rules of baseball are considerably easier to understand than the rules of cricket. I once read an entire novel about cricket, *Flashman's Lady,* by George MacDonald Fraser, and was no closer to understanding the rules by the end than I'd been in the beginning. I once asked a table of five or six British SF writers to explain the rules of cricket to me, and none of them could, admitting that they didn't understand them either. They challenged the Americans to tell them a baseball joke, and, without missing a beat, Peter Heck said, "What do you do with an elephant with three balls?" The answer being: "You walk him, and pitch to the giraffe."

Blank stares. Baffled silence.

I then asked them to tell us a cricket joke, but none of them could come up with one.

The short fiction categories are a lot stronger than the novel this year. In novella, I'd go for Ursula K. Le Guin's *Forgiveness Day,* one of the best of the new Hainish stories that she started to write about then, after a lapse from that setting of some years, although Brian Stableford's *Les Fleurs du Mal* is also excellent. The Bishop, the Flynn, and the Resnick are also good, but not as good as the Le Guin and the Stableford. R. Garcia y Robertson, a writer who produces good, intelligent, often funny adventure stories year after year without ever drawing much attention, had *Werewolves of Luna.*

The David Gerrold story was a controversial winner that year, with many, including me, arguing that it wasn't really a science fiction story at all. I rejected it for *Asimov's,* and in spite of it going on to win the Hugo, never regretted the decision. Strongest story there is probably Le Guin's "Solitude"; Le Guin was really having a wonderful year that year, with not only the two stories already mentioned but also "The Matter of Seggri," very strong itself, and other strong stories such as "Another Story," "Betrayals," and "Unchosen Love." Greg Egan's "Cocoon" is also first-rate, one of his first major stories, and one of the first in those days to feature an openly gay man as the hero (something we heard about from readers, too). Maureen F. McHugh's "Nekropolis" is also very strong, and a story that I always thought deserved more attention than it got. Robert Reed's "The Remoras" was I think the first of his Great Ship stories, a series still running to this day, and very strong. Steven Utley's "Edge of the Wind" is a strong Silurian story, George Turner's "Flowering Mandrake" is a powerful first-contact story, John Brunner's "Good with Rice" was one of his last major stories, and Terry Bisson's "The Hole in the Hole" is very funny. Kandis Elliot, who

seems to have subsequently disappeared, had a brief run of good biological mystery stories in *Asimov's*. Gregory Feeley's "Aweary of the
Sun" is a good Shakespeare story, although, as I recall, one with a
slight fantastic element.

In short story, I have no problem with the Haldeman, although
Stephen Baxter had one of his strongest stories, "Cilia-of-Gold." There
was the wry but bleak "Dead Space for the Unexpected," by Geoff
Ryman, and Howard Waldrop's funny, folksy "The Sawing Boys."

Slipping through without much notice is Joe Lansdale's "Bubba Ho-
Tep," which would later be made into a movie that many regard as a
cult classic. Michael Swanwick's "The Changeling's Tale" is also good,
as is Nancy Kress's "Margin of Error."

58. RICH HORTON

In novella, *Forgiveness Day* was certainly my choice as the best of the
year. But two stories not yet mentioned were also well worth a look:
Alex Jeffers's *Composition with Barbarian and Animal,* and the Nebula
winner, oddly enough from 1994, Elizabeth Hand's *Last Summer at
Mars Hill.*

In novelette, I did indeed like Le Guin's "Solitude" a lot. Also Egan's
"Cocoon." And I enjoyed Gerrold's winner too. But I thought the
best novelette of 1994 was another Ursula Le Guin story, to me long
underappreciated, perhaps in part because it appeared first in Algis
Budrys's small-press magazine *Tomorrow.* This is "Another Story; or,
A Fisherman of the Inland Sea," probably my single favorite New
Hainish story of hers.

A host of other novelettes seem worth a mention from that year:

"Cretaceous Park," by Kandis Elliott (who indeed seems to have
   disappeared—alas—she was both a promising author and a pretty
   good artist)
"Going West" and "The Valley of the Humans," by Philip C. Jennings
"Nekropolis," by Maureen McHugh (I agree with Gardner—this story
   has not gotten the notice it deserves.)
"The Lovers," by Eleanor Arnason (one of many magnificent Hwarhath
   shorts from her)

"The Blackery Dark," by Wil McCarthy
"Ylem," by Eliot Fintushel
"The Wild Ships of Fairny," by Carolyn Ives Gilman

In short story I have little to say—"None So Blind" was a good winner, the nominees a good set. I'd like to also mention "Ash Minette," a striking Cinderella retelling by the then very young Felicity Savage (another seemingly disappeared writer!); and, from the mainstream, Nicholson Baker's "Subsoil," from *The New Yorker,* but reprinted by Datlow and Windling in their 1995 *Year's Best Fantasy and Horror.* (Baker is one of my favorite writers—I recommend in particular his first novel, *The Mezzanine,* with the warning that in some ways it may appeal most to writers of his generation. (He was born in 1957, me in 1959.) (He's done genre only one other time [besides "Subsoil"], in perhaps my least favorite of his novels, *The Fermata.*)

61. GARDNER DOZOIS

I second Rich's recommendations for "Another Story" (boy, what a year Le Guin was having!), and for "Going West," "The Valley of the Humans"—Jennings, who did some really weird but good stuff also seems to have largely disappeared—and "Ylem" (Fintushel is another weird but good writer who doesn't seem to be around much anymore), and especially for Arnason's "The Lovers," one of my favorite Hwarhath stories.

In short story, M. Shayne Bell's "Mrs. Lincoln's China" was a quiet but moving story, and Bell is another writer who has disappeared; since he was majorly sick at one point, I wonder if he's even still alive.

1996

BEST NOVEL

Winner: *The Diamond Age,* by Neal Stephenson

Nominees:
Remake, by Connie Willis
The Terminal Experiment, by Robert J. Sawyer
Brightness Reef, by David Brin
The Time Ships, by Stephen Baxter

The 1996 Hugo Awards were presented at LACon III in Anaheim, California.

The Best Novel Hugo was won by Neal Stephenson's *The Diamond Age,* which has always struck me as two-thirds of a really brilliant book. It's a scintillating nanotech future with huge social changes consequent to the changes in technology, and there's a book and a girl shaped by the book, and an actress, and neo-Victorians, and everything is going along swimmingly . . . and then a miracle occurs and the end falls down in flinders. Nevertheless, even as a book where the end doesn't work for me, I think this is a good Hugo winner, because it's relentlessly inventive and exciting and doing science-fictional things that hadn't been done before. It's a groundbreaking book. It won the Locus Award. It's in print, and it's in the library in English and French.

There are four other nominees, and I've read two of them.

Connie Willis's *Remake* is a short novel about new technology and classic movies. It's funny and clever and has some lovely images—who can forget the job of removing all the drink and cigarettes from Rick's

Café in *Casablanca*? Having said that, I found it rather thin compared to most of Willis's work, even in her screwball comedy mode. It's in print, and it's in the library in French only.

Robert Sawyer's *The Terminal Experiment* is a near-future thriller about scientific proof of the existence of souls. It's classic SF in the tradition of Clarke and Benford. It won the Nebula, which is why I read it; I hadn't heard of Sawyer before this. It's in print, and it's in the library in French and English.

I haven't read David Brin's *Brightness Reef*. I was waiting for all three of the second Uplift series to be out, and then I never picked them up. It's in print, and it's in the library in French and English.

I also haven't read Stephen Baxter's *The Time Ships*. I haven't read it, because it's a Wells sequel, and I'd been playing the *Forgotten Futures* RPG, and a little bit of mock-Victorian SF goes a long way. It sounds really clever, but also an example of SF turning back in on itself rather than reaching out to new futures. It won the Campbell Memorial Award. It's in print, and in the library in French and English.

So, one woman and four men—one English, three American, and one Canadian—that's the widest spread of nationalities for a while. Brin and Willis are previous winners. Sawyer and Baxter and Stephenson are Hugo newcomers. They're all SF—one near-future thriller, one near-future screwball comedy, one medium-future technodream, one time travel, one planetary SF. This year's list doesn't excite me, and it didn't excite me in 1996. There's nothing wrong with any of them, but only *Diamond Age* has any luster.

What else might they have chosen?

Eligible non-overlapping Nebula nominees were Paul Park's *Coelestis* and Walter Jon Williams's wonderful *Metropolitan*, which would have been an excellent Hugo nominee.

The World Fantasy Award was won by *The Prestige*, Christopher Priest. Other nominees were *All the Bells on Earth*, James P. Blaylock; *Expiration Date*, Tim Powers; *Red Earth and Pouring Rain*, Vikram Chandra; *Requiem*, Graham Joyce; and *The Silent Strength of Stones*, Nina Kiriki Hoffmann.

The Campbell Memorial Award was given to Baxter, with Stephenson second and Ian McDonald's *Chaga* third.

The Philip K. Dick Award was won by Bruce Bethke's *Headcrash*, with a special citation to *Carlucci's Edge*, Richard Paul Russo. Other finalists were *The Color of Distance*, Amy Thomson; *Permutation City*, Greg Egan; *Reluctant Voyagers*, Elisabeth Vonarburg; *Virtual Death*, Shale Aaron.

Permutation City wasn't Hugo eligible because of prior UK publication. *The Color of Distance* and *Reluctant Voyagers* would both have made excellent Hugo nominees.

The Tiptree Award was a tie, shared between *The Memoirs of Elizabeth Frankenstein*, Theodore Roszak; and *Waking the Moon*, Elizabeth Hand. Also on the short list: *Little Sisters of the Apocalypse*, Kit Reed; and Melissa Scott's *Shadow Man*.

Other Locus nominees not previously mentioned were: *Invader*, C. J. Cherryh; *Legacy*, Greg Bear; *Sailing Bright Eternity*, Gregory Benford; *Worldwar: Tilting the Balance*, Harry Turtledove; *Slow River*, Nicola Griffith; *Amnesia Moon*, Jonathan Lethem; *Kaleidoscope Century*, John Barnes; *Fairyland*, Paul J. McAuley; *The Ganymede Club*, Charles Sheffield; *The Killing Star*, Charles Pellegrino and George Zebrowski; *Gaia's Toys*, Rebecca Ore; *The Stone Garden*, Mary Rosenblum; *Testament*, Valerie J. Freireich; *The Golden Nineties*, Lisa Mason; *An Exaltation of Larks*, Robert Reed.

I think *Kaleidoscope Century* absolutely was one of the most significant books of the year, if also one of the nastiest.

The Locus fantasy award went to Orson Scott Card's *Alvin Journeyman*. Other nominees not previously mentioned: *Fortress in the Eye of Time*, C. J. Cherryh; *The Lions of Al-Rassan*, Guy Gavriel Kay; *Resurrection Man*, Sean Stewart; *The Book of Atrix Wolfe*, Patricia A. McKillip; *Blood*, Michael Moorcock; *Storm Rising*, Mercedes Lackey; *City of Bones*, Martha Wells; *Crown of Shadows*, C. S. Friedman; *Maskerade*, Terry Pratchett; *Zod Wallop*, William Browning Spencer; *Assassin's Apprentice*, Robin Hobb; *Stone of Tears*, Terry Goodkind; *The Tower of Beowulf*, Parke Godwin; *A Sorcerer and a Gentleman*, Elizabeth Willey; *World Without End*, Sean Russell; *Harp of Winds*, Maggie Furey.

Some really great stuff there.

The Mythopoeic Award was won by *Waking the Moon*. Only one nominee not previously mentioned: Kenneth Morris, *The Dragon Path*.

The Prometheus Award was won by Ken MacLeod's *The Star Fraction*, a book which by itself practically justifies the existence of a separate UK publishing industry. It's a book that makes me excited about what SF can do. And it didn't get US publication for years, because it's a book about the near future of Britain. This should have been on the Hugo ballot.

Was there anything all of these missed?

Greg Egan's *Distress*, Alison Sinclair's *Legacies*, C. J. Cherryh's *Rider at the Gate*.

So I'd say 1996 is a year where the Hugo nominees didn't do their job for me. Apart from the Stephenson, they're fairly unexciting books, while more exciting books (*Metropolitan*, *The Star Fraction*, *Kaleidoscope Century*) didn't make the ballot.

OTHER CATEGORIES

BEST NOVELLA

Winner: *The Death of Captain Future*, by Allen Steele (*Asimov's*, October 1995)

Nominees:
Bibi, by Mike Resnick and Susan Shwartz (*Asimov's*, mid-December 1995)
Fault Lines, by Nancy Kress (*Asimov's*, August 1995)
A Man of the People, by Ursula K. Le Guin (*Asimov's*, April 1995)
A Woman's Liberation, by Ursula K. Le Guin (*Asimov's*, July 1995)

BEST NOVELETTE

Winner: "Think Like a Dinosaur," by James Patrick Kelly (*Asimov's*, June 1995)

Nominees:
"The Good Rat," by Allen Steele (*Analog*, mid-December 1995)

"Luminous," by Greg Egan (*Asimov's*, September 1995)
"Must and Shall," by Harry Turtledove (*Asimov's*, November 1995)
"TAP," by Greg Egan (*Asimov's*, November 1995)
"When the Old Gods Die," by Mike Resnick (*Asimov's*, April 1995)

I think I'd have voted for the Kelly above the Egan or the Turtledove, but it would have been a close thing. Terrific year for novelettes, again.

Best Short Story

Winner: "The Lincoln Train," by Maureen F. McHugh (*F&SF*, April 1995)

Nominees:
"A Birthday," by Esther M. Friesner (*F&SF*, August 1995)
"Life on the Moon," by Tony Daniel (*Asimov's*, April 1995)
"TeleAbsence," by Michael A. Burstein (*Analog*, July 1995)
"Walking Out," by Michael Swanwick (*Asimov's*, February 1995)

The McHugh and the Freisner are both absolutely chilling.

Best Nonfiction Book

Winner: *Science Fiction: The Illustrated Encyclopedia*, by John Clute

Nominees:
Alien Horizons: The Fantastic Art of Bob Eggleton, by Bob Eggleton
Spectrum 2: The Best in Contemporary Fantastic Art, edited by Cathy Burnett and Arnie Fenner
To Write Like a Woman: Essays in Feminism and Science Fiction, by Joanna Russ
Yours, Isaac Asimov, by Isaac Asimov, edited by Stanley Asimov

Best Dramatic Presentation

Winner: *Babylon 5:* "The Coming of Shadows"

Nominees:
12 Monkeys
Star Trek: Deep Space Nine: "The Visitor"
Toy Story

BEST PROFESSIONAL EDITOR

Winner: Gardner Dozois

Nominees:
Ellen Datlow
Scott Edelman
Kristine Kathryn Rusch
Stanley Schmidt

BEST PROFESSIONAL ARTIST

Winner: Bob Eggleton

Nominees:
Jim Burns
Thomas Canty
Don Maitz
Michael Whelan

BEST ORIGINAL ARTWORK

Winner: *Dinotopia: The World Beneath,* by James Gurney

Nominees:
Bob Eggleton, cover of *F&SF*, October/November 1995 (illustrating *Dankden,* by Marc Laidlaw)
George H. Krauter, cover of *Analog,* March 1995 (illustrating "Renascance," by Poul Anderson)
Gary Lippincott, cover of *F&SF*, January 1995 (illustrating "Tea and Hamsters," by Michael Coney)

Bob Eggleton, cover of *Analog*, January 1995 (illustrating "Tide of Stars," by Julia Ecklar)

BEST SEMIPROZINE

Winner: *Locus*, edited by Charles N. Brown

Nominees:
Crank!, edited by Bryan Cholfin
Interzone, edited by David Pringle
The New York Review of Science Fiction, edited by David G. Hartwell, Ariel Hamon, and Tad Dembinski
Science Fiction Chronicle, edited by Andrew I. Porter

BEST FANZINE

Winner: *Ansible*, edited by Dave Langford

Nominees:
Apparatchik, edited by Andrew Hooper and Victor Gonzalez
Attitude, edited by Michael Abbott, John Dallman, and Pam Wells
FOSFAX, edited by Timothy Lane and Elizabeth Garrott
Lan's Lantern, edited by George "Lan" Laskowski
Mimosa, edited by Richard and Nicki Lynch

BEST FAN WRITER

Winner: Dave Langford

Nominees:
Sharon Farber
Andy Hooper
Evelyn C. Leeper
Joseph T. Major

BEST FAN ARTIST

Winner: Bill Rotsler

Nominees:
Ian Gunn
Teddy Harvia
Joe Mayhew
Peggy Ranson

JOHN W. CAMPBELL AWARD

Winner: David Feintuch

Nominees:
Michael A. Burstein
Felicity Savage
Sharon Shinn
Tricia Sullivan

David Feintuch (1944–2006) was a very nice guy, and he really believed in his Midshipman's Hope series. I believe he's the oldest Campbell winner. He had published three volumes of the series by the end of 1995, and he went on to write another four volumes and two fantasy novels. He was a pretty good winner, and the rest of the nominees were also very good—a much better year for the Campbell than 1995.

Michael A. Burstein won in 1997, so let's leave him for next time. And we talked about Felicity Savage last time.

Sharon Shinn had published one excellent first novel, *The Shape-Shifter's Wife*. She has gone on to have a significant career and is a major writer; she'd have been an excellent winner.

Tricia Sullivan was also an excellent nominee and would have been a great winner—she'd just published a first novel, *Lethe,* and has gone on to become an important writer.

So a pretty good Campbell year. Other possibly eligible people not nominated: Alison Sinclair, Linda Nagata, Richard Calder.

COMMENTS ON 1996

16. GARDNER DOZOIS

Novella was strong that year. I liked *The Death of Captain America*—I published it—but the best amongst the novellas that made the ballot are the two Le Guins, perhaps the best of her New Hainish stories, which in turn are the best of her short work. *A Woman's Liberation* is particularly strong. But a few of my favorite novellas didn't even make the ballot, among them David Marusek's first major story, *We Were Out of Our Minds with Joy*, and what is probably still Brian Stableford's single best story, "Mortimer Gray's *History of Death*." Also first-rate are *For White Hill*, by Joe Haldeman, and "Genesis," by Poul Anderson, amazingly up to date with the cutting edge of the field for someone who had been writing since the fifties. Also good are Robert Reed's *Brother Perfect,* Pat Cadigan's *Death in the Promised Land,* and Mary Rosenblum's *The Doryman.*

I have no problem with "Think Like a Dinosaur" winning, but both "Luminous" and "TAP," by Greg Egan, are extraordinary stories. Off the ballot, Egan, who was at the height of his prolificness, also had the amazing "Wang's Carpets" and "Silver Fire." I used both "Luminous" and "Wang's Carpets" in my Best that year, and never for a moment doubted that it was justified. Also off-ballot was a very entertaining story by Robert Reed, "A Place with Shade"; John Kessel's "Some Like It Cold"; and Tom Purdom's "Romance in Lunar G."

In short story, "The Lincoln Train" is very powerful, but I also liked Tony Daniel's underrated "Life on the Moon." Some of the best short stories of the year didn't make the ballot at all, though, including Ian R. MacLeod's "Starship Day," Geoff Ryman's "Home," Paul J. McAuley's "Recording Angel," and Michael Swanwick's "Radio Waves."

I'll allow myself the indulgence of bragging that ALL of the novellas that year, and all but one of the novelettes, were from *Asimov's*. In all, twelve *Asimov's* stories made the ballot that year, which may be the record for the most finalists in one year from a single source.

(The Federal Express people were nervous about shipping the Hugo home that year, by the way, since, with all the wires and batteries—the spotlights swiveled and actually lit up—combined with the Hugo rocket, it looked too much like a bomb. I had to partially disassemble it before they'd take it.)

David Feintuch WAS a nice guy, and a reasonable choice at the time. In retrospect, I think perhaps it should have gone to David Marusek.

41. RICH HORTON

This might have been the greatest year for novelettes in SF history. But I'll start in novel. And I admit, this is a post I basically set up last night, so mostly it does not reflect the comments string.

First, I'm happy enough with *The Diamond Age* as a winner. It may not have a great ending, as Jo says, but what Stephenson does? Still, ideas, ideas, ideas.

I quite liked David Brin's *Brightness Reef,* a good start to the ultimately disappointing Second Uplift Trilogy.

Egan's *Distress* is very fine work. *The Prestige* is excellent work. I quite enjoyed, though didn't quite love, Jonathan Lethem's *Amnesia Moon.* Catherine Asaro's first novel, *Primary Inversion,* appeared this year—it's quite interesting. I don't like where she ended up going with this series, but this book (and one or two more in its continuity) was quite fun.

From the mainstream, one quite major SF novel: Richard Powers's *Galatea 2.2.*

From the world of YA, two significant works: Philip Pullman's *Northern Lights* aka *The Golden Compass* (and which title should be preferred? Perhaps uncharacteristically, I prefer the US title [*The Golden Compass*], but what do others think? Like Pullman??)

Also YA, a great debut: *Sabriel,* by Garth Nix.

A novel I haven't read, by an author who has done little if anything else, but which Lawrence Watt-Evans has praised highly, is Stuart Hopen's *Warp Angel.*

And finally, the wonderful but insufficiently prolific William Browning Spencer published two first-rate novels this year: *Zod Wallop* and *Résumé with Monsters.* These are just great stuff.

42. RICH HORTON

Now to the short fiction. IMO, this was quite a year.

In novella, among the nominees, I'd have gone for either of the Le Guin stories ahead of Steele's enjoyable but not brilliant story. But some better work didn't get nominated:

Mortimer Gray's 'History of Death,' by Brian Stableford
De Secretis Mulierum, by L. Timmel Duchamp
Hypocaust and Bathysphere, by Rebecca Ore
We Were Out of Our Minds with Joy, by David P. Marusek (who also would have been a good Campbell nominee)

And even Willis's *Remake,* which I think was actually novella length (though very long—maybe 38K?) and which was nominated in that category for the Nebula.

All of those are good, none obviously better than the two Le Guin stories—but one story, I think, was the best of the year, by SF's greatest-ever writer of novellas: Gene Wolfe. This is *The Ziggurat,* a tremendously exciting and quite chilling novella, with a classically, profoundly unreliable narrator. It can be read entirely differently depending on how much you believe what the narrator says—I think enough clues are there to suggest he's entirely out there—but the story certainly doesn't demand any particular reading.

In novelette, I've already said this might arguably be the greatest year ever for novelettes. Consider the winner: "Think Like a Dinosaur" is a great story, clearly one of the best Hugo winners. It's in very fruitful dialogue with not one but two classic SF stories ("The Cold Equations" and "Rogue Moon"), and it's great even if you don't know those stories. A masterwork.

And I don't think it's the best story of 1995.

Consider Egan's two nominees. Both of them ("Luminous" and "TAP") are magnificent, the best work he had done to that date, I think. Either would have been fine Hugo winners, though I'd place them behind the Kelly.

But neither was even the best Egan novelette of the year.

That honor, in my opinion, goes to "Wang's Carpets," which I think one of the best SF stories of all time. A few novelettes might be better ("A Rose for Ecclesiastes"? "Fondly Fahrenheit"? "5,271,009"? "The Stars Below"?), but surely not many—and at this level, picking favorites is pointless. I don't think any SF story ever has pushed my sense of wonder to this level—and I was a jaded thirty-five-year-old when I read it.

The thing is, there were a ton MORE great novelettes in 1995. My other two favorites were:

"Starship Day," by Ian R. MacLeod

"Fragments of a Painted Eggshell," by Alexander Jablokov (an almost ignored story)

But also, these novelettes are first-rate:

"For White Hill," by Joe Haldeman (a beautiful SF story based quite rigorously on a Shakespeare sonnet)

"Gone to Glory," by R. Garcia y Robertson

"Coming of Age in Karhide," by Ursula K. Le Guin

"Recording Angel," by Paul McAuley

"Spondulix," by Paul Di Filippo

"Downloading Midnight," by William Browning Spencer

"Ether OR," by Le Guin

"Ellen O'Hara," by MacLeod (Ian)

"Tale of the Blue Spruce Dreaming (or, How to Be Flesh)," by Neal Stephenson

"Radio Waves," by Michael Swanwick

"Thorri the Poet's Saga," by S. N. Dyer (Sharon Farber) and Lucy Kemnitzer

"Elvis Bearpaw's Luck," by William Sanders

"The Cement Garden," by Mary Rosenblum

"The Chronology Protection Case," by Paul Levinson

And finally in short story, the nominees include three excellent choices:

McHugh's winner, "The Lincoln Train"; Friesner's striking "A Birthday"; and Tony Daniel's excellent "Life on the Moon." Any of them would have been a worthy winner.

Other good potential nominees:

"Alderley Edge," by Jim Cowan (the first of three stories I've seen by him, every one excellent—I wish there were more!)

"One," by George Alec Effinger

"Ebb Tide," by Mary Soon Lee

"Excerpt from the Third and Last Volume of 'Tribes of the Pacific Coast,'" by Jean Mark Gawron (and those who have seen me express my hatred for his awful novel *Algorithm* should note that Gawron could actually write, and besides *Algorithm*, his work is generally well worth checking out)

"Noses," by Eliot Fintushel

"Snow, Glass, Apples," by Neil Gaiman

"The Bone Carver's Tale," by Jeff VanderMeer

"The Dream of Houses," by Wil McCarthy

"The Grass Princess," by Gwyneth Jones (which won the World Fantasy Award)

"Water off a Black Dog's Back," by Kelly Link (her first published story)

(And last year, I should have mentioned Friesner's very affecting "Death and the Librarian.")

65. TNH

James Nicoll @12, 17; Skwid @63: You may feel that *Apollo 13* isn't SF, but the Hugos have a useful operating principle: Unless something truly absurd happens, content-based Hugo eligibility is what the voters say it is.

Voters can't override date- or format-based rules, such as length requirements or publication date cutoffs. However, if they feel that *Apollo 13* delivers more skiffy goodness than any other piece of dramatic entertainment that year, and they vote accordingly, then *Apollo 13* qualifies.

It's a good rule. If you don't believe me, consider the alternative, and what it would take to administer it.

72. Rich Horton

Well, of course, you can disagree with the voters' choices. That's part of the deal. But you can disagree on all grounds—I can disagree with voters who choose Sawyer, say, though I don't dispute his eligibility.

But what I think happens is that voters decide, in essence, which story/film/whatever best satisfied their SF jones—or, as TNH says, delivered more skiffy goodness. As she says, what's the alternative? A tribunal deciding what's SF and what's not? That'll work real well, you bet.

1997

Best Novel

Winner: *Blue Mars*, by Kim Stanley Robinson

Nominees:
Holy Fire, by Bruce Sterling
Memory, by Lois McMaster Bujold
Remnant Population, by Elizabeth Moon
Starplex, by Robert J. Sawyer

The 1997 Hugo Awards were presented at LoneStarCon II, in San Antonio, Texas. The Best Novel winner was Kim Stanley Robinson's *Blue Mars*, which I have not read because of problems with *Red Mars*, as previously mentioned. It's the conclusion to Robinson's trilogy about terraforming Mars. It won the Locus SF award. It's in print, and it's in the library in French and English.

There were four other nominees, and I've read three of them.

Bruce Sterling's *Holy Fire* is a near-future extrapolation about rejuvenation. I liked it, but I had issues with it—having the hormones and body of a young person wouldn't inherently give an old person the same fashion tastes as a young person. It was a book that got a lot of buzz at the time, but I haven't heard much about it since—I think it has been eclipsed by Sterling's later work. I have a soft spot for it because it was the first long thing of his I really liked. It's in print, and it's in the library in French and English.

Lois McMaster Bujold's *Memory* is planetary SF about growing up and facing responsibilities. It's very much not a stand-alone book, it really needs the rest of the series to support it, and I think it may have suffered in the voting because of that. I think it's an excellent nominee, and I would have voted for it. It's in print, and it's in the library in French and English.

Elizabeth Moon's *Remnant Population* is about a colony moved off their planet and one grandmother who decides to stay alone. I liked the idea of it, and the elderly female protagonist, more than I actually enjoyed the experience of reading it, but I'm glad it got a Hugo nomination—a very unusual book. It's in print and in the library in English only.

I haven't read Robert J. Sawyer's *Starplex,* because I didn't enjoy *The Terminal Experiment* enough to want to seek out more of his work. This sounds much more my kind of thing, though—the discovery of a series of wormholes opens up time and space to an Earth that might not be ready for it. It's in print, and it's in the library in English and French.

So, two women and three men—one Canadian and four Americans. Robinson and Bujold were former winners. Sawyer and Sterling were former nominees. Moon was a Hugo newcomer. All the nominees are science fiction: two planetary SF, one space opera, one near-future Earth, and one medium-future Mars. What else might they have chosen?

The Nebula was out of sync with calendar years at this point—it was won by Nicola Griffith's excellent *Slow River,* which is a 1995 book. The only eligible non-overlapping nominee was Patricia McKillip's *Winter Rose.*

The World Fantasy Award was won by Rachel Pollack's astonishingly weird *Godmother Night.* Other nominees: *The 37th Mandala,* Marc Laidlaw; *The Bear Went Over the Mountain,* William Kotzwinkle; *Devil's Tower,* Mark Sumner; *A Game of Thrones,* George R. R. Martin; *The Golden Key,* Melanie Rawn, Jennifer Roberson, and Kate Elliott; *Shadow of Ashland,* Terence M. Green.

A Game of Thrones would have been a good Hugo nominee.

The Campbell Memorial Award was given to Paul McAuley's *Fairyland,* with *Blue Mars* second and Mary Doria Russell's *The Sparrow* third.

Some people might feel that *The Sparrow* might have deserved a Hugo nomination, and surely it was a book many people were talking about. I hate it—it sets up a situation that eventually makes no emotional sense, and I felt I'd been conned into caring about something that's just stupid. I don't mean science errors; I mean people are not like that and do not act in ways like that. *The Sparrow* requires hundreds of people to behave in ways that only psychopaths behave. It's just barely plausible that one person could find a victim of severe abuse and assume this is a degenerate who should be blamed for what happened to them, but an entire ship full of people? The whole Catholic Church? The book sets up a question and palms the card really badly on the answer.

The Philip K. Dick Award went to *The Time Ships*, Stephen Baxter, though as it was a 1996 Hugo nominee, I don't understand how it was eligible. The special citation was *At the City Limits of Fate*, Michael Bishop. Other nominees: *Reclamation*, Sarah Zettel; *The Shift*, George Foy; *The Transmigration of Souls*, William Barton.

The Tiptree Award was given to *The Sparrow*. Ugh. At least it was a tie with Le Guin's excellent short "Mountain Ways." The long works on the short list were: *A History Maker*, Alasdair Gray; *Leaning Towards Infinity*, Sue Woolfe; *Nadya: The Wolf Chronicles*, Pat Murphy; *The Pillow Friend*, Lisa Tuttle.

Locus nominees not mentioned already: *Endymion*, Dan Simmons; *Cetaganda*, Lois McMaster Bujold; *Idoru*, William Gibson; *Inheritor*, C. J. Cherryh; *Night Lamp*, Jack Vance; *Exodus from the Long Sun*, Gene Wolfe; *Voyage*, Stephen Baxter; *Beggars Ride*, Nancy Kress; *Excession*, Iain M. Banks; *The Ringworld Throne*, Larry Niven; *Children of the Mind*, Orson Scott Card; *Otherland: City of Golden Shadow*, Tad Williams; *Dreamfall*, Joan D. Vinge; *Distress*, Greg Egan; *Pirates of the Universe*, Terry Bisson; *River of Dust*, Alexander Jablokov; *Night Sky Mine*, Melissa Scott; *The Other End of Time*, Frederik Pohl; *Gibbon's Decline and Fall*, Sheri S. Tepper; *The Tranquillity Alternative*, Allen Steele; *Oaths and Miracles*, Nancy Kress; *Infinity's Shore*, David Brin.

Well, some good stuff there, but also some things I'm really glad are there and not on the Hugo list—*Endymion, Ringworld Throne, Children of the Mind, Beggars Ride*—this is a year when people sensibly didn't nominate things in series where only the first one was great. Also worth noting the presence of *Cetaganda* here. People talk about Bujold's fans voting her Hugos as if they do this mindlessly and fanatically, but here we have a weaker novel in the series, and it wasn't nominated. People nominate what they think are the best books they've read that year, and it works out pretty well on the whole.

The Locus fantasy award was won by *A Game of Thrones*, which doesn't surprise me one bit. Other nominees not yet mentioned: *Lunatics*, Bradley Denton; *Blameless in Abaddon*, James Morrow; *Royal Assassin*, Robin Hobb; *A Crown of Swords*, Robert Jordan; *Feet of Clay*, Terry Pratchett; *The Wood Wife*, Terri Windling; *One for the Morning Glory*, John Barnes; *Walking the Labyrinth*, Lisa Goldstein; *Ancient Echoes*, Robert Holdstock; *Clouds End*, Sean Stewart; *The Golden Compass* (UK title: *Northern Lights*), Philip Pullman; *Mother of Winter*, Barbara Hambly; *Fair Peril*, Nancy Springer; *Blood of the Fold*, Terry Goodkind; *Firebird*, Mercedes Lackey; *The Dragon and the Unicorn*, A. A. Attanasio; *Sea Without a Shore*, Sean Russell.

The Wood Wife won the Mythopoeic Award, and very well deserved—it's a great book.

So, was there anything they all missed?

There was Raphael Carter's *The Fortunate Fall*, which really was one of the most exciting books of the year, or any year, and which should have made the Hugo ballot. And there was Candas Jane Dorsey's beautiful and disturbing *Black Wine*, which should have made the World Fantasy or Mythopoeic lists at least. There's Jane Emerson's *City of Diamond*, Neil Gaiman's *Neverwhere*, and Ian McDonald's *Sacrifice of Fools*—one of his very best books.

On the whole, 1997's nominees work. They're a good set of books, they're representative of where the field was, though I'd have really liked to see *The Fortunate Fall*, *A Game of Thrones*, and *Sacrifice of Fools* up there.

OTHER CATEGORIES

BEST NOVELLA

Winner: *Blood of the Dragon,* by George R. R. Martin (*Asimov's,* July 1996)

Nominees:
Abandon in Place, by Jerry Oltion (*F&SF,* December 1996)
The Cost to Be Wise, by Maureen F. McHugh (*Starlight 1*)
Gas Fish, by Mary Rosenblum (*Asimov's,* February 1996)
Immersion, by Gregory Benford (*Science Fiction Age,* March 1996)
Time Travelers Never Die, by Jack McDevitt (*Asimov's,* May 1996)

My two favorites here, the Martin and the McHugh, are both sections of novels. I didn't make it to Worldcon that year, but I remember being at a Unicon the weekend before and talking about how great these nominees were, which was probably the first time I noticed how much I liked novellas. And *Starlight,* what a great anthology!

BEST NOVELETTE

Winner: "Bicycle Repairman," by Bruce Sterling (*Intersections: The Sycamore Hill Anthology; Asimov's,* October/November 1996)

Nominees:
"Age of Aquarius," by William Barton (*Asimov's,* May 1996)
"Beauty and the Opéra or The Phantom Beast," by Suzy McKee Charnas (*Asimov's,* March 1996)
"The Land of Nod," by Mike Resnick (*Asimov's,* June 1996)
"Mountain Ways," by Ursula K. Le Guin (*Asimov's,* August 1996)

Best Short Story

Winner: "The Soul Selects Her Own Society: Invasion and Repulsion: A Chronological Reinterpretation of Two of Emily Dickinson's Poems: A Wellsian Perspective," by Connie Willis (*Asimov's*, April 1996; *War of the Worlds: Global Dispatches*)

Nominees:
"The Dead," by Michael Swanwick (*Starlight 1*)
"Decency," by Robert Reed (*Asimov's*, June 1996)
"Gone," by John Crowley (*F&SF*, September 1996)
"Un-Birthday Boy," by James White (*Analog*, February 1996)

Best Nonfiction Book

Winner: *Time & Chance: An Autobiography*, by L. Sprague de Camp

Nominees:
The Faces of Fantasy, by Patti Perret
Look at the Evidence, by John Clute
The Silence of the Langford, by David Langford
The Tough Guide to Fantasyland, by Diana Wynne Jones

Here, another helping of comparing kumquats to parakeets! I'm amazed the DWJ didn't win.

Best Dramatic Presentation

Winner: *Babylon 5:* "Severed Dreams"

Nominees:
Independence Day
Mars Attacks!
Star Trek: First Contact

Best Professional Editor

Winner: Gardner Dozois

Nominees:
Scott Edelman
Patrick Nielsen Hayden
Kristine Kathryn Rusch
Stanley Schmidt

Best Professional Artist

Winner: Bob Eggleton

Nominees:
Thomas Canty
David A. Cherry
Don Maitz
Michael Whelan

Best Semiprozine

Winner: *Locus*, edited by Charles N. Brown

Nominees:
Interzone, edited by David Pringle
The New York Review of Science Fiction, edited by Kathryn Cramer,
    Tad Dembinski, Ariel Hameon, David G. Hartwell, and Kevin
    Maroney
Science Fiction Chronicle, edited by Andrew I. Porter
Speculations, edited by Kent Brewster

Best Fanzine

Winner: *Mimosa*, edited by Dick and Nicki Lynch

Nominees:
Ansible, edited by Dave Langford
File 770, edited by Mike Glyer
Nova Express, edited by Lawrence Person
Tangent, edited by Dave Truesdale

BEST FAN WRITER

Winner: Dave Langford

Nominees:
Sharon Farber
Mike Glyer
Andy Hooper
Evelyn C. Leeper

BEST FAN ARTIST

Winner: William Rotsler

Nominees:
Ian Gunn
Joe Mayhew
Peggy Ranson
Sherlock

JOHN W. CAMPBELL AWARD

Winner: Michael A. Burstein

Nominees:
Raphael Carter
Richard Garfinkle
Katya Reimann
Sharon Shinn

Burstein is a terrific winner—he was nominated on the strength of awesome short work, and he has continued to produce awesome short work ever since.

Raphael Carter's first novel, *The Fortunate Fall*, had just come out to great acclaim, a great nominee. Carter hasn't produced much since, unfortunately.

Richard Garfinkle had also just written a first novel, the unusual *Celestial Matters*, in which there are real crystal spheres and you can crash through them on your way to the moon. Another good nominee.

Katya Reimann is another first novelist; her *Wind from a Foreign Sky* had just come out. She has completed that trilogy, but I haven't seen anything recently.

Sharon Shinn is, of course, a major writer, as I said last week, and would have been another terrific winner.

So a pretty good Campbell slate. Other possible eligible candidates: Candas Jane Dorsey, Ian McDowell, Sarah Zettel, J. Gregory Keyes.

COMMENTS ON 1997

4. RICH HORTON

I think a nomination list that comprised *Holy Fire*, *The Fortunate Fall*, *Blue Mars*, *Celestial Matters*, and perhaps *Memory* would have been about right.

In the Campbell, I strongly disagree about Burstein, by all accounts a very nice guy but just not that strong a writer. His first story did have some interesting ideas, and got a fair amount of notice. I voted for Raphael Carter, no doubt. It's a shame Carter has done so little since— just one more story that I can think of, and that very good, I should add. Really, I should add, the entire nominee list is very strong, and the other candidates you mention are also strong. A good year for the Campbell, even if the winner is in my opinion a weak choice.

But you missed one eligible writer, who in retrospect is in my opinion overwhelmingly the best and most important new writer to appear in the field in 1995–1996: Kelly Link.

Around this time, I had started to write for the print *Tangent* (which, I see, was a Hugo nominee, though not by any means due to my contributions), and to post my thoughts on SFF.net as well, so I actually have records of what I thought the best stories of 1996 were. In novella, I liked:

Bellwether, by Connie Willis
Immersion, by Gregory Benford
Abandon in Place, by Jerry Oltion
Chrysalis, by Robert Reed
The Cost to Be Wise, by Maureen McHugh
Primrose and Thorn, by Bud Sparhawk
Human History, by Lucius Shepard

Back then, I probably would have voted for Willis, and I might still, but I also might vote for McHugh. I had problems with *Blood of the Dragon,* partly because it seemed too much "part of a novel," and partly because the economics seemed absurd.

In novelette, I had a long list, with three absolutely outstanding stories that did not make the Hugo nomination list. These are:

"The Spade of Reason," by Jim Cowan
"Erase/Record/Play," by John M. Ford
"Seven Guesses of the Heart," by M. John Harrison

All of those should have been nominated, a win by any of them would have been fine—I'd have voted for the Cowan, a great and sadly underknown story, in first.

As for other possibilities—well, here's what I wrote back then (still saved on my home page):

> Other notable novelettes, in no particular order: "The Copyright Notice Case" by Paul Levinson, "Galley Slave" by Jean Lamb, "Martian Valkyrie" by G. David Nordley, "Beauty and the Opéra or The Phantom Beast" by Suzy McKee Charnas, "Bicycle Repairman" by Bruce Sterling, "Pyros" by George Ewing, "Bettina's Bet" by L. Timmel Du-

champ, "The Miracle of Ivar Avenue" by John Kessel, "The Flowers of Aulit Prison" by Nancy Kress, "Generation Zero" by Michael Cassutt, "Flying Lessons" by Kelly Link, "Yesterdays" by Mary Rosenblum, "The Crear" by Barrington J. Bayley, "The Weighing of Ayre" by Gregory Feeley, and "Tea" by Esther Friesner. Of those listed, I'd point special attention to the Kelly Link story, mainly because I think she is a new writer of considerable interest, based on the grand total of two stories of hers that I've read.

In retrospect, I'm really, really proud that I singled out Kelly Link—I think it's fair to say I was right about her potential!

Of those novelettes listed above, besides the Link, I am most impressed in memory by Kress's "Flowers of Aulit Prison" (though as noted by someone else, this was a good story that led to a mediocre trilogy), Duchamp's "Bettina's Bet" (she might have been a good Campbell nominee!), and the two Hugo nominees, "Bicycle Repairman" (which is good, and a good winner, just not as good as the three I mentioned at first), and "Beauty and the Opéra."

In short story, my clear choice as the best of the year was "Gone," by John Crowley. (Crowley really is an utterly amazing writer.)

My other top favorites:

"The Spear of the Sun," by David Langford
"Counting Cats in Zanzibar," by Gene Wolfe
"Cider," by Tom Purdom
"Breakaway, Backdown," by James Patrick Kelly (reminded me of "Scanners Live in Vain")
"A Crab Must Try," by Barrington Bayley (a very weird late story by this often very weird writer—I think this one won the BSFA short fiction award)
"The Drowning Cell," by Gregory Feeley

32. Gardner Dozois

If you eliminate *Blood of the Dragon* and McHugh's wonderful *The Cost to Be Wise* because they're parts of novels, then the best novella of the year didn't even make the ballot, Tony Daniel's *The Robot's Twilight*

Companion. Reed's *Chrysalis* was good too, as was Greg Benford's *Immersion,* Peter S. Beagle's fantasy *The Last Song of Sirit Byar,* and Gregory Feeley's near-mainstream *The Weighing of Ayre.* One of the weirdest novellas of the period was Eliot Fintushel's *Izzy at the Lucky Three.*

Novelette was strong this year too. My own vote would have gone to Nancy Kress's "The Flowers of Aulit Prison," which didn't make the ballot, although "Bicycle Repairman," "Beauty and the Opéra," and Le Guin's "Mountain Ways" are very strong too. Other strong stories that didn't make the ballot included John Kessel's "The Miracle of Ivar Avenue," Jim Cowan's "The Spade of Reason," Steven Utley's "The Wind over the World," Charles Sheffield's "The Peacock Throne," Jonathan Lethem's "How We Got In Town and Out Again," and Phillip C. Jennings's very strange "The Road to Reality."

In short story, of the stuff that made the ballot, Michael Swanwick's "The Dead" and John Crowley's "Gone" are definitely the best, but I also like Tony Daniel's "A Dry, Quiet War"; a very strong story that didn't make the ballot, one of the most eccentric time-travel stories ever written, Robert Reed's "Killing the Morrow"; and Wolfe's "Counting Cats in Zanzibar." The Willis is quite funny, but not a major work.

Of historical interest is "Invasion," one of the last, if not the last, Joanna Russ stories to appear in a mainline SF magazine—a Star Trek pastische, of all things—and Alastair Reynolds's first major story, "Spirey and the Queen."

Of the sixteen short pieces on the ballot this year, ten of them were from *Asimov's,* including the entire novelette category.

I have to agree with Rich about Michael Burstein. Nice guy, but I've never seen a story from him that I would have bought for *Asimov's.*

1998

Winner: *Forever Peace*, by Joe Haldeman

Nominees:
City on Fire, by Walter Jon Williams
Frameshift, by Robert Sawyer
Jack Faust, by Michael Swanwick
The Rise of Endymion, by Dan Simmons

The 1998 Hugo Awards were voted on by the members of BucConeer in Baltimore.

The Best Novel award was won by Joe Haldeman's *Forever Peace*, a book about the horrors of near-future war solved by telepathic niceness. It's a thematic sequel to *The Forever War*, not a direct sequel. This is by far my least favorite of Haldeman's works. I've read it only once. *Forever Peace* is in print, and it's in the library in French and English.

There are four other nominees, I've read three of them, and I like *one* of them. (Why did I ever start doing this?)

Let's start with the one I like, Walter Jon Williams's *City on Fire*, a wonderful innovative book, sequel to *Metropolitan*. These are smart science fiction books about a world where magic is real and powers technology. They're not like anything else, and they're on a really interesting border between SF and fantasy. *City on Fire* is about an election. This would have had my vote, had I been at Baltimore, but I expect it suffered in the voting from not being a stand-alone. It's not in print, and it's in the library in French only, thus reinforcing my perception that Walter Jon Williams is massively underrated.

Next, Robert Sawyer's *Frameshift*, which again I haven't read, again because I didn't care for *The Terminal Experiment*. It sounds like a near-future technothriller with genetic experiments and Nazi war criminals. I expect it's great. It's in print, and it's in the library in French and English.

Michael Swanwick's *Jack Faust* is a fantasy where Faust starts the Industrial Revolution early and everything goes to hell. It's beautifully written, as with all Swanwick, but it's negative about technology and the possibility of progress in a way that makes it hard for me to like. It's a good book, and probably deserved nomination. (But really, 1998 nominators? My least favorite Haldeman *and* my least favorite Swanwick? What were you thinking?) It's in print, and it's in the library in English and French.

Then there's Dan Simmons's *The Rise of Endymion*. After two books I don't like much, here's a book I really hate. I really don't like sequels that spoil the books that come before them, so this is a book I try not to think about. This is the book that gives all the answers left open by *Hyperion,* and they're awful answers. I know there are people who really like this book—there must be, it was Hugo nominated and won the Locus SF award—but it's beyond me. It has beautiful prose, but what it's saying, ugh. It's in print, and it's in the library in English only.

So, five men, four American and one Canadian. Simmons and Haldeman were previous winners; Sawyer and Swanwick were previous nominees. Williams had several short-form nominations, but this was his first appearance on the novel ballot. We have one near-future technothriller, one medium-future horrors-of-war novel, one messianic space opera, and two things that could be described as hard fantasy, very different from each other.

Wasn't there anything else they could have chosen? Or was I just really out of tune with what was being published that year?

Vonda McIntyre's *The Moon and the Sun,* a historical fantasy about a mermaid at the court of the Sun King, won the Nebula. I didn't like that either! The only other eligible non-overlapping nominee is Kate Elliott's excellent *King's Dragon,* first in the Crown of Stars series.

The World Fantasy Award went to *The Physiognomy*, by Jeffrey Ford. Other nominees were: *American Goliath*, Harvey Jacobs; *Dry Water*, Eric S. Nylund; *The Gift*, Patrick O'Leary; *Trader*, Charles de Lint.

The John W. Campbell Memorial Award was given to Haldeman, with Greg Bear's *Slant* in second place and Paul Preuss's *Secret Passages* third. *Slant* would have made a fine Hugo nominee.

The Philip K. Dick Award went to *The Troika*, Stepan Chapman. The special citation was *Acts of Conscience*, William Barton. Other nominees were: *Carlucci's Heart*, Richard Paul Russo; *An Exchange of Hostages*, Susan R. Matthews; *Mother Grimm*, Catherine Wells; *Opalite Moon*, Denise Vitola.

The Tiptree Award was won by Candas Jane Dorsey's *Black Wine*, a book that would have been a terrific and thought-provoking Hugo nominee, and Kelly Link's short "Travels with the Snow Queen." Eligible works on the short list were: *Cereus Blooms at Night*, Shani Mootoo; *The Dazzle of Day*, Molly Gloss; *Sacrifice of Fools*, Ian McDonald; *Signs of Life*, M. John Harrison; *Waking Beauty*, Paul Witcover.

The Dazzle of Day is marvelous—how I wish it had been a Hugo nominee! *Sacrifice of Fools* would have been a really good nominee, if eligible.

Locus nominees not previously mentioned were: *Antarctica*, Kim Stanley Robinson; *Saint Leibowitz and the Wild Horse Woman*, Walter M. Miller Jr. with Terry Bisson; *Finity's End*, C. J. Cherryh; *Diaspora*, Greg Egan; *Fool's War*, Sarah Zettel; *Titan*, Stephen Baxter; *3001: The Final Odyssey*, Arthur C. Clarke; *The Reality Dysfunction*, Peter F. Hamilton; *God's Fires*, Patricia Anthony; *Corrupting Dr. Nice*, John Kessel; *Destiny's Road*, Larry Niven; *Eternity Road*, Jack McDevitt; *The Black Sun*, Jack Williamson; *The Family Tree*, Sheri S. Tepper; *Glimmering*, Elizabeth Hand; *The Fleet of Stars*, Poul Anderson; *Mississippi Blues*, Kathleen Ann Goonan; *The Calcutta Chromosome*, Amitav Ghosh; *Dreaming Metal*, Melissa Scott; *Tomorrow and Tomorrow*, Charles Sheffield; *Once a Hero*, Elizabeth Moon; *Einstein's Bridge*, John Cramer; *Deception Well*, Linda Nagata.

There are a lot of books here I like better than the actual nominees, and would have preferred to see nominated—but the one it seems a real injustice to ignore is Egan's *Diaspora*, a really major work about the nature of consciousness and virtual life and space exploration.

The Locus fantasy award was won by Tim Powers's *Earthquake Weather*, another book that would have made a fine Hugo nominee. Other nominees not yet mentioned: *The Dark Tower IV: Wizard and Glass*, Stephen King; *Assassin's Quest*, Robin Hobb; *Freedom & Necessity*, Steven Brust and Emma Bull; *Winter Tides*, James P. Blaylock; *The Subtle Knife*, Philip Pullman; *Rose Daughter*, Robin McKinley; *Dogland*, Will Shetterly; *Lord of the Isles*, David Drake; *Gate of Ivory, Gate of Horn*, Robert Holdstock; *Running with the Demon*, Terry Brooks; *The Mines of Behemoth*, Michael Shea; *My Soul to Keep*, Tananarive Due; *The Night Watch*, Sean Stewart; *The Stars Dispose*, Michaela Roessner; *The Blackgod*, J. Gregory Keyes.

The Mythopoeic Award was given to A. S. Byatt's *The Djinn in the Nightingale's Eye*, which is wonderful, but a novella.

The Prometheus Award was won by Ken MacLeod's *The Stone Canal*, which strikes me as exactly the sort of book that should be Hugo nominated.

And was there anything they all missed? George R. R. Martin's *A Clash of Kings* and J. R. Dunn's chilling *Days of Cain*.

So, to sum up, 1998's nominees don't look anything like the best five books of the year to me, but this could just be my idiosyncratic reaction. How do they seem to you? I don't remember spending all of 1998 gnashing my teeth.

OTHER CATEGORIES

BEST NOVELLA

Winner: . . . *Where Angels Fear to Tread*, by Allen Steele (*Asimov's*, October/November 1997)

Nominees:
Ecopoiesis, by Geoffrey A. Landis (*Science Fiction Age*, May 1997)

The Funeral March of the Marionettes, by Adam-Troy Castro (*F&SF,* July 1997)
Loose Ends, by Paul Levinson (*Analog,* May 1997)
Marrow, by Robert Reed (*Science Fiction Age,* July 1997)

BEST NOVELETTE

Winner: "We Will Drink a Fish Together . . . ," by Bill Johnson (*Asimov's,* May 1997)

Nominees:
"Broken Symmetry," by Michael A. Burstein (*Analog,* February 1997)
"Moon Six," by Stephen Baxter (*Science Fiction Age,* March 1997)
"Three Hearings on the Existence of Snakes in the Human Bloodstream," by James Alan Gardner (*Asimov's,* February 1997)
"The Undiscovered," by William Sanders (*Asimov's,* March 1997)

BEST SHORT STORY

Winner: "The 43 Antarean Dynasties," by Mike Resnick (*Asimov's,* December 1997)

Nominees:
"Beluthahatchie," by Andy Duncan (*Asimov's,* March 1997)
"The Hand You're Dealt," by Robert J. Sawyer (*Free Space*)
"Itsy Bitsy Spider," by James Patrick Kelly (*Asimov's,* June 1997)
"No Planets Strike," by Gene Wolfe (*F&SF,* January 1997)
"Standing Room Only," by Karen Joy Fowler (*Asimov's,* August 1997)

BEST RELATED BOOK

Winner: *The Encyclopedia of Fantasy,* edited by John Clute and John Grant

Nominees:
Infinite Worlds: The Fantastic Visions of Science Fiction Art, by Vincent Di Fate

Reflections and Refractions: Thoughts on Science-Fiction, Science, and Other Matters, by Robert Silverberg

Space Travel, by Ben Bova with Anthony R. Lewis

Spectrum 4: The Best in Contemporary Fantastic Art, edited by Cathy Fenner and Arnie Fenner, with Jim Loehr

BEST DRAMATIC PRESENTATION

Winner: *Contact*

Nominees:
The Fifth Element
Gattaca
Men in Black
Starship Troopers

BEST PROFESSIONAL EDITOR

Winner: Gardner Dozois

Nominees:
Scott Edelman
David G. Hartwell
Stanley Schmidt
Gordon Van Gelder

BEST PROFESSIONAL ARTIST

Winner: Bob Eggleton

Nominees:
Jim Burns
Thomas Canty
David A. Cherry
Don Maitz
Michael Whelan

Best Semiprozine

Winner: *Locus,* edited by Charles N. Brown

Nominees:
Interzone, edited by David Pringle
The New York Review of Science Fiction, edited by Kathryn Cramer,
    Ariel Hameon, David G. Hartwell, and Kevin Maroney
Science Fiction Chronicle, edited by Andrew I. Porter
Speculations, edited by Kent Brewster and Denise Lee

Best Fanzine

Winner: *Mimosa,* edited by Nicki and Richard Lynch

Nominees:
Ansible, edited by Dave Langford
Attitude, edited by Michael Abbott, John Dallman, and Pam Wells
File 770, edited by Mike Glyer
Tangent, edited by David Truesdale

Best Fan Writer

Winner: David Langford

Nominees:
Bob Devney
Mike Glyer
Andy Hooper
Evelyn C. Leeper
Joseph T. Major

Best Fan Artist

Winner: Joe Mayhew

Nominees:
Brad W. Foster
Ian Gunn
Teddy Harvia
Peggy Ranson

JOHN W. CAMPBELL AWARD

Winner: Mary Doria Russell

Nominees:
Raphael Carter
Andy Duncan
Richard Garfinkle
Susan R. Matthews

Mary Doria Russell's *The Sparrow* had come out the previous year to much acclaim. She has written a couple of books since.

I talked about Carter and Garfinkle last week, both terrific nominees.

Andy Duncan was nominated on the basis of some excellent short work, and he has continued to produce excellent short work ever since, winning the World Fantasy Award and the Sturgeon Award. Great nominee.

Susan R. Matthews had a controversial and much-discussed first novel, *An Exchange of Hostages*. She published another few novels, but I haven't seen anything from her recently.

On the whole, a pretty good Campbell year. Other people who might have been eligible: Julie Czerneda, Stephen Dedman, David B. Coe, Ian MacLeod, James Alan Gardner, Candas Jane Dorsey.

Comments on 1998

29. Richard Horton

For novella, my clear favorite was Geoff Landis's *Ecopoiesis,* an original and realistic look at a terraforming attempt. Of the nominees, I also liked *Marrow* by Robert Reed. Not nominated was a good odd vampire story by Brian Stableford, *The Black Blood of the Dead.*

As usual, there is a long list of worthy novelettes. Of the nominees, the best was William Sanders's "The Undiscovered" (Shakespeare in the Americas)—and I think its latter-day reputation has only gotten stronger. I understand that the novelette voting was very close, and any of three stories could plausibly be said to have deserved the win. The winner, "We Will Drink a Fish Together," is pretty nice work, and so is Gardner's "Three Hearings on the Existence of Snakes in the Bloodstream." I can't remember the third story that almost tied—it may have been "The Undiscovered."

"Broken Symmetry" is good for Burstein but not at all a worthy Hugo nominee. "Moon Six" is strong work, though.

My favorite novelette of the whole year was "The Pipes of Pan," by Brian Stableford, which wasn't nominated, though it made a couple of Bests.

Other strong novelettes:

"Reasons to Be Cheerful," by Greg Egan
"After Kerry," by Ian McDonald
"Second Skin," by Paul McAuley (an early Quiet War story)
"Glass Earth, Inc.," by Stephen Baxter (a rather Eganesque story by
     him, uncharacteristically so, and very good but almost ignored at
     the time)
"Alice, Alfie, Ted, and the Aliens," by Paul Di Filippo (about Tiptree,
     Bester, and Sturgeon, of course, and riffing on a Tiptree title)
"Collected Ogoense," by Rebecca Ore
"On the Ice Islands," by Gregory Feeley
"The Dragons of Springplace," by Michael Swanwick
"The Mendelian Lamp Case," by Paul Levinson

"London Bone," by Michael Moorcock
"Great Western," by Kim Newman

Also, there were lots of fine short stories. I wasn't happy with the choice of a winner—I voted for "Itsy Bitsy Spider," and "No Planets Strike" was also good.

The best story of the year was nominated: Paul Park's "Get a Grip."
Also very strong was Terry Bisson's "An Office Romance."
Other top stories:

"Heart of Whiteness," by Howard Waldrop
"Beluthahatchie," by Andy Duncan
"The Fubar Suit," by Stephen Baxter (who had a great year despite publishing a truly awful novel)
"The Jackdaw's Last Case," by Paul Di Filippo
"The Nostalginauts," by "S. N. Dyer" (that is, the late Sharon Farber)
"Pages Out of Order," by Ben Jeapes
"Scarey Rose in Deep History," by Rebecca Ore
"Echoes," by Alan Brennert

49. GARDNER DOZOIS

The Steele and the Landis novellas were both strong, although I think I might have given it to *Marrow*. Ian R. MacLeod's Lovecraftian novella *The Golden Keeper* was very strong. Eliot Fintushel's *Izzy and the Father of Terror* was very strange indeed.

Novelette was even stronger than novella, with a lot of good novelettes published that year. Although I liked Bill Johnson's story, I think in retrospect I might have given it to William Sanders's "The Undiscovered" or, off the ballot, Paul McAuley's "Second Skin," one of McAuley's first major stories. Also excellent were James Alan Gardner's "Three Hearings on the Existence of Snakes in the Human Bloodstream," Ian R. MacLeod's "Nevermore," Walter Jon Williams's "Lethe," Silverberg's "Beauty in the Night," Baxter's "Moon Six," Ian McDonald's "After Kerry," Greg Egan's "Reasons to Be Cheerful," Swanwick's "Mother Grasshopper" (perhaps the only SF story ever written about people living on the back of a giant grasshopper), Brian

Stableford's "The Pipes of Pan," and Alastair Reynolds's "A Spy in Europa," one of his first sales. A very strong year for novelettes.

In short story, I think I'd go for "Itsy Bitsy Spider," although "Beluthahatchie," a colorful story about the train to Hell by Andy Duncan, and Karen Joy Fowler's "Standing Room Only," one of her rare straight SF stories, were also strong. As were "Yeyuka," by Greg Egan; "Balinese Dancer," by Gwyneth Jones; "Echoes," by Alan Brennert; "Winter Fire," by Geoffrey A. Landis; and "The Wisdom of Old Earth," by Michael Swanwick.

All three short fiction winners were from *Asimov's* this year.

The Campbell should have gone to Ian R. MacLeod, although Andy Duncan wouldn't have been a bad choice either.

50. DATLOW
Stephen Dedman had at least three stories published in professional markets beginning in 1994, so I believe would have been ineligible for the Campbell in 1998.

61. TNH
Good books aren't evenly spaced. Some years, you get a stack of great books that could have been Hugo winners in any other lineup. Other years, not so much.

James Nicoll @15: I wouldn't have missed the Chris Garcia moment for the world. It was an outburst of pure joyful id, totally unmodified by higher brain functions. I don't think anyone could do that twice in one night. I'm not sure they could do it twice in one lifetime.

TRANSFORMATIVE IN THIS AS EVERYTHING ELSE: WALTER JON WILLIAMS'S *METROPOLITAN* AND *CITY ON FIRE*

It would seem odd to describe Walter Jon Williams's *Metropolitan* and *City on Fire* as political thrillers set in a post-singularity world-spanning megacity, but it's not inaccurate. The reason it would be odd is because they're arguably fantasy. Indeed, one could call them "urban fantasy" if the term didn't already mean something else, because they're among the most urban books ever written.

It's the future. There's an impassable light-giving shield over the sky that was put there when the gods ascended. The sun and moon and day and night are legends. The entire world is covered in city—divided into many polities under a bewildering multitude of governments, but it's all solidly city, with food growing on the rooftops. There's a kind of magic thing called plasm that is magically generated by the relationships between buildings (by understandable and controllable methods) and which is used for everything from rejuvenating cells to astral projection. They think it's magic, and they know how to work with it without knowing how it works—it's power, and it's the basis of civilization. A female civil servant from a working-class immigrant background finds a secret source of plasm, and the whole plot gets kicked into motion.

There are a couple of things I can say about these books rereading them now that I couldn't say when I first read them in 1997. The first thing is that in some ways, they resemble Williams's latest books, *This Is Not a Game* and *Deep State*. If you like the political action of those, you'll also find it here. Secondly, they are not going to be finished. They were supposed to be a trilogy, but the third book is never likely to appear—not only the editor but also the whole imprint these books were published under was cancelled, and Williams moved on to other projects. This is a pity, not only because they're brilliant but also because they're clearly a character study of Aiah and how she comes to terms with power.

Aiah begins about as powerless as anyone can be—she has a boring bureaucratic job and she's barely making the rent, her lover's away and he's not sending back what he said he'd send. She's a member of a visible minority, the Barkazils, who are known as the "cunning people" but who live in a ghetto and suffer all the kinds of prejudice and violence that minorities do tend to suffer in big cities. She's a great character, and she's an unusual kind of character in an unusual kind of world. She finds the plasm well, and what she does with it and the choices she makes are the books. Each book is reasonably complete with a good volume-completion ending, but it's clear that at the end of *City on Fire*, Aiah has had enough of being acted upon and is shaping power for herself. There are also tantalizing hints of what is outside the Shield.

This is a world where when you're caught up in a revolution, your grandmother rings you with advice about hoarding. It's a world with vast divides between rich and poor. It is in many ways very realistic—much more realistic than most SF, let alone fantasy. The gangs feel like gangs, and the poverty really feels like poverty—the difference between just making it between paychecks and not quite making it, the odd combination of relief of being in your ethnic neighborhood and feeling simultaneously you can't wait to get away from it again. But then there's the plasm and the things plasm can do, and the things that live in plasm and the bargains you can make with them. The little details are wonderful—how Aiah gets used to the luxury of fruit, and how she can't understand how time zones used to work or why they used to have them. There are also talking dolphins and plasm-modified people who are their own ethnicity—and who have religious leaders ranting against them.

This is the future of our world, but it's the far future—names and continents have changed in the centuries in which the Shield has been up, and the mythology is of the Ascended and only occasionally reaching back further. We are ancient history to them, and they have their own problems. These books are deeply political, engaging with how politics works in practice and in theory. They are more than anything about power—who has it, who wants it, what you can do with it. And plasm is power, and plasm is transformative, and can be used for war, or ads in the sky, or to make yourself young again, if you know how to do it. It's magic by Clarke's Law if it isn't really magic, and they meter it and tax it and steal it.

I'd have loved to see what happened next to Aiah and to this world. But I'm very glad I have these two books.

1999

Winner: *To Say Nothing of the Dog,* by Connie Willis

Nominees:
Children of God, by Mary Doria Russell
Factoring Humanity, by Robert J. Sawyer
Darwinia, by Robert Charles Wilson
Distraction, by Bruce Sterling

The 1999 Hugo Awards were presented at Aussiecon Three, in Melbourne, Australia. The Best Novel winner was Connie Willis's time travel romp, *To Say Nothing of the Dog,* a book I like a great deal and an excellent winner. Willis is a master of the screwball comedy, and here she's working with wonderful material like Victorian England, cats and dogs living together, jumble sales, and the significance of art and love on history. It also won the Locus. It's in print, and it's in the library in English and French.

There were four other nominees, and I've read only two of them.

I haven't read Mary Doria Russell's *Children of God* because I hated *The Sparrow,* to which it is a direct sequel. I should have no opinion on whether it was a good Hugo nominee, as I haven't read it, but one spoiler I heard for it made me feel really glad it didn't win. It's theological SF. It's in print, and it's in the library in English and French.

I haven't read Robert J. Sawyer's *Factoring Humanity,* because I wasn't excited by *The Terminal Experiment.* (I'd have read it if I'd been going to vote in 1999, which is not true of the Russell.) It appears to be a near-future technothriller about SETI. It's in print and in the library in English and French.

Robert Charles Wilson's *Darwinia* is not the book I was looking for. It has an absolutely fantastic premise—in 1910, Europe suddenly disappears and is replaced by a weird jungle continent, and the rest of the world goes on, baffled. It's beautifully written, as is the case for all Wilson. But where he goes with *Darwinia* struck me as much less interesting than a straightforward exploration of the premise would have been. My reaction to *Darwinia* was to immediately seek out all Wilson's previous novels and to buy all his subsequent books on sight, and I'm very glad I've done this, but I've not read it again. The very fact of its Hugo nomination means that for lots of other people, it *was* the book they were looking for, so I think on balance it was a good nominee. It's well written and thought-provoking SF, in any case. It's in print, and it's in the library in English and French.

Bruce Sterling's *Distraction* is another excellent nominee. It's a brilliant near-future political thriller—funny, clever, and fast moving—one of Sterling's best. I'd have voted for it above the Willis. But it's a book that's all about American politics. I wonder if it would have done better at a US Worldcon? It's in print and in the library in English only.

So, three men and two women—three Americans and two Canadians, although the con was in Australia. Willis is a previous winner. Sterling and Sawyer are previous nominees. Wilson and Russell are Hugo newcomers. The novels are all SF: one time travel, one theological space opera, one near-future technothriller, one near-future political SF novel, and something that looks like an alternate history that turns out to be much weirder. What else might they have chosen?

The Nebula, out of step again, went to last year's Hugo winner, Haldeman's *Forever Peace*. Other eligible nominees were Martha Wells's *The Death of a Necromancer* and Jack McDevitt's *Moonfall*.

The World Fantasy Award was won by *The Antelope Wife*, by Louise Erdrich. Other nominees were *The Martyring*, Thomas Sullivan; *Mockingbird*, Sean Stewart, which would have been an excellent Hugo nominee; *Sailing to Sarantium*, Guy Gavriel Kay; and *Someplace to Be Flying*, Charles de Lint.

The John W. Campbell Memorial Award went to George Zebrowski's *Brute Orbits*, with Poul Anderson's *Starfarers* second, and *Distraction* third.

The Philip K. Dick Award was given to Geoff Ryman's *253*. The special citation was Paul Di Filippo's *Lost Pages*. Other nominees were Nalo Hopkinson's *Brown Girl in the Ring*, Paul J. McAuley's *The Invisible Country*, and Steve Aylett's *Slaughtermatic*. The Dick Award never fails to turn up interesting things.

Locus nominees not previously mentioned: *The Alien Years*, Robert Silverberg; *The Golden Globe*, John Varley; *Cosm*, Gregory Benford; *Parable of the Talents*, Octavia E. Butler; *Ports of Call*, Jack Vance; *Dinosaur Summer*, Greg Bear; *Six Moon Dance*, Sheri S. Tepper; *Maximum Light*, Nancy Kress; *Moonseed*, Stephen Baxter; *Komarr*, Lois McMaster Bujold; *Mission Child*, Maureen F. McHugh; *Vast*, Linda Nagata; *Child of the River*, Paul J. McAuley; *Deepdrive*, Alexander Jablokov; *Girl in Landscape*, Jonathan Lethem; *Otherland: River of Blue Fire*, Tad Williams; *Earth Made of Glass*, John Barnes; *The Children's Star*, Joan Slonczewski; *Bloom*, Wil McCarthy; *Noir*, K. W. Jeter; *Prisoner of Conscience*, Susan R. Matthews; *Kirinya*, Ian McDonald; *The Cassini Division*, Ken MacLeod; *The Shapes of Their Hearts*, Melissa Scott.

Some really good books—I think *Mission Child* would have been a great Hugo nominee, and so would *Parable of the Talents* or *The Cassini Division*. Any one of these three in place of the Russell would make me feel much happier about this slate.

The Locus fantasy award was won by *A Clash of Kings*, which wasn't Hugo eligible, because it was published the year before. Other nominees not previously mentioned were: *Stardust*, Neil Gaiman; *Heartfire*, Orson Scott Card; *Fortress of Eagles*, C. J. Cherryh; *Newton's Cannon*, J. Gregory Keyes; *Song for the Basilisk*, Patricia A. McKillip; *Dragon's Winter*, Elizabeth A. Lynn; *Prince of Dogs*, Kate Elliott; *Dark Lord of Derkholm*, Diana Wynne Jones; *The One-Armed Queen*, Jane Yolen; *Changer*, Jane Lindskold; *Juniper, Gentian, and Rosemary*, Pamela Dean; *The Gilded Chain*, Dave Duncan; *The Innamorati*, Midori Snyder; *Bhagavati*, Kara Dalkey; *The Book of Knights*, Yves Meynard; *Harry Potter and the Philosopher's Stone* (US title *Harry Potter and the Sorcerer's Stone*), J. K. Rowling (Bloomsbury; Scholastic/Levine 1998).

It's funny to see the first Harry Potter book way down there at the end of the list!

The Mythopoeic Award was won by *Stardust*. Other nominees not yet mentioned were *The High House*, James Stoddard; *The History of Our World Beyond the Wave*, R. E. Klein.

With all these awards, was there anything that hasn't been mentioned yet? Every week I think there can't possibly be, and every week it turns out to be worth dredging through the ISFDB's unintuitive interface and making my eyes cross. This week there's Julie Czernada's terrific alien shape-shifter novel, *Beholder's Eye;* James Alan Gardner's *Commitment Hour;* and China Miéville's *King Rat*.

While this year's nominees are not my five favorite books of the year, nor the five books I'd have nominated for a Hugo, they are a pretty good representation of where the field was and what people were excited about in 1999. There are good books that didn't make it, but there are always good books that don't make it—there's nothing that really fills me with horror at the injustice of its being skipped over. So a pretty good year on the whole, even if I do wish *Children of God* wasn't up there.

OTHER CATEGORIES

BEST NOVELLA

Winner: *Oceanic*, by Greg Egan (*Asimov's*, August 1998)

Nominees:
Aurora in Four Voices, by Catherine Asaro (*Analog*, December 1998)
Get Me to the Church on Time, by Terry Bisson (*Asimov's*, May 1998)
Story of Your Life, by Ted Chiang (*Starlight 2*)
The Summer Isles, by Ian R. MacLeod (*Asimov's*, October/November 1998)

That's a very odd result. Two of the best novellas of all time—the Chiang and the MacLeod, beaten by what I think of as one of Egan's lesser works—and I'm a big Egan fan. Maybe it was the home advantage—and goodness knows Egan's award status has suffered enough for his being Australian, it deserves to work for him for once.

BEST NOVELETTE

Winner: "Taklamakan," by Bruce Sterling (*Asimov's*, October/November 1998)

Nominees:
"Divided by Infinity," by Robert Charles Wilson (*Starlight 2*)
"Echea," by Kristine Kathryn Rusch (*Asimov's*, July 1998)
"The Planck Dive," by Greg Egan (*Asimov's*, February 1998)
"Steamship Soldier on the Information Front," by Nancy Kress (*Future Histories 1997; Asimov's*, April 1998)
"Time Gypsy," by Ellen Klages (*Bending the Landscape: Science Fiction*)
"Zwarte Piet's Tale," by Allen Steele (*Analog*, December 1998)

Great novelettes this year. All memorable and absolutely first class. I'd have found that a very difficult vote.

BEST SHORT STORY

Winner: "The Very Pulse of the Machine," by Michael Swanwick (*Asimov's*, February 1998)

Nominees:
"Cosmic Corkscrew," by Michael A. Burstein (*Analog*, June 1998)
"Maneki Neko," by Bruce Sterling (*F&SF*, May 1998)
"Radiant Doors," by Michael Swanwick (*Asimov's*, September 1998)
"Whiptail," by Robert Reed (*Asimov's*, October/November 1998)
"Wild Minds," by Michael Swanwick (*Asimov's*, May 1998)

And finally a well-deserved win for Swanwick, after a whole lot of nominations. But "Maneki Neko" is my favorite thing Sterling has ever written.

Best Related Book

Winner: *The Dreams Our Stuff Is Made Of: How Science Fiction Conquered the World*, by Thomas M. Disch

Nominees:
The Hugo, Nebula and World Fantasy Awards, by Howard DeVore
Science-Fiction: The Gernsback Years, by Everett F. Bleiler
Spectrum 5: The Best in Contemporary Fantastic Art, edited by Cathy Fenner and Arnie Fenner
The Work of Jack Williamson: An Annotated Bibliography and Guide, by Richard A. Hauptmann

It really is very hard to rank things so different from each other.

Best Dramatic Presentation

Winner: *The Truman Show*

Nominees:
Babylon 5: "Sleeping in Light"
Dark City
Pleasantville
Star Trek: Insurrection

Best Professional Editor

Winner: Gardner Dozois

Nominees:
Scott Edelman
David G. Hartwell
Patrick Nielsen Hayden
Stanley Schmidt
Gordon Van Gelder

They were absolutely right to separate out long form and short form editors, because when I saw this, I immediately thought, "Right, Patrick is there because *Starlight 2* was so great," even though he was *also* eligible for all the novel editing he did that year. *Starlight 2* was an amazing anthology, though. And Gardner was continuing to do a great job with *Asimov's,* which was also doing well in the awards.

BEST PROFESSIONAL ARTIST

Winner: Bob Eggleton

Nominees:
Jim Burns
Donato Giancola
Don Maitz
Nick Stathopoulos
Michael Whelan

BEST SEMIPROZINE

Winner: *Locus,* edited by Charles N. Brown

Nominees:
Interzone, edited by David Pringle
The New York Review of Science Fiction, edited by Kathryn Cramer,
    Ariel Hameon, David G. Hartwell, and Kevin J. Maroney
Science Fiction Chronicle, edited by Andrew I. Porter
Speculations, edited by Denise Lee

BEST FANZINE

Winner: *Ansible,* edited by Dave Langford

Nominees:
File 770, edited by Mike Glyer

Mimosa, edited by Richard and Nicki Lynch
Plokta, edited by Alison Scott and Steve Davies
Tangent, edited by David Truesdale
Thyme, edited by Alan Stewart

BEST FAN WRITER

Winner: Dave Langford

Nominees:
Bob Devney
Mike Glyer
Evelyn C. Leeper
Maureen Kincaid Speller

BEST FAN ARTIST

Winner: Ian Gunn

Nominees:
Freddie Baer
Brad W. Foster
Teddy Harvia
Joe Mayhew
D. West

JOHN W. CAMPBELL AWARD

Winner: Nalo Hopkinson

Nominees:
Kage Baker
Julie E. Czerneda
Susan R. Matthews
James Van Pelt

Great Campbell year. Nalo Hopkinson's *Brown Girl in the Ring* was a much-talked-about first novel, and her second novel, *Midnight Robber*, would be a Hugo nominee in 2001. Since then, she has gone on to be a successful and respected writer of SF and fantasy with additional mainstream credibility—a terrific winner.

Kage Baker was another writer with an impressive first novel, *In the Garden of Iden*, beginning the Company series. She went on to have a successful career, with many books and award nominations before her untimely death in 2009.

Julie E. Czerneda might be even more successful if she were easier to spell! I love her work—she writes in my favorite aliens-and-spaceships subgenre. She had two novels out at the time of nomination, beginning two of her series. She has published a book almost every year since then.

I talked about Susan R. Matthews last week.

James Van Pelt was nominated on the strength of his short work, and he has continued to produce excellent short work in the decade since. A very good nominee. I often think it would be better to replace the Campbell with a straight-up "Best First Novel" Hugo, but then people like Burstein and Van Pelt wouldn't be honored, and they're worth honoring. Much of the finest and most innovative work in SF has always been at shorter lengths.

Other people they could have considered—well, J. K. Rowling, obviously, maybe David B. Coe, maybe Anne Bishop, maybe Carolyn Ives Gilman. But I think the five we have are really a very good set with the benefit of this much hindsight.

Comments on 1999

21. Rich Horton

To me, *Story of Your Life* is clearly one of the great SF novellas of all time. (We'll just miss covering another one a couple of years later—Ian MacLeod's 2001 masterwork *New Light on the Drake Equation*.) I thought it the clear deserving winner then, and I still think so. It did end up with a Nebula, didn't it?

The Summer Isles is also very good. *Oceanic* I found interesting, but unsuccessful—too much strawman-bashing. (I said so on rec.arts. sf.written, and Egan responded, disputing my view—he made some good points, but I still think it less than his best. It was his time, though—he probably should have had two or three by that time, and if it took a bit of home cooking to get him one, well, I'm not complaining too loudly. Anyway, *Aurora in Four Voices* finished second, in a very close race—which would have been a very disappointing result.)

Other novellas I enjoyed:

A Princess of Helium, by R. Garcia y Robertson
Sea Change, with Monsters, by Paul McAuley
Family, by Geoff Ryman
Mother Death, by Robert Reed

In novelette, my favorite of the nominees was "Taklamakan," one of my favorite Bruce Sterling stories. As Jo says, the rest of the list is very good too—"Echea" is one of the best of Rusch's stories; the Wilson, Egan, and Kress stories were very strong too.

But there were some other excellent novelettes:

"Auschwitz and the Rectification of History," by Eliot Fintushel (my second favorite story by this weird writer—my favorite is the tragically neglected "Milo and Sylvie" [2000])
"Home Time," by Ian R. MacLeod
"Minutes of the Last Meeting," by Stepan Chapman (another very weird story, about an alternate Russian Revolution)
"Approaching Perimelasma," by Geoffrey Landis (like Egan's "The Plank Dive," this is about diving into [or very near] a black hole)
"Animae Celestes," by Gregory Feeley
"Rules of Engagement," by Michael F. Flynn
"A Dance to Strange Musics," by Gregory Benford
"Mrs. Mabb," by Susanna Clarke (I hope we see more from her sometime soon.) (She was eligible for the Campbell in 1997 and 1998, by the way.)

In short story, I was glad to see Swanwick win, but "Radiant Doors" was the best of those three stories, and "The Very Pulse of the Machine" worst.

Burstein's "The Cosmic Corkscrew" is awful, and noticing how bad it is and how silly its nomination was changed my perception of him as a writer—to some extent perhaps unfairly. I agree that "Maneki Neko" is first-rate—so too is "Whiptail."

Some excellent work that wasn't nominated:

"The Mars Convention," by Timons Esaias
"Instructions," by Roz Kaveney
"Access Fantasy," by Jonathan Lethem
"Artifacts," by Jerry Oltion
"The Dream of Nations," by Wil McCarthy
"Outsider's Chance," by Geoffrey A. Landis
"Dante Dreams," by Stephen Baxter
"First Fire," by Terry Bisson
"Jack Neck and the Worrybird," by Paul Di Filippo
"Congenital Agenesis of Gender Ideation," by Raphael Carter
"Monogamy," by William Eakin

I'd like to particularly mention the Timons Esaias story—he seems to have disappeared after a couple years of promising work, and "The Mars Convention" in particular I thought wonderful, but nobody else noticed it. Raphael Carter's story won the Tiptree, and it's quite excellent. And William Eakin is mostly known for some weird Southern Gothic–ish sort of stuff set in "Redgunk, Mississippi"—"Monogamy" is quite different, and very good.

33. GARDNER DOZOIS

Short fiction was very strong this year, though, especially novella and novelette. Unlike others here, I really like Egan's *Oceanic*, and was not at all displeased to see it win; in fact, I think it's one of his two or three best stories, adding a human element and local color reminiscent of late Le Guin to his sometimes chilly and abstract idea content. *The Summer Isles* is perhaps one of my favorites among stories that I published, and was the only form the story was available in for several more years, as I boiled it down to novella length from a novel MacLeod had already written and was unable to sell, and wouldn't be able to sell for a few more years. Also wonderful is Ian McDonald's *The Days of Solomon Gursky*, which takes us to the very end of the universe and back around again (you can't hardly get more wide-screen than that!), and Tony Daniel's *Grist* is also jammed with wild new ideas. McAuley's *Sea Change, with Monsters*, is also excellent, one of the best of the Quiet War stories. And yes, Ted Chiang's *Story of Your Life* is very, very strong as well, one of the most memorable novellas of the decade.

Looking back, this must have been one of the strongest years for novella ever. You were spoiled for choice.

Novelette was also strong. I voted for "Taklamakan" at the time, one of Sterling's strongest later stories (better than last year's "Bicycle Repairman," which it's related to), but also excellent were Robert Charles Wilson's "Divided by Infinity," Geoffrey A. Landis's "Approaching Perimelasma," Kristine Kathryn Rusch's "Echea," Greg Egan's "The Planck Dive," Cherry Wilder's "The Dancing Floor," and William Barton's very depressing "Down in the Dark." Jim Grimsley, who seems subsequently to have been driven from the field by reactionaries upset with him being openly gay, had a strong story, "Free in Asveroth." Michael Swanwick did a strong posthumous collaboration with Avram Davidson, "Vergil Magus: King Without Country," and a collaboration with me, "Ancestral Voices." Gregory Frost published "How Meersh the Bedeviler Lost His Toes," probably one of the few stories ever to feature a talking penis as a character.

In short story, Michael Swanwick had a really strong year, really his breakout year, publishing "The Very Pulse of the Machine," "Wild Minds," and "Radiant Doors," all three of which he placed on the Hugo ballot in the same category (the only time that's ever happened, I think). Also first-rate were Robert Reed's "Whiptail," Stephen Baxter's "Dante Dreams," Geoff Ryman's "Family," and Bruce Sterling's "Maneki Neko." Also good were Rob Chilson's "This Side of Independence," which showed up in a couple of the Year's Bests, and William Browing Spencer's very Zelazny-like "The Halfway House at the Heart of Darkness."

Of historical interest is (as far as I know), Liz Williams's first sale, "Voivodoi"; Dominic Green and Alexander Glass were making their first sales to *Interzone* (Glass would later disappear, but Green still turns up from time to time, with an issue of *Interzone* devoted to his stuff appearing a couple of years back), and Charles Stross was inching closer to the kind of work that would make his reputation with stories like "Toast: A Con Report."

For the second year in a row, all three short fiction winners were from *Asimov's*.

I had real problems with a lot of the conclusions in *The Dreams Our Stuff Is Made Of*, so whatever I voted for there, it wasn't that.

Nalo Hopkinson makes a perfectly acceptable Campbell winner, as would have James Van Pelt and several of the others, but I must admit that I wanted to see Kage Baker, who was pouring out a remarkable amount of first-rate work at that point, to win. In my opinion, she was perhaps the best natural storyteller to enter the field since Poul Anderson.

35. RICH HORTON

Again Gardner reminds me of some outstanding work I should have mentioned. For example, "This Side of Independence" is a really fine story by a Missouri writer, Rob Chilson (and the Indepedence of the title is indeed Independence, MO)—Chilson isn't terribly prolific, but his occasional stories are pretty good.

Gardner's collaboration with Swanwick, "Ancestral Voices" is also strong work, and also a story I can list on my (now somewhat dormant) compilation of pieces with titles taken from "Kubla Khan."

I really liked "Grist," by Tony Daniel—a very weird, indeed entirely implausible, central idea, but neatly executed. (He too seems to have left the field, apparently after failing to sell the third novel in his trilogy that began with *Metaplanetary*.)

Alexander Glass was an exciting writer for the few years he stayed in the field—I have no idea what he is up to now.

Anyway, a reminder that there is no substitute for scouring the ISFDB's list of stories each year . . . I've been lazily using my contemporary compilations of my favorites, and I can be counted on to have missed some stories, or to have reevaluated some in the years since then.

41. GARDNER DOZOIS

I should also have mentioned Cory Doctorow's first sale, "Craphound." For a while there, he wanted to start a literary movement that would call themselves "Craphounds," but it never caught on.

2000

BEST NOVEL

Winner: *A Deepness in the Sky,* by Vernor Vinge

Nominees:
Darwin's Radio, by Greg Bear
A Civil Campaign, by Lois McMaster Bujold
Cryptonomicon, by Neal Stephenson
Harry Potter and the Prizoner of Azkhaban, by J. K. Rowling

The 2000 Hugo Awards were presented in Chicon 2000, in Chicago.

The Best Novel Hugo went to Vernor Vinge's *A Deepness in the Sky,* a space opera about interstellar slower-than-light civilization, awesome aliens, and a future with finite technological advances. It's an excellently written book doing exactly what I always want science fiction to do, and it's an excellent Hugo winner. It's in print, and it's in the library in English and French.

There are four other nominees, and I've read three of them. The one I haven't read is Greg Bear's *Darwin's Radio.* I haven't read it, because it was a near-future technothriller about "something sleeping in our genes waking up," which just never seemed appealing enough to pick up. I'd have read it if I'd been voting, but I wasn't and I didn't. It's in print and in the library in English and French.

Lois McMaster Bujold's *A Civil Campaign* is another volume in the Vorkosigan series, it's a science fiction romantic comedy, it's very enjoyable, but it doesn't stand alone very well and it isn't really breaking new ground. However, seeing this nominated shows that the image of nominating fans as stuck-in-the-mud older geeky males had pretty much evaporated by the end of the twentieth century. It's in print, and it's in the library in English and French. (And the French title is *Ekaterin*.)

Neal Stephenson's *Cryptonomicon*, an absolutely brilliant generational novel about cryptography and society and the possibility of keeping secrets. People argued that it wasn't SF, but it does contain the philosophers' stone, which makes it fantasy. I really love it, and I think it's an excellent nominee, the kind of quirky unusual thing I like to see on these lists. It won the Locus SF award. It's in print and in the library in English and French in three volumes.

I read J. K. Rowling's *Harry Potter and the Prisoner of Azkaban* because it was nominated. It's a boarding school story that brilliantly replaces the class snobbery books like this had in my childhood with snobbery over magical talent. I thought it was pretty good, and I went back and read the first two books afterwards. I may finish the series one of these days, or maybe not. The phenomenon of the worldwide passion these books inspire leaves me completely baffled. It's in print and in the library in English, French, Arabic, Chinese, and Spanish, and in braille in English and French, making it the best library-represented Hugo nominee of all time.

So, two women and three men, four Americans and one English. Vinge, Bujold, and Stephenson are prior winners, Bear's a prior nominee, but Rowling is a Hugo newcomer. We have one fantasy children's book about wizard school, one space opera, one near-future techno-thriller, one generational novel about cryptography, and a planetary SF romance. What else might they have chosen?

The Nebula went to Octavia Butler's *Parable of the Talents*—great book, but it wasn't Hugo eligible in 2000. None of their other nominees were Hugo eligible either!

The World Fantasy Award was given to Martin Scott's *Thraxas*. Other nominees were: *Gardens of the Moon*, Steven Erikson; *The Rainy Season*, James P. Blaylock; *A Red Heart of Memories*, Nina Kiriki Hoffman; *Tamsin*, Peter S. Beagle; *A Witness to Life*, Terence M. Green.

John W. Campbell Memorial Award went to *Deepness*, with *Darwin's Radio* second; Norman Spinrad's *Greenhouse Summer* third; and

Jack Williamson's *The Silicon Dagger* and Peter Watts's *Starfish* receiving honorable mentions.

Starfish would have been an interesting Hugo nominee, but it was an early work—and an early sign of an emerging major talent.

The Philip K. Dick Award was won by Stephen Baxter's *Vacuum Diagrams* with a special citation for Jamil Nasir's *Tower of Dreams*. Other nominees were *Code of Conduct*, Kristine Smith; *Typhon's Children*, Tony Anzetti; *When We Were Real*, William Barton.

The Tiptree Award was given to Suzy McKee Charnas's *The Conquerer's Child*.

Locus SF nominees not yet mentioned were *Ender's Shadow*, Orson Scott Card; *Forever Free*, Joe Haldeman; *Precursor*, C. J. Cherryh; *On Blue's Waters*, Gene Wolfe; *The Naked God*, Peter F. Hamilton; *Teranesia*, Greg Egan; *The Cassini Division*, Ken MacLeod; *The Martian Race*, Gregory Benford; *Waiting*, Frank M. Robinson; *Time: Manifold 1* (US edition *Manifold: Time*), Stephen Baxter; *All Tomorrow's Parties*, William Gibson; *Bios*, Robert Charles Wilson; *The Far Shore of Time*, Frederik Pohl; *Finity*, John Barnes; *Ancients of Days*, Paul J. McAuley; *Souls in the Great Machine*, Sean McMullen; *Singer from the Sea*, Sheri S. Tepper; *The Extremes*, Christopher Priest.

I love *Precursor*, but nobody's going to nominate book four in a series that starts out rockily. *The Cassini Division* would have been a terrific nominee if it had been eligible—staggered US/UK publication probably means it wasn't.

The Locus fantasy award was won by the Harry Potter. Other nominees not yet mentioned: *The Fifth Elephant*, Terry Pratchett; *Fortress of Owls*, C. J. Cherryh; *Dark Cities Underground*, Lisa Goldstein; *The Eternal Footman*, James Morrow; *Enchantment*, Orson Scott Card; *Mr. X*, Peter Straub; *A Calculus of Angels*, J. Gregory Keyes; *The Marriage of Sticks*, Jonathan Carroll; *Dragonshadow*, Barbara Hambly; *Black Light*, Elizabeth Hand; *The Stars Compel*, Michaela Roessner; *The Sub*, Thomas M. Disch; *Saint Fire*, Tanith Lee; *The Wild Swans*, Peg Kerr; *Sea Dragon Heir*, Storm Constantine; *Rhapsody*, Elizabeth Haydon.

The Mythopoeic Award went to *Tamsin*, and the only nominee not yet mentioned was Yves Meynard's wonderful *The Book of Knights*.

Is there anything all these awards missed?

There's Lawrence Watt-Evans's *Dragon Weather*, a surprisingly original fantasy take on the *Count of Monte Cristo*, with dragons; Pat Cadigan's *Promised Land;* Kage Baker's *Sky Coyote;* Walter Jon Williams's
The Rift; Madeleine Robins's *The Stone War;* and Amy Thomson's
Through Alien Eyes.

But on the whole, I think this was a year where the nominees did a
pretty good job. I'm not excited about Harry Potter, but goodness knows
a lot of people are. Really, this is the first year in a long time where
everything looks good and there isn't anything that strikes me as clam-
oring to be on the short list.

OTHER CATEGORIES

BEST NOVELLA

Winner: *The Winds of Marble Arch*, by Connie Willis (*Asimov's*,
October/November 1999)

Nominees:
The Astronaut from Wyoming, by Adam-Troy Castro and Jerry Oltion
    (*Analog*, July/August 1999)
Forty, Counting Down, by Harry Turtledove (*Asimov's*, December
    1999)
Hunting the Snark, by Mike Resnick (*Asimov's*, December 1999)
Son Observe the Time, by Kage Baker (*Asimov's*, May 1999)

I'd have put the Turtledove first, one of his best stories. And that's one
of Baker's best as well.

BEST NOVELETTE

Winner: "10^{16} to 1," by James Patrick Kelly (*Asimov's*, June 1999)

Nominees:

"Border Guards," by Greg Egan (*Interzone 148*, October 1999)

"The Chop Girl," by Ian R. MacLeod (*Asimov's*, December 1999)

"Fossil Games," by Tom Purdom (*Asimov's*, February 1999)

"The Secret History of the Ornithopter," by Jen Lars Jensen (*F&SF*, June 1999)

"Stellar Harvest," by Eleanor Arnason (*Asimov's*, April 1999)

And novelette was having a great year, too.

BEST SHORT STORY

Winner: "Scherzo with Tyrannosaur," by Michael Swanwick (*Asimov's*, July 1999)

Nominees:

"Ancient Engines," by Michael Swanwick (*Asimov's*, February 1999)

"Hothouse Flowers," by Mike Resnick (*Asimov's*, October/November 1999)

"macs," by Terry Bisson (*F&SF*, October/November 1999)

"Sarajevo," by Nick DiChario (*F&SF*, March 1999)

In fact, all the short categories were in very good form as they closed out the century.

BEST RELATED BOOK

Winner: *Science Fiction of the 20th Century*, by Frank M. Robinson (Collectors Press)

Nominees:

Minicon 34 Restaurant Guide, by Karen Cooper and Bruce Schneier

The Sandman: The Dream Hunters, by Neil Gaiman, illustrated by Yoshitaka Amano

The Science of Discworld, by Terry Pratchett, Ian Stewart, and Jack Cohen

Spectrum 6: The Best in Contemporary Fantastic Art, edited by Cathy
   Fenner and Arnie Fenner

I'm really glad I didn't have to vote on this. I have no idea how you
can compare things this different to rate them. It's an excellent
restaurant guide, I've used it, and *The Science of Discworld* is entertaining and informative. How is the *Sandman* volume nonfiction?
Oh well.

Best Dramatic Presentation

Winner: *Galaxy Quest*

Nominees:
Being John Malkovich
The Iron Giant
The Matrix
The Sixth Sense

Best Professional Editor

Winner: Gardner Dozois

Nominees:
David G. Hartwell
Patrick Nielsen Hayden
Stanley Schmidt
Gordon Van Gelder

Best Professional Artist

Winner: Michael Whelan

Nominees:
Jim Burns
Bob Eggleton

Donato Giancola
Don Maitz

Best Semiprozine

Winner: *Locus,* edited by Charles N. Brown

Nominees:
Interzone, edited by David Pringle
The New York Review of Science Fiction, edited by Kathryn Cramer,
    Ariel Hameon, David G. Hartwell, and Kevin J. Maroney
Science Fiction Chronicle, edited by Andrew I. Porter
Speculations, edited by Kent Brewster

Best Fanzine

Winner: *File 770,* edited by Mike Glyer

Nominees:
Ansible, edited by Dave Langford
Challenger, edited by Guy H. Lillian III
Mimosa, edited by Nicki and Richard Lynch
Plokta, edited by Alison Scott, Steve Davies, and Mike Scott

Best Fan Writer

Winner: Dave Langford

Nominees:
Bob Devney
Mike Glyer
Evelyn C. Leeper
Steven H. Silver

Best Fan Artist

Winner: Joe Mayhew

Nominees:
Freddie Baer
Brad W. Foster
Teddy Harvia
Taral Wayne

John W. Campbell Award

Winner: Cory Doctorow

Nominees:
Thomas Harlan
Ellen Klages
Kristine Smith
Shane Tourtellotte

Well, an excellent winner. Cory won on short work; his first novel didn't come out until 2003. He has gone on from strength to strength, including a Hugo nomination in 2009 for *Little Brother*. He's clearly a major writer, and it's nice to see him getting the recognition right at the beginning of his career.

Thomas Harlan was nominated on the strength of his first novel, *The Shadow of Ararat*, and he has gone on to publish another novel almost every year since. A good solid Campbell choice.

Ellen Klages had published only short work at the time of her nomination. She has gone on to write some wonderful YA novels and more terrific adult SF and fantasy at short lengths. She's amazing. Great choice.

Kristine Smith was clearly nominated on the strength of her well-received first novel, *Code of Conduct*. She won the Campbell Award in 2001. She has published four more novels since.

I wasn't familiar with Shane Tourtellotte. He seems to have been nominated on the basis of short work in *Analog*, and he has gone on since to write more short fiction, mostly in *Analog*.

Who else might they have nominated? It's hard to know who's eligible, but China Miéville? Peter Watts? Juliet McKenna? Justina Robson? Steven Erickson?

COMMENTS ON 2000

8. KEVIN STANDLEE

The *Sandman* graphic novel was in Related Book because of the insistence that "if it's full of pictures, then it's an Art Book." This was yet one more brick in the wall that led up to the adoption of Best Graphic Story a few years later so that graphic novels would have a category of their own.

29. RICH HORTON

As for short fiction, I thought this one of the best years ever in SF. That said, I wasn't too happy with most of the Hugo nomination list, nor with the winners.

In novella, *The Winds of Marble Arch* is okay, but nothing special. And Resnick's *Hunting the Snark* is not just a twice-told tale, it's a 472-times-told tale—and nothing in this story is new enough to make it stand out.

Here's my list (from back then) of the best novellas:

Dapple, by Eleanor Arnason
The Actors, by Eleanor Arnason
Orphans of the Helix, by Dan Simmons
Once upon a Matter Crushed, by Wil McCarthy
Twenty-One, Counting Up, by Harry Turtledove
Argonautica, by Walter Jon Williams
Forty, Counting Down, by Harry Turtledove

Son Observe the Time, by Kage Baker
The Wedding Album, by David Marusek
Old Music and the Slave Women, by Ursula K. Le Guin
The Gateway of Eternity, by Brian M. Stableford
Fortitude, by Andy Duncan
Epiphany, by Connie Willis
The Astronaut from Wyoming, by Jerry Oltion and Adam-Troy Castro

That's in more or less my order of preference. My clear favorites were the two Arnason novellas—the best two Hwarhath stories of all, in my opinion. You'll note I mildy preferred Turtledove's *Twenty-One, Counting Up* to the Hugo nominee, *Forty, Counting Down.* But really I consider them as parts of the same story.

My contemporary list of best novelettes:

"Stellar Harvest," by Eleanor Arnason
"Attack of the Ignoroids," by Wayne Wightman
"Where Does the Town Go at Night?," by Tanith Lee
"At Reparata," by Jeffrey Ford
"Chanoyu," by Esther Friesner
"Fossil Games," by Tom Purdom
"Strongbow," by R. Garcia y Robertson
"Border Guards," by Greg Egan
"Naming the Dead," by Paul J. McAuley
"Recalled to Home," by Michael Armstrong
"The Giftie," by James Gunn
"The Fourth Branch," by Kage Baker
"Soldier's Home," by William Barton
"Scarlet and Gold," by Tanith Lee
"The Secret Exhibition," by Brian Stableford
"The Secret History of the Ornithopter," by Jen Lars Jensen

I separate "Stellar Harvest" from the pack because I thought it by a wide margin the best novelette of the year, and indeed one of the best novelettes of the 1990s. I still think that—it's a great story.

I really like James Patrick Kelly, but "10^{16} to 1" failed to convince me—after all, on the evidence in front of me, the odds of the title are grossly wrong. Still, a well-done story.

The five best short stories of the year, which was in my opinion a great year for short stories, were:

"Suicide Coast," by M. John Harrison
"Jennifer, Just Before Midnight," by William Sanders
"Sailing the Painted Ocean," by Denise Lee
"Lifework," by Mary Soon Lee
"Yurek Rutz, Yurek Rutz, Yurek Rutz," by David Marusek

"Suicide Coast" is a masterwork. Clearly the best story of 1999, and, as with "Stellar Harvest," one of the great stories of recent times.

William Sanders was in his most productive period (in the field). Mary Soon Lee was a fairly new writer, who did a passel of intriguing short stories (almost all short—I think her longest was a short novelette) and who has since fallen mostly silent, pretty much coinciding with the birth of her first child—I hope she finds the time to write more when her children are old enough. Marusek's "Yurek Rutz . . ." is a delight.

And finally, I seemed to be the only person who noticed Denise Lee's "Sailing the Painted Ocean," but I thought it remarkable. (It's one of those stories that I wish I could anthologize, to bring it to more people's notice.) (I should note that it did appear in Datlow and Windling's *The Year's Best Fantasy and Horror*.)

A few more strong stories—"Human Bay," by Robert Reed; "Her," by Stephen Woodworth; "Grandma's Bubble and the Speaking Clock," by Alexander Glass (whom Gardner mentioned last week); and "Everywhere," by Geoff Ryman.

On the Hugo nomination list, my preference was for "macs," by Terry Bisson, another story I really liked. Both Swanwick stories are good (and note that he had five nominees in two years, winning both times!)—if truth be told, I preferred "Ancient Engines." I didn't much care for either the Resnick or Di Chario.

30. RICH HORTON

Now to the Campbell Award, where at last I have a means of deter-
mining who was really eligible. This is thanks to James Van Pelt's web
page that listed eligible writers at the time (as a nomination aide). (The
page was taken over by Writertopia in 2005.)

Authors whose first eligible works appeared in 1998 included Doctorow, Tourtellotte, and Klages from the short list, and most notably
Devon Monk besides them. Monk did some neat short work that I remember really liking back then, and then popped up a few years later
with some apparently fairly successful urban fantasies. Also: Scott Nicholson, Delia Marshall Turner, Kathy Oltion, Christopher Rowe.
(Rowe hadn't yet done his best stuff—a couple of years later, he put out
some truly remarkable short work.)

Eligible from 1999, besides Harlan and Smith, were Peter Watts (!),
Paolo Bacigalupi, Lyda Morehouse, Douglas Lain, Yoon Ha Lee, and
Rajnar Vajra (among others, of course).

That's a pretty impressive list, I think. The actual Campbell nomination list was pretty strong, though in retrospect Watts would have
been a great addition, and the likes of Yoon Ha Lee, Christopher Rowe,
and Paolo Bacigalupi have done enough since then to make them obviously great choices—but I'm not sure they'd done enough by then to
merit inclusion.

32. GARDNER DOZOIS

Short fiction was stronger than the novels overall, which has often been
true. In novella, of the stuff on the ballot, I much prefered Kage Baker's *Son, Observe the Time,* one of her single best stories. Of the stuff
that didn't make the ballot, I too am very fond of Eleanor Arnason's
Dapple, which some readers complained was "slow-moving," but
which I found profound and emotionally affecting, and which I would
agree is one of the best, perhaps the best, of her Hwarhath stories. David
Marusek's *The Wedding Album* is also very fine, and it would be a hard
decision for me to make between any of the three. I might have considered using Le Guin's *Old Music and the Slave Women* or Simmons's
Orphans of the Helix in the Best, but all the stories from that book were

encumbered for a couple of years. Andy Duncan's *The Excecutioner's Guild* is near mainstream, but exquisitely written. I'll allow myself the indulgence of mentioning my own *A Knight of Ghosts and Shadows*, perhaps my best story, which would lose a Nebula by a small margin the following year to Walter Jon Williams's *The Green Leopard Plague*.

Also lots of strong novelettes. Interesting that Rich selects Arnason's "Stellar Harvest"—I liked it too, I bought it—for the Year's Best, when I remember one reviewer going on at great length about how awful it was; proving once again that one man's meat is another man's poison. I really liked "10^{16} to One," but Tom Purdom's "Fossil Games" was also very strong, one of his best stories, as was Egan's "Border Guards" and Robert Reed's "Winemaster." Richard Wadholm really looked at this point like he was going to be one of the hot new writers in the genre, and his "Green Tea" was terrific—he disappeared not too long thereafter, a pity. Karl Schroeder's "The Dragon of Pripyat" was also very strong, and is a prequel to his story in the current *Eclipse Four*. Alastair Reynolds's "Galactic North" was also good, as was Walter Jon Williams's brutal "Daddy's World."

Short story was a bit weaker overall, although I liked both of the Swanwick stories, and also liked Stephen Baxter's "People Come from Earth," Geoff Ryman's "Everywhere," and one of Chris Lawson's first stories, still one of the best bioscience stories, "Written in Blood." "Suicide Coast" is also very fine.

Of historic interest is one of Kij Johnson's early appearances.

For the third year in a row, all three of the short fiction winners were from *Asimov's*, as were four out of five of the novellas, four out of six of the novelettes, and three out of five of the short stories. This may be the high point of my success as *Asimov's* editor. Within a few years, I'd be gone. Funny how things work out.

Cory has been uneven, some of his subsequent stuff good and some mediocre, but I'm not displeased that he won the Campbell—although if Kage Baker had still been eligible (not sure if she was or not), I'd have given it to her.

34. RICH HORTON

I'm glad Gardner mentioned Richard Wadholm—"Green Tea" was good, but he had two or three further stories in coming years that were just outstanding—then, as Gardner says, he pretty much stopped. (As far as I know.)

I don't think I saw "The Dragon of Pripyat" in 1999—perhaps in Gardner's Best the next year—it is indeed excellent. So too is "Written in Blood." And I should have mentioned *A Knight of Ghosts and Shadows*, which is first-rate, indeed one of Gardner's best stories.

SO HIGH, SO LOW, SO MANY THINGS TO KNOW: VERNOR VINGE'S *A DEEPNESS IN THE SKY*

It's very unusual to have a big space opera like this in a slower-than-light setting, and in a universe where technological progress turns out to be finite. It's especially unusual to have it explored in such detail—a large chunk of the book is about Pham Nuwen setting up the Qeng Ho, a slower-than-light interstellar trading culture.

Vinge came to write this book from his belief in the singularity. Because he believes, as he said in an interview on Tor.com:

> *Barring catastrophes such as world nuclear war, I'd be surprised if the Technological Singularity hasn't happened by 2030. The enabling technologies of computation and communication seem to be going like gangbusters. By the way, I think my 1993 essay still does a good job of addressing many Singularity issues.*

Now, my computer seems dumber and more lacking in personality than my computer was in 1993, but that doesn't matter. We don't have to believe in the singularity to enjoy what Vinge is doing here—I think it's completely kooky, but never mind. What's important here is that Vinge really believes in the singularity, and therefore in order to write SF where people are people and flying around in spaceships and having adventures, he has had to think hard about ways to avoid having it happen. He's had to do this for the last twenty-five years, since

Marooned in Realtime. Working under this constraint led him to constructing one of the coolest universes ever, in the same way that poetic constraints led Frost to, "And would suffice" and Keats to "Silent, upon a peak in Darien."

To avoid having everyone disappear in a singularity and the end of all stories, Vinge came up with the fascinating universe of *A Fire Upon the Deep*, in which there are superhuman alien transcended intelligences, post-singularity intelligences, who have physically divided the galaxy up into geographically distinct regions with different physical rules. In the Beyond, where *A Fire Upon the Deep* takes place, you can have antigravity, human-equivalent AI, faster-than-light travel. Out in the Transcend, where the post-singularity intelligences are gods, you can have superhuman-level AI and unimaginably fast computer networks across interstellar distances. And down in the Slow Zone, absolutely none of those things will physically work. In the Slow Zone, AI and FTL and real nanotech are just flat-out impossible.

In *A Fire Upon the Deep*, the human and alien characters don't know why the superhuman superaliens did this Partition—they have lots of surmises, but that's all.

But from inside *A Deepness in the Sky*, you can't tell anything about the zones. To the characters of *Deepness*, the Slow Zone is just the universe, it's the way things are. They've never been outside it. Pham dreams that there might be more in the core—which we know are the Unthinking Depths, where human-level thought isn't possible. We know, from the perspective of having read both books, that he's going in the wrong direction but will end up in the Beyond anyway. We also know, or guess, that the "cavorite" the Spiders find is of Beyond origin, fueled in some way by the periodicity of their star. But they don't know where it comes from. They have all these civilizations, all this history, how could they guess?

Medical tech has incrementally extended human life to about five hundred years. Humanity has made it off Earth and spread across much of the galaxy, and trading fleets move between the stars. As the story begins, fleets from two civilizations converge at the astronomical anomaly of the OnOff star, a star that cycles, spending two hundred years dormant and then bursts back to life for thirty years of brightness. The

OnOff star has a planet, and the planet has alien inhabitants; the two groups of humans have different agendas, and the story is not just fascinating but absolutely unputdownable too. This goes to 11 on the readability scale.

For the way their tech works, Vinge has taken the idea of a "mature programming environment" and extrapolated it outward to everything. Everything has layers built on layers, protocols built on protocols. I laughed when I read the professional designation "programmer-archaeologist" because I use Linux, and I'm married to someone whose answer to "How can we do this?" is often "I could write a Perl script, but let me Google to see if anyone has already done one." Everything the Qeng Ho have is patched and refined and integrated and messed about with. The "localizers" Pham uses are very nearly magic tech—working with pulsed microwaves, giving a distributed network that can be controlled with thought—but this is the best anyone has ever achieved. They have medical advances, and cold sleep, and ramscoops—and that's all they have and they're never going to have anything else. No AI, no natural language translation, no uploading . . . to them these are the Failed Dreams, because Vinge believes that would lead to a singularity.

What they have is a universe desperate for incremental tech increases—but Vinge is clever enough to understand that what most people living in it want is to make a profit, make a living, to fall in love and have kids, to understand the new aliens. Most people accept the tech they have. Pham is driven—Pham has come from medieval Canberra and got to the best human tech has ever managed in the Slowness, and he wants more. He has a vision of an interstellar empire, and he has to give it up because the price is too high. But the other human characters are quite happy living where they find themselves, selling rocks to each other and getting rich, identifying with the Spiders.

The novel is essentially a locked room or desert island—the Emergents and the Qeng Ho and the Spiders are all trapped at OnOff, nobody leaves and nobody else arrives and they have only the things they brought with them. The only time we see the rest of the civilization is in Pham's memories, which move through the book giving us his life story in extended flashbacks. I love this, partly because it gets away from the claustrophobic situation in the space around the OnOff star, and partly because it's just extremely nifty—Pham's dream is empire, and on the way to that, he develops the Qeng Ho with their broadcasting information and standards to help fallen civilizations recover and be better customers.

We see two civilizations that are at absolute peaks, where there's nowhere to go, because technology can't advance and every resource is being used and there's no flexibility left. This is fascinating speculation, and it's not much like anything else, as most people assume constant technological progress.

The Emergents are evil, and their incremental advance of Focus involves creepy mind-slavery—but Vinge does a very good job of showing them as people who want things, even while they're monsters who accept horrors. He also shows them being "corrupted" by the black market of the conquered Qeng Ho.

Focus is a psychoactive virus that can control brains and direct them, focus them, so that they care for nothing but their specialty. The Focused are just that little bit more monomaniacal than the worst monomaniac you've ever met, and they can be tuned to be Focused on automation or piloting or translation so that they'll ignore everything and keep working on it. Up close, we see a Focused park designer and a Focused translator. The people who are Focused, called "zipheads," are unquestionably slaves. The Emergents have three planets controlled this way. We see them first from outside, from the Qeng Ho point of view, but as the book goes on, we start to get Emergent viewpoints—Tomas Nau and Ritser Breughel, who are villains, and Trud Silipan and Jau Xin, who are Emergents just trying to live their lives.

One very interesting thing about Focus is that in online discussions after the book came out, many people said that if it was voluntary and reversible, they'd absolutely use it. But it's very easy to see how it automatically becomes a tool of repression—from people using it voluntarily to do better work to employers only being prepared to hire people who'll use it "voluntarily." Focus is evil, but Pham Nuwen finds it seductive because it gives an edge he's always wanted and makes interstellar empire possible.

Then there's the third civilization—the alien Spiders.

There's a difficult line to walk with aliens between making them too familiar and making them too alien. Vinge does wonderfully here by making them low-slung, squat, and spidery, with maws, eating-hands, and the ability to hibernate, but culturally and technologically in many ways familiar. He gives them cute names (like Sherkaner Underhill, Victory Lighthill) and makes them so easy to identify with. They are just a little like dressed-up animals in a children's book, very easy to digest—and then he turns this inside out when the humans actually get down to the planet and meet them, and we discover that the Focused translators have (for their own reasons) been making them seem nicer and easier to identify with on purpose. Their "nooks" are sinister chimneys with lairs at the top, their stairs are ladders, their bright airy rooms are dark and sinister. They are people, they are familiar, but they are also very alien. You can't ever quite forget they are spider-aliens even in cute mode, but the revelation of how sinister they look to humans is very clever.

And then we come to Vinge's piece of genius. The Spiders, especially Sherkaner, are the only characters who don't accept the way the universe is. The Spiders, though alien, are more like us than the human characters. They're having a technological explosion like the one we have had, and they haven't yet run up against the limits of technology. All the human characters have lived for generations accepting these limits—Pham less than the others, and Pham is less content within them. The Spiders naturally believe that the Focused are AIs in revolt, happily accept antigravity, immediately imagine space as a safe enviroment for their future. They have the wide imagination of science fiction readers, while the human characters here have been forced to learn better. They call the things they can't have "Failed Dreams," and they are people from cultures who have lived with failed dreams for a long time.

One of the things SF can do is show you characters with different mind-sets. Anyone can write a character whose dreams have failed. Vinge is writing people from whole societies whose dreams have failed over millennia. And yet, this is a cheerful, optimistic book in which awful things happen but good wins out. It's a tragedy only from a perspective outside the book, where you know that there's so much more they could have had and Pham is going the wrong way at the end.

The scope is so wide and the details are so fascinating that it's easy to get caught up in talking about the other things about this book, but I want to note that the actual plot is extremely exciting. Vinge manages to pull off multiple strands—the spider POV, all the human POVs— and juggle them so it's all consistently interesting and all builds up to an astonishingly exciting climax where everything happens at once and you can't put it down for hundreds of pages together. Tomas Nau is a great villain, and Pham is a great hero, and Ezr and Qiwi are good people trying to do what they can against awful odds, and the spiders are lovable. I like this book for all kinds of defensible rational reasons, but what I'd most like to say in conclusion is how much I enjoy reading it. It's fun on all sorts of levels at the same time, in a way that not very much else is.

CONCLUSION

I have learned a lot from writing this series. I have learned exactly how to find everything quickly in *Locus*'s wonderful Index to Awards, without which I couldn't even have thought about doing this.

I have learned that novellas are consistently the Hugo category about which I feel most enthusiastic, which I would never have guessed was the case. I've learned that I still love *Dune* despite everything, and that the alien sex really is the only bit worth remembering from *The Gods Themselves*. I've learned that hardly any years have sufficient good movies to make it worth having a special category for Dramatic Presentation—*delenda est*! I've learned that the results of the Campbell Memorial Award almost always baffle me and that the Philip K. Dick Award always picks up interesting things other awards miss.

I've also learned a lot from the comment threads—the discussion on these posts has been stellar. I especially valued the weekly participation from Gardner Dozois, Rich Horton, and James Nicoll. Thank you, everyone.

But did I learn the thing I set out to learn, whether the novel nominees are the best five books of the year?

Not really.

I concluded that they did a mostly good job in 1959, 1960, 1961,

1963, 1964, 1965, 1966, 1968, 1970, 1971, 1972, 1974, 1975, 1977, 1979, 1982, 1983, 1984, 1986, 1988, 1989, 1990, 1991, 1992, 1993, 1994, 1997, 1999, and 2000—twenty-nine out of forty-two years that had nominees, or 69 percent. I concluded they didn't do a good job in 1962, 1967, 1969, 1973, 1976, 1978, 1980, 1981, 1985, 1987, 1995, 1996, 1998, thirteen out of the forty-one years, or 31 percent. So yes, on numbers I thought the Hugos were doing a good job more often than not— 69 percent of the time. And I was looking at "representative of where the field was" as well as "best," and although I am very opinionated, I was trying hard not to mistake "best" for "Jo's favorite," so I think that there were times I gave a year the benefit of the doubt.

Sixty-nine percent is okay, I suppose, but it feels like a wishy-washy "well, sort of" as a conclusion. I'd have preferred something more definite in either direction. My intuitive guess before I actually looked at the data would have been more like 80 percent. So, yes—well, doing pretty well, could do better.

When I started doing this series, everybody thought I meant to read or reread all the Hugo winners, but that wasn't what I wanted to do at all. For one thing, this is a fairly normal thing to do—several people I know have done it. For another thing, I think that there's too much significance on winners, when what I think is much more interesting is the whole slate of nominees. I wanted to look at them as a set, and as a set in the context of their year. In addition, I am fairly well read in the genre, but there are lots of things I haven't read, and I wanted to look at what I had and hadn't read and my reasons for not having read things. Whether I've read something is a piece of data to go with whether it's in print and in the library.

But in Worldcon in Reno in 2011, in addition to a ton of people saying how much they enjoyed them, three people told me that they usually go to Worldcon, but this was the first time they'd voted for the Hugos. They chose to exercise their vote this year because reading this series made them feel the Hugos were important and exciting.

This in itself makes the whole experience worthwhile, inconclusive results or not. 2011 had the highest-ever turnout of Hugo voters—2,100 people, and it would only have been 2,097 if not for this series. That makes me happy. Because I do think the Hugos are important. The

Hugos are fan-nominated, fan-voted, fan-collated awards—okay, only fans who can afford to go to Worldcon or buy a supporting membership just to be able to vote. But it's still terrific that we can be involved in SF's most prestigious and highly regarded award. And they are important for more than one year; they are the lasting record of what we have liked. One thing this series has shown is that people still care about the old Hugos. The controversies have mostly not been "settled by history," as Mike Glyer put it. Some nominees have indeed been forgotten, while other books from those years remain important. But on the whole, they're doing a good job—69 percent of the time for novels, but 99 percent of the time for novellas.

Read. Nominate. Vote. Care.

Comments on Conclusion

2. Rich Horton

Thanks again for doing this series. For me, it was a particularly valuable spur to reexamine what's been done in the field over the history of the Hugos, to make me remember stories I loved but haven't thought about, and to discover occasional stories I missed.

And I echo the plea to people who love this field to support the Hugos by, as you say, reading, nominating, voting, caring. It frustrates me to see people who I know love and care about the field saying they don't participate in the Hugos, because they're aggrieved over some past bad result, or because "they're just a popularity contest," or whatever. The Hugos are only as good as we can make them, and we can only make them better by adding our voices to the discussions, and our votes to the decisions. Yes, they are (almost by definition) a popularity contest, but they are a valuable (and, to me, fun) way of time-binding, of keeping a collective memory, of reinforcing community, and of praising our best work.

8. Gardner Dozois

This whole series has reconfirmed for me what I really already knew: that there's been a LOT of good science fiction written over the last few decades, in spite of all the moaning about how the field isn't what it used to be. It also reconfirmed my feeling that the bulk of the really good work is done at shorter lengths, particularly novella and novelette, and especially novella. Unfortunately, what everybody talks about in a year, and what the quality of a year is judged on, is the novels, which often are the weakest stuff. Even here in this series, there were always far more comments about the novels than about the short fiction, and I can only conclude that many more people read the novels than ever get around to the short fiction. Too bad, in a way, since they're missing the bulk of the good fiction published that year.

ACKNOWLEDGMENTS

I compiled this book in the summer of 2014, in one mammoth weekend editing session with the help of Patrick and Teresa Nielsen Hayden, and then I worked on it while on a signing tour around the United States, largely in hotel rooms and while traveling on Amtrak. I'd like to thank Ada Palmer for putting up with me as I was working on it, for encouragement, helpful suggestions, and listening to more Hugo trivia than anyone ought to have to put up with. This book could not have been written this way without the technical skill of Lindsey Nilsen, who has made it possible for me to work in Protext on modern machines.